35.

St. Peter's
Banker

St. Peter's Banker

Luigi DiFonzo

FRANKLIN WATTS

NEW YORK   LONDON   TORONTO   SYDNEY

1983

The dialogue in this book has been reconstructed from various sources.
The reader should not assume that the speaker of any particular line
of dialogue is the only source or the source of that line of dialogue.
The reader should also be aware that no claim is made that the dialogue
set forth in this book contains the exact words used by the participants
in the conversation. However, the reader should note that the dialogue
does represent the recollections of the sources of the author regarding
such conversations, and that it is intended to capture both the essence
and spirit of what was said as well as the personalities speaking and
their respective styles and to do so in a way that is at least as
accurate, if not more accurate, than the technique of paraphrasing.

Library of Congress Cataloging in Publication Data

DiFonzo, Luigi.
St. Peter's banker.

Bibliography: p.
Includes index.
1. Sindona, Michele. 2. Bankers — Italy — Biography.
3. Catholic Church — Finance. I. Title. II. Title: Saint Peter's banker.
HG1552.S5D53 1983   332.1'092'4   [B] 83-1102
ISBN 0-531-09889-3

To Diane,
my wife, research assistant,
and best friend

CONTENTS

PART II

PART III

AUTHOR'S NOTE

THIS BOOK IS A STUDY of the life of Michele Sindona, his relationship with the Vatican, the Mafia, his family, and the men and women associated with him throughout his life. Directly based on more than three thousand hours of tape-recorded interviews, more than one million documents, records of court proceedings from a half a dozen different countries, the personal papers and unpublished memoir of Michele Sindona, *St. Peter's Banker* is an examination of one man's obsession with the desire to achieve greatness, as well as the rules, traditions, and inherent corruption that dominated his world, and the weaknesses that continue to permeate the whole system of international banking.

Many of the documents have never been seen before by anyone outside of the institutions and individuals originally involved. Much of this information could not have been acquired without the help and courage of a number of individuals in the United States, France, Germany, Liechtenstein, Luxembourg, Switzerland, Panama, Venezuela, and, more specifically, Rome, Milan, and Palermo, Sicily.

I would, however, like to thank my wife, Diane J. DiFonzo, for contributing far more than I asked of her. During the four years I spent researching and writing this book, Diane tirelessly searched through libraries, organized research material, translated documents, conducted many interviews with Italian nationals, and transcribed all of the 452 interviews I conducted for this book. It has been a long journey, working sixteen and, at stretches, twenty hours a day, seven days a week; when I was fatigued, Diane was my greatest source of strength; when I felt lost, she gave me guidance and constructive criticism. I could not have had a better companion.

The Sindona family may not completely agree with this author's portrait of Michele Sindona; nevertheless, it must be said that without the cooperation of the entire family it would not have been possible to gather the wealth of intimate and factual details needed to write this biography. Michele Sindona generously gave me his time and allowed me access to all of his personal records, papers, diaries, unpublished memoir, and financial records. Maria Elisa Magnoni and Nino Sindona made copies of documents, spent many hours reviewing personal papers and financial records with me, and allowed me to interview them on countless occasions. Nino, for example, spent approximately two thousand hours with me reviewing documents and being interviewed. For allowing this author to enter their lives: my eternal gratitude.

Special thanks is due Arthur Roth for being unselfish with his time and for trusting me with his personal records, papers, diaries, and unpublished memoir; Father Giordano Cardinelli for his advice and assistance; Professor Clara M. Lovett for helping me to understand Italian politics; Father Romano S. Almagno for guiding me in my research of the Vatican.

To Jeanne Vestal, Robert Levine, Lydia Stein, and the whole production staff at Franklin Watts, the author wishes to acknowledge his appreciation for their efforts.

Finally, I am deeply indebted to Jesse Kornbluth, friend, confidant, and mentor for nearly ten years, who read each draft and offered many valuable suggestions.

LUIGI DIFONZO
December 28, 1982

BY MEANS OF THE BANKING SYSTEM THE DISTRIBUTION OF CAPITAL IS TAKEN OUT
OF THE HANDS OF THE PRIVATE CAPITALIST AND USURERS. BUT AT THE SAME TIME
BANKING AND CREDIT THUS BECOME THE MOST EFFECTIVE MEANS OF DRIVING
CAPITALIST PRODUCTION BEYOND ITS OWN BOUNDARIES, AND ONE OF THE MOST
POTENT INSTRUMENTS OF CRISES AND SWINDLES.

KARL MARX
CAPITAL

PART
I

THE LEGEND BEGINS

1

THE FISHERMAN AND THE PRINCE

THE VATICAN GATES are locked at 11:30 P.M. A resident of Vatican City who wishes to leave or return to the city after that hour needs special permission and a written pass from the governor. But at midnight on a warm and humid night in the spring of 1969 when Michele Sindona pulled his Mercedes in front of the gate, the Swiss guard did not check his identification, nor did he ask to see a pass. He simply opened the gate, as he would have for the pope's limousine, and allowed Michele to pass.

Sindona's meeting with Pope Paul VI would not be registered in the papal calendar or Paul's personal appointment book. Officially, there would be no record that the meeting ever took place. If somehow the press caught wind of the secret meeting, it would be denied, for popes, like bankers, tell lies to protect the interest of their holy institution.

Few men in history are known to have had such a conference with the Holy Father. Bernardino Nogara met with Pope Pius XI on June 7, 1929, when His Holiness appointed Nogara manager of the $90 million cash settlement that was part of the Lateran Treaty. And Agostino Chigi met secretly with Pope Julius II in 1511, when the pope signed a contract giving Chigi complete control of the alum-producing Tolfa mines. Yet the alliance between Pope Paul and Michele Sindona had implications that later proved significant to the future structure of the Holy See.

3

Sindona was more than just a successful tax attorney and banker. For some years, it had been known throughout the financial world that Michele Sindona and the Vatican were partners in several business ventures and banks in Italy and Switzerland. This relationship perplexed many business leaders, for they also knew that Sindona was associated with the Mafia and the notorious right-wing Masonic lodge Propaganda Due (P-2). Still, Paul chose Sindona to manage the Vatican's finances, even though, since 1738, the church had forbidden Catholics to join the Freemasons and had openly condemned the Mafia. Pope Paul himself once asked of the Mafia, "Do we not see that it is wrong that such a thing exists still in a country bearing the name of Italy?"

Why then did the Holy Father choose such a man to represent the church? It would be difficult to believe that His Holiness had not heard the rumors about Michele Sindona's ties to the Mafia and P-2. The answer is that in the real world of international banking those who appear in the light of day to be enemies will quite often show themselves under the cover of night to be allies. Their playing field is a world without national boundaries, the rules of the game are complex, and the players are friends to various dictators, kings, and presidents, with allegiance to none.

The players have no illusions, no rules but one, and that is to win, and the Vatican is a player, which makes the pope a willing or unwilling leader among the players. As Pope Paul had mastered the rules, his obvious purpose for not recording his meeting with Sindona was to ensure confidentiality. Doing so, His Holiness protected the Holy See from the scandalmongers, kept its allies in check and its enemies guessing. Such a strategy does not surprise Italians.

Unlike American Catholics, who choose to believe that the pope and the church are above human frailty, Italian Catholics have no illusions about the Vatican. By June 21, 1963, when Conclave 81 announced Giovanni Montini's election as Pope Paul VI, Italians knew that the Vatican had built a financial empire through the use of secret bank accounts and the advice of expert money men like Michele Sindona.

Perhaps only in Italy can one begin to see the political and financial realities of Vatican philosophy. The 1,400-room Apostolic Palace where the pope and his Vatican family live—"the pope's shop," as it is called by Italian Catholics—overlooks more than a dozen courtyards. The papal suite comprises nineteen rooms on the top floor. It is richly carpeted, the walls are covered with blond wood, and three large windows overlook St. Peter's Square. Books fill two ceiling-high, wall-length bookcases. Rich satin-covered chairs and tables are spaced around the 60- by 40-foot work chamber. The Vatican collection of art treasures, worth millions upon millions of dollars, is exhibited throughout the palace.

Some one thousand citizens of Vatican City live in a group of recently modernized apartment buildings. On the 108 acres are two man-made reservoirs fed by Lake Bracciono, magnificent gardens, fruit trees, and many fountains. The annual cost of maintaining all of this is estimated at $12 million. The cost is supported through the sale of special stamps, which raises a million dollars each year, and the annual worldwide collection of Peter's pence, a sort of franchise fee levied against every archdiocese for the benefit of the pope. By nature of his office, the pope is considered the most powerful and wealthiest individual in the world. The greatest portion of the church's wealth, however, is hidden in a complicated network of holding companies and banks that conceal the true worth of the Vatican.

The Instituto per le Opere di Religione (IOR) is the head of the Vatican's financial octopus. The IOR, known also as the Bank of the Vatican, looks like any other bank, except that the cashiers are priests. The pope's army of ninety-five ceremonial Swiss guards, each armed with a halberd — a combination battle-ax and pike — and approximately a hundred unarmed plainclothes police maintain constant security around the business district of Vatican City.

In addition to performing all the normal banking functions, the IOR also acts as the Vatican's holding company. It owns major blocks of shares in eighty-two banks. Among them are the largest banks in Italy: Banca di Roma, Banco Ambrosiano of Milan, Banco di Napoli, and Banco di Sicilia. Its gold reserves are in excess of $3 billion.

With an estimated $11 billion invested in stocks, the Vatican is the largest stockholder in the world. Vatican money has been invested in the largest institutions in Italy and America: General Motors, Alfa Romeo, the Watergate complex, the Finsider steel group, Finmeccanica, Società Finanziaria Telefonica, Italcementi, Italmobiliare, Società Generale Immobiliare, and Serono. The last is a pharmaceutical company that manufactured Luteolo, a contraceptive that was marketed euphemistically as a medication "for regulating female malfunctions." When its ownership of Serono was revealed, the Vatican quickly sold its participation.

A few years ago an American auditing firm evaluated the Vatican's business expertise. "The Vatican scored exceedingly well," Nino Lo Bello wrote in the *Vatican Empire*, "receiving what amounted to straight-A grades: 650 points out of a maximum of 700 for operating efficiency, 2,000 out of a possible 2,100 for effectiveness of leadership, and 700 out of a possible 800 for fiscal policy." He concluded that "the Vatican could teach other businesses quite a few lessons."

Until recently the Vatican would have scored high in political science. The right wing of the Christian Democratic party, which was formed by the church and Pope Paul's father, has been the protector of Vatican interests in Italy. Since 1947, however, the Christian Democrats have also been partners with the Mafia. This is not to say that either the Vatican or the Christian Democrats condone the actions of the Mafia. What it says, simply, is that the pope and the Vatican bankers, like the Christian Democrats, have realized that in Sicily either you deal with the Mafia or you don't do business at all.

In a number of incidents, however, members of the clergy have crossed the line of friendly coexistence with the Mafia. In 1962, for example, four Franciscan monks were tried, convicted, and sentenced to thirteen years' imprisonment for conspiracy, extortion, and manslaughter. In 1975 Father Agostino Coppola was arrested for being a high-ranking member of the Mafia (in Sicily it is not unusual for the local Mafia boss to be a priest) and a member of Anonima Sequestri, a quasi-neofascist group headed by the ruthless mafioso Luciano Leggio. Father Coppola was accused of masterminding one murder and the kidnappings of three prominent Italians. At his trial it was also revealed that Coppola had laundered the Mafia's "black money" through banks and produced votes for Sicilian "High Mafia" politicians. And in 1978 a Franciscan monk, Fernando Taddei, prior of St. Angelo Church in Rome, was arrested for buying ransom money—at 70 percent of face value—from the Mafia and washing it through Vatican-owned banks. The case is still pending.

The Mafia, the Christian Democrats, and the church are the major perpetuators of Sicily's wretched poverty. So strongly connected are the three institutions that a Mafia leader who is blessed with two sons places one in politics, and one in the church. Only in Sicily can this triangle work, because no other place in the world can be compared with Sicily.

In reality Sicily is without freedom and without an identity. It is not Italy; it is the forgotten region, the poor stepchild. And power can be wrested from poverty, from illiteracy. The Mafia, the Vatican, and the Christian Democrats know this better than anyone. They manipulate the peasants with fear. The Mafia has the kiss of death, the church has the fear of God, and the Christian Democrats have the fear of communism. The uneasy liaison presents itself as proof that at least in Sicily the gates of hell have prevailed.

In Sicily people are friends if they share the same enemy. The Vatican, the Christian Democrats, and the Mafia all claim the leftist and communist parties as their common enemy. In truth, education and opportunity are their common enemy. To educate the people, to give them a life of meaning would threaten their stronghold. And the Sicilians themselves are much to blame. A thousand times their land has been invaded. A million promises—Garibaldi waving his flag of unification, the Americans promising independence as payment for Sicily's help in World War II—

have been broken. The Sicilians, as a result, have learned to trust no one, to shrug and accept whatever must be in order to survive.

Attempts have been made to arrest the Mafia's habitual raping of Sicily's resources. Although ground has been paved since the Beati Paoli, a twelfth-century secret society, rose in opposition to the house of Savoy, it has proved difficult to change what for centuries has been a part of the, Sicilian mentality: the notion that to steal from or outsmart the state is an act of which many Sicilians are proud. They commit crimes and allow crimes to be committed, judge a man honorable by his silence while not judging his lawlessness. It is a nihilistic belief that all which could be good has been contaminated by greed, that everyone is hiding a scam and therefore no one should be trusted.

This aberrant pride has continued to create problems in Sicily and southern Italy, for it has allowed the Mafia, the Christian Democrats, and the church to take advantage of the peasants. The Christian Democrats, for example, have awarded three Mafia families the legal right to collect taxes throughout Sicily. And with the help of Michele Sindona and Graziano Verzotto — former Italian senator and regional secretary of the Christian Democratic party and most recently president of Ente Minerario Siciliano (EMS), the Sicilian mining corporation — the Mafia was able to infiltrate EMS.

Verzotto had appointed mafioso Giuseppe Di Cristina treasurer of So-Chi-Mi-Si, a division of EMS. In return for "black interest" payments (a 2 percent kickback above the official interest rate on EMS accounts), Verzotto and Di Cristina fed EMS funds to Banca Unione, which was owned in partnership by the Vatican and Michele Sindona. Black interest payments drawn against a checking account (number 0.028049/73) were endorsed by Pietro Giordano (an alias used by Giuseppe Di Cristina) and cashed at the Rome branch of the Bank of Sicily. The funds were then distributed to the Mafia and transferred through the Bank of the Vatican to secret accounts at Amincor Bank of Zurich, which was controlled by Michele Sindona.

The Sindona–Mafia–Christian Democrat–Vatican network extends beyond Sicily and Italy. The Mafia enforcer, Giuseppe Di Cristina, for example, was a close associate of Tommaso Buscetta, a major international heroin smuggler and relative of New York's Gambino Mafia family. When Tommaso Buscetta was arrested and jailed in New York on drug-related charges, a leader of the Christian Democrats (believed to have been Verzotto) intervened and won his release. According to sources inside the Palermo police department, the 40 million lira bond deposited in Buscetta's favor was cleared through one of the banks belonging to Michele Sindona and the Vatican.

All of this proves what Pope Paul VI surely knew, that Michele Sindona was the only contemporary man to organize a successful liaison between the Vatican, the Freemasons, the Mafia, and the Christian Democrats. Sindona was so powerful that in 1967 an Interpol memo sent to the Italian police identified him as a leading member of a group of mafiosi and bankers who were "involved in the illicit movement of depressant, stimulant, and hallucinogenic drugs between Italy, the United States, and possibly other European countries." Michele Sindona's name reportedly appeared at the top of the list.

On Vatican coins, on which a likeness of the pope's head appears, two mottoes are engraved: "This is the root of all evil" and "It is better to give than to receive." The statements represent the hypocrisies the church has promoted for centuries. This can be seen clearly in the decisions Pope Paul made on fiscal matters.

Because of his years of service as pro-secretary of state under Pope Pius XII, Paul probably knew more about Vatican finances than any pontiff since Julius II. Like John Kennedy, who brought his brother and friends to the White House, Paul shocked the Vatican establishment by bringing his own advisers to Rome. The "black nobility," as the establishment is called, had been dominated by Pius's family, the Pacellis, and a few chosen friends, all of whom are given the title "Prince." Paul's entourage — the press tagged them the "Milan Mafia" — included Cardinal Vagnozzi, who had spent nine years in Washington as papal nuncio and had had the opportunity to study the financial genius of Cardinal Spellman (known in the Vatican as "Moneybags").

Others were Cardinal Cody of Chicago; Cardinal Sergio Guerri, who was appointed governor of Vatican City; Cardinal Giuseppe Caprio, who was appointed president of the Beni della Santa Sede (Bank of the Holy Ghost); and Bishop Paul Marcinkus from Cicero, Illinois, who was appointed president of the Instituto per le Opere di Religione (IOR).

Marcinkus was studying in Rome when he first met Paul. Reportedly Paul was walking through the streets of Rome when the crowd, eager to touch him, broke through the barriers. Marcinkus, nicknamed *il gorilla* because of his thick 6-foot-4-inch body, picked the tiny pope up and carried him on his shoulders through the crowd. From that day on, Marcinkus served as the pope's bodyguard.

The most controversial person the Holy Father brought into his confidence, however, was Michele Sindona. Their relationship would transform the Vatican from a powerful Italian corporation into a multinational financial power. Before that could happen, however, the Vatican had to resolve its tax problem.

In 1962 the center-left coalition government of Premier Amintore

Fanfani passed a dividend tax (*cedolare*) on profits earned on the Italian stock market. Through April 1963 the Vatican paid taxes. Then Fanfani's government was defeated. Giovanni Leone formed an all–Christian Democrat caretaker government. Leone granted the Vatican a tax exemption. Minister of Finance Mario Martinelli, a Christian Democrat, signed the exemption and sent it to the tax agency. When the caretaker government was replaced by Aldo Moro's center-left coalition government, Pietro Nenni, a socialist who was then deputy prime minister, and Antonio Giolitti, also a socialist and the minister of the treasury, supported finance minister Roberto Tremelloni's rejection of the Vatican's exemption. In search of a compromise, the government asked the Vatican for a complete list of its shares. The Vatican refused to provide the information.

Pope Paul turned to Michele Sindona, the man who had begun his career by fighting and beating the tax authorities. Working behind Vatican front men, Sindona successfully convinced the tax officials to file the Vatican tax exemption until a more favorable government was formed. In the meantime the Vatican continued to earn millions on the Italian stock market without paying either the 5 percent or the 30 percent tax.

In mid-1964 Moro's government fell and was replaced by another Moro government. This time, however, the new minister of the treasury, Socialist Giovanni Pieraccini, refused to allow the Vatican tax issue to lie dormant. Sindona tried to convince Pieraccini to ratify the exemption; Pieraccini refused. The fight now threatened more than the Vatican finances. Sindona realized that the left was too powerful and would support the plan for continued nationalization. The left was, therefore, a threat to his growing empire, now valued at about $100 million.

Michele Sindona made a brilliant and powerful move against the left. In 1964 the Italian stock market was depressed. Sindona decided that the government could not survive if he attacked the economy. Acting on Sindona's advice, the Vatican threatened to sell hundreds of millions of dollars' worth of stocks on the open market. The threat was timed perfectly to coincide with the resignation of the president of the republic, Antonio Segni. The plan worked. A bill ratifying the Vatican's exemption was passed and signed by Moro, Tremelloni, and the new president, Giuseppe Saragat, a Social Democrat. Pieraccini, however, refused to endorse the bill. Without his signature, it was sent to parliament for approval. For some reason the bill never passed the legislative committee. In 1967 the issue was revived with a series of articles in the Italian left-wing press that called the Vatican "the biggest tax evader in postwar Italy." According to one source, the Vatican owed as much as $720 million in unpaid taxes.

For two more years the debate over Vatican taxes and Vatican tax exemption was argued in parliament and in the press. During this period Pope Paul was faced with another, even more embarrassing situation.

In May 1968 demonstrations by students, unions, and the left wing exploded throughout Italy and the rest of Europe. The activities in Italy were financed by multimillionaire Milan publisher Giangiacomo Feltrinelli, who, in addition to *The Leopard* and *Doctor Zhivago*, published many handbooks on terrorism including Carlos Marighella's minimanual of terrorist tactics. Feltrinelli, a friend to Fidel Castro, had inherited a large block of stock in the Vatican's Banca Unione. To make matters more complicated, the paper *La Sinistra* ("The Left"), owned by Feltrinelli, supported the government's side on the Vatican tax issue.

For help in resolving the problem, Pope Paul again turned to Michele Sindona, who responded magnificently. The Banca Unione (BU) shares were owned by Feltrinelli and his French brother-in-law, Count André D'Ormesson. After a quick check, Sindona discovered that the count did not share Feltrinelli's political views and in fact regarded Feltrinelli as something of a nut. Sindona exploited family tensions by telling D'Ormesson that unless he persuaded Feltrinelli to sell all of his family's shares to the Group Sindona he (Sindona) would be forced to blacklist D'Ormesson.

D'Ormesson knew that Sindona had the power to blacklist. In addition to knowing about Michele's reputation as a member of P-2 and the Mafia, D'Ormesson was aware of Sindona's association with Hambros Bank and Continental Bank of Illinois. So D'Ormesson successfully talked Feltrinelli into selling his shares to Sindona. Feltrinelli used the money to buy guns and dynamite for his organization, the Proletarian Action Group. He was killed on March 15, 1972, when a bomb that he was tying to a high-tension pylon exploded prematurely.

The rescue of Banca Unione resolved a sticky problem for the Vatican and gave Sindona control of another bank. Furthermore, because of his relationships with Pope Paul, Bishop Marcinkus, and David Kennedy, former secretary of the treasury under Richard Nixon and chairman of Continental Bank of Illinois, the Vatican agreed to finance Sindona's purchase of the Feltrinelli shares.

David Kennedy had been introduced to Michele Sindona in the early 1960s by an American associate of Sindona's named Dan Porco. Kennedy and Sindona became very close friends, and eventually Continental Bank purchased approximately 20 percent of Sindona's Banca Privata Finanziaria in Milan.

The Sindona–Vatican family grew even closer when Mark Antonucci, an Italian-American born in Pittsburgh who was also very close to the Vatican and Sindona, named his seventh son after Kennedy. The baptism was performed by Bishop Marcinkus, and Michele Sindona was the child's godfather.

David Kennedy later became a director of Sindona's holding company Fasco, A.G., which in 1972 purchased controlling interest of Franklin National Bank, the eighteenth largest bank in the United States. With these connections and the fact that the Vatican was already a partner with Sindona in Banca Unione, the Vatican did not hesitate to become partners with Sindona when he purchased Finabank of Geneva, Switzerland.

By 1969 several Italian governments had fallen. New ones were formed, and they also fell. All of this helped to stall action on the tax issue until the spring of that year when the government made the irrevocable decision that the Vatican would have to pay taxes on its stock holdings. It was time for the Vatican to move, so Pope Paul again turned to Michele Sindona for assistance.

Only one light was burning in the pope's chambers as Michele Sindona entered late on that spring night in 1969. Paul was seated in one of the satin-covered chairs. His body bent forward and his face distorted by shadows, he appeared tired and ill.

Sindona wore a navy blue suit, a white shirt with gold cuff links, and a blue tie. He appeared fresh and confident. He approached the Holy Father with respect and a strong, warm smile. Paul did not offer his hand for Michele to kiss; instead, they greeted each other with the handshake of old friends.

This is a terrible problem, Paul told him, referring to the parliamentary ruling regarding the Vatican investment tax. If the Vatican allowed Italy to tax its investments, it would be a signal for other countries to do the same. If that happened, the Vatican's power would be diluted. It was not Michele's fault, the pontiff assured him. He had taken on a difficult task and had done a marvelous job of stalling the inevitable.

His Holiness did not say so, but Michele received the impression that the tax problem had weakened Paul's pontificate. His leadership of the church had been seriously challenged by the traditionalists, and the conservatives were less than supportive. Most of the infighting was over the course Paul had dictated for the church throughout the sessions of the Vatican II councils. But Sindona was confident that the tax problem added a burden Paul did not want or need.

Michele proposed a strategy to move Vatican resources out of Italy and into the profitable, tax-free Eurodollar market by way of a network of offshore tax corporations. The move would not only give the Vatican added secrecy — which the Vatican cherished as much as the Mafia treasured *omerta* — but would also demonstrate to other countries that the Vatican was strong. In the long run, Sindona said, they would see that Italy was the one that suffered.

Paul must have been a bit nervous. What Sindona was proposing, if the pope approved, would put the Sicilian financier in charge of several billion dollars. Had not Pope Paul already trusted Sindona? And had not Sindona always acted in good faith? And had the pope not already made his decision, no matter how uncomfortable it might have been?

Pope Paul handed Michele Sindona the agreement he had already prepared. Sindona read it quickly: it was more than he had hoped for, more than he would have dared to suggest. The Holy Father, by virtue of that document, had granted him complete control of the Vatican's foreign investment policy. Michele Sindona would work closely with Bishop Marcinkus, president of the Bank of the Vatican; Cardinal Giuseppe Caprio, president of the Beni della Santa Sede; and Cardinal Sergio Guerri, governor of Vatican City. Sindona, however, would have final authority.

When he turned to the last page, he looked at Paul and smiled. His Holiness had already endorsed the document. It was the highest compliment, the greatest honor, the grandest show of trust anyone could receive.

After Michele had signed the agreement and placed a copy in his breast pocket, Pope Paul asked him to kneel beside him and pray. A moment later and still kneeling, Michele gently lifted the pope's hand to his lips and kissed the Fisherman's ring.

What Michele Sindona felt as he left the Vatican that night is unclear. In general the press viewed Sindona as a cunning, unemotional, and ruthless businessman who remained cool even when negotiating deals worth tens of millions of dollars. "The iceman," he had been called. Perhaps the nickname was fitting. He says he felt nothing unusual. It was business, nothing to get excited about.

But Sindona had become an actor. He existed behind a portfolio of characters, and he had worked very hard to master each of them. "Michele Sindona," Dan Porco says, "could be anything he decided he had to be."

Whatever role Michele Sindona played that night, he must have been overwhelmed first with anticipation and later, as he drove home, with joy. In his breast pocket Sindona carried a document that gave him complete control of the Vatican's foreign investments. From that night on, as he traveled the world, he would no longer be just Michele Sindona, Sicilian peasant turned banker, financier, mafioso, and Freemason; he would now carry the Vatican title *Mercator Senesis Romanam Curiam sequens*. Michele Sindona was now officially what Italians had been calling him in cafés — "the pope's banker."

2

HEAVEN AND HELL

MICHELE EUGENIO SINDONA was born on May 8, 1920. Twenty-one days later—and forty-three years before he was to be crowned Pope Paul VI—Giovanni Battista Montini officially entered the life of the clergy. Though they were born nearly twenty-three years apart, their childhoods were remarkably similar. Both of their mothers, Maria Sindona and Giuditta Montini, had difficulty in childbirth. The midwives worked from early morning through the dark of night and into the light of a new day. With each hour, the pain weakened both mothers. Death, the midwives prophesied, would embrace both mothers and infants.

Michele's birth was the more violent. Maria Sindona's birth canal was extremely narrow, and it was impossible for the infant to pass beyond the cervical area. "Forceps inserted high into the cervical area were clamped firmly around the infant's head," a physician who has treated Sindona explained after examining medical records in Sicily. "Forceps are normally fixed on the lateral aspects of the scalp. This case was extreme. The forceps were pushed so high that they wrapped around the child's head to the anterior portion of the scalp. When the midwife squeezed, the skin ruptured, leaving permanent scars and facial deformity."

And there was more. The umbilical cord was wrapped twice around Michele's neck. Asphyxiation had turned the infant's face purple. "A traumatic entrance," says the physician. "I am positive that a certain number of brain cells were destroyed. I feel absolutely comfortable saying that."

The trauma was complicated by the fact that Maria was weak and incapable of nursing the child. The same was true of Giuditta Montini. Both infants were taken directly from their mothers' wombs and placed in the arms of wet nurses.

Throughout adolescence, both Michele and Giovanni were often sick. Giovanni suffered with bronchitis; Michele battled rheumatic fever and chorea, a complication of the central nervous system also known as Saint Vitus' dance. Because of the weakness of their mothers and the illnesses of both boys, they were raised by surrogates: Montini by Clorinda Peritti, his wet nurse; Sindona by Nunziata, his grandmother.

Early in their studies, Giovanni Montini and Michele Sindona displayed signs of brilliance. In school both stood at the top of the class. And years later, when both were powerful men — Montini as Pope Paul VI, Sindona as his banker and confidant — there was a similarity in appearance: the thin lips and dark eyes filled with imagination and ambition. Both men were 5 feet 10 inches tall, and both were thin, almost frail.

Unlike Pope Paul, whose family was affluent and lived in the northern Italian town of Concesio, once considered the Fortress of Faith, Michele Sindona was born in Patti, Sicily, to a family paralyzed by poverty.

Patti rests on the northeast coast of Sicily, twenty miles west of Messina. The road from Messina to Patti snakes along a pyramidal hill a thousand feet above the Tyrrhenian Sea. To the north of the road appears Patti, with its field of ruins: a basilica, a Byzantine fort, and Tyndaris, the Greek theater. From Tyndaris, which crowns the hill, there is a view of the Tyrrhenian Sea, the Gulf of Patti, and the Lipari Islands.

Mountains frame the village. Its streets are unpaved and narrow. Houses are generally small, though there are class distinctions: a family that rents is considered poor; a home with no balcony is considered lower middle class; a home with a balcony, of course demonstrates achievement.

On December 28, 1908, at 5:21 A.M., one of the worst earthquakes in recorded history destroyed Patti, its neighboring villages, and Messina, "city of legend and disaster." Some 160,000 people lived between Messina and Patti before the earth exploded. Landslides struck the village of Patti, destroying major portions of it within minutes. Panic-stricken men, women, and children raced into the streets. Among them was Don Michele Sindona, grandfather of Michele Sindona. He led the terrorized peasants to the calm safety of the sea, where they waited on the beach, in fishing boats, and on the cliffs for the holocaust to end.

Suddenly a roar echoed, and the sea reached out in the form of a great tidal wave. Bodies crashed against the rocky hill. Human blood stained the beachhead black. Both the dead and the living were dragged into the bowels of the sea. By the thousands the number of victims rose. Headless bodies stretched across the landscape. Finally the earthquake ended. Night fell, the earth settled, and the sea rested. Then a blanket of fire spread from Messina to Patti.

In the morning it was discovered that more than 90 percent of the buildings had been destroyed and more than eighty thousand people — 50 percent of the population — were dead. The stench of burned flesh lay over the village like a thick smog. In sunlight the haze of death burnished the air. The naked body of a child hung by its feet from a balcony for nearly a week. Time passed, and nothing changed. Finally the mutilated and decayed bodies were removed from the ruins and burned. Don Michele and his wife, Nunziata, gathered food and medicine and cared for the injured. At the ruins of Tyndaris, they helped erect a hospital tent. They slept in the fields under lemon and olive trees, without clothes to protect their skin from infection.

In order to rebuild their lives and their village the peasants needed supplies and money. The government in Rome, true to its history and its traditional attitude toward the South, showed little concern and offered even less assistance. So the people of Patti turned to Don Michele, as they always had, for advice and help.

Michele Sindona's grandfather had earned his money warehousing lumber, tools, and wrought iron. He sold to wholesalers in Messina. Later he opened a store in the village, offering his goods to his neighbors at the same discount. The elder Sindona, a good businessman with a strong affection for his people, granted credit to his customers in Messina, but for the villagers of Patti he did even more. After the disaster, Don Michele set a table in his parlor where neighbors came and borrowed money, "free of interest." They used it to buy food, materials, and tools needed to rebuild their modest homes.

Soon the Sindonas were the most respected family in Patti and one of the richest in the Messina area. Of his grandfather, Michele Sindona says, "He was an honest, generous, and wise man. At thirty he was king of Patti, a descendant of the royal family of Aragon, the conquerors of Sicily."

One summer day, probably in 1914, Don Michele Sindona, Sr., returned home after a long swim in the Tyrrhenian Sea. That night he died in his sleep, leaving his fortune to his wife, Nunziata, and his only child, Antonino.

On May 23, 1915, Italy declared war on Austria-Hungary. Nini, as Antonino was called, being the only surviving son of *famiglia* Sindona, was exempt from military duty. Had he been forced to serve in the Italian army during World War I, the Sindona family might have maintained its wealth. But Nini preferred to spend his time playing cards, for he had neither his father's ability nor his ambition. In addition, his mother, Nunziata, could not find it within herself to refuse to give financial aid to the other families of Patti, many of whom had lost husbands and fathers to the war.

If they needed clothing, food, or advice, the peasants of Patti came to Nunziata. The confided in her as they had in her husband. "She was like the godmother of Patti," Michele recalls. When friends argued, when they could not reach a calm solution, and when anger drifted toward violence, they called on Nunziata. She would listen. First, the one with the loudest voice would be forced to wait in silence while the other delivered his or her complaint. Then, after all had had a turn to speak, Nunziata would dictate a resolution. Everyone respected her judgment and obeyed her decision. "Nunziata," Michele adds, "was honest and wise, but too generous, not a manager of money." By the time Michele was born, because of Nunziata's warm heart and Nini's gambling losses, *famiglia* Sindona was as poor as most others in Patti.

Among Sicilian peasants there is a saying: "No money, no power, no respect." Sicilians build power and accumulate wealth through tribal ritual born from the belief that a son is everything and a daughter is nothing; a son is named after his grandfather, the daughter is named after no one, for she serves only one purpose: to be offered as a bride, usually to the son of a stronger family. In exchange, her father gains power and influence. If she gives birth to a male child, especially the firstborn, she has fulfilled her life's duty. When she succeeds, the grandfathers drink and dance, and, at the end of the celebration, each smears his own blood on a picture of the other's patron saint; they are now family. If the girl fails to provide a son, however, her husband has the right to find a lover who will do so.

Nunziata knew that her family's one asset was Nini — not because he was a great man but because he was a man. In reality, what Nunziata perceived as a solution to her family's poverty was a reversal of Sicilian bartering. The marriage of Nini to the daughter of a middle-class family would strengthen the Sindonas. They would regain prestige, and the girl's dowry would fill the hole in the Sindona coffers. To that purpose, Nunziata entered negotiations with Eugenio Castelnuovo, a middle-class businessman who had been a friend of her husband. Eugenio's daughter, Maria, was the most beautiful woman in Patti, but she had epilepsy, she was shy, and at thirty she was prepared to die a virgin.

Maria was Eugenio Castelnuovo's only daughter, the youngest of his five children, thirty years younger than her oldest brother. Though Eugenio had already been blessed with a dozen grandsons, he was pleased at the thought of Maria producing a few more. Whether Nini liked the idea of marrying a woman eight years his senior is unknown. What is certain is that Nini, as custom dictated, expected a dowry, a handsome one, to be sure, since no one else was interested in Eugenio's beautiful but sick daughter. Eugenio, however, knew that Nini gambled, and in a classic Sicilian move, to the surprise of Nini and Nunziata, he outmaneuvered them. To protect his daughter, he set her dowry in trust. The income was small, but Nini took his revenge by using it to finance his gambling.

Though Maria had difficulty carrying a child full term, the union did produce two children, Michele and Enio. The strain of two difficult births, however, caused severe damage to her already weakened body. She was sent to Rome, where reconstructive vaginal surgery was performed. When she returned home, it was with the fear that sexual intimacy with her husband would kill her, so she and Nini never again shared a bed. Soon Nini began the first of many open affairs in the city of Messina.

Yet Nini must have felt some pride. He was the first in a long line of Sindonas to sire more than one child. Adding to his joy was the fact that both of his children were males. Whether it was this accomplishment or a desperate need for money that led him into business, one can only speculate. For whatever reason, he opened a flower shop in the basement of his father's house. While Nunziata cared for Michele and Enio, Nini designed wreaths and sold them to the local funeral parlor. The money wasn't good, and the shame Michelino (little Michele, as Nunziata called her first and favorite grandson) was forced to bear at the hands of his classmates scarred him for life. Selling flowers "is the job of peasants," Michele explains. The descendants of the queen of Aragon were now reduced to doing peasant's work.

Michele and his "angel," Nunziata, lived with his father, his sickly mother, and his brother Enio in the unfinished house his grandfather had built. It had two bedrooms, a very small kitchen, and a parlor, but no balcony. Enio slept on the sofa, except when Nini was not spending the evening with a lover; then Enio's bed was the floor. Maria had her own bedroom. And Nunziata and Michele had their bedroom, where they shared the same bed until Michele turned fifteen. "Had Grandfather lived," Michele says, "we would have moved to a new house, with a room for everyone, and *two* balconies."

Each morning Nunziata, a short, broad-shouldered woman with thick white hair and penetrating eyes, would fix Michelino a breakfast of milk and bread. More often than not, dinner was also milk and stale bread. A special treat—if Nini had been lucky with the cards—would be a teaspoon of sugar. Food high in nutrition was rare. On market days Nini would wait until it was very late. If he timed his arrival perfectly, the vendors would toss him a few pieces of unsold fish.

Sweets were seldom found in the Sindona household, and Michelino loved sweets. But on his *onomastico* (the day of his patron saint, the most important day of celebration for a Sicilian, more important than a birthday or Christmas), Maria's brothers always gave Michelino a gift of a few lire, which he spent on his favorite desserts. He would gather his gang and lead them in a race to the bakery. With authority, he slapped the lire on the counter and ordered, "Give me a dozen cannoli and twelve of these . . . and twelve of these . . . and twelve of these." Then, before allowing his friends to feast, he would place two samples of each pastry in a separate bag. Later he would watch Nunziata and his younger brother enjoy his gift.

Michele remembers his mother mostly as an invalid. In addition to the problems created during childbirth, epileptic seizures weakened her. A family member recalls that "when Michelino angered her, all she did was toss a hanky on top of his head." Even when she was well, Maria would lie in bed two days a week, every week of the year, for she owned only two dresses, one for summer and one for winter. When she washed her dress, all the neighbors knew, for she would stay in bed all day until the dress was dry.

The family was so poor that they couldn't afford to buy Michelino decent clothes either. Long after his friends began wearing long pants to school, Michelino was forced to continue to wear short pants. In fact, he owned only one pair of pants. At night, Nunziata washed them and hung them out the bedroom window to dry. Many times they were still damp when he put them on in the morning.

An old school friend remembers, "In the second year of high school, Michele was still wearing short pants. In the usual cruel manner of children, a lot of his classmates picked on him." Michele's way of getting even with those who mocked him was to fold a piece of paper into a crown with four points. He would color one section blue and one red. Then, after deciding if someone was a friend or an enemy, he would ask him to pick a number from one to ten. "Of course," the friend explains, "Michele had already made his decision, but at eight years old the other kids did not realize this." If the child was a friend, the number chosen would end on the blue. Michele would smile and say, "See, you are my friend. You will go to heaven." If an enemy was his target, the number chosen would end on the red. Invariably, Michele would have something appropriate to say. His eyes cold and bitter, he would pronounce with certainty, "You will go to hell!" Michelino was serious about heaven and hell. This was his way of dividing people. He set forces of good and evil in clear perspective, into two categories: friend or foe.

Michelino found more than one way to prove he was not only as good as his classmates but better. Small-framed and weakened by a poor diet and rheumatic fever, he used his imagination, challenging friends to outrageous eating contests. On one occasion Michelino won the contest after devouring fifty pears. His favorite dare, however, the one that excited him most, was seeing who could eat the most lemons. He would gather his friends under the lemon tree in the back yard of his family's house, and each boy would pick a handful of lemons. Michelino kept a keen eye on his pals while each bit into a lemon. The idea was to see who could eat the most lemons without cringing or spitting juice. Michelino usually won. To prove himself a leader, he organized his friends and raided the orchards and gardens of his father's friends. When Nini learned of the raids, he beat Michelino and forbade him to play soccer. The punishment, however, was rarely enforced. For in a house that reeked of poverty and sickness, Michelino had his "angel," Nunziata. She would wink and smile and kiss his cheek as she and Michelino conspired against Nini. She would sneak Michelino out of the house so that he could play with his friends while Nini worked. When Nini returned home and asked where Michelino was, Michele recalls with a mischievous grin that Nunziata would say that she had just sent the rascal to the store to buy a loaf of day-old bread.

"Nunziata," Michele admits, "was the most important person in my private life." When the family could not afford to buy Michelino and Enio a soccer ball for Christmas, Nunziata gathered old rags from neighbors and rolled them into the shape of a soccer ball. But the moments of greatest joy and serenity in Michele Sindona's young life were when he was in bed and nestled safely in the arms of Nunziata. Before he went to sleep, she told him stories about his grandfather, how he never judged anyone, never listened to what others had to say about a person. And he remembers her saying, "A man who has committed a terrible act may have had a good and honorable reason for doing so."

They started each day together, hours before anyone else in the house woke up. "I never slept more than three or four hours," Michele explains. "I just couldn't rest." He would wake up and kiss Nunziata so that she would awaken. Then she would tell him more stories about his grandfather. Nunziata would also comfort Michelino when he was depressed. "I was depressed a lot," Michele says. "I thought of suicide ever since I was about ten years old. I don't know why. Perhaps it was the people, the kids, the endless poverty, what I had already seen of human nature. Perhaps I was just anxious. I don't know. But Nunziata knew. She understood me and she cared."

On Sunday, while the rest of Patti was attending mass, Nunziata and

Michele would sit and talk. "I would read to her," Michele remembers. "She would ask me what I thought. We'd discuss everything — homework, ideas, dreams." Sundays were nice. They never attended mass, though Nunziata was religious. Mass was for the hypocrites, she'd say. Every day, she and Michelino would walk to the cathedral and pray. On Sunday, after Enio and Maria and the rest of Patti had attended services, Nunziata would take her grandson to church and spend an hour talking with the bishop. During these visits Michele became close to the church. The bishop would talk to him about Rome, the Vatican, and the pope, about the great fortress of Vatican City, and about the need the Holy See had for men with financial expertise. After each visit Nunziata told Michelino that if he studied hard and remembered what she had taught him about honor he would one day be able to help the church. But to do so, she said, Michelino must be a man of courage as well as intelligence.

When Michelino was eight years old, Nunziata taught him what having courage meant. One day after school Michelino went to his father's flower shop to watch him make wreaths. "Michelino," Nini said, "everyone says that you are smart, a genius even. Already you tutor your classmates in math. Why don't you help your father? I am not good with figures. Instead of playing every day, instead of helping others, I want you to come here after school and help me."

The next day Michelino found himself with a pencil and a ledger. What he really enjoyed, however, was designing flower arrangements, but this angered Nini. "Michelino, don't touch the vases," he always yelled. Nevertheless, Michelino continued to play with the flowers, moving a vase here or there, changing the arrangements that Nini had worked on all day.

One day Michelino dropped a vase and cut his right wrist. "I told you never to touch the vases!" Nini screamed. Nunziata heard Nini yelling at her grandson and came to his rescue. When she saw Michelino bleeding and crying, she ordered Nini to stop yelling. Then Nunziata swept Michelino into her arms, held him very close, and carried him to the doctor.

The doctor said that Michelino needed stitches and wanted to give him a shot of Novocain, but Nunziata would not allow the doctor to inject anything into her grandson. The realization of what was about to happen frightened Michelino. He felt weak and began to cry again. "Michelino," Nunziata said, "you are a man, not a little girl. Pain is nothing for a man. Remember that a man must always be a man. He must always be himself. He is not himself if he depends on drugs. Therefore he is not a man. Drugs will steal life from you, make you something you are not." So Michelino bravely received eight stitches without the benefit of Novocain. Nunziata was very proud of him, but her devotion did not end there.

After a serious bout with rheumatic fever, Michelino was afflicted with Saint Vitus's dance. It was difficult for him to sleep, his body kept jerking involuntarily, and his perspiration chilled him. To help, Nunziata held him against her breast and massaged his back. He loved her. With Nunziata he was happy.

In Sicily cousins and siblings sometimes marry. The roots of this custom are buried deep in Sicily's unwritten laws: marrying a relative prevents the possible infiltration of family enemies. From outside the culture, one cannot grasp five hundred years of tradition, and so there is the question of Sindona's relationship with his grandmother. When asked whether this sort of relationship was common among the people of Patti, Michele says, "No . . . no . . . it is not common. Quite unusual. It was not sinful, however. Love, real maternal love, an American could not understand. She brought me through the pain of illness and poverty, the shame of being of a family that in one generation had risen to affluence and respect and power, then crumbled."

3

THE LEMON DEALER

In 1938, when he was eighteen years old, Michele Sindona won a scholarship to the University of Messina where, in 1942, he earned a degree in tax law. While attending the university he worked for a time at Credito Italiano, a government-controlled bank. Later he worked full-time as a real estate tax consultant for Ufficio del Castasto, the local tax office. He also worked part-time as a bookkeeper for a producer of lemon juice. He acquired an interest in tax consulting while working for his father's cousin, Vitorio Cappadona. Nini and Vitorio had entered into a partnership when Michele was fourteen. Nini got the money to finance the consulting firm from his wife's family. In charge of the family fortune since Eugenio's death in 1930, the Castelnuovo brothers wanted to rid themselves of Nini and free the inheritance that had been placed in trust by their father for Maria. In exchange for the loan, Nini forced his wife to sign a document releasing her claim on the dowry and inheritance.

Though Nini did not have a university education, Italian law did not prevent him from working under Vitorio's degree. Michele did their typing and helped research tax and bankruptcy laws. It was Michele's high school principal, however, who had the most influence on Michele's choice of profession. At the time, Principal Nasilli, Michele recalls, "was the most important person in my public life." During his first two years of

22

high school Michele's interest in his studies fell second to his interest in girls and dating. As a result, his grades dropped from nearly perfect to barely passing. Nasilli told his student that he was acting foolishly, that he could have a brilliant future if he used the mind God had been kind enough to give him. Banking and government were the two areas that offered job security. Nasilli suggested that Michele concentrate on one. He decided to study philosophy, economics, and law.

Michele rarely attended class at the university, showing up only when it was necessary to take an exam. He had the gift of instant comprehension. He would read a textbook, without rereading or the assistance of the professor, with complete understanding. He also had the gift of speed, which, years later as a lawyer and *uomo di fiducia* in Milan, he would demonstrate while executing business deals and resolving not only his problems but the problems of the pope as well. And, finally, he had the gift—and the power—of presence. Even at a restaurant, Sindona was in command. Before anyone had a chance to read the menu he would decide: "Have the beef!" Before anyone could object, he would tell the waiter, "*Battuta di manzo . . . battuta di manzo . . . battuta di manzo.* All rare." Quickly he would eat. Quickly he would render a decision on whatever matter needed his attention. Then, just as quickly, assuming that everyone wanted coffee and that everyone was in as much of a rush to leave as he was, he would again call the waiter, point to each person and order: "*Caffè . . . caffè . . . caffè.* And the check!"

During his university years, Michele always dressed in a blue suit. Like Nunziata, Principal Nasilli had instilled in Michele a sense of dignity, urging him to carry himself with the pride of his grandfather, to speak Dante's Italian rather than dialect, and to dress well. He could afford only one suit, but it was always clean and pressed. He lived in the university dorm, sharing simple rooms with two or three classmates. The house mother allowed Michele to live rent-free in a room by himself; in trade, Michele did her tax returns. And he earned extra money playing cards.

Nini had given to his son two things: his love of adventure and his love of gambling. Unlike Nini, however, Michele was a master of illusion, an artist. A good card player, he loved to win more than money: he took pleasure in destroying his adversaries.

One evening at the University of Messina, Michele's luck was even better than usual. "Incredible" was the word he used when he recalled that evening. His three classmates knew he was bluffing, but they had been unable to challenge his outrageous bets. They were losing heavily and about ready to call it a night when Mario Barone sensed that the cards had turned. The player to Michele's left placed a large bet. Barone smiled; Sindona hesitated. Barone was anxious and demanded that Sindona make his bet or fold. Still, staring directly into Barone's eyes, he stalled. Then he tripled the bet. Was Michele bluffing? Of course he was bluffing; he always bluffed at poker. One player dropped out of the betting. Barone quickly called, then drew three cards. The other player drew three cards, and Michele whispered, "One." It was Michele's bid. Again he hesitated. Seeming concerned with Barone, he stared deep into his eyes. Someone asked, "Are you ready to play?" Looking again at his cards, fanning them out one by one, Michele answered, "Wait. I am still reading." Finally, after calculating how much Barone had to bet, Sindona placed an equal amount in the center of the table. The player to his left folded. Barone must have had some doubt when he met Sindona's bet. The tension was high. He had Sindona trapped. Barone spread his cards out, displaying a full house. All three of the players smiled. Michele did not. As Barone reached for the money, Sindona placed one card on the table, then another, and another, one by one, naming them as he did so: "Ace of hearts, king of hearts, queen of hearts," and so on, until all five were displayed. "A royal straight flush." Machiavellian overtones echoed in his joy. Destiny, however, would deliver to Barone his revenge. Thirty-five years later, as chief administrator for Banca di Roma, Barone would help destroy Sindona's empire.

On July 10, 1943, with the assistance of the Mafia, Anglo-American forces invaded Sicily. American troops seized Gela; Canadian and British troops took Cape Passaro. By July 22 the Allies occupied half of Sicily. On August 18 Messina fell, and with it all resistance.

In general the people celebrated Sicily's liberation from fascist Italy. Mussolini had murdered and jailed thousands of Sicilians in what he claimed was an attempt to rid Sicily of the Mafia. Michele Sindona was among those who celebrated the Allied victory. Even before the Allies had thought of seizing Sicily and using it to launch an attack against the rest of Italy, Michele Sindona had resisted Mussolini's government. While at Ginnasio, the high school in Patti, Michele had refused to wear the military uniform Mussolini required of all students. As punishment the government refused him the perfect grade of 110. With five demerits, Michele graduated with a grade of 105.

Italian law prevents a lawyer from opening a *studio* (law office) until he has served a two-year apprenticeship in an established firm. Again Michele rebelled. With the help of Nunziata and the bishop of Patti, Michele purchased a truck from the Americans. He delivered lemons to the center of Sicily and traded them for wheat and other commodities. Of this experience he wrote, "I engaged in a crash schedule . . . obtaining food supplies from inland areas to help prevent problems of starvation in the Messina region."

To accomplish his task, Michele Sindona needed the protection of the Mafia because it controlled the produce industry and could supply him with the documents he needed to present to the border patrols. To this end, the bishop of Patti got in touch with Vito Genovese, a top-ranking member of the American Mafia who had helped to organize the American invasion of Sicily with the help of the Sicilian Mafia. Genovese, a major international drug smuggler and boss of the New York crime family founded by Lucky Luciano, used his influence with Sicilian Mafia dons and members of the American invasion force to arrange for fresh produce, forged papers, and a safe route for Michele Sindona.

Michele enjoyed the excitement and the praise he received from the people of Patti. With each delivery, families gathered around his truck. He proudly distributed the food, always sneaking an extra portion to his friends. Like his grandfather, Michele Sindona had come to their rescue. He earned his family the respect they had known during grandfather Sindona's lifetime. Now he was "king of Patti."

During this period, Michele made friends of many American soldiers and mafiosi. They spoke to him about life in America, about democracy, and the virtues of capitalism. They told him that in America a man with his ambition could become rich and famous and powerful. Of the war years, Michele says, "It was then that I realized, if I wanted to do something big, I would need to be friends with America." He told the Americans that someday he would come to the United States. Someday he would be an important person, and when he was, they should remember him, they could come to him. He would help them the way they had helped him to aid his people.

By 1944 the war was over for Sicily. Avvocato (attorney) Gensabella, a friend of the Sindona family, forged work papers that allowed Michele to open a *studio* specializing in tax and corporate law. He worked hard, and as his income increased Michele enjoyed an active social life. As if he felt he had to make up for the years spent studying, Michele dated nearly every young woman he met. Once he had successfully seduced one girl, he would hunt for another, even prettier one to conquer. But his career was what truly mattered to Michele, and it did not take him long to realize that in order to be accepted by the establishment he needed a wife.

Michele started seriously to court Caterina (Rina) Cilio, whom he had first met in *asilo* (kindergarten). The middle-class Cilio family had moved from Syracusa to Patti when Rina was five years old. Her father did not approve of Michele because he was poor and had a reputation as a womanizer. In Sicily, when a girl's father does not approve of her lover, the couple may solve the problem either by sleeping together for one night or by eloping. Once either is done, the father of the girl offers her seducer one of two choices: be killed or agree to a church wedding.

On September 2, 1944, Michele Sindona eloped with Rina Cilio. The next day they informed Rina's father of what they had done. Of the two choices given him, Michele chose a church wedding, and on September 4 he and Rina were married in the cathedral. Rina's father, however, disliked Michele so much that he refused to grant the newlyweds a dowry.

Michele's practice earned him enough to pay for an apartment in Messina, but he and Rina could not afford to buy furniture. A woman named Trina Mantaglia also had financial problems. Her husband had been killed in the war, leaving her with a two-year-old daughter and no money to pay rent. Trina's husband had been a friend of Michele. He offered her a solution: move her furniture into his apartment and live there rent-free. She accepted, and the four of them lived together until Michele moved his family to Milan.

To keep costs down Michele used the apartment as his office. He spent long hours interviewing clients and making extensive notes about their tax problems. At night Rina would sit at the kitchen table, which Trina Mantaglia's husband had nailed together from assorted pieces of old wood, and read Michele his notes while he tapped away on his portable typewriter. Twice a week when the washing was strung from one end of the kitchen to the other and shadows intensified the already poor lighting, Michele strained his eyes working late into the night and early morning. "I would get so tired," Rina explains. "I could not work as hard as Michele. He hardly ever slept. Every hour or so I would say to him, 'Michele, please! Just let me rest for five minutes. Then I can go on.' He would laugh, and I would rest my head on the table for a few minutes. Sometimes I would not wake up until morning. Michele would still be working." Even after the birth of Maria Elisa, their first child, Rina continued to help Michele transcribe his notes.

Michele Sindona eventually realized that the financial limitations of Messina were suppressing his talent and therefore his career. His reputation had grown. He was considered a brilliant and creative tax lawyer. After reading about Amadeo P. Giannini, who had emigrated to San Francisco in the late 1800s and founded the Bank of America, the largest bank in the world, Sindona recognized his own potential. In himself Michele saw the same genius. Furthermore, after reading the works of Friedrich Nietzsche, the German philosopher, Sindona came to believe that he was a rare and gifted individual. When he revealed his ambitions to Avvocato Gensabella, his friend suggested that Sindona move to Milan. The opportunities there were many: real estate investments, construction, the new stock exchange. The potential for wealth was great, the need for tax advice even greater. But Rina feared her husband's motives when he told her of Milan. Reflecting on that time, she says, "I wanted Michele to be satisfied, to remain a good lawyer — without trouble."

Michele, however, was not concerned, for he was leaving Messina with the blessings of the bishop and an introduction that would lead him to Giovanni Battista Montini, then pro-secretary of state for the Vatican.

4

THE VATICAN CONNECTION

TODAY, Milan is the financial and industrial capital of Italy. The city has a climate of extremes: cold winters, with rain, sleet, and snow; hot and humid summers, thick with smog. After the war Sicilians in search of opportunity moved to Milan. What they found was a desert of the kind that only war can create. All that remained in the ruins of its bombed factories was the memory of its greatness and the hope that the future would see the return of honor and financial stability to the city.

In 1948, when Michele Sindona arrived in Milan, his daughter Maria Elisa was a child of three and Rina was seven months pregnant. Immediately upon disembarking at the railroad station, people like the Sindonas saw the immediate and overwhelming profundity of social prejudice. Milanese businessmen in tailored suits, silk ties, and diamond cuff links greeted them with contempt, calling them "people of dirt." Outfitted in custom-made dresses and designer hats, the women strutted like peacocks passing a pigeon coop. The worst insult came from those who had the time to stop and gawk. "Peasants," they whispered not so softly. For Milan's social structure was, and still is, the most rigid in all of Italy. As one Sicilian CIA operative, who was stationed in Milan from 1948 to 1974, explains, "A young man moving from Sicily to Milan has thirty-two strikes against him — all because he is Sicilian."

The shock of a new land and the reality of being an unwanted stranger in a country that was supposed to be theirs frightened Rina so much that she pleaded with her husband to return to Sicily. But the challenge, his will to conquer, and his will to succeed prevented Michele from retreating.

Sindona moved his family into a moderate-sized apartment on the Via San Barnaba, a tiny, unattractive street in the center of Milan. Even after Rina gave birth to their son Nino, Michele continued to use the living room as his office, though he did hire Elisa Forli, a stocky woman who was very talkative and friendly, as his secretary. Forli was married to a successful doctor. She worked to keep busy, not for any need of money. This was an asset Michele found attractive. Forli could not be bribed; therefore the corporate holdings and financial interests of his clients would remain privileged.

In the beginning, however, there were lean years. Sindona's contacts were good, but they were not supplying him with the income he needed and wanted. At the time his dream was modest: he wanted only to be the most successful lawyer in Italy. When that goal seemed impossible, when his wife pleaded to return home to Patti to be with her people—people who spoke her dialect, for at the time she did not understand northern Italian—Michele decided he needed Nunziata by his side.

Michele had been receiving letters from his mother complaining about Nini's open love affair with a woman in Messina. The solution, he decided, was to move all four—Nunziata, Maria, Nini, and his younger brother Enio—to Milan, thereby separating Nini from his mistress. Michele moved Maria, Enio, and Nunziata into one apartment and Nini into another apartment, which was what they all wanted. But unlike Nunziata, who had a gift for solving people's problems, Michele then made a mistake: he hired a young and very pretty live-in maid for Nini, which did not please Maria.

"My father supported Nini," Maria Elisa explains. "He wanted Nini to be far away from this woman in Messina so that he would forget her, but Maria and Nini never lived together again." And because of Nini's infidelity, Nunziata refused to visit him. Whenever Michele attempted to get Nini and Nunziata together, she would say, "No, my son was wrong. I will stay with my daughter-in-law." In time, Nunziata became Maria's slave—bathing, dressing, and feeding her, dedicating herself to Michele's sickly mother to make up for the shameful way Nini had treated her.

On Sundays and holidays, however, the family would get together and pretend that everything was fine. Nini would come to the house with a box of sweets or something nice for Maria, and everybody would be happy for the day. Then Nini would leave, and Maria would think about his young maid and become sick with jealousy.

After Nunziata moved to Milan, Michele's belief in himself, his destiny, and life was no longer contaminated by confusion or doubt. Nunziata made Michele realize he had two advantages that his Sicilian countrymen lacked: he was light-skinned, which made it difficult to distinguish him from a Milanese, and he spoke perfect Italian, without the slightest hint of a Sicilian accent. While they were discussing the difficulties of building a career, Nunziata pointed out that Michele needed a gimmick to make the public aware of him. Thus Michele became a master of illusion.

"Michele was a magician," says Sheldon D. Zigelbaum, a psychotherapist who has studied Sindona's medical records and has conducted extensive interviews with Michele and his family. Michele realized, says Dr. Zigelbaum, "that people want to believe in magic, that magic is a necessary part of life." Without the trick, people feel cheated. Truth and honesty are not enough, and, in fact, may cause failure if they are not camouflaged by illusion.

Once Sindona realized this, he became a financial wizard, a sorcerer. "His trick," Zigelbaum explains, "was turning a financial statement inside out. If you put a company's statement—no other facts—in front of Michele, he could tell you where the company was incorporated, what problems it had, who caused the problems, and how to resolve them. It was a con, but he had to know his stuff. People who deal on the level that Sindona dealt on must have a great depth of knowledge. If they don't, the con doesn't work.

"Privately, his clients—like all of us, once the con is uncovered—were willing to acknowledge the con while continuing to participate. When the con becomes public knowledge, when the magician's trick is revealed, when we are embarrassed because everyone knows we've been made fools of—only then do we rebel.

"So Michele was able to convince clients that their problems could be resolved but that the solution would be expensive and that they would have to work together. The clients would pay a large fee and/or give Michele stock, and they would feel good because the magician had performed well. He never told them he could fix things with a phone call, never said, 'I have a connection who will increase distribution.' He knew what to say, how to say it, and, most important, he enhanced the mystery."

Michele's magic act started with a sideshow titled "L'Avvocato Risponde," a daily newspaper column offering the people of Milan free legal advice. People too poor to afford the advice of an attorney mailed their questions to "L'Avvocato Risponde." Michele Sindona published the inquiries and his advice in the newspaper. His capacity to work long hours, together with his competence and his ability to identify problems quickly and find creative solutions, accelerated the growth of his practice, his reputation, and his wealth.

As his practice grew, Michele quickly recognized the need to establish himself as a specialist. In Italy at the time, all law offices had a general practice: criminal, civil, corporate, bankruptcy, and divorce law. Studio Sindona, however, concentrated only on corporate and tax law. On commission, Michele hired Matteo Maciocco, a lawyer and *commerciale* (accountant), and Vittorio Ghezzi, a *commerciale*. With their assistance Sindona was able to follow market trends. Clients found this service invaluable, and soon many of Milan's richest and most prestigious families sought Sindona's advice. Sometimes a client could not pay Michele's fee. Sindona, unruffled, was delighted to take stock in the client's company instead. From such seemingly kind gestures, the Sicilian lawyer was able to build real wealth while his ordinary income continued to increase. But Michele's big break came when Nunziata wrote to the bishop of Messina, asking him to introduce Michele to important financial figures in the Vatican.

The bishop suggested that Michele speak with Monsignor Amleto Tondini, an official of the Curia, the central administration governing the financial affairs of the church. Ironically Monsignor Tondini turned out to be a distant relative; his sister was married to one of Sindona's cousins. Tondini proved to be a valuable contact, for he was secretary of the briefs of princes and would later deliver the traditional address, "On Choosing a Pontiff," to the members of Conclave 81 two days before the cardinals were to select Montini as divine heir to the Fisherman's throne.

Monsignor Tondini wrote a letter introducing Michele Sindona as a "man of trust" to Vatican Prince Massimo Spada, a high-ranking member of the Vatican's "black nobility," an elite group of men who by birthright have access to the Vatican's financial holdings. A large man with thin gray hair who always dressed in a gray, double-breasted suit with pants that started above his rib cage and extended down to the tops of his shoes, Massimo Spada was not wealthy. A dedicated servant of the Holy See, he worked to produce profits for the church, manipulating the system so that the Vatican would play an important role in Italy's economic life.

Spada was only one of many Vatican advisers, but he may have been the most dedicated and the most sincere. He did not have the distinction of being the pope's banker, but the Vatican considered him a man of honor. Spada was a cautious banker and financial expert, not a speculator. He had always bought small blocks of shares rather than controlling interest. He was liked and respected and frequently served as arbitrator during delicate negotiations between government and private concerns. A powerful and influential man, he held the secrets of the national economy in his hands during postwar reconstruction.

If Nunziata was the most important person in Michele's private life and if Principal Nasilli was the most influential person during Michele's school years, then it is correct to say that Massimo Spada, twenty years older than Michele Sindona, proved to be the most important person during the lawyer's early career in Milan. After meeting Michele, Spada immediately took the young man under his wing, introducing him to many important people, including Giovanni Montini.

By 1948 Giovanni Montini had advanced to the position of monsignor, serving as the Vatican's pro-secretary of state. He was in the right place at the right time that year, when Pope Pius XII decided the Vatican should invest its fortunes in the redevelopment of postwar Italy. Not only was Monsignor Montini one of the most powerful men in the Vatican; he was also the favorite of Pope Pius. For Montini's years of service as pro-secretary of state had made him wise in fiscal matters. Also, as the son of Giorgio Montini, one of the founders of the Christian Democratic party, he had a knowledge and understanding of politics that Pius found useful during the elections of 1948.

Following Pius's orders, Montini assigned the Vatican investment project to Massimo Spada. Before Spada could implement the investment of Vatican funds, however, it was important to ensure that the Vatican's political arm, the Christian Democratic party, beat the communists at the polls. This was a delicate situation, for although the Vatican needed to win, it did not want a repetition of what had occurred the previous year in Sicily.

In 1947 the Christian Democrats had suffered a major setback. The Mafia, the Christian Democrats, and the outlaw Salvatore Giuliano together formed the framework of a separatist movement that invited the United States to annex Sicily. Support for the separatists was believed to be strong. A poll taken just before the elections of that year revealed that a majority of Sicilians did not share a political identity with Italy. The United States rejected the separatists' offer to annex Sicily, but with U.S. assistance Italy agreed to grant autonomy to the island. The Sicilian parliament would have complete control of provincial matters; however, Italy would have power over the island's foreign policy.

Later that same year, however, the spirit of reform was high when the people of Portella della Ginestra went to the polls and elected to parliament members of the Popular Front (the Communist party). This was a terrible defeat for the Christian Democratic party. It had been the ruling party since 1919, when Father Luigi Sturzo, a Sicilian, and Giorgio Montini, the father of Pope Paul VI, founded the Parito Populari Italiano, which after World War II became known as the Christian Democratic party.

Determined to regain control of the island, the Christian Democrats turned to the Mafia for help. In return for the right to appoint mafiosi as leading members of the party, the Mafia agreed to teach the communists a lesson.

In behalf of democracy, the Mafia enlisted as their agent Salvatore Giuliano. He and his cousin Gaspere Pisciotta led their men into Portella della Ginestra. Without prejudice, they shot and killed a dozen people and wounded more than fifty others. New elections were held, and the Christian Democratic party won a resounding victory. Later, at the orders of the Mafia, Pisciotta murdered Salvatore Giuliano. At his trial, Gaspere Pisciotta said of the massacre, "We were a single body: bandits, police, and Mafia, like the Father, the Son, and the Holy Ghost." Ultimately, this "black trinity" would give birth to a more powerful group known as the High Mafia, or the political Mafia. For from that time forward the right wing of the Christian Democratic party would be dominated by Mafia-connected politicians, a fate that not only would lead to the corruption of Italian politics and the infiltration of industry and banking by well-educated Mafia-connected men like Michele Sindona but would also lead to the contamination of the Holy See.

In Rome, in 1948, Italian journalists were predicting a major victory by the Communist party. Palmiro Togliatti, the president of the Italian Communist party, preached political and economic opportunity, the need for Italy to become the workers' country, and the absolute necessity of nationalization. His vehicle was the Instituto per la Ricostruzione, the government holding company created by Mussolini in 1933. Like most countries that have lived under fascism, Italy wanted change. Togliatti, a gifted orator, offered dramatic change. The Vatican's fear was clear: communism posed a threat to its religious, political, and economic strength.

The embattled Pope Pius put his faith in Montini to organize a campaign that would defeat the communists. Of Montini's brilliant efforts, biographer Alden Hatch wrote, "Through more than three hundred bishops, a hundred and twenty-five thousand other prelates, and nearly five million members of Catholic Action he led a drive that astonished the experts." Hatch went on to describe how, just before the elections, Montini summoned hundreds of thousands of people to St. Peter's Square: "The crowd filled the broad square and extended back along the Via Conciliazione to the bridges across the Tiber and even along its farther banks and up the Corso Vittorio Emmanuele. The Holy Father, in the white and gold vestments of his sacred office, spoke to them. . . . Pope Pius made a fiery speech . . . in the tradition of the Crusades . . . and his passionate words lifted the hearts and pierced the spirits of all who heard him." Pius's speech had also been broadcast over the Vatican radio station, and through-out Italy the voters responded to his message. The right wing of the Chris-tian Democratic party came to power with Premier Alcide de Gasperi.

Montini had defeated the communists. Fascism, communism, social-ism — throughout history, the church had outlasted and outmaneuvered all of them. The Holy See had survived. The Vatican States no longer existed, but the church now controlled all of Italy through its political arm, the Christian Democratic party, and the power of the church was vested in Premier Alcide de Gasperi, a former Vatican clerk.

Able to enjoy the glory of victory and the privilege of security, the Vatican moved its economic plans forward. Massimo Spada immediately placed in motion the Vatican's plan to purchase stock in important Italian businesses. The man Spada enlisted to help him fulfill the Vatican's finan-cial goals was Michele Sindona. It was the beginning of a relationship that in a few short years would lead Sindona into the world of international banking.

On November 3, 1954, Giovanni Montini was appointed archbishop of Milan. When he arrived in the city, Montini discovered that the commu-nists had added more than 1.5 million members to their party. He was not prepared for the shock. The results of his evangelistic work of 1948 had deteriorated beyond anyone's expectation. Milanese layman were dis-gusted with the system and with the church. They did not want prayer; they wanted and needed money to feed their families. The majority of union officials were communists led by Pietro Secchia, a violent organizer with a smile marked by gold teeth. Montini's assignment was to convince the workers to come back to the church and support the Christian Dem-ocratic party.

In January 1955, when Secchia tried to stop Montini from saying mass inside the factories, the archbishop requested help from Michele Sindona, who by then was an extremely successful tax attorney with con-siderable influence in the business community. Sindona, a devoted anti-communist, placed calls to many of his clients who owned factories and mills. He reminded them that capitalism and democracy had offered them the opportunity to gain wealth and independence. "The liberals promise everything, but have never delivered," he said. "Only capitalism will sup-port private enterprise, and only through private enterprise will the people have security and freedom." As a result, Montini was able to celebrate mass and bring his message to the people.

Each afternoon Archbishop Montini and his friend Michele Sindona would visit factories and mill shops. Montini demonstrated an honest interest in the laborers and their work. He listened to their complaints about the church and the system. He attacked the dangers inherent in leftist ideology. He and Sindona spoke of the need to support freedom, the church, and the Christian Democrats. Finally, after months of work, the election results showed that Montini had again succeeded. Many of Secchia's union officials had been replaced by right-wing Christian Democrats.

In early 1959 Montini again enlisted Sindona's help. A priest who attended this and many other meetings between Montini and Sindona, both when Montini was archbishop and after he became pope, recalls, "Montini had been intrigued with Sindona ever since Sindona helped the archbishop win the support of the workers in Milan. So when Montini needed $2 million to build a home for the elderly he again turned to Michele Sindona."

They met just after 11:00 P.M. inside Milan's cathedral, a magnificent example of Gothic architecture and excess, with an altar of gold and marble trimmed with emeralds and rubies. When Sindona arrived, he joined the archbishop at the foot of the altar and said a silent prayer before discussing business. Then they moved to the second pew, both of them facing the altar and talking in whispers. "I was kneeling four rows behind them — praying, but mostly watching," recalls the priest. "Every so often Sindona would lean toward Montini as if straining to hear what the archbishop was saying. In a few minutes, they had finished. Sindona kissed Montini's hand, Montini smiled, and then I heard Sindona say, 'Don't worry. I won't abandon you.' "

In a single day, Michele raised all of the money. It has been said that Sindona got the money from a CIA operative who was stationed in Milan at that time. Sindona does not deny having had strong CIA contacts. In an interview published in a Milanese magazine called *Panorama*, former CIA operative Victor Marchetti supports the possibility that the $2 million did come from the CIA. He says that "in the 1950s and 1960s the CIA gave economic support to many activities promoted by the Catholic church, from orphanages to the missions. Millions of dollars each year . . . to a great number of bishops and monsignors. One of them was Cardinal Giovanni Battista Montini. It is possible that Cardinal Montini did not know where the money was coming from. He may have thought that it came from friends."

If the money did come from CIA contacts Sindona may have acquired during the American occupation of Sicily, he probably would not have admitted this to Montini. If he had, it is likely that Montini would not have cared.

The year 1959 was an important one in Michele Sindona's life. He had not only established a bonding relationship with Archbishop Montini but had also made an important contact with American businessmen.

In that same year Crucible Steel of America was interested in acquiring a steel mill in Italy. Daniel Porco, certified public accountant and vice-president in charge of Crucible's international operations, went to Milan to study a number of steel companies, including Vanzetti Steel, which was owned by Ernesto Moizzi, a friend and client of Michele Sindona. Moizzi had been introduced to the young lawyer by Massimo Spada. Of his meeting with Moizzi, Porco says, "I didn't like him, and I didn't like the plant, so I left and went about my business. But I couldn't find a mill in Italy, so I went to France." There Porco looked at half a dozen companies. He searched for two months. Unable to make a deal, Porco returned to the United States.

In the meantime, Moizzi told Sindona about Porco's visit. By this time, Sindona had fulfilled his dream: largely because of his association with Spada and Montini, Sindona's practice was now the largest in Italy, and he had long since moved his office out of his apartment and into a splendid suite. When a large stock transaction or real estate purchase was made, the streets of Milan echoed with the rumor: "That belongs to the Group Sindona," as his organization was called.

Hearing of Porco's interest in Vanzetti Steel, Sindona quickly recognized the opportunity to make a connection with American businesses wanting to do business in Italy. While Moizzi was still sitting in his office, Sindona reviewed the Vanzetti company file. He quickly glanced over the balance sheet and income statement and then advised Moizzi to sell. "I will handle everything," he assured him.

When Porco reported to Joel Hunter, president of Crucible, Hunter showed him a letter from Michele Sindona. The letter suggested that they take another look at Vanzetti, that it was an appropriate time for Moizzi to sell. Then, Porco recalls, "Sindona sent an emissary to visit with Hunter. He convinced us to take another look. The price was different, and the deal was different, so I went back to Italy. Instead of buying the plant, we bought only the inventory, receivables, and certain equipment. And instead of paying cash, we bought Vanzetti with stock. It was a much better deal. Sindona was very businesslike. He lived up to everything he said he would do. When problems arose that could not have been seen at the time of purchase, he did everything possible to resolve matters. . . . Eventually Michele became Crucible's fiscal adviser in Italy. . . . He arranged bank lines. . . . He was helpful in every way."

Later Michele Sindona would arrange for Daniel Porco—a Group member would later refer to Porco as Sindona's "Diamond Head," his key man in America—and his wife to adopt a baby boy in Italy. In America Daniel Porco would help Sindona purchase Libby, McNeil & Libby; Brown Paper Company; Argus, Inc.; and Interphoto Corporation. He would introduce the financier to at least one high-ranking member of the

Republican party. And in 1972 Daniel Porco would search for an American bank for Sindona to purchase.

Ernesto Moizzi was also the founder, president, and majority stockholder of Milan's Banca Privata Finanziaria (BPF). In 1960, one year after the Vanzetti deal, Moizzi and his partner Mino Brughera decided to sell BPF. Pleased with the way Sindona had handled the Vanzetti transaction and aware of Sindona's close association with Massimo Spada, Moizzi asked the lawyer to arrange the sale of the bank to the Instituto per le Opere di Religione (IOR).

Ironically, at the same time, the Vatican instructed Massimo Spada to locate a bank in Milan to act as the IOR's correspondent. Archbishop Giovanni Montini, who continued to play an important role in Vatican finances, suggested to Spada that the man to handle such a project was Michele Sindona.

When Sindona told Spada that BPF was available, Spada, usually reserved and modest, became excited. He knew Banca Privata Finanziaria well. It was a small bank with a good reputation and clients of substantial importance. He considered the bank an excellent vehicle for the Vatican. Spada told Sindona to negotiate the purchase of BPF on behalf of the Vatican. To Michele's surprise, however, Spada told him that Archbishop Montini had convinced the Vatican to make Sindona its partner and fiscal adviser. It was agreed that the Holy See would own and control 60 percent of the stock and that Sindona would control 40 percent, either by ownership or through his Group.

During negotiations, however, the name of Tito Carnelutti came up. Carnelutti had made friends with Sindona when Sindona first moved to Milan. While Sindona was struggling to build his practice, Carnelutti brought clients to him and also, in return for tax advice, made Sindona his partner in many real estate transactions. So it was natural for Sindona to want Carnelutti to become his partner in BPF, especially since Carnelutti held controlling interest of Banque de Financement (Finabank) of Geneva. Having an inside connection to a Swiss bank offered tremendous opportunity: lines of credit, secrecy, and the chance to move currency out of Italy by way of the fiduciary contract, a secret Swiss document that conceals the true owner of the funds being moved by listing only the names of the banks involved in the transaction. The Vatican refused to purchase the bank, however, unless Sindona agreed not to make Carnelutti a shareholder, for Carnelutti, according to Sindona, was not considered a man of discretion — and secrecy is as important to the Vatican as it is to the underworld.

"Tito," Sindona explains, "would have bragged. He would have divulged information, and therefore a good banker considered him dangerous." So Sindona assured Spada, Moizzi, and Franco Marinotti, president of the textile firm Snia Viscosa and a client of Sindona's who had agreed to purchase 20 percent of the bank's stock, that Carnelutti would not be either a stockholder or a director of BPF.

The Bank of the Vatican acquired the portfolio of stock. To conceal the partnership, the Vatican's IOR remained the registered underwriter in the resale and distribution of the stock to Franco Marinotti and to Fasco Italiano, a holding company wholly owned by Michele Sindona. But Sindona had deceived the Holy See, for the 20 percent purchased by Fasco was split with Tito Carnelutti. Sindona says he lied because Carnelutti had been a friend to him from the beginning. He felt that he owed Carnelutti the courtesy of friendship. As Nunziata had taught him, he refused to judge Carnelutti by what others had to say about him. This blind consideration would ultimately play an important role in Sindona's fall.

The purchase of BPF was more than an important step for Michele Sindona; it also increased Massimo Spada's prestige within the Vatican, which did not please Cardinal Di Jorio, president of IOR. If Spada had an enemy, it was Cardinal Di Jorio. Like most cardinals, Di Jorio did not understand finance. As a result, he and Spada constantly battled—Di Jorio for control of the bank's fortune and the power that fortune represented, Spada to enrich the Vatican vault.

Shortly after the purchase of BPF, Cardinal Di Jorio and Massimo Spada had their final confrontation. Monsignor De Luca, the well-known scholar and theologian, asked Spada to obtain a loan of 10 million lire (approximately $16,666) to finance the completion of his book and to purchase new volumes for his famous library. Cardinal Di Jorio did not like the scholar, whom he considered weak and pompous about his work. On hearing of the request, the cardinal called Spada to his office and forbade him to make or obtain a loan for the monsignor. Spada argued that De Luca's work and library would eventually be donated to the Vatican and that their value would surpass the amount of the loan. But Di Jorio refused to change his mind.

News of the situation reached Pope John XXIII. The pope asked Spada to help Monsignor De Luca. Spada was caught between granting Pope John's request and obeying Cardinal Di Jorio's order not to help the scholarly priest. He chose to please the pope. In order to avoid further conflict with Di Jorio, Spada decided not to use BPF. In an attempt to circumvent another conflict with Di Jorio, Spada convinced Credito Lombardo—a bank in which the Vatican owned shares but which was separate from the IOR—to grant De Luca the loan. Spada did not realize, however, that Credito Lombardo also owned shares in Finabank, Carnelutti's Swiss bank, and someone at Credito Lombardo mentioned the loan to Tito Carnelutti.

Carnelutti, to no one's surprise, found the situation too amusing to keep to himself. He bragged about being such an important banker and confidant that the pope had instructed Spada to seek his help in arranging a loan for Monsignor De Luca. When his tale reached Cardinal Di Jorio, the cardinal ordered Spada to return the money to Credito Lombardo. And because the cardinal knew just how important the BPF deal was to Spada, to sweeten his revenge, he caused Spada humiliation by ordering him to resell the BPF shares through a security account at Credito Lombardo.

While Sindona's mentor was battling Cardinal Di Jorio, Michele was busy moving his family into the Hotel Principe è Savoia. The Sindonas' apartment house had been sold and was being torn down so that a park could be constructed. Because Michele had not found time to locate another home, he rented the largest apartment in the hotel, with a suite for Maria Elisa, a suite for his sons Marco and Nino, and a suite for Rina and himself. There was also a living room with plush white carpeting, a dining room — for which Michele and Maria Elisa had to buy the furniture because Rina refused to spend the money Michele gave her — and a room for the governess.

What Michele liked most about living in a hotel was the room service and the central air conditioning. "My father hates the heat," Nino says. "When it's hot he feels like dying. His headaches get really bad; he becomes nervous and really depressed." Rina hated living in a hotel, however. She did not want to raise her family in an atmosphere of room service and maids. "I wanted a home," she says, "a real home, one with a kitchen so I could bake Sicilian pastries and cook Sicilian dinners for Michele and the children." It took her two years to convince Michele to buy an apartment.

In the meantime, Nino and Marco entertained themselves by stealing shoes that the hotel guests left outside their doors to be shined. The boys would move the shoes to different floors, causing so much trouble that Michele had to pay an extra rental fee in order to keep peace between his children and the hotel management. And whenever Rina pleaded with Michele to buy a house or an apartment, he would say, "Rina, cara, why the hell do you have to have a house when here you have the best service in the world? When you like, you have a guest, and you don't have to work around the kitchen. You just call room service, and they come up with a million plates, and they serve you the best dishes." So for two years Rina didn't fix lunch, because Michele wanted the family to eat in the hotel restaurant.

Each day at 2:00 P.M., Michele, his family, and the governess would eat lunch at the same table in the southeast corner of the dining room. It was there that Massimo Spada found his young protégé. Bewildered, he told Michele that Di Jorio had learned of the De Luca loan because of Carnelutti and had ordered him to repay the money. Spada explained that he did not have it and that honor prevented him from asking Monsignor De Luca to return it.

Michele realized that his friendship with Carnelutti had jeopardized Spada's position. Abruptly Michele excused himself from the table, after first insisting that Spada try the *battuta di manzo*, very thin slices of beef sautéed quickly on a grill, while he waited for him to return. Shortly Michele returned and handed Spada a briefcase containing the ten million lire needed to pay back the loan. Stunned, Massimo Spada thanked Sindona the only way he knew how—he asked him to find a way that he, Michele, could take control of BPF.

Michele Sindona was unprepared for the opportunity of owning controlling interest of BPF. His concerns, as he later said, were as follows:

- "Ernesto Moizzi had sold the bank because he had confidence in the acquiring parties. They lent prestige to the bank. He would never have sold it to a private individual.

- "I did not have a reputation as a banker. My taking control of a bank known for its competence and discretion could have caused problems in the banking community, especially if Moizzi resigned as president.

- "The transfer of stock to the IOR was already known. An immediate resale might raise doubts about the bank's stability.

- "My money was invested in small companies and real estate. It would not be easy to raise the amount necessary to meet the cost of the shares.

- "Franco Marinotti might request that his shares also be repurchased. That would have made it impossible for me to take control."

The only possible solution was for Sindona to appeal to a first-class foreign bank. "Such a negotiation," he explains, "would have taken several months." Sindona didn't have months because Cardinal Di Jorio was pressuring Spada.

The BPF acquisition was one of the few deals Michele discussed with his wife. Rina remembers that Michele wanted the bank because he believed that if he owned a bank he would have the respect and acceptance that the Milanese community, regardless of Sindona's success, still refused to bestow on the Sicilian. But as much as he wanted the bank, his vision of becoming another A. P. Giannini and perhaps even building a banking empire larger than Giannini's Bank of America seemed to be evading him. After examining all of his possibilities, Michele sadly told Rina that he did not think he could put together a large enough block of shares. "Just be content," Rina remembers saying to her husband. "Too much too fast is not easy to digest." But BPF did not evade Michele's reach.

After hearing Sindona's concerns about himself and his suggestion that Marinotti take control of the bank, Massimo Spada rejected it all. "I want you," Michele recalls Spada saying. "You will inject energy into BPF. You can bring international business to the bank." But there was not enough time, Michele argued, not unless he made Tito Carnelutti a partner. To his surprise, Massimo told Sindona to talk with Tito to see if he would divide the block with him. "Massimo," Michele laughed, "Tito is the cause of your problem. How could you possibly suggest such a thing? No, it won't work. You'd better look elsewhere." But Massimo persisted. He assured Sindona that he would convince Tito to remain a silent partner and that he, Massimo, would remain an adviser to the bank. That, he said, would resolve any doubts Moizzi and Marinotti might have.

Spada kept his promise. On October 28, 1960, Fasco Italiano took control of Banca Privata Finanziaria.

The embarrassment of the sale of BPF and the return of the money to Credito Lombardo was not enough revenge for Cardinal Di Jorio, however. Complete humiliation fell upon Massimo Spada when the cardinal wrongly accused him of being incompetent and of becoming wealthy to the detriment of the church. Di Jorio forced the prince to resign as chief administrator of the Bank of the Vatican.

Michele Sindona became a banker; Massimo Spada, once the mentor, became his student's employee. In time Sindona also replaced Spada as the Vatican's new *uomo di fiducia*. And years later, Prince Massimo Spada would be arrested and jailed by the Italian authorities for his connection with Group Sindona.

5

THE POWER BROKER

TO SUCCEED IN MILAN it was important to maintain a good relationship with Enrico Cuccia. Cuccia—a tall, dark-skinned Sicilian with cold black eyes—was the powerful head of Mediobanca, Italy's government-owned financial institution. Like many Sicilians who had moved north, Cuccia was a socialist. He believed that nationalization would bring economic equality to Italy, especially in the impoverished southern provinces. He was as dedicated to his program as Sindona was to capitalism. This meant that the two men were destined to become enemies, for Sindona had built an empire by associating himself with powerful groups that could serve him, while Cuccia had built a base of power through the Instituto per la Ricostruzione Industriale (Institute for Reconstruction, also known as IRI), Italy's government-owned holding company.

The IRI bought a majority interest in private companies. It set up agencies to manage those companies and compete with private enterprise. The ideology was to give the public better service and prevent the corruption of public officials by private interest groups. The new leaders of this nationalization were Enrico Cuccia and Ugo La Malfa, Italy's minister of finance.

As a whole, private business opposed the infiltration of government, warning that it would lead to communism. More than one irony existed in the political and economic chaos of Italy. One was that many of the men who opposed nationalization—those who were true capitalists—were appointed managing directors of IRI companies. Another is that in many instances entrepreneurs, such as Sindona, were partners with the IRI, the very institution they opposed, for capitalists recognized the opportunity for graft. Once the movement toward nationalization took hold, many of them sought positions of power within the IRI structure. And because the IRI had huge resources and desired to work in cooperation with private sectors, independent businessmen gladly accepted the IRI as a partner.

After Michele Sindona took over Banca Privata Finanziaria in 1960, Cuccia realized that Sindona—Vatican man, private banker, and entrepreneur—was a person he should meet, if only because Sindona's reputation as a shrewd businessman interested him. Although Cuccia maintained his power, Sindona had captured the imagination of the people. The Vatican, the government, and the bankers wanted to be partners with the young and brilliant tax attorney and financier, Michele Sindona. The Christian Democrats, the Mafia, and private enterprise also wanted to become part of Group Sindona. And Sindona courted them all, because he wanted and needed their friendship and their money. In return, he promised them profits and, more important, confidentiality.

Sindona concealed the identity of his partners and financial backers by manipulating bank secrecy laws, which enabled him to hide people's identities from the government and other groups. When someone enquired about one of his clients, Sindona claimed attorney–client privilege. Finally, he practiced the Sicilian code of *omerta*—shielding clients not only from the public and the minister of finance but often from the other partners as well. This, however, was more than a protection for clients. The secrecy created power; power created respect and opportunity; power, respect, and opportunity created profits; and profits coupled with power, respect, and opportunity built empires.

The mystery surrounding Sindona was a result of more than his ability to keep secrets. It was fed, also, by the way he bought and sold companies: purchasing distressed corporations and turning a quick profit by dividing their divisions and selling them off one by one—"sometimes," he boasts, "in the same day." Still, Milan is a city that thrives as much on curiosity and rumor as it does on banking and industry, and Sindona's idiosyncrasies stimulated the minds of the Milanese, for they saw Sindona in restaurants eating cubes of sugar or folding pieces of paper into papal hats during conferences or while talking on the phone. "Set a candy wrapper or an empty cigarette pack on his desk," a banker explains, "and before you knew it, he was making one of those hats out of it." He painted them red, yellow, green, many different colors, and stacked them on his desk or credenza the way a hunter would exhibit a kill.

There was also the well-known gesture. When an opponent proved himself right and Michele wrong, Sindona flipped both palms upward, his head fell to one side, his eyes shut, and an expression of annoyance stretched across his lips and brow — "as if to say," explains a lawyer who represented him, "I know you're right, but I won't give you the satisfaction of knowing that I know you are right." Finally, there was the story he told about his appendectomy. "I was twenty-seven," he recalls. "I refused anesthesia. I wanted to see everything, because I don't like not knowing what is happening to me. I forced the doctor to place a mirror above me so that I could see what was happening. Pain does not bother me. I don't accept prolonged pain — three hours of pain is different — *cut in and continue!*"

Enrico Cuccia, like many others, wondered how Michele Sindona had risen so rapidly. Rumors indicated that Michele Sindona was backed by the Vatican and the Mafia, but whenever Sindona was asked about these things, he remained silent, thus creating speculation and more rumors. There were those who admired him, however, considered him bright, and did not care who was backing him. After all, many people made money buying stock in companies that Don Michele, as he was now called, was said to control. Yet there were also those who feared him, if only because he was mysterious and Sicilian. Though Cuccia was also Sicilian, he was protected from the gossip because he was a government man — the most powerful financial figure in Italy. So everyone who doubted, admired, and feared Michele Sindona was left with the same question: *who is he?* Enrico Cuccia was determined to find out.

When Sindona learned that Enrico Cuccia wanted to meet him, he was busy reorganizing BPF and tried to dismiss the invitation, for he believed nothing good could come from meeting a man whose beliefs were so opposite to his own. Though Massimo Spada, Archbishop Montini, and a few of Sindona's clients and friends also opposed nationalization, they cautioned Sindona, explaining that Cuccia was a man of great importance and should not be ignored. A good strategist, Sindona was told, would not force Cuccia to come to him, because to do so would be a show of disrespect that no one could afford. Cuccia, they pointed out, could make it difficult for Sindona's American clients to invest in Italy. Duly warned, Sindona agreed to a meeting.

They met for the first time in Cuccia's office — two Sicilians, each powerful, each a financial genius. Cuccia represented government and nationalization; Sindona represented free enterprise and Western economic philosophies. The plotting that went on in each man's mind must have been intriguing. What Luigi Barzini, author of *The Italians*, wrote about Sicilians offers some insight:

> Their capacity to grasp situations with lightning speed, invent a way out of intricate tangles, gauge exactly the relative power of contending parties, weave wonderfully complex intrigues, coldly control their smallest acts, emotions and words . . . bewilders continental Italians. The islanders are so expert, in fact, that they neutralize each other . . . each participant inventing diabolical schemes of his own to get the better of his opponent and, at the same time, foresee all possible schemes which his opponent will try to employ.

Their conversation drifted away from economic policy when Cuccia began to warn Sindona of the dangers of associating with the wrong groups. "It is not easy to be accepted in Milan," Cuccia said. "Too much success, Michele, and people of importance can be made to turn against you. The right friends are important, more important than brains."

Cuccia went on to warn Sindona that Mediobanca might be interested in initiating joint ventures with BPF. It would be helpful, however, if Michele ended his friendship with Tito Carnelutti, for certain members of Milan's financial sector did not like or trust Carnelutti. "That's impossible," Sindona said. "Tito is a friend. He helped me when I first moved to the North. I will judge him by what he has done for me, how he has treated me, not by what people tell me!"

The meeting ended with Cuccia and Sindona at odds with each other over Sindona's friendship with Carnelutti. Later, Michele made this note:

> Cuccia struck me as a very introverted and reserved person. Certainly not a simple character!—endowed with a tremendous knowledge of banking technique. (In effect he declared himself the author of the Banking Law of 1934.) He has contacts with the most important groups in Italy! . . . was not likable . . . has an insatiable appetite for power!

Later, at a conference of the executive board of Società per le Condotte d'Acqua, a Vatican-owned company, Sindona asked Massimo Spada, Loris Corei, and Tullio Torchiani, all members of the Vatican's "black nobility," their opinion of Enrico Cuccia. They all agreed that Cuccia was ferociously determined to destroy private enterprise, to exploit nationalism, to have everything under his control; not for money, but for power.

Nationalization aligned itself with the far left, which threatened to destroy not only free enterprise but also the power of the right-wing Christian Democrats, a development that would dilute the Vatican's influence over Italian politics. Michele Sindona and his Vatican friends therefore entertained the idea of conquering Enrico Cuccia. Unfortunately for them, however, no one was able to find Cuccia's weakness. Sindona explains that "in order to succeed with people, to get what you want from them and therefore to dominate them, you must discover their Achilles' heel, so to speak." So Michele Sindona assigned to himself the task of finding Cuccia's weak spot, a project that proved extremely difficult.

Enrico Cuccia lived on a modest salary, his home was simple, and he was never seen in the company of a woman other than his wife. His only indulgence was the excellent education he gave his children. He frowned on extravagance, preferring conservative clothes and a small, graceful office. By all accounts one could not possibly reach him with money.

With this in mind, Sindona invited Cuccia to his new office at 29 Via Turati. It was a small office with enough space for a secretary, a few employees, and a private room for Sindona, who worked at a beautiful hand-carved monk's table. The room contained two eighteenth-century armchairs, both purposely uncomfortable, to discourage lengthy meetings, for Sindona did not like conferences that lasted more than thirty minutes. There were two paintings by Piassetta, a Saint Jerome and a Crucifixion; a wooden statue by Laurana; and a small bust by Antonio Pollaiuolo, the fifteenth-century Florentine artist. One window overlooked a maze of red-tile roofs. The other offered a view of the famous San Giuseppe Cathedral. And there were many books on law, taxes, banking—including a book about A. P. Giannini and the Bank of America that had several pages folded back and many passages underlined—and on philosophy, most significantly a collection of works by Friedrich Nietzsche.

"Nietzsche's superman," explains Albert J. Seaver, an American neuropsychiatrist who treated Sindona for migraines for many years, "had a remarkable influence on Michele. His headaches, his digestive problem, his insomnia—all of them seem to relate to Michele's strong identification with Nietzsche." Michele has admitted a certain admiration for Nietzsche's superman, or overman, theory. "I think Nietzsche was a genius," Michele says. "There is a higher morality, void of any responsibility to the masses." Dr. Seaver suggests that at some point, when Michele was being attacked by Enrico Cuccia and the left, his identity may have metamorphosed into Nietzsche's superman.

Dr. Seaver adds further insight, suggesting passages that Sindona either memorized or marked with ink.

From *Beyond Good and Evil*:

● Independence is for the very few; it is a privilege of the strong.

● Today the concept of "greatness" entails being noble, wanting to be by oneself, being capable of being different, standing alone, and having to live independently.

● He shall be the greatest who can be the loneliest, the most hidden, the most deviating, the human being beyond good and evil, the master of his virtues, he that is overrich in will.

From *Thus Spoke Zarathustra:*

● Let me reveal my heart to you entirely, my friends: *if* there were gods, how could I endure not to be a god! *Hence* there are no gods.

Nietzsche's superman has courage, a strong and dominating will, and an impulse toward power. He is independent and therefore opposed to socialism. He has no fear and believes that to conform to the moral code of society is to fear the organized power of an inferior people. "Michele Sindona," adds Dr. Seaver, "envisioned Enrico Cuccia and the left-wing political parties in Italy as the real evil."

Sindona had hoped that his office, with its simple elegance, would impress Cuccia. "Impressing a person," Michele says, "is the first step, the first brick on the road to conquering that person." But Cuccia left the office without commenting and with disappointment drawn tightly across his dark, thin face. Confused by Cuccia's reaction, Sindona told a friend, "Cuccia is hard to read. My office didn't impress him. Money means nothing to him, and he guards his emotions. How do you deal with a man like him?" Michele had failed. A month passed, and another. Still Sindona did not hear from Cuccia. He was the first important person in Milan to regard Sindona's charismatic personality with reserve. Defeat seemed unavoidable. Then, on the same day that Sindona told Ernesto Moizzi that he had decided the best way to handle Cuccia was to stay away from him, Cuccia called and invited Sindona to dinner.

At the restaurant in the Palace Hotel, Cuccia finally complimented Sindona on the style of his office. He seemed to be uncomfortable with Sindona, however. He asked Michele if he supported Nietzsche's ideology. "Do *you?*" Sindona asked.

"Most of Nietzsche is misunderstood," Cuccia said. "Power in the hands of people with social conscience is good. But the theory of a superman, a noble man above the will of authority is dangerous."

"Nietzsche was crazy," Michele said, folding a napkin into the shape of a crown, "but he was also a genius. I prefer to spend my time with a genius, even an insane genius, rather than with a weak and stupid person."

Cuccia was still uncomfortable, but he appeared to relax a bit. He criticized wealthy Italian families for being behind the times. According to Sindona, Cuccia said they were unworthy of the fortunes they inherited. "Soon," Cuccia predicted, "everything will be under the control of

Mediobanca and the IRI. There will be no more of this lopsided capitalism."

Sindona listened, while chewing on a sugar cube. "Whenever a
friend sends me a gift," Cuccia was saying, "I immediately send him an
object of the same value — to let him know I will not be compromised by
favors or gifts."

Michele studied his subject. Then he told Cuccia, "I have nothing
but high esteem for you. You are a puritan. You admit no exceptions."
Cuccia smiled and insisted on paying the check.

Sindona decided that the way to control Cuccia was to "feed his
vanity and his thirst for power." He sent Cuccia a book on Renaissance art,
published by the Italian Publishing Institute, which belonged to the
Group Sindona. Cuccia immediately sent a book to Sindona, but Michele
returned it, explaining, "I own the company. [The book I sent you] did not
cost me anything. It is a sample of our products. I would never force you to
spend any part of your salary in order to trade gifts with me." Michele's
trick succeeded because of its simplicity and innocence. Cuccia relaxed.
He began to trust Sindona, because the gesture proved that Michele Sindona respected him. As a result, though Sindona was still unable to find a
way to compromise Cuccia and damage his credibility (and thereby deal a
crucial blow to nationalization), he and Cuccia became partners in a major
real estate project conceived by Sindona.

It was winter, and it was snowing when Michele Sindona and Enrico Cuccia drove east in a chauffeured limousine toward the Adriatic Sea to the
village of Comacchio. They followed the route along the Po River, the
largest river in Italy. Starting in the Maritime Alps, it weaves through the
flatlands cutting by Pavia, 20 miles south of Milan, and Cremona, where
the great Stradivarius made his violins, to Parma. There they stopped to
lunch on *prosciutto crudo* (raw ham) and slices of Parmesan cheese. From
Parma they followed the river to Ferrara, "the most horizontal city in
Italy." The war destroyed many of Ferrara's Renaissance palaces. The few
that remain are scattered among new buildings that are flat and square. Its
cathedral, however, is unique, with its unusual carvings that represent the
calendar year. November, for example, is characterized by a goat suckling
a child. Sindona and Cuccia, however, were not sightseeing. They stopped
in Ferrara to study the land. The marshes had been drained and converted
to farmland. As a result, Ferrara produces some of the best food in Italy.
But Sindona was not interested in farming. He and his friend Tito Carnelutti wanted to build a resort on the swamps of Comacchio. "If you can
turn this into farmland," he said to Cuccia, "I can turn swamps into
hotels."

The village sits on the edge of Lake Comacchio, in the delta of the
Po, and was once surrounded by marshland. At the time, the beauty of its

many humped bridges was diminished by the smell of the garbage its inhabitants tossed into the canals. Before Sindona and Carnelutti conceived the idea of building a resort, Comacchio had one attraction, eel-trapping. In autumn fleets of fishermen trapped millions of eels as they began the long journey down the Po River to the Adriatic Sea and out into the Mediterranean, heading to the Sargasso Sea, in the middle of the Atlantic Ocean.

Sindona and Cuccia drove more than 200 kilometers, spent less than two hours in Comacchio looking at swamps, and made a deal.

They rushed back to Milan on the *autostrada*. Through the snowstorm, the driver sped along the viaduct and through the tunnels. Twice the car nearly slid off the road. "He drove like a maniac!" Michele recalls. Yet, Sindona and Cuccia were able to discuss the project in detail.

"The land will cost nothing," Sindona said. "The eels can be brought to market. That will cover the cost of the property and show a profit besides. But substantial capital will be needed to drain the swamps and start construction."

Cuccia said the financing would be handled by Fidia, a division of Mediobanca, Italy's government-owned investment bank, which financed all of the IRI's construction projects. "There will be no problems getting the money," Cuccia assured Sindona. "For financing the project, however, Fidia will take eighty percent."

Michele was disappointed. They haggled back and forth. Michele wanted an equal partnership, fifty-fifty, which was not excessive since the idea was his and he would be overseeing the construction of the resort.

"Impossible," Cuccia laughed. "Fidia and Mediobanca are taking all the risk."

He and Carnelutti, Michele said, deserved more. "If you won't do better," Michele warned, "then I will take the project elsewhere."

By the time they reached Milan, they had agreed that Fidia would buy 80 percent of the project from Sindona at an agreeable price. In this way Cuccia would get what he wanted and Michele would realize an immediate profit. He would retain 20 percent, and Fasco, A.G., his holding company, would also manage the development. Cuccia assured Sindona that the contracts would be ready as soon as Mediobanca's executive board approved the deal.

At the board meeting, which Sindona attended, he complained that one point in the contract was unsatisfactory. It forbade him from selling any of his shares to a third party. If he did, Mediobanca would not be obliged to continue its financing. Sindona argued that this was unfair, but Cuccia would not relent. Then, when Sindona again threatened to back out of the deal, Adolfo Tino, who at the time was president of Mediobanca but did not have the power Cuccia had, revealed the true problem.

"Sindona, I like you," Tino said, according to Sindona. "But if I have any doubt about you, it is because you declare yourself Tito Carnelutti's friend. Carnelutti says he is the real owner of Banca Privata Finanziaria. Either he possesses an important block of stock, or he financed the shares you acquired. Carnelutti has no discretion, he is not serious, and he's no good. If you want to work with us, if you desire to climb, you had better get rid of him. Quickly!"

"Tito is my friend," Michele argued. "I always work with him on real estate projects. I know he brags, but I won't lie to you: he is my partner; I won't betray him so that I can be your friend."

Adolfo Tino exploded, screaming that Sindona was acting stupid. "I warned you, Sindona," Tino said. "Now, if you want to be a success, if you want to work with us, you get rid of Carnelutti."

After Tino left the room, Sindona tried to convince Cuccia that he was obligated to Carnelutti. "Michele," Cuccia calmly said, "I drove with you to Comacchio. We looked, we talked, we made a deal. The deal is between you and Mediobanca. And *I* am Mediobanca. Without me, Fidia does not move. With Carnelutti involved, *I* do not move. Now you make your decision."

After evaluating the situation, Sindona decided that a healthy relationship with Enrico Cuccia was more important—especially since he could not find a way to break Cuccia—than his friendship with Tito Carnelutti. So he bought Carnelutti out of the Fidia contract. Once Cuccia was sure that Carnelutti was out of the deal, he and Sindona signed the contract. The project was immediately started and in time became a well-known resort area for the middle class.

Presently Massimo Spada, Franco Marinotti, and Ernesto Moizzi proposed to the board of Snia Viscosa the nomination of Michele Sindona as president. Because Mediobanca was a minority stockholder in Snia Viscosa, Enrico Cuccia had to approve the election. Cuccia told Sindona that he would support him, for Cuccia believed that he had control of Sindona. This would give Mediobanca greater control over the activities of Snia Viscosa, which in turn would help push Cuccia's plans for nationalization even further. But Michele Sindona rejected the idea of becoming Cuccia's man.

Forgetting that he was talking to a government employee, Sindona told Cuccia, "I have chosen to be a free-lance professional. I don't want to be anyone's employee, not even at the highest level of government. Michele Sindona will never answer to anyone but Michele Sindona."

Cuccia must have been upset, even angry with Sindona's arrogance. This was the first of two insults that would forever set the two men apart as archenemies. His voice cold and dry, Cuccia ended the discussion, saying, "That is a problem, a serious problem! We can talk about it another time."

6

SINDONA INVADES AMERICA

THE MOUNTAINS WERE Michele's sanctuary—miles from the breathless heat of the city and the strain of social and business pressures. He relaxed there. It was cool, and he loved the smell of nature, the taste of wild strawberries, and the freedom of hiking through the fields with his children. He had planned to drive to the Alps on July 1, 1961. Michele had no way of knowing that fate had already set that day aside for Nunziata's funeral.

One by one the family moved away from Nunziata's coffin. They seemed to know that Michele needed to be alone with his grandmother. They had never seen him so upset. Tears fell faster than the early morning sun could burn them off his face. Not even for his father, Nini, who had died suddenly in 1957 from a stroke, had Michele wept.

Nunziata had died at home, as she had insisted, in her own bed. For three days, Michele remained by her side. To keep her comfortable, he bathed her with cool compresses as she had comforted him during his bouts with rheumatic fever and chorea. They talked about his childhood in Patti, and he made her smile when he reminisced about the hours they had spent together under the lemon tree reading and talking. Only when the end was imminent did he allow the other family members to enter the room so that they could say farewell. He did not sleep, nor did he eat during those last three days or during the week following her funeral. Every day for the next month, he took fresh flowers to her grave. He seemed lost and confused. At the dinner table on Sundays, no one was allowed to sit in Nunziata's place.

After Nunziata died, Michele was possessed with excessive energy. His capacity to go many nights without sleep dramatically increased. Frequent incidents of severe bitemporal headaches occurred. He became irritable and angry, and he exhibited poor judgment both in business and with his family.

Medical records reveal that he was treated for manic depression. The records describe Michele as "chronically experiencing a hypomanic state" after Nunziata's death. He suffered "a major emotional disorder involving both mood and cognitive processes." And he was "unable to attend to the advice of family and friends that he should relax."

In the opinion of a psychiatrist who has treated him, Michele Sindona was experiencing what could be described as identity assassination. As a member of the international banking and industrial world, Sindona was respected because of the image he presented: that of a cold, calculating magician who could turn rags into silk and gold. He enjoyed creating the illusion of greatness. While Nunziata was alive, Michele did not have to suppress his subpersonalities. She knew him so thoroughly that he could freely exhibit to her his emotions and feelings without fear of being judged unfavorably. With her, Michele could be himself; he had no need for magic acts or lies; he could cry or laugh or simply relax. After Nunziata's death, Michele lacked what everyone needs: one person with whom he could be himself. Deprived of this, Michele came to see himself as having value only when he achieved goals. The result was that he began to judge people from the single perspective of their relative usefulness to his business.

Once he decided that an individual was important to the success of an operation, Sindona created the illusion that only with his help could that person achieve his or her goal—and only if the person first assisted Sindona in reaching his goal. "Michele acted as if he had sworn an oath to Nunziata that he would make the Sindona name a world legend," a family member says. "He worked harder than ever, was irrational at times, and believed no one understood him." Michele's only attempt to reverse the situation occurred when he turned to his daughter Maria Elisa for help and understanding.

One day approximately a year after Nunziata died, Michele told Maria Elisa to sit next to him at the dining table. From that day onward, he talked with her the way he had talked with Nunziata. It was natural for Michele to turn to Maria Elisa for help. Ever since he had helped Rina give birth to his daughter in the living room of their apartment in Messina, he had displayed a special love for her. But Sindona's love was contaminated by his need to share his dreams and problems with his daughter. Now, at the age of thirty-six, Maria Elisa is too thin, her short black hair is graying too fast, and her olive eyes are dull. Yet, although she is tired and worn, she is proud that she shared a much more intimate relationship with her father than her mother did.

Rina and Michele grew further apart as he became more successful, for Rina never adjusted to her husband's power and wealth. While Michele traveled the world meeting important business and political leaders, Rina stayed home and mended socks. All she ever wanted was to be an average Sicilian housewife, so even after she and Michele became wealthy, Rina continued to mend socks. Embarrassed by this, Michele constantly complained to Rina, saying, "Don't you understand that every hour you spend to save ten lire you could use that hour to make ten times more?" Rina always agreed, then added, "But I cannot do what you do, Michele. So what I am doing, I'm doing my best to save the ten lire."

Rina was always trying her best to save her husband money. She even bought men's clothes for Maria Elisa to wear so that she could pass them down to her brothers, or she would make Maria Elisa wear her old dresses. "My mother would give me her dresses. Still today she brings me her old dresses," Maria Elisa explains. "She says, 'Look. This will fit you beautifully.' I answer, 'Yes, it will fit me, mama, but not beautifully.' She orders me, 'Come on, wear it.' "

One time Michele insisted that Rina buy a wardrobe appropriate for their new life-style. Rina returned empty-handed, saying, "Michele, they want too much money." A week later Michele sent Rina to Marisandra, a custom dress shop. "They're clients of mine," he told her. "They said that they will give you a fifty percent discount." For twenty years, Rina had all of her dresses made there without knowing that her husband had bought the shop.

Michele also bought Rina a home, a co-op apartment in the upper-middle-class district in the center of Milan on the Via Visconte di Mondrone. The apartment comprised four bedrooms, a study, a dining room and living room, three baths, maid's quarters, and three balconies. The rooms contained a small antique bar, a bright red couch, wall-to-wall carpeting, an oval blue-gray marble-top dining table, a marble-top desk-table, bookshelves, and a 4- by 3-foot portrait of Nunziata. From the living room one enjoyed a view of the street, a movie theater, and a small public garden.

On weekends the family would drive to the villa that Michele had purchased in the mountains between Milan and Como. It was one of the most expensive estates in the area. There was a stable on the grounds, so Michele bought Maria Elisa an old and somewhat fat horse she named Nembo. Whenever Michele could join the family, he would watch Maria Elisa ride Nembo, cheering her on as if she were a champion rider. He loved her and needed to be near her, the way he had needed to be with Nunziata.

As a child, Michele's son Nino was intimidated by his father's success. When he was a teenager, he saw many people visit his father for advice. They would come to his house and nervously ask permission to speak with Don Michele, who never refused to see anyone. He had a remarkable ability to put people at ease, allowing them to speak without interrupting. Then, at exactly the correct moment, he would address the problem, getting to the point quickly and offering a resolution, just the way Nunziata had taught him. "As visitors left his study," Nino recalls, "they always looked like the religious people who go and see the saint on the top of the hill and come back mystified."

Michele's reputation and fame were just too enormous for Nino to live with. Everywhere he went he would meet people who knew his father. "Ah, you are Don Michele's son. Your father is a genius." Nino would constantly hear this. When he was old enough to go out with his friends at night, he avoided the expensive nightclubs and restaurants where his father was known. "I preferred to go to the worse type of cafés where only the hookers went and nobody ever knew who I was," he says. "People did not recognize my face, and I never gave anyone my last name. I was just Nino."

After Nino graduated from boarding school in Switzerland, he was drafted into the Italian army. Again he discovered that he could not escape the influence of his father. So that Nino would be close to home, Michele arranged through Admiral Pighini, Italian chief of NATO, to have Nino stationed in Milan. "My father's connections screwed me again," Nino says. "I didn't give a shit about Milan. I wanted to be free, to go out and have fun."

Rebelling against his father's authority, five times Nino faked illness and was taken to the hospital, from which he attempted to escape. Once he even tried to break his finger, bending and twisting the forefinger until finally it dislocated. Though he succeeded in escaping, the military police captured him and put him in jail. He never did get his early release. No matter how much he cried that he was a political prisoner, his father's contacts wouldn't discharge him.

Nino's younger brother, Marco, looks more like a rock star than an associate professor of economics at the University of Milan. Unlike his brother and sister, he appears to have control of his own life without interference by either his mother or his father. Close up, however, Marco appears to lack a multiplicity of interests. He has protected himself from his father's will by withdrawing not only from the family nucleus but from the general sweep of life as well. He exists mainly within the confines of his apartment, the library, and the classroom.

Basically Michele's family is riddled with guilt, rivalry, hate, and confusion, all of which were created not only by Michele's unusual needs and demanding personality but also by the larger-than-life figure that he created for himself. Yet, when pressed, their loyalty does not falter. For them, Michele Sindona was, and still is, a genius gifted with tremendous monetary vision, an international banking and financial guru who, because of the extraordinary pressure he forced on himself, lived in constant pain.

When Michele Sindona was home he spent most of his time working, meeting friends who wanted advice, and talking with Maria Elisa about his business. He did all this even though he was nearly always in ill health. In addition to the headaches, he suffered with arrhythmia (in his case, a rapid and irregular heartbeat), and he was obsessed with the idea that if he did not cleanse his intestines every day the waste would enter his blood and poison him.

Careful not to aggravate his digestive system, Sindona ate very lightly during the day and almost nothing after midafternoon. Still, every day he took a strong laxative known as Gutalax for fear that if he did not have a daily bowel movement the toxic poison would enter his body and, he believed, cause him to suffer with a terrible, blinding pain above the left eyebrow. "When this [pain] occurred," Nino says, "my father would suffer all night, sweating, pale like a sheet. The pain would really make him crazy. I don't know how he was able to perform, so many nights each month he was in pain, and in the office during the day he would suffer." But somehow Michele was able to work, for by now he was determined to break into the American market.

Ever since the war years, Sindona had been obsessed with his desire to understand and master the principles of American business procedures. Now this single goal became the focus of his energies. He read books on American law and accounting, investigated Western politics and philosophy, and studied the bylaws of the New York and American stock exchanges. Through his association with Dan Porco and Joel Hunter, he was introduced to executives from several American companies. Some of the larger corporations he represented in Italy were Crucible Steel of America, General Foods, Ford Motor Company, and General Mills. With a monk's discipline, he examined their financial statements, balance sheets, and profit-and-loss statements. He made notes. He analyzed. He questioned. He memorized everything and designed a questionnaire that Maria Elisa used to test his memory. To get a feel for the country, he traveled with his wife and family to the United States.

Sindona took his family to America for the first time in 1962. In New York City he took them to see the RCA Building, the Empire State Building, and Coney Island. At Coney Island, Maria Elisa and Nino— Marco was too small—rode on the Cyclone, which they thought was "incredible compared to the roller coasters in Italy." Michele so wanted his family to fall in love with America that, even though he hated the sun, he took them to the beach.

Then Sindona rented a car and drove his wife and children to Lake Champlain, where they stayed at a resort hotel for twenty days. While they were there, Nino and Maria Elisa learned to water-ski. But what they liked most was that their father spent so much time sightseeing, walking, and playing with them. "It was nice because he seldom was able to spend a month with us," Nino recalls. "He was relaxed, and I remember he enjoyed himself. He even went canoeing with me."

When they left the resort, they returned to New York City. Rina and the children spent their time visiting the famous stores, though Rina refused to spend any money. Nevertheless, the family fell in love with America. This proved to be a decisive experience for Michele Sindona, for he had already looked into the possibilities of buying controlling interest of Libby, McNeil & Libby, a food-processing firm with international distribution. Before he invested in America, however, it was important to him that his family like Manhattan, because he knew that one day, if his plan worked, they would all live in the United States.

Libby, McNeil & Libby interested Sindona for a variety of reasons. Though its profit structure had declined in recent years, in Europe it was the best-known company in its field. Management was neither strong nor energetic, but Sindona believed that new, highly trained men might restore the profitability of the company. Additionally, no single group appeared to hold a majority of stock; therefore, a timely and well-organized public bid to acquire control seemed possible. Finally, Sindona saw in Libby an opportunity for geographical diversification. Sindona not only wanted to distribute Libby's products throughout Italy but also intended to reduce the company's overhead by purchasing control of the orchard industry in southern Italy. This would allow the Sindona Group to balance decreased earnings in Italy against more positive results in America.

Sindona recognized the advantages of geographical diversification as early as 1960, when he began purchasing real estate in Ontario and Quebec for himself and the Vatican. Through a series of Liechtensteinian corporations including Tuxanr, A.G., and Ravoxr, A.G., both owned and controlled by the Vatican, Michele Sindona purchased millions of dollars' worth of Canadian property. Sindona sent Amadeo Gatti, an attorney who had worked for Sindona's law firm in Milan, to Montreal to manage the property. Gatti subdivided the land into building lots and sold them. The profits were transferred to several Swiss bank accounts controlled by Fasco, A.G., Sindona's major holding company, which continued to act as the conduit for the reinvestment of Vatican funds.

Sindona's strategy circumvented not only Italy's currency laws, which disallowed the exportation of lire, except through the necessary day-to-day transactions of international banking, but also its investment tax, which ranged from 5 to 30 percent. The difference was decided after the disclosure of the stocks' owners, in which case a tax of 5 percent was applied. If disclosure was not made — and legally it was not required — a tax of 30 percent was calculated. The penalty for lack of disclosure was established by the government as a vehicle for discovery. It was believed that Italians who had smuggled currency out of Italy — either through the sophisticated use of bank secrecy laws, as Sindona did, or by the simple method of stuffing millions of dollars' worth of lire into briefcases, as others did — would be forced to disclose their ownership in order to avoid the higher tax rate. But what the Bank of Italy, that country's equivalent of the Federal Reserve, and the minister of finance had not foreseen was that through the illegal use of the Swiss fiduciary contract system a foreign bank appears as the owner and therefore pays the smaller tax.

The fiduciary contract was originally invented by the Swiss to help Jews filter liquid assets out of Germany. Today, however, it is used to smuggle funds out of Italy. In simple terms, Banca Privata Finanziaria would transfer a customer's funds from Italy to its corresponding bank in Switzerland. On the Italian side, BPF would record the transfer as a normal interbank transaction, naming itself as the owner of the funds, thereby concealing its customer's name from the monetary authorities. In Switzerland, however, a secret agreement would be signed by BPF and the Swiss bank. This agreement would direct the Swiss bank to lend the funds to the true owner. This agreement, known as a fiduciary contract, would also relieve the Swiss bank of any responsibility to repay BPF should BPF's customer decide not to repay the Swiss loan. Since BPF's client is the real owner of the funds, neither bank has taken a risk, while they have both earned a small commission for their illegal services.

Michele Sindona did not invent the fiduciary deposit system, but he did exploit it. Through BPF and the Bank of the Vatican, funds were secretly deposited in Switzerland and invested in profitable enterprises outside Italy. Once the corporations were established and the fiduciary system was manipulated, however, it was easy to invest profits in Italy as a foreign corporation, without fear of paying the higher tax. A foreign corporation could earn profits in Italy and then transfer them to Switzerland and convert them into a more stable currency. As a result, what started out as an illegal transaction now appeared to be perfectly legitimate. Sindona mastered this system because he realized that his ability to circumvent investment and currency laws could make the difference between the success and failure of an operation. Furthermore, he realized that owning an American corporation that did business on an international scale, coupled with his use of the fiduciary contract system, offered him an opportunity to build a multinational corporation that would allow him to funnel massive amounts of money out of Italy.

Foreseeing the advantages of a multinational corporation, Sindona also hoped to persuade other American businesses to expand their operations inside Italy, which would increase the earnings of his law practice. So after his return to Milan, Sindona asked Enrico Cuccia to help convince the Italian government to relax its controls on foreign investors. At the time, however, Italy was searching for its identity. The financial sector of the government was obsessed with the concept of nationalization, which not only allowed the Italian government to infiltrate free enterprise but also opposed the investment of U.S. dollars into Italy's economy. This was mainly due to the fact that the leaders who advocated nationalization, like Enrico Cuccia, leaned politically toward the far left, which interpreted the investment of U.S. dollars as an invasion of the Italian economy by a powerful and corrupt capitalist nation made up of businessmen interested only in profit and the exploitation of Italians.

So after analyzing Libby's financial statements, Enrico Cuccia told Sindona that he thought the company was bad for Italy's economy. Therefore, he refused to refer Sindona to André Meyer, president of the investment bank Lazard Frères. Meyer, because of his association with Cuccia, handled the majority of acquisitions in Italy. This presented Michele with a serious problem, for he realized that without Meyer's assistance the Libby deal would be more difficult to seal.

Though Cuccia had insisted that Sindona forget the Libby deal, at a meeting of the board of directors of Snia Viscosa, Sindona mentioned his disappointment to Franco Marinotti. Marinotti believed that the Libby deal was solid, and, since he enjoyed an excellent relationship with the American investment bank Lehman Brothers, he arranged a conference between Sindona and its president, Robert Lehman. Sindona, however, thought he needed a better command of English before entering the American and international business world.

Typical of the way in which Sindona attacked a project, he secretly hired a tutor, and for three weeks locked himself and the tutor in a London hotel. Because of his extraordinary ability to work for long stretches,

Michele studied twenty hours a day. When the tutor slept, Michele watched television, listening to the actors and answering them in English. When there was nothing on television, Sindona read. And when he slept, he dreamed in English. In those dreams, he recalls, everyone was American and everyone was friendly. "Prejudice did not exist," he says. "The Americans loved me because of my brains. They did not treat me like a nigger, the way Italians treat Sicilians."

When his siege with the tutor was over, Sindona boarded a plane for New York. In America the Sicilian financier was free of the tension imposed by Milanese prejudice. He did not have to prove who he was to American businessmen, who assumed he was a member of the High Mafia. After all, he was Sicilian, and he had evolved rapidly from an obscure peasant to a man of power and wealth. It was enough that American businessmen realized Michele Sindona and his money deserved their respect. So Lehman Brothers catered to him, sending young women to escort him and keep him happy. The bankers made a chauffeured limousine available to Sindona twenty-four hours a day, and they entertained him at New York's finest restaurants. But at a tiny diner known as the Luncheonette, on the corner of 86th Street and Madison Avenue, Sindona discovered what he considers "the greatest meal in America."

When he brought Italian friends to America, Sindona always introduced them to the Luncheonette. He would order two hamburgers, with no roll, and black coffee with two scoops of vanilla ice cream in it. "If we were in Manhattan," explains Daniel Porco, "we ate hamburgers." If for some reason they could not get to the Luncheonette, or if they were not in New York, Porco ate what he wanted to eat and Michele sustained himself on sugar cubes and Coca-Cola.

During his trip to America to negotiate the acquisition of Libby, Michele met Britta Behn at a party Lehman Brothers held in his honor. A beautiful, blonde Swede who had married an American but was now divorced, Behn lived in New York with her two children. Michele and Britta were immediately attracted to each other, and they soon began an affair that, according to Nino Sindona, lasted approximately seven years.

Michele had had a great number of affairs before meeting Britta, but none had lasted more than six months. All of his mistresses were young, attractive, and sexually uninhibited, and he offered them the same fidelity he had promised his wife. Britta was fifteen years younger than Michele, and their affair was different from his relationships with his wife or other mistresses.

Michele was attracted to Britta because, in addition to being beautiful, she could read, speak, and write five different languages fluently. Unlike Rina, Britta was comfortable in the world of international business. She was a great asset to Michele, because she knew how to dress and how to work a party. She could seduce a man with her eyes; with her smile she could befriend his lady, and when she spoke, her intelligence enchanted everyone. When an opponent of Michele's complimented her, she would say that it was a shame they could not be friends, or that Michele would like to meet later to resolve these silly tensions. Britta was very effective, and Michele appreciated and loved her for that reason.

When Britta's ex-husband suffered a heart attack and died in 1968, he left a substantial estate to their two children, but nothing to Britta. Because Britta was not an American citizen, the court was obligated to appoint a guardian to manage the children's inheritance. The judge handling the case was S. Samuel Di Falco, who in May of 1966 was mentioned in the *New York Times* in a series of articles pertaining to the misuse of power in connection with his son, Anthony Di Falco, who had been appointed trustee of a $5 million estate, representing the inheritance of thirty-five children.

Since 1959 Judge Di Falco and Michele Sindona had been close friends. At a party organized by the Italian-American community in New York they had been introduced by a lawyer who represented Carlo Gambino, deceased boss of the five New York Mafia families. So Sindona took Britta Behn and Dan Porco to talk with Judge Di Falco. Sindona asked Di Falco if he would do him a favor and appoint as guardian of the estate Dan Porco, who by then was working full-time for Sindona. Judge Di Falco agreed, making it possible for Britta to control her children's inheritance through Dan Porco by way of Michele Sindona.

Britta probably couldn't have loved Michele any more than she already did. She did, however, truly learn to respect his power, and she understood why his friends felt it necessary to honor him with the title Don Michele. But to her he was always Michele. There were no games between them. Michele was more than just the man with the computer-like brain. With her he was tender, sensitive, and in need of warmth and love. She remained loyal and faithful to him throughout their relationship, supporting him when his wife could not, especially during the difficult negotiations that led to his acquisition of Libby, McNeil & Libby.

· After conferring with Sindona in New York, Robert Lehman and Frank Manheim, head of Lehman's international division, reviewed Libby's financial situation and investigated the distribution of its stock. They advised Sindona that he could acquire control with the assistance of Glore Forgan, the Chicago investment bank, because it was in a position to know what shares could be purchased and where to find them without causing alarm. With the help of Glore Forgan, Lehman assured Sindona, he would gain control of Libby by the first part of 1963. So Sindona retained both firms to acquire Libby stock for his Liechtensteinian holding company, Fasco, A.G. As soon as they started buying the shares, however, Jean Reyre, chief executive officer of Banque de Paris et des Pays Bas (Paribas), one of the most respected central bankers in the world, attempted to block the purchase.

Someone inside Lehman Brothers had informed Reyre of Sindona's attempt to purchase controlling interest in Libby. Lehman Brothers and Paribas had had a long and profitable working relationship. In fact, it had been at the suggestion of Lehman Brothers that Paribas decided to establish a New York branch. When Jean Reyre informed Georges Pompidou, then prime minister of France, of Sindona's interest in Libby, Pompidou instructed Reyre to intercede. As a result, Reyre notified Frank Manheim that he wanted to discuss the Libby deal with Michele Sindona.

Manheim passed the invitation on to Sindona, strongly suggesting that Sindona meet Reyre, because an association with Paribas would be of tremendous value to Sindona, from the aspect of both finance and prestige. A tender offer made jointly by Paribas and Group Sindona, Manheim explained, would receive a much better reception by the American financial community. At first, Sindona's reaction to the proposal was negative. "I had the feeling that Paribas — a bureaucracy! — would not permit the dynamic development I desired for Libby's revival," he recalls. But when Sindona discussed the situation with Franco Marinotti and Massimo Spada, they insisted he work it out with Reyre. "A partnership with Paribas," they reasoned, "means entering the world of international finance through its main gate." Since Sindona had always dreamed of being more than just a Vatican consultant or Italian financier, the possibility of finally being accepted and acknowledged by the international financial community motivated him to meet with Jean Reyre.

In January 1963 the two men met in the New York offices of Lehman Brothers. At the start, the meeting was a disappointment for Sindona because Reyre arrived fifteen minutes late. "Hence, my impression could only be negative, as it is of anyone who arrives late for appointments," Sindona says. As a result, Sindona's attitude during the first stage of their conversation, as Reyre questioned him about his interest in Libby, was cold.

Reyre wanted to know why Sindona was interested in a company that was not doing well. Sindona explained his plans for Libby in Italy. That seemed to please Reyre, but he wanted to know who was backing Sindona. Michele refused to say, claiming he was bound by the client–attorney privilege. He did, however, assure Reyre that no matter who was backing him, whether it was the Vatican or private individuals, he had the authority to make all decisions regarding Libby.

"Are there any Americans in your Group?" Reyre asked, adding that "de Gaulle does not want an American colonization of France. France will intervene with its own capital. Libby is constructing a food-processing plant in France. The country has extended credit at very favorable rates. Paribas and France want to push Libby forward." Sindona assured Reyre that he was not representing American investors.

"I want Libby," Sindona explained. "It is important to Italy; it is important to my relationship with the Americans, important to my plans."

Reyre said that he was interested only in France, that he had no desire to become involved in Libby's management. If Sindona was willing to give him Libby's French division, Reyre said, then Paribas was prepared to make a joint venture with Group Sindona. For a fifty-fifty partnership, Paribas would finance Sindona's shares. Sindona insisted he be granted "all powers of management for nine years." Reyre agreed, with the condition that "Libby's profits, on a two-year average, would not be less than it had earned in the year prior to purchase."

As soon as Sindona and Reyre had signed a contract forming a partnership between Paribas and Fasco, A.G., Lehman Brothers quietly began to purchase stock in Libby. At some point during the acquisition of stock, however, the market grew nervous. Sindona interpreted this as a signal that someone else was buying large blocks of Libby stock at a price higher than the Paribas–Fasco offer, which was substantially higher than the price quoted during the preceding months on the New York Stock Exchange. After a week of intensified research, Lehman Brothers discovered that for some years a number of Canadian corporations had been quietly purchasing small blocks of shares in Libby and had recently increased their purchases.

At about the same time, while Michele Sindona was in Milan, he received a call from Enrico Bignami, managing director of Nestlé, the Swiss chocolate corporation. Bignami told Sindona that he wanted to meet with him to discuss Libby. Sindona immediately realized that Nestlé was behind the Canadian corporations, for that was the only possible reason for Bignami's call. He therefore agreed to meet Bignami the following day on Lago Maggiore.

In Lago Maggiore are the four Borromean Islands, named after St. Carlo Borromeo. The climate in the area is mild, and palm trees, tropical plants, and shrubs with ball-shaped, light-sensitive clusters of flowers grow on the shore of the lake, which extends into Switzerland and is often wrapped in a seductive mist.

From his suite at the Ciga Hôtel des îles Borromée in the center of Isalabella, a town on the main island, Michele admired the gardens and the statue of St. Borromeo, which appears to be as large as the Statue of

Liberty. At the time he did not own the Ciga chain, but it was then, just as Enrico Bignami arrived, that he decided he would someday own the chain of Ciga Hotels.

Bignami wasted no time getting directly to the point. "You will never succeed!" he warned Sindona.

"Oh, but I will," Sindona said with confidence. "I want Libby, and so does Paribas. We might have a war but, Mr. Bignami, I think I know how to fight."

"You won't win," Bignami insisted. "We've been interested in Libby for several years. We've been buying stock. Buying and buying and buying! We aren't going to back off just because you've got Jean Reyre with you. If we have to, we will buy the stock at even higher prices."

Bignami hesitated, waiting for Sindona's reaction. Calmly, Michele handed him a copy of the records on the Canadian purchases. "I know exactly how you're going about this," Sindona smiled. "I'm prepared to fight you; I enjoy a good fight. But you should realize that if you intend to outbid me, I will release the information on the Canadian corporations. You must realize that if I do that, you may get Libby, but it will cost you more than you're willing to pay. Now why don't you just sell me your shares? It will make things easier for everyone."

"We're not afraid of you or Jean Reyre," Bignami said. "We're prepared to fight you all the way. We want Libby."

"Fine," Sindona said. "If I succeed against a good adversary like Nestlé, success will be sweet. If I lose — something I do not think is possible — I will be equally happy. An operation that brings me into contact with a giant like you, Mr. Bignami, could teach me a great deal. Perhaps you too will learn something, Mr. Bignami."

As soon as the meeting ended, Sindona called Reyre and informed him that Nestlé intended to fight them for control of Libby. Reyre told Sindona that the Swiss banks had tried to pressure him to pull out. But Reyre would not be intimidated, not by the Swiss, not by anyone. He and Sindona kept the pressure on the market. In a few days, it was evident that Bignami intended to keep his word and fight his adversaries all the way, for Sindona and Reyre found themselves in the middle of a bidding war. But Bignami was the first to break. He called Sindona and requested another conference. Sindona said he was too busy. Finally, Bignami called Reyre and requested a meeting. This time, Reyre advised Sindona that they should all meet before the war got out of hand.

In March 1963 they met at the home office of Paribas. Bignami said that he wanted to work out a compromise. Reyre suggested that they all become partners rather than fight one another. He told Sindona that Nestlé had experience and would make a good contribution to the management of Libby, McNeil & Libby. So the enemies became partners. They pooled their stock, splitting it equally. Then after allowing the market to settle, they instructed Lehman Brothers to finish the acquisition using Paribas as the purchaser of record. Nestlé managed production and distribution in America and the rest of the world, except Italy and France. Paribas controlled the French market, and Michele Sindona controlled the Italian market, naming Dan Porco to represent him on the board of directors of Libby, McNeil & Libby.

The successful acquisition of Libby was an important element of Michele Sindona's plan to build an international empire. Along with the success came problems, however. When André Meyer learned of Sindona's participation in the Libby deal, he wanted to know why Enrico Cuccia had not sent Sindona to him.

7

P-2

A MONTH AFTER Michele Sindona acquired Libby, McNeil & Libby, he, André Meyer, and Enrico Cuccia met in Paris to discuss the situation. Although Cuccia denied having any knowledge that Sindona was bidding on Libby, Sindona assured Meyer that he had in fact mentioned it to Cuccia and had requested an introduction to Meyer, but that Cuccia had refused. Since Meyer did not have a personal relationship with Sindona, as he did with Cuccia, he chose to believe Cuccia's story, which promoted a conflict between Sindona and the two most influential men in Italian finance. Though Sindona had tried to prevent this, it was clear to him when the meeting ended that he and Cuccia were now confirmed enemies.

Nevertheless, when Sindona decided to make a public offer for controlling interest in the Brown Paper Company, an American firm, he attempted to allay the tensions among the three of them by offering Meyer the opportunity to act as broker in the deal. Meyer was still angry, however, and refused to have anything to do with Michele Sindona. Mocking Sindona, Meyer told him not to waste his time on a deal that could not possibly be closed.

The war between Cuccia and Sindona continued to build over the years as each man struggled for power. Although their dislike for one another was personal, it was so intense that everyone knew they had come to hate each other. Their antagonism was seen by the business community as a classic battle between the left and the right, government and free enterprise, nationalization and capitalism. But as Dan Porco remembers, their hatred was more personal. "I always thought it was Sicilian jealousy," he says, "each trying to outdo the other, each man wanting to have a better batting average."

Cuccia, however, had the advantage of being a member of the Freemasons' Laic Bankers, a group that promoted the interest of its members, all of whom favored nationalization, which was also supported by left-wing political parties whose members were pushing for social reform and a complete break with the Western Alliance. So, without serious opposition, Cuccia increased his power through the IRI by gaining controlling interest in important Italian banks such as Banca Commerciale Italiana, Credito Italiano (Bank of the Holy Spirit), and two Vatican banks: Banca di Roma and Banco di Santo Spirito By utilizing the principles of capitalism, Cuccia also helped to expand the IRI's umbrella through the formation of specialized holding companies financed by Mediobanca. These holding companies gained control of the steel industry, food processing, supermarkets, construction companies, engineering, machinery, and the manufacturing of electrical equipment. Alitalia Airlines; RAI, the government's radio and television holding company; Alfa Romeo; and finally Snia Viscosa also fell into the hands of the IRI.

As Cuccia and the left gained more influence and power, Michele Sindona's political and economic philosophies drifted farther to the right. Unlike most Italians, who seldom voiced their displeasure for fear their enemies would hear and would one day be in a position to take revenge, Michele Sindona openly attacked Cuccia and nationalization. "He would take time out of a busy schedule," says Dan Porco, with a glow of admiration, "to argue his economic and political beliefs. And he was a great arguer—to the right of everyone you can think of, except Mussolini. Sometimes he would convince people by the force of his argument rather than by his words."

In 1964 at a meeting in Rome attended by American and Italian businessmen, Michele presented his arguments. "The left wing, the socialists, the communists—all of them are corrupt," Michele said. "Nationalization is a threat to free enterprise. The left makes promises that it cannot possibly keep. The people have been helped only when capitalism, the extreme right, has ruled. The left, all they do is talk and talk and talk, say what the people want to hear—lie, lie, lie! That's all they do. Whenever they have won power, show me where they have kept their promises. Nowhere!"

Though many businessmen privately agreed with Sindona, Licio

Gelli was among the few who offered public support, for he hated the left. A former clothing, furniture, and mattress springs manufacturer, Licio Gelli was the grand master of the Masonic lodge Propaganda Due, commonly called Propaganda 2 or P-2, a lodge organized for the high-ranking and elite Freemasons, who have been described by Italy's interior minister as "the most powerful hidden power center in Italy."

Licio Gelli was born in 1919 in Pistoia, a provincial capital of Tuscany, 45 kilometers north of Florence. At seventeen he left high school to fight with the fascist Italian Blackshirt division in Spain, and during World War II Gelli zealously supported the Italian dictator, Benito Mussolini.

When the dictator fell, Gelli fled to Argentina, where he allied himself with the dictator Juan Perón, became Perón's economic adviser to Italy, and was granted dual citizenship. Licio Gelli's relationship with the Peróns became so strong that after Juan Perón died, Gelli was called to Argentina by Isabel Perón, the dictator's widow, to help organize the transition of power from Juan Perón to Isabel and finally to the military. When Gelli returned to Italy in the early 1960s, he joined the Masonic Order of Freemasonry, known in Italy as the Grande Oriente.

Freemasonry first appeared in Europe in the seventeenth century. The Masonic lodges as an organized group remained politically neutral; members, however, were bound by oath to fight for the abolition of censorship, for religious choice, freedom from arbitrary arrest and imprisonment without trial, and the destruction of authority that refused to grant representation.

Freemasons have throughout history been involved in revolutions. Voltaire and Diderot, writers who influenced the French Revolution, were both members of the order. Some historians have credited the Freemasons with the success of the Russian Revolution of 1917. The Masons have also been credited with, or blamed for, the Spanish civil war and the start of World War I (the assassination of Archduke Franz Ferdinand). The ideals behind Freemasonry were the foundation of the American Revolution: Benjamin Franklin, George Washington, Alexander Hamilton, Paul Revere, and John Paul Jones were all Masons. And under the direction of Grand Master Giuseppe Garibaldi, the Masonic Order played a leading role in the unification of Italy. Only in Italy have the Freemasons as a group been actively involved in politics.

During World War II a large number of Masons were jailed and tortured by Mussolini for opposing his dictatorship. Yet, for some unexplainable reason, the Masonic Order accepted Licio Gelli as a member. As a result, with the support of the Grande Oriente, the Anti-Fascist Commission cleared Gelli of war crimes with which the partisan commission had charged him.

With the backing and support of the Masonic Order and the government of Argentina, Gelli soon prospered. He traveled frequently to Hungary, Rumania, and Libya to negotiate multimillion-dollar contracts for Argentina and for himself. Within a few years he had purchased several magnificent villas in northern Italy, Monaco, and Argentina, and he threw lavish parties to display his wealth. In Rome, however, Gelli operated secretly out of room 127 of the Excelsior Hotel.

In 1964, when the communists and other leftists were gaining influence in Italy, Michele Sindona's preaching of pro-Western philosophy roused Gelli's political beliefs. Eventually, as grand master of Propaganda Due, Licio Gelli declared himself "a lifelong anti-communist."

Propaganda Due originated in the early nineteenth century with the birth of the secret society known as the Carbonari. The lodges were similar to Masonic lodges. Carbonari membership however, included Freemasons, mafiosi, and military officers who were more serious about their political beliefs than other Masons. They opposed Napoleonic rule; recruited members in Spain, Greece, France, and Russia; won constitutions in Spain and a few Italian states; and led Greece in its fight for independence.

The success of the Carbonari was due to the dedication of its individual members and to the initiation ceremony, which threatened "certain and violent death" for any member who violated the society's secrets. The presence of mafiosi among the Carbonari guaranteed that violators of omerta, the Sicilian code of silence, would meet death by mutilation.

As grand master of P-2, Licio Gelli turned the lodge into the most powerful, political, and violent secret organization in Italy. Important Italian generals, magistrates, and businessmen became members of P-2, which Gelli severed from the hierarchy of Freemasonry. According to a former U.S. intelligence officer who until recently was stationed in Italy where he became friendly with Gelli, P-2 under Gelli's command became "an underground state within a state."

Determined to destroy Italy's parliamentary system of government in order to form a presidential dictatorship, Gelli recruited members who swore allegiance to him rather than to the nation of Italy. A distinguished-looking man of medium height and build, with silver hair and a charismatic personality, Licio Gelli recruited powerful bankers, industrialists, generals and colonels of the Italian army, and agents of Italy's highly secret Service of Defense Information (SID). His greatest single recruiting victory, however, was the membership of Carmelo Spagnuolo, who was at the time chief public prosecutor in Milan and who later became president of a division of the Italian supreme court.

Gelli was not brilliant so much as shrewd and devious. He had money and power, but he realized that wealth and position meant little without the weapon of fear. Gelli believed that fear was the instrument by which real power could be masterfully employed, and he believed fear was most useful when cloaked in silence. So Grand Master Gelli divided members of P-2 into divisions and forbade them to disclose their membership.

Secret societies are illegal in Italy. Freemasonry is allowed to exist only if each lodge agrees to disclose the names of its members. Gelli, however, would not do this. His connections were strong enough and high enough that no one dared to challenge P-2's dark existence. Gelli had made it impossible for anyone outside the order to learn the identity of P-2 Masons, and even within P-2, members of one group could not learn the identity of any member of another group. As the only person to know every member's name, Licio Gelli had ensured his position and power.

He used contacts in government and business to gather secrets about members and nonmembers alike, and he used their dossiers to increase his wealth and influence. A leather folder containing details of embarrassing and criminal acts committed by an individual would be delivered to that person's house or office. A calling card that read simply "P-2" identified the sender. Contact would be made and a deal struck for either money or favors. By his consistent and ruthless use of blackmail, political favors, bribes, and the purchase of important government positions for members of the secret Mafia-Masonry-style society, Gelli, an Italian journalist says, "was king and pope. Many hated him for his bad character and fascist past, but no one dared cross him."

Like a public relations expert, Gelli manipulated people and situations. At parties he boasted of his friendship with judges, military leaders, and powerful businessmen like Michele Sindona. Gelli's activities, of course, did not go unnoticed. Italians began to refer to P-2 as "a state within the state." Rumors of pagan rituals filled the imagination of the public. Even some of Gelli's confidants called him "Naja Hannah" (King Cobra), and Naja Hannah was said to be a magician who cut through red tape and produced results. So, in traditional Italian style, nonmembers seeking promotions in government or business offered suitcases stuffed with lire or, if their position allowed, political favors. In Italy Propaganda Due exists, like the Mafia, as an accepted fact of life, because Italians have learned to treat corruption not as an evil but as an art. They believe not in the state but in the power of those who are feared—the creators of intrigue and chaos.

This conspiratorial chaos permeates every level of Italian society from the peasantry to the nobility, with an attitude that says, in effect, "To survive, one must have the protection of friends who have friends." Such a belief has fed the cancer of corruption, undermined the foundation of social ethics, and distorted the individual Italian's concept of morality. Desensitized to crime and scandal, Italians have come to the devastating— yet for them practical—conclusion that parties change faces but the system remains the same. What is truly important is not changing the system but instead simply making it work for oneself. A Mafia complex has spread throughout northern Italy, especially Rome and Milan, where political parties serve special interest groups like the Vatican by manipulating a degenerate system for personal gain.

In summary, as a result of the morbid realism that pervades Italy, beneath the structure of that nation's official government there exists another more potent government, which serves the special interests of its members and financial supporters. Still deeper below, another government operates in complete darkness. It has been called the Mafia, the High Mafia, and Propaganda Due. Italians have surrendered to it, some by watching without opposition, others by not caring, and still others by using it. So for Licio Gelli to have recruited important military and judicial figures, to have organized P-2 as a secret power, even as "a state within the state," may not have been such an extraordinary accomplishment.

Michele Sindona and Licio Gelli became allies. The web that they would weave would seriously threaten the economy of Italy and eventually bring about the collapse of Italy's fortieth government since World War II. Before that would happen, however, they would weave a network of deals that would include two attempted coups.

Yet their personal differences were extreme. Licio Gelli proudly fought for Mussolini; Sindona refused to wear the fascist uniform in school. Gelli was anti-Semitic; Sindona in 1973 raised $2 million for Israel. Gelli believed in a dictatorship; Sindona wanted for Italy, he says, an American form of democracy. But they were both capitalists, they were both anti-communists and anti-leftists, and they both believed that some men, the truly gifted, were above the morals and laws that applied to the rest of society.

That Gelli wanted a dictatorship was not important to Sindona. By the time Gelli approached him, Michele had become hard, cunning, and scornful of the motives of the Italian government. That P-2 operated illegally was also not important to Sindona, because Italians, especially super-Italians, do not respect the law. All that was important was that P-2 was powerful and would create opportunity and protect capital.

In other words, Michele Sindona did not join forces with Licio Gelli because he was a valiant defender of democracy and human rights. Sindona was not a martyr. He became a P-2 Freemason for the clearest of all reasons, the very same reason for which men who are driven by success have always done things — for profit.

Licio Gelli created an oath by which initiates declared their loyalty to him, the supreme master of Propaganda Due. There is no way to be sure how the oath read or how it was taken because Gelli quite often would

change the ceremony and the oath to fit his moods. In interviews, however, two former members of P-2 have described a compound—its exact
location was never revealed—and the oath Michele Sindona is believed to
have taken when he was inducted into P-2.

The setting is a villa hidden somewhere in the Apennines, probably
in the region of Tuscany. A 12-foot wall seals the neatly manicured
grounds from view. In the center of the main courtyard stands a fountain
shaped like a tree trunk, with a serpentine figure crawling from its base
upward. The cobralike sculpture, with its inflated hood, watches over the
compound in a protective posture, as if ready to strike. The cobra's head is
twice the size of a human skull. It has a single eye, which is blue during
daylight and red after nightfall, for inside the cobra's hood and behind its
eye there is a closed-circuit camera that follows a visitor, invited or unwel-
come, as the fountain rotates in the direction the intruder moves. The
fountain-camera is controlled from a room within the villa where eight
monitors, each with five stations, cover eight guest rooms, patio, pool,
dining room, sitting room, and party room. Approximately ten cameras are
strategically scattered throughout the grounds. Four of these cameras,
including the one inside the cobra, have infrared lenses. All of the exterior
cameras are camouflaged by the landscaping.

The villa's interior is magnificent. Every room has marble floors and
is furnished with antiques. Observing the high ceilings, the finely crafted
gold-leaf moldings, the portraits of Mussolini, Hitler, and Perón, the visitor
experiences a feeling, a sort of living, breathing odor of danger and power
that penetrates the soul and cell by cell contaminates the mind with
fear.

The year is 1964. In the meeting room, twelve members of P-2,
dressed in satin ceremonial robes and wearing black hoods reminiscent of
those worn by members of the Ku Klux Klan, sit in leather chairs at a red
marble conference table. They are the elite members of the wolf pack,
Gelli's disciples—some say his execution squad. None of the black-clad
disciples knows the identity of any of his eleven brothers. Grand Master
Licio Gelli is the only one who bares his face.

On this night in 1964, though he will not officially become grand
master, or worshipful master, of P-2 until ten years later, Gelli is the self-
proclaimed leader of P-2's movement against the state of Italy, Il Momento
di Passare all' Azione (The Time for Real Action). Phase one of Real
Action is to enlist the support of military leaders. Phase two of Real Action
has three parts: 1) smuggle lire out of Italy and convert them to a more
stable currency, preferably dollars or Swiss francs; 2) reinvest the hidden
liquid assets in businesses inside Italy, thereby taking control of important
industries; and 3) funnel profits out of Italy, completing the cycle that
would disrupt the country's balance of payments and ultimately cripple

the nation's economy. To do this Gelli planned to foment the use of political violence, bombings, murder, and kidnappings and then, when he had created sufficient chaos, make use of propaganda designed to prepare Italians psychologically for the new era of fascism.

In addition to the twelve disciples, two Masons stand post at the entrance to the meeting room. Their faces are also covered. They are Naja Hannah's personal bodyguards — some say his death squad — former Mussolini fascists whose job is to protect the grand master and kill any of the twelve disciples who betray the cause, Il Momento di Passare all' Azione. Like Naja Hannah and his disciples, each bodyguard carries an ax; they also bear automatic weapons.

The ceremony begins.

There is an uneven series of knocks at the door. "Your Worshipful," a disciple announces, "a pagan wishes to enter."

The grand master strikes the table with one blow with his ax. Immediately the oversized door swings open and slams against the inner wall. Two guards escort the initiate to the center of the room where he faces the twelve Masons with his back to the grand master's throne. The pagan, as he is called, is wearing a plain black hood and a blindfold. His identity is known to Grand Master Licio Gelli but to no one else. He is asked one question by each of the disciples, but the pagan does not answer; instead, one of the guards speaks for him.

Once all of the ritual questions about purpose and belief and reason for wanting to become a member of Propaganda Due are answered, the pagan is turned to face the grand master, who asks, "Pagan, are you prepared to die in order to preserve the secrets of Propaganda Due?"

The initiate now answers for himself: "I am."

"Do you have the necessary quality of contempt for danger?"

"I do."

"Do you have the necessary quality of courage?"

"I am courageous."

"Do you proclaim yourself an anti-communist?"

"I do."

"And, pagan, are you prepared to fight and perhaps face shame, even death, so that we who may become your brothers may destroy this government and form a presidency?"

"I am."

Then the blindfold is removed. It takes a moment for the initiate's vision to clear, because this is the first time since entering the compound that he has been allowed to see light. The blindfold serves a purpose other than security. It also represents the power of P-2: "Without membership one is blind; with the help of the order, however, the way is clear."

According to Lieutenant Colonel Luciano Rossi, one-time member of P-2's execution squad, who committed suicide six weeks after being interviewed, the initiation ceremony varied. The ceremonial ritual described here was seldom used, according to Rossi, except when Gelli wanted to show his power and test an initiate's courage. In that most extreme initiation, at the exact instant when the blindfold is removed, another Mason drops a viper within three meters of the pagan's feet. The initiate has had no warning that such an act will take place but has been told that something will be done to take him by surprise and test his courage. If, when his vision clears, he is overcome by fear, he will not be allowed to enter the "enlighted society of Propaganda Due." If he demonstrates courage in the face of Satan's interrogator — the viper is regarded as a symbol of the evils of communism, socialism, anything left of the extreme right — and stands his ground for sixty seconds, a brother Mason will remove the viper. According to Rossi, it is then fed to a cape cobra.

The next stage in all initiations is the swearing of the "eternal oath." Each disciple presents to the grand master a sealed envelope containing a photograph of himself. Then a drop of blood is taken from each of the twelve Masons, the grand master, and the pagan. The drops are blended in a purified vial. Then Naja Hannah places the pictures, one at a time, inside a gold compote. As he does this, he spills a drop of blood on each picture: Vito Miceli, general of the SID; Joseph Miceli Crimi, chief surgeon for the Palermo Police Department; Carmelo Spagnuolo, judge of the supreme court and chief prosecutor in Milan; Raffaele Giudice, general and commander of the Finance Guard; Ugo Zilletti, head of the Supreme Council of Magistrates; Roberto Calvi, president of Banco Ambrosiano (a bank partly owned by the Vatican); Antonio Viezzer, colonel in the SID; Luciano Rossi, lieutenant colonel in the Finance Guard; Loris Corei, member, with Sindona, of the executive board of Società per le Condotte d'Acqua, a Vatican-owned company; and so on.

Finally, Naja Hannah places his picture on the table next to the photograph of the initiate — in this case, Michele Sindona. Then he lights a match and places it inside the gold compote.

"You will be known as sixteen-twelve," Gelli informs Sindona.

"Sixteen-twelve," Sindona repeats.

The flame licks the corners of the bowl.

Licio Gelli strikes three blows with his ax. The disciples immediately raise their axes; then simultaneously they strike the table. One ax is then placed on top of the other to form six crosses, and, finally, the disciples form a circle around Michele Sindona.

"Repeat after Naja Hannah," all twelve order, as Sindona hears for the first time Licio Gelli called by his official title. The oath is taken:

I swear to all who are present, I swear to all whose identities are sealed in the vaults of Propaganda Due, and especially, I swear to your Worshipful Master — Naja Hannah — that I will be loyal to our brothers and to the cause, il Momento di Passare all' Azione. I swear on this steel [Naja Hannah hands Sindona an ax] to fight against the evils of communism, to strike a blow in the face of liberalism, and to fight for the establishment of a presidential government.

I swear to help my brothers and never to betray them. And if I fail, if I should perjure myself [the grand master cuts Sindona's picture into four parts], my body should be cut into pieces [Sindona's picture and Gelli's picture are tossed into the fire with the others] and burned to ashes like the ashes of this image.

The ceremony has been completed. Michele Sindona is now Freemason 1612 of Propaganda Due.

With the support of P-2 Sindona was able to fight the weaker Laic Bankers, a division of the Grande Oriente of which Enrico Cuccia was a member and which actively promoted nationalization. Nearly as fast as the IRI could absorb private corporations, Michele Sindona expanded his empire. He devoured more companies than any other living Italian, and among the many tags the Italian press gave him, none was more fitting than "the Sicilian Iron Chewer."

In ten short years Sindona purchased half a dozen banks in four countries: Italy, Germany, Switzerland, and the United States. He acquired control of Ciga, Italy's largest hotel chain. He bought the Grand Hotel in Rome; the Meurice Hotel in Paris; the Rome *Daily American*, an English-language newspaper with CIA money and influence; and approximately five hundred corporations.

Of his growth between 1964 and 1974, Sindona arrogantly proclaims, "I bought Pacchetti, a chemical company, at ten and sold at thirty; bought Saffa, a lumber company, and sold at a ten-million-dollar profit; sold Sviluppo, a real estate development firm, at five million dollars. Millions, millions, millions for many years." He once told *Newsweek*: "Everything has its price, and if I think it is cheap — I buy; if it is expensive and I am offered a good price — I sell. I have no principles about what businesses to be in or not to be in. That is the correct attitude for an investment banker to have."

So on July 13, 1964, Michele Sindona — surprising no one more than Enrico Cuccia and André Meyer — acquired Brown Paper Company. Then, on December 2 of that year, Sindona expanded his power and influence with the formation of Moneyrex, an international money brokerage firm that serviced banks throughout the world.

8

MONEYREX

CARLO BORDONI ENTERED the offices of Studio Sindona at 29 Via Turati, Milan. A short, balding, roly-poly figure with fleshy jowls, a thin upper lip, and short eyebrows, Bordoni was not well known in the general banking community. He was, however, well known to that community's foreign exchange experts, a tightly knit tribe of currency traders. He had written a book examining the advantages and the dangers of foreign exchange trading. The book had been well received by the members of that elite community.

In 1963, when the First National City Bank of New York (Citibank) hired Carlo Bordoni to direct its foreign exchange department in Milan, Citibank officials believed Bordoni to be the best-qualified currency expert they could find—and he probably was. Bordoni had a problem, however. He liked to trade on the market for his personal account. Because he did not have the kind of resources that would allow him this privilege, Bordoni used Citibank's money to speculate. When he won, the profits were credited to his account; when the market betrayed him, he let Citibank eat the losses. Once Citibank's auditors uncovered Bordoni's scam, the bank threatened him with prosecution unless he returned his ill-gotten profits. He did, and Citibank immediately terminated its relationship with him.

Out of work, with no money, a sick wife, and a young daughter, Carlo Bordoni, who was usually confident to the point of snobbery, was now frightened. He had approached every bank in Milan, but none had offered him a position. Many bank presidents would not even grant him an interview. Michele Sindona was his last hope, and the situation did not look promising.

Sindona and Bordoni had met twice before. On both occasions Sindona had treated Bordoni in a gentlemanly manner but had not committed himself. He would have to think things through, Sindona had said, before offering Bordoni a position in his Group. That meant Sindona intended to check him out.

Dan Porco was assigned the task of compiling a dossier on Carlo Bordoni. When Porco was at Crucible Steel, that company was a large depositor at Citibank, Milan. Citibank's chairman Walter Wriston cooperated with Porco on the dossier. In two days Porco presented his findings to Sindona.

"Carlo is clearly an intelligent guy," Porco said, "but he never completes anything. His reputation is bad. He's nothing but trouble."

"Give me the specifics," Sindona insisted, as he folded the report into the shape of a crown.

"The banking community does not like him," Porco answered. But Michele already knew that Bordoni had been blacklisted. That morning he had received warnings about Bordoni from two banks that had become partners in Banca Privata Finanziaria: Hambros of London and Continential Bank of Illinois.

The Italian representative of Hambros was Scottish-born John McCaffrey. He was 5 feet tall with a sturdy frame, rich and calculating blue eyes, and a lion's mane of thick white hair. He had been chief British organizer of the European resistance movement on the Continent during World War II and was awarded the highest decoration of the House of Savoy. His American counterpart was Allen Dulles, later the director of the CIA. After the war, Italy gave McCaffrey the keys to Milan.

Many former resistance leaders eventually became powerful financiers, industrialists, and politicians. Immediately after the war, however, none of these men knew one another. Their only common link was John McCaffrey. Like Licio Gelli, but for different reasons, McCaffrey decided that a group of men who had worked well and secretly together in the past should work together in the business world. Merchant banking was a natural vehicle for them. It could finance operations for members and allow them to keep an eye on the political situation.

When McCaffrey told Sindona that Hambros would demand that Michele repurchase its share participation in Banca Privata Finanziaria

(BPF) if Sindona hired Carlo Bordoni, Sindona had to know that McCaffrey was not just making noise. Therefore, when Continental's chairman David Kennedy, later to become Richard Nixon's secretary of the treasury, repeated the warning, Sindona recalled the problems his friend Tito Carnelutti had caused him.

"Don't hire Bordoni." Porco's voice was strained with frustration. He had very strong negative feelings about Bordoni. "He's nothing but trouble," he warned again. If BPF hired Bordoni, Porco cautioned, Sindona's reputation in the banking community would be seriously tarnished. Sindona had enough enemies already, thanks to his continuous sparring with Enrico Cuccia.

Michele stared out his office window at the sea of red-tiled roofs. He appeared more disturbed than he should have been. He didn't owe Bordoni anything; nevertheless, Porco sensed that Michele wanted to hire him.

The report, now folded into three crowns, sat on the credenza next to a dozen more crowns that were already painted. Sindona chuckled, recalling the rumor that each crown contained the name and secret account number of a man he had helped to move lire out of Italy.

"People who talk," he was saying, "may talk because they're jealous — or just because they must."

"It wasn't just talk," Porco persisted. "The sources were reliable. Bordoni is bad news."

Michele Sindona demonstrated sincere kindness when he told Carlo Bordoni that he could not offer him a position at BPF. It was a reluctant decision, Sindona said, not the one he would have made had it been entirely up to him. He had partners, however, and — well . . . Bordoni understood.

But Bordoni did not understand.

Three days later, on November 16, 1964, Carlo was back with a new proposal. If Sindona would finance the initial cost, Bordoni would establish an international currency brokerage firm. Euro-Market Money Brokers, s.p.a., Milan, was the name he had selected, but it would be called Moneyrex. This firm, Bordoni explained, would act as a sort of clearinghouse and detective agency. It would locate banks with excess deposits in a given currency, say dollars, and for a fee of $1/32$ of 1 percent, Moneyrex would find a bank that was short of dollars to accept the funds and pay the sending bank a fair interest rate.

Moneyrex, Bordoni said, would also add stability to the market because a client bank's identity would remain confidential throughout the search-and-find process. In addition, Moneyrex would save banks time and considerable expense because they would not be tying up their own people. Finally, Bordoni said, Moneyrex would add "considerable luster" to the Sindona Group and "consistent foreign currency credits in favor of BPF and Finabank of Geneva."

Sindona was excited. He immediately called John McCaffrey and Jocelyn Hambro, chairman of Hambros Bank, to ask them if they objected to BPF's participation in the constitution of Moneyrex.

Yes, they said categorically. Continental Bank's chairman David Kennedy repeated his previous warning. The most they could agree to would be to allow Sindona to promote the brokerage firm independently of BPF — and only if Sindona made a moral commitment to them that if Moneyrex entered the currency market it would close all transactions at the end of each day. This would minimize Sindona's exposure if Bordoni began to speculate, limit Sindona's personal risk, and also eliminate the risk of astronomical losses spilling onto the shoulders of the Sindona Group.

Michele agreed to the stipulations, and on December 2, Euro-Market Money Brokers, s.p.a. (Moneyrex), was incorporated with an initial capital of 50 million lire funded by Fasco, A.G., of Vaduz, Liechtenstein. Roberto Cacchi, Sindona's personal accountant, was named managing director. Raul Baisi, Sindona's friend and partner in American International Corp. of Zurich (which later became Amincor Bank of Zurich), was elected president. Carlo Bordoni, to his dissatisfaction, held no title. He complained to anyone who would listen that Moneyrex had been his brainchild and that it was not fair for him to be "only a mere operator" with an annual salary of $12,000.

Michele's decision to back Bordoni's idea was a disappointment to many. Dan Porco says, however, that it was not out of character. "I've seen Michele protect and defend all kinds of people," Porco says. "He had employees who, because of old age or physical problems, could not work, and Michele just kept on paying them. He would not throw anybody over. He had a personal interest in people. He loved people. He wanted to know what problems they had and if he could help. Michele was a man with very little time, but he always made time to help people."

Nevertheless, kindness had nothing at all to do with Michele's decision regarding Bordoni and Moneyrex. Licio Gelli had passed on to Sindona information about Bordoni that he believed proved that Bordoni, if used correctly, could be a valuable pawn. The P-2 report revealed that Bordoni had been a military prisoner in South Africa during World War II. Bordoni, the report went on to say, had been interrogated and beaten by the British over the course of a two-year period.

This was not a trivial footnote in Bordoni's dossier. When Bordoni speculated, he usually took a short position on the English pound, hoping he would make a killing by forcing the value of the pound to fall. Playing psychiatrist, Sindona concluded that Bordoni was not a thief but, instead, a man who was determined to avenge himself against the British by destroying the value of the pound. For exactly the same reasons that the banking community and Sindona's banking associates did not like Bordoni, Michele realized Carlo was the perfect pawn. He had nowhere to run because nobody wanted him. So Michele believed that he could coerce Bordoni into assigning profitable foreign exchange trades to the Sindona Group while bank customers swallowed the losses. Backing Moneyrex, Sindona believed, would, in addition to creating profits, make Bordoni grateful and loyal. And Sindona intended to set that loyalty against Bordoni's weak position in the community, so that Moneyrex would filter foreign currency deposits to Sindona's banks. But first, Moneyrex had to be successful.

For the first two years Moneyrex met strong resistance. Banks refused to deal with Bordoni, and the brokerage firm lost money. Sindona, however, refused to accept defeat. To promote the company, a monthly bulletin was printed in Italian, English, and French. The bulletin was written by Bordoni and edited by Sindona. Circulation exceeded ten thousand copies a month. And when responding to inquiries, Sindona had instructed Bordoni to represent Moneyrex as a joint venture of Hambros Bank, Continental Bank, and the Vatican.

In time, Moneyrex became the largest institution of its kind in the world, with 850 client banks—including Westminster National Bank of England, First National Bank of Boston, and the Central Bank of Hungary—spread throughout Europe, North and South America, the Middle East, Asia, and Africa. The firm's gross volume, according to Nino Sindona, who worked with Bordoni at Moneyrex, averaged $200 billion a year. As a result, Banca Unione and Banca Privata Finanziaria were fed a total of $1.1 billion in foreign exchange deposits. And deposits in national currency, not including ordinary deposits by private citizens or local interbank deposits, totaled approximately 660 billion lire.

Shortly after Carlo Bordoni joined the Sindona Group, Maria Elisa told her father that she wanted to become a physician. To her surprise, her father became angry and accused her of abandoning him.

"You will study business so that you can help me," Michele said.

"If you won't give me permission to study medicine, then let me study language. Since your business has expanded into several countries, I would not only be satisfying myself but also serving you."

"You're stupid!" Michele screamed. "If you want to learn a language, you live in that country for a few months and learn it. I want you to study business."

For a Sicilian this was an unusual demand. Most Sicilian men turn to their sons, not their daughters, for help. Perhaps Michele realized that Maria Elisa was the strongest and most intelligent of his three children, but it appears more likely that Michele's insistence arose from his need to share a close and confidential business relationship with a woman.

Maria Elisa was sent to England to study business administration. When she returned to Italy, however, she did not become Michele's right hand in business. Instead, on April 8, 1967, she married Pier Sandro Magnoni, who was half Italian and half Spanish. He was 6 feet tall, with thick eyebrows, and like his father he was a lawyer. The Magnonis were long-time members of Milan's aristocracy. Comfortably wealthy, they were very religious and had built a lavishly decorated chapel in their villa, where Maria Elisa and Pier Sandro were wed. It was a good marriage, and the Magnoni family possessed the kind of credibility that Michele wanted.

The newlyweds, however, shattered Michele's heart when, immediately after the honeymoon, they moved to Barcelona. Michele pleaded with Maria Elisa not to move away from him. Instead of complying, Maria Elisa asked her father to buy an apartment for her in Spain. "I don't want to buy you an apartment," Michele cried. "If I do, you will never return." In desperation, he offered Pier Sandro a job within the Sindona Group if he remained in Milan. Pier Sandro declined the offer. His family was depending on him to take over control of a foundry they owned in Barcelona. Besides, he explained, he was too young and knew nothing about banking.

Beaten, Michele purchased a co-op for his daughter and son-in-law. The apartment, however, was not finished when the time came for them to move in. Michele against suggested they remain in Milan. Impossible, both Maria Elisa and Pier Sandro said. Not wanting to upset his daughter, Michele negotiated with the builder and arranged for the newlyweds to live rent-free in a suite in a hotel that the builder owned while the apartment was being finished.

His daughter's absence, in one psychiatrist's opinion, tormented Michele, fracturing the thin wall of security he had erected since Nunziata left him. When things did not go as well as he had hoped or when the law prevented him from doing what he wanted, he would lose control, change from his normally rational self, and burst into a rage. A phone call from Maria Elisa would help, and for a day or two he would appear happy, sometimes even euphoric. Eventually, however, the cycle would start again. He would lose control, denounce the world for its moral nihilism, and become seriously depressed, at times suicidal. Ultimately, he became a nihilist, which led him, in the struggle to understand himself, to accept, uncontaminated by doubt, his belief that he was a superman.

Maria Elisa and Pier Sandro were to take possession of their apartment in one month. Not until a year had passed, however, was the apartment completed. By then, Maria Elisa was pregnant and Michele had finally convinced Pier Sandro to move back to Milan. A close friend and business associate says that he believes "Michele had bought the complex and postponed construction to force his daughter back to his side." No documents are available to support such a claim. Even if the story is true, it would be less remarkable than the joy Michele experienced when Pier Sandro joined his empire.

First, he sent Pier Sandro to England to study banking. Later, he brought his son-in-law into the Sindona Group and made him his lieutenant. Pier Sandro proved to be a trusted aide and a valuable asset to Sindona. Nevertheless, a doctor who treated Michele for manic depression is convinced that Michele's real purpose in bringing Magnoni into the Group was to keep Maria Elisa close to him. "If he had lost her, after losing Nunziata," the physician explains, "I don't think Michele would have survived."

Pier Sandro Magnoni went to work at Moneyrex with Carlo Bordoni, who was eventually rewarded for the company's success. Bordoni's annual salary was increased to $15,000, and he was also awarded a bonus based on 10 percent of the annual net profit, with a stock option of 17 percent of Moneyrex. Ultimately, Bordoni's income rose to $65,000 a year. He was much happier now, although he was a little put out by Sindona's practice of relaying orders through the younger and less experienced Pier Sandro Magnoni. Nevertheless, Pier Sandro always treated Bordoni with respect, and it was easy for Bordoni to control Sindona's son-in-law, especially since Maria Elisa mocked her husband for his naiveté about the business world. In spite of everything, Carlo promised Michele and the Sindona Group eternal loyalty.

Sindona was pleased. He boasted that he alone had correctly judged Bordoni's value. Eventually John McCaffrey acknowledged Sindona's coup by purchasing a 10 percent participation in Moneyrex. Meanwhile Michele Sindona, who stood to the right of the most extreme right as an inflexible anti-communist, sold another 10 percent to the Central Bank of Hungary.

When business associates demanded an explanation, Michele said, "I only let the Bank of Hungary in so that I could watch what the communists were doing in the market" — not a very plausible answer, but everyone was still participating in Michele's magic act.

Not everyone, however, shared the Sindona Group's feelings about Bordoni. Rina Sindona had remained a serious skeptic, and finally, one evening before guests arrived for cocktails, she confronted Michele.

They were expecting their daughter, their son-in-law, and Carlo Bordoni, who was now divorced and living with a divorcée named Virginia Cornelio, who had a voracious appetite for food and money. It was a typical Milan night, hot and humid. The air conditioning had been on all day, though, so it was cool and comfortable inside the apartment. The lights in the living room were dimmed, and Rina was standing on the balcony, wearing a new cotton print dress with a white collar. She was proud of the dress because she had made it herself and saved Michele 180,000 lire ($300).

A million lights dotted the city's skyline. Rina often spent time counting these lights. She had never been able to count past a thousand; each time she reached that number someone would need a shirt ironed or something to eat, or she would simply lose interest. It didn't matter, for she never thought that she would count more than a thousand. It was just something she liked to do when she was upset, just as some people relax by petting a cat or a dog.

"One thousand," she said. Then she automatically turned, wondering if Michele had called her. No, Michele wasn't even home yet. She would have to entertain Bordoni and his mistress without Michele's help. Because she didn't like Bordoni, this would not be a pleasant task for her. She knew, however, that Michele wouldn't fail to arrive; he would come home, and when he arrived she would tell him she did not like Bordoni. No, she wouldn't do that, she decided. Michele would be tired, and that would just upset him. She would keep her feelings to herself, as always.

"*Buona sera, cara,*" Michele said with a smile and a kiss as soon as he shut the door.

"You're a poor judge of character," Rina let slip.

"What?" Michele looked confused.

"This man is no good," Rina said. "I can feel it when I look at him. Carlo is not what you think."

"Ahhh, you don't know anything. You're just a housewife. I know people." His voice cracked, and his hands waved uncontrollably in the air. "I know what I am doing."

"What you're doing," Rina screamed, "is buying loyalty. You always pay the check, never allow anyone else to pay. You are too generous, Michele, always paying bills for people, always trying to help every stranger who asks for help. People do not appreciate it. They will not remember to be loyal when it matters. Bordoni is no different. Carlo will act loyal as long as he is getting something from you, Michele. But he is not capable of being a friend. I can feel it. He's an evil man. He is not the kind of man you can turn your back on without risk."

But Michele would not listen. He knew what he was doing. "Carlo is a little nuts, I know," he said, "but he's no thief. Besides, I have . . . " He left the thought dangling in the air all through the evening.

After dinner, when they were in bed, Rina asked Michele what he meant when he said, "I have . . . "

Michele did not respond.

Had Sindona completed his thought, he would have had to admit that his plan was to filter "black money" for Propaganda Due, Mafia figures, currency for businessmen and politicians, and foreign account deposits placed at his banks, through Moneyrex, outside Italy. This was illegal but Italian bankers, brokers, and lawyers believed that currency laws were a political sham designed to impress the lower classes. In Italy, laws — and governments — changed too quickly for businessmen to take them seriously.

The rule of the game was to circumvent laws rather than break them. For transferring lire out of Italy and into secret bank accounts in Switzerland, the fiduciary contract, as Michele Sindona had already learned, provided the perfect loophole. It preserved the thin illusion of legality while serving Sindona's end.

Serving the Mafia and P-2, however, created problems more serious than simply bypassing currency restrictions. Smuggling profits from kidnappings, extortion, and drug trafficking, washing off the blood and dirt so that the funds could be reinvested made Sindona, at the very least, a conspirator in every act. Circumventing such problems required a more artful approach, and Michele Sindona's mind appears to have been fertile with devious ideas.

Yet to say that he was just a criminal would be too simple. In order to exist, to overcome indecision and the empty feeling that accompanied the manic depressive state he often dwelled in, Michele needed excitement. When he was stimulated by the adventure of plotting complex schemes, when he was turning fantasy into reality or pitting his wits against the system, his headaches and indigestion, for the moment, disappeared.

Challenged, Michele's mind became a field of creative energy directed toward winning, the method employed being unimportant to him. He stamped his identity on an empire more powerful than the system, created an illusion and became the focus of his own creation until he no longer thought of himself as Michele Sindona. Determined to prove his existence, Nunziata's grandchild transcended the boundaries of self and became Group Sindona, Banker Sindona, Avvocato Sindona, Freemason Sindona, adopting any label that implied greater importance than the name Michele Sindona, which designated a mere person.

By the time Carlo Bordoni entered Sindona's world, Michele had mastered the art of breaking or circumventing laws for the benefit of Group Sindona. His methodology can be broken into four parts:

- Have a clear and precise understanding of the project, the risks involved, and the rules or laws to be circumvented.

- Know the law and foresee legal complications.

- Motivate conspirators by taking advantage of their greed, their need for affection, and/or their fear of the leader.

- Allow no one else to know the entire plot. Arrange matters and distribute facts on a need-to-know basis. Even then, lie when possible, but always make people believe.

Sindona's plan for Bordoni was to make him his minister, the man who signed the contracts, ordered wire transfers of hundreds of billions of lire and hundreds of millions of dollars. Bordoni was the vehicle, the human loophole. He needed money, and he needed to feel that he belonged. Sindona filled both needs.

In his position, Carlo Bordoni knew more than any other individual in the Sindona Group, but Michele did not reveal everything even to Bordoni. He concealed from everyone the assignment Pope Paul VI had given him during that secret midnight meeting in the spring of 1969 — the night that all of the Vatican's wealth was turned over to him, the moment when he officially gained the title *Mercator Senesis Romanam Curiam sequens* — the pope's banker.

9

PHASE TWO

IN 1969 when Pope Paul VI chose Michele Sindona to become the Vatican's banker, the Holy Father placed the financial future of the Holy See in the hands of a man who would later be described by Carlo Bordoni as "the banker of the Mafia." The Mafia had followed Sindona's career ever since Vito Genovese made it possible for him to smuggle produce from the center of Sicily to Patti. But on November 2, 1957, at a summit meeting in Palermo, Sicily, a committee of high-ranking Sicilian and American mafiosi chose Michele Sindona to manage the Mafia's plan to infiltrate legitimate businesses throughout the world. This historical meeting of the world's most powerful crime figures took place on one of Sicily's most celebrated pagan holidays.

To the rest of the Catholic world, November 2 is known as All Souls' Day. In Sicily, however, it is called either "Day of the Dead" or "Bones of the Dead." Lucky Luciano, who had directed the course of the American Mafia, changing it into a nationally organized crime syndicate known as the Cosa Nostra, picked this day because he knew that the festivities would provide a good cover for his associates.

In the *vucciria* (marketplace), puppet theaters were erected on each street corner. Puppeteers re-created battles between Sicilian knights and their Arab rulers. Fireworks seemed to burst from the heart of the red-orange Sicilian moon, splashing a rainbow of brilliantly colored stars across the sky. Laughter marinated in wine dripped from cafés and flooded the city with a festive sound. Vendors pushed their artistically painted carts through the streets, creating a trail of pungent odors. There was the smell of garlic and broiled seafood; the sparkle of fried rice balls stuffed with ricotta cheese, raisins, and toasted bread crumbs; and the sweet aroma of 12-inch sugar dolls called *pupico di zucchero*. The dolls were made by hand and colored red and green and white. There were knights for the boys and princesses for the girls. The holiday's traditional specialty was called *scardellini*, "bones of the dead" — skeletonlike cookies made of sugar and chocolate and shaped like bones: the humerus, the phalanx, the cranium, and the spine.

While children nibbled on *pupico di zucchero* and *scardellini*, Michele Sindona and the international Mafia committee sat in a suite in the Hôtel des Palmes and talked about reinvesting drug profits in legal investment channels. The Mafia's representatives were Joseph "Joe Bananas" Bonanno, self-proclaimed Prince of the Honored Society (the Sicilian Mafia); his underboss, Carmine Galante; Lucky Luciano; representatives of the Genovese, Lucchese, and Gambino families; and Tommaso Buscetta and Frank Coppola, major international heroin smugglers with strong connections to the Gambino crime family and the Christian Democrats. As Sindona worked on his origami, fashioning one papal crown after another, the crime syndicate agreed to grant him complete control of their heroin profits. The deal was not unlike the agreement Michele would sign years later with Pope Paul VI, except that this contract was verbal and, if the Mafia suffered losses, Michele would lose his life.

So by 1969, when Sindona transferred Vatican-owned stocks to a series of holding companies in Luxembourg and Liechtenstein, tax havens that practice Swiss-style secrecy, he was doing something he'd been doing as a matter of course for more than a decade. Once the Vatican's ownership of the stocks was concealed from the Italian government Sindona was able to sell the shares on the Italian stock exchange. He then reinvested the tax-free profits in European and American stocks, which included Chase Manhattan, General Motors, General Foods, Standard Oil, and Westinghouse.

Michele Sindona also used some of the Vatican funds to finance his acquisition of Banca di Messina in Sicily and Rome's water company, Condotte d'Acqua. But his largest transaction was the takeover of the Vatican's giant real estate conglomerate, Società Generale Immobiliare (SGI), one of the largest real estate companies in the world, whose best-known property was Washington's Watergate complex.

Like all Vatican business, the transfer of SGI was completed with extreme secrecy. Sindona arranged for the SGI shares to be first transferred to Paribas Transcontinental of Luxembourg, a subsidiary of Banque de Paris et des Pays Bas (Paribas). Then he instructed Paribas to transfer the SGI shares to his holding company, Fasco, A.G. Not long after Sindona had SGI safely tucked under the Fasco umbrella, however, there was a leak. The press reported the transaction and pressured the Holy See to respond.

Through a spokesman, Pope Paul said, "Our policy is to avoid maintaining control of companies as in the past. We want to improve investment performance, balanced, of course, against what must be a fundamentally conservative investment philosophy. It wouldn't do for the church to lose its principal in speculation."

Sindona, however, was less cooperative. When Italian journalists visited him at his office — which would remain his headquarters until he left Milan for good — Sindona said nothing. Standing in the archway that formed the entrance to his office, Michele apologized, saying that if he answered their questions he would be violating not only the confidence of a client but also the law. The reporters persisted, arguing that the Vatican had already acknowledged the transfer. Still Sindona refused to respond. "Isn't it a violation of one of Italy's securities laws to transfer stocks out of the country?" a journalist asked. Sindona quickly became bored. Automatically his hands flipped palms up, his head fell to one side, his eyes shut.

In 1970 Dan Porco introduced Sindona to Charles Bludhorn, chairman of Gulf & Western. In August Sindona sold fifteen million shares of SGI stock to Bludhorn. At first glance, it appears that Bludhorn outmaneuvered Sindona. In payment for the SGI shares, Bludhorn gave Sindona all the shares of Commonwealth United, a record and film distribution company that was near bankruptcy.

Sindona, however, explains, "I always sell a company for less than it is worth to someone I want to please." In other words, whenever Sindona wanted to establish a relationship with someone, he would, like a human kaleidoscope, reflect shaded images of strength and intelligence, power and kindness, or honesty and shrewdness. Then he would lead an associate through a series of shady deals.

The Securities and Exchange Commission (SEC) later charged Bludhorn and Sindona with a violation of U.S. securities laws. The SEC alleged that both men had traded worthless stocks back and forth at face value in order to create a false market. In essence, even though the SEC eventually forced them to stop trading, they had circumvented the law. As already explained, Michele Sindona was a genius at circumventing the law. He did it with his Liechtensteinian and Luxembourgian corporations. He did it for the Vatican, the High Mafia, and the Freemasons. And he did it when he and Bludhorn traded valueless stocks between themselves. Even after the SEC caught them, Michele Sindona was able to beat them by negotiating what amounted to a gentleman's agreement. He and Bludhorn agreed to discontinue their activities, and the SEC dropped all charges. By then, however, Sindona and Bludhorn had already made a tremendous profit.

Two years later, in 1972, after Sindona had purchased control of Franklin New York Corporation, which owned Franklin National Bank, Bludhorn sold his SGI shares back to Sindona for 700 lire each. A few months later, on the Italian stock market, Sindona pushed the price per share of SGI stock to over 1,450 lire. So in the end, Bludhorn was outmaneuvered by Sindona. "I don't understand that market," Bludhorn says, "and I've never talked to an Italian businessman who can explain it."

Michele Sindona, unlike Bludhorn, understood the Italian stock market very well. On a given day he controlled an average of 40 percent of all the stocks traded. According to Carlo Bordoni, however, that success in the stock market should be partly credited to Sindona's misuse of customers' accounts. Michele would buy and sell stocks in companies he controlled for his banking clients. This created a market pushing the price of his shares upward. Once the price reached a predetermined figure, presenting Sindona with a huge profit margin, Michele would sell off part or all of his shares to his customer accounts. Some customers benefited from this, but many others, especially those who had not authorized speculation, lost considerable amounts of money.

In May 1971 a client by the name of Jacometti issued a press release through the news agency AIPE, accusing Michele Sindona of misusing customer funds. Jacometti accused Michele Sindona and Ugo De Luca, managing director of Banca Unione, of selling shares of several of Sindona's corporations to bank customers without their knowledge. The companies involved were Pacchetti, Talmone, and Banca Unione. According to Sindona, however, Jacometti had refused to repay a $500,000 loan. When Sindona pressured Jacometti for payment, Jacometti issued the press release, thus creating a scandal that nearly cost Sindona his banks and his reputation in the banking community.

When the scandal broke, Sindona and Pier Sandro Magnoni were in Madrid negotiating the purchase of Banco Industrial, C.A. Michele called Carlo Bordoni to ask him how serious the situation was. Bordoni told Sindona that "the situation was very serious." Ugo De Luca had defended himself against Jacometti's accusations by holding a press conference in which he blamed Sindona for the illegal transactions. As a result, Bordoni says, "in the banking and stock exchange circles, it was rumored that the Sindona Group would collapse." The stock exchange prices of Pacchetti, Talmone, and BU remained stable only because BU was supporting the market. "It is my impression," Bordoni said, "that the month-end stock exchange closing could provoke a liquidity crisis for BU."

The following day, Sindona flew back to Milan. He silenced De Luca by depositing 900 million lire (at the time approximately $1.3 million) in De Luca's name at a Swiss bank in Lugano. Then he fired De Luca and appointed Carlo Bordoni managing director of Banca Unione.

In the meantime, the Jacometti scandal was resolved. With the help of Masonic brothers Licio Gelli and General Raffaele Giudice, who had been appointed head of the Finance Guard by Prime Minister Giulio Andreotti, reportedly a close associate of Gelli's, the scandal was covered up and died. To help end the bad publicity surrounding the Jacometti problem, Licio Gelli assisted Sindona in purchasing the news agency AIPE. In return for his help, Gelli was allowed to bring suitcases of "hot money" through the Vatican gates. Sindona then transferred the money to secret accounts at Finabank and Amincor, two Swiss banks Sindona controlled.

For some time, Michele Sindona had been using his Swiss banks to steal millions in foreign currency deposits that Bordoni, through Moneyrex, had placed in the hands of the Group. For example, the foreign currency Bordoni deposited with Romitex, a Group company, was split equally between Amincor and the Vatican bank, Banca di Roma per la Svizzera in Lugano. The IOR also used Finabank to speculate in the currency market. In 1970, when Bordoni was auditing Finabank's records, he discovered that the Vatican had accumulated $30 million in foreign exchange losses. These losses were covered by the illegal transfer of BPF's foreign bank deposits, which had been deposited at BPF by Moneyrex. Years later, in 1973, when losses reached $45 million, the Federal Commission of Swiss banks ordered Sindona and the Vatican to close Liberfinco (Liberian Financial Co.), a Finabank subsidiary that was owned jointly by Michele Sindona and the Vatican's IOR. "If this had not been done," Bordoni says, "Finabank would have been declared bankrupt." Nevertheless, through this banking garbage can, Sindona and the Vatican financed Edilcentro of Washington, a subsidiary of SGI. Edilcentro constructed the Watergate complex. Although neither Carlo Bordoni nor Nino Sindona will elaborate, both claim that Michele Sindona was one of the protagonists of the Watergate scandal.

Bordoni also says that, in addition to "the numerous dirty Vatican operations carried out by the Christian Democrats, Finabank was the laundry for hot dollars coming from the Mafia and Freemasons." After the funds were deposited at Finabank, they were reinvested through Liberfinco.

While the authorities were investigating the Jacometti scandal, Licio Gelli boldly organized what would later become the biggest rip-off in the history of Italian finance. With General Giudice, oil magnate Bruno Musselli, and Michele Sindona, all members of the renegade Masonic lodge P-2, Gelli robbed Italy of more than $2.2 billion in oil tax revenues.

In Italy the same petroleum product is used both to heat houses and to drive diesel trucks. The heating oil, however, is dyed so as to be distinguishable from the diesel fuel and is taxed at a rate fifty times lower than the diesel fuel. Under the direction of Licio Gelli, Bruno Musselli doctored the dyes and General Giudice falsified the paperwork in order to get all of their fuel taxed at the lower rate. Once the fraud was committed, Giudice, Musselli, and Sindona sold the fuel to gas stations at the higher rate and pocketed the difference between the real tax paid to them by the gas stations and the lower tax they paid to the government. They then transferred the profits through the Bank of the Vatican to a series of secret accounts at Sindona's Finabank.

"In turn," wrote journalist Thomas Sheehan in an article in the January 1981 *New York Review of Books*, "Musselli and his associates paid out millions of dollars (the exact sum is unknown) over some four years to General Giudice, his right-hand man General Donato lo Prete, and Sereno Freato, the trusted counselor of the late Aldo Moro, to get them to close an eye to the revenue evasion." Gelli and Sindona were so successful in keeping things quiet that, in 1978, says Sheehan, when the scandal came to light in a provincial newspaper in northern Italy, it was discreetly covered up. "Even the chairman of the senate finance committee hid away a police report on the swindle for over seven months. When a muckraking journalist in Rome named Mino Pecorelli got wind of the scandal, he began to publish some articles in his magazine, *OP*, but was apparently bought off by an interested group that included Christian Democrat Senator Claudio Vitalone, Judge Carlo Testi, and General Donato lo Prete of the Finance Guard."

Mino Pecorelli, it has been said, had excellent contacts within the secret service. What Sheehan and others did not realize at the time was that Pecorelli was a member of Propaganda Due. For reasons unknown, in 1979 Pecorelli and Gelli had a falling-out. Pecorelli denounced his membership in P-2 and began to publish stories about the illegal activities of Gelli and the Masonic lodge. Eventually Gelli persuaded Pecorelli to accept a bribe, and the stories stopped. "When the money dried up," writes Sheehan, Pecorelli "threatened to go public with his information" on the oil rip-off. "On March 20, 1979, as [Pecorelli] sat in his car on a dark Roman street, he was shot twice in the mouth and died. The murder was in the Mafia style of *sasso in bocca* — a rock in the mouth of the dead man to indicate that he would speak no more." (Recently there have been over one hundred arrests of persons believed to have been involved in the oil scandal. One member of P-2, Antonio Viezzer, at one time a high-ranking

officer of SID, Italy's secret service, has been arrested and charged on suspicion of involvement in the killing of Mino Pecorelli.)

Although giant deals were Sindona's forte, he gave special consideration to
the little, seemingly unimportant transactions. In order to increase the
deposits at his banks, Michele borrowed an idea from A. P. Giannini, founder of Bank of America, and Arthur Roth, former chairman of Franklin
National Bank. Sindona developed a campaign designed to attract small
depositors; the campaign proved extremely successful. Nevertheless, at
Banca Privata Finanziaria, Bordoni says, "Foreign currency 'black operations' [illegal transactions], a true exportation of capital, took place daily,
and large figures were involved."

Apart from overdrawn accounts for amounts far in excess of one-
fifth of the capital and reserves of the bank, the legal lending limit, Bordoni also discovered an enormous one-way infusion of liquidity from BPF
to Moizzi & Co. (a Sindona Group company). These were illegal transfers
of funds that, in almost all cases, transpired when large sums of money
were diverted from the accounts of the bank's depositors with the help of
from the accounts of the bank's depositors with the help of the Vatican.

With Pope Paul's approval, Michele Sindona placed bank customer
funds at the disposal of Moizzi & Co. The funds were then transferred to
the account of the Instituto per le Opere di Religione (IOR), which in turn
placed them at the disposal of Sindona at Finabank, Geneva, in an account
designated as MANI: MA for Marco, NI for Nino, the first two letters of
Sindona's sons' names.

When clients presented checks or payment orders against their
accounts, the employee responsible for the checking accounts refused to
accept such checks. When the clients vigorously protested, the head teller
gave them their money, apologizing, as instructed, and explaining that it
was all "a big accounting error."

At some point Bordoni decided to block the flow of funds from Moneyrex to BPF. On one day he repaid $110 million to foreign counterac-
counts. When Sindona learned of this, he ordered Bordoni to come to his
office. As soon as he entered Sindona's office, Bordoni says, Sindona
accused him "of sabotaging BPF and his Group by first interrupting, and
then decreasing, the flow of foreign liquidity toward BPF." Responding to
Sindona's "violent attitude," Bordoni became angry and "accused him of
being a criminal" for utilizing BPF's liquidity "for his dirty and disorderly
personal business." Refusing to replenish BPF's foreign currency deposits,
Bordoni said that if what Sindona was saying were true — "that is, that his
banks' national and foreign currency deposits were increasing, thanks to
his unlimited credit" — then Sindona should not be upset, since "he could

have substituted, totally, the funds that Moneyrex had pumped into his banks."

Sindona became angry. Though Bordoni says that he was by now accustomed to Sindona's threats, he was stunned when Sindona black-mailed him by threatening to reveal to the governor of the Bank of Italy, Guido Carli, an irregular operation Bordoni had performed. The transac-tion involved a forward six-month contract in gold, which Bordoni had anticipated in one of his monthly bulletins.

The gold operation was carried out in behalf of Sindona on Fina-bank's and Amincor's books. This was illegal since Italian law prevented an Italian citizen from owning a foreign account. The gold was sold for $46 an ounce against a cost of $35.25 an ounce, with a margin of 30 percent, and the pound sterling equivalent was covered after a devaluation of 16 percent, which produced a profit of $2 million. Although Sindona had promised Bordoni a share of the profits, he received nothing. Instead, according to Bordoni, Sindona kept the profits for himself and filed a copy of the transaction for the purpose of blackmailing Bordoni, who says that the operation proves that Sindona's methods of creating profits were not those of a banker or financier but those of a gambler. Others say Sindona was a thief. Michele Sindona, however, held a different opinion. Accord-ing to Bordoni, Sindona bragged that he had built a vast empire based on his "personality, which is unique in the world, on well-told lies, and on the efficient weapon of blackmail."

Bordoni's allegations must be taken seriously because he was in a unique position that allowed him to be close to Sindona's operations. Also, Sindona had humiliated Bordoni several times, and in front of other people. Sindona made many promises to grant Bordoni a share of partici-pation in the banks, but this never materialized. And though Carlo seems to have been willing to suffer Sindona's humiliation, his new wife was not. Virginia Bordoni constantly pushed her husband, demanding that he demonstrate a stronger will and desire for success, that he insist on more than a simple salary and bonus while he earned millions for Michele Sin-dona. Virginia talked Carlo into opening a trading account (number 0/ 013880/2) for her in her maiden name at BPF, through which Carlo could filter funds. Still, Virginia wanted more, and she wanted it much faster. In time, frustrated by her unfulfilled desire to be rich, Virginia Bordoni wove a tale about Sindona's attempt to rape her. This story eventually turned Bordoni against the man who held the keys to the secrets and wealth of the Vatican, the Mafia, and Propaganda Due — Don Michele Sindona.

Money did not always flow into the Sindona Group's coffers, how-ever. Regardless of Sindona's business practices, he was more interested in financing political movements. Through an account labeled SIDC — an acronym for Sindona–Christian Democrats — Michele laundered the equivalent of hundreds of millions of dollars for the Christian Democrats. He also authorized large payments to individuals who were in a position to protect his and Licio Gelli's interests.

A good example is the case of Menna S.A.S. di Varese, a real estate holding company with property in Sicily. Matteo Maciocco was the general partner in this company as well as president of the board of auditors of Banca Unione, a government position, and a member of Sindona's Group. On February 11, 1972, after agreeing with Sindona to give Banca Unione a favorable report, a deposit of 310,116,543 lire ($500,000) was made in favor of Menna di Varese (account number 0/026018.07). And on March 17, 1972, a loan was granted to Maciocco in the amount of four billion three hundred million lire ($1.1 million). Finally, on December 21, 1973, the sum of 9 million lire ($15,000) was transferred from a secret account (number 29920), which was managed directly by Carlo Bordoni, to Matteo Maciocco's checking account (number 0/7418/67).

In addition to graft, Michele Sindona also financed the Christian Democrats' opposition to divorce. In the coming years, he would also act as the conduit for millions of U.S. dollars authorized by former President Richard M. Nixon and his ambassador to Italy, Graham Martin, to institute extreme right-wing movements against the left in Italy.

PART
II

THE YEARS OF GLORY

TO MAKE AN INTERNATIONAL BANKING SYSTEM WORK REQUIRED A BANK AT EACH
END OF THE TRANSACTION, AND IN THE EARLY YEARS IT WAS CONSIDERED BEST FOR
THE SAME FAMILY TO OWN BOTH, ESTABLISHING A SON OR NEPHEW OF AN IN-LAW AS
AT LEAST A PARTNER IN THE REMOTE ENTERPRISE.

MARTIN MAYER
THE BANKERS

10

ROME FALLS
AND FALLS AND FALLS

IT IS GENERALLY BELIEVED that in Europe the armed struggle between the left and the right exploded in 1968 when leftist university students flooded the streets of Rome to battle police and Italian neo-fascists. Participants in the "strategy of tension," as this war between the left and the right is known in Italy, regard killing and mutilation as necessary steps toward freeing Italy from the control of the right-of-center Christian Democrats. Over a twelve-year period, terrorism has saturated every level of society and impregnated it with so much fear that many wealthy Italians attempt to protect themselves from assassinations, kneecappings, kidnappings, bombings, and extortion by trading in their Mercedes for less expensive cars and equipping them with bulletproof glass, reinforced door and engine panels, and guns mounted in the door wells. They keep a constant watch on the rearview mirror, change their routes almost daily, and train themselves not to respond to unfamiliar voices calling their names. They hire bodyguards, and they shop at Fendi's of Milan, where inexpensive-looking coats are lined with costly furs.

Others, however, take a more chilling position. They have desensitized themselves to the point of claiming that learning of organized and premeditated violence is no different from hearing that some stranger has been killed in a car accident. As one member of parliament says, "You can get used to anything, even fear. For two or three days after every episode of violence, you ask yourself who it is when the doorbell rings. But habit can destroy anything, even fear."

Italians in the late sixties and throughout the seventies found it difficult to escape the realities of terrorism when anarchists marched in the streets of Rome and Milan, their faces covered with handkerchiefs, and their hands — the thumb and index finger extended to form a gun — raised above their heads as they shouted, "Don't vote; shoot!" Or, when reading the daily newspapers, Italians were confronted by advertisements pleading with terrorists for information about the fate of kidnap victims, some of whom had been missing for as long as five years.

On December 12, 1969, a number of innocent people discovered the power of terrorism when a bomb exploded at the Bank of Agriculture in Piazza Fontana in Milan. Moments later, another went off in Rome's National Bank of Labor just off the Via Veneto. A third bomb exploded at the monument of King Victor Emmanuel II. Altogether, sixteen people were killed and another ninety were wounded. At first the bombings were blamed on the left. An official of Movimento Sociale Italiano (MSI), the neo-fascist party, declared the acts a crisis for the whole system of government and called for "civil war." In response, new fascist groups — the New Order, the Black Order, the Mussolini Action Squad, the Steel Helmet, and the Third Position — to the right of MSI sprang up and began their armed struggle.

In an attempt to contain the violence, police arrested seventy anarchists and searched the home of the wealthy left-wing publisher Giangiacomo Feltrinelli. (Though no evidence was found that could tie Feltrinelli to the bombings, he was later ordered to stand trial on charges of criminal incitement in connection with the September 1968 police seizure from Feltrinelli's bookstores of paint spray bottles inscribed "paint your policeman yellow.") Another leftist by the name of Pinelli died after he mysteriously fell or was tossed from the third-floor window of a police station. Later, however, it was discovered that the massacre of December 12 was probably the work of the extreme right.

Police traced the bombings to three neo-fascists, among them General Guido Giannettini, an agent of the SID, Italy's secret service, and a high-ranking member of Licio Gelli's P-2. It is believed that Giannettini was head of a faction within P-2 known as the Third Position. This faction, says journalist Thomas Sheehan, advocates what is called Nazi-Maoism. Sheehan goes on to say that the Third Position aligns itself with the political beliefs of Hitler, Perón, Mao, and Qaddafi. Its slogans include "Long live the fascist dictatorship of the proletariat" and "Hitler and Mao united in struggle."

The terrorist activities of Italy's extreme right, however, did not start in Italy. They began, instead, in Greece where, in 1967, Michele Sindona helped finance the "Colonel's Coup."

In April 1967 Propaganda Due directed its attention to the upcoming election in Greece. The Greek left was headed by forty-seven-year old Andreas Papandreou, a political foe of King Constantine II, who was the ruling monarch of Greece and commander and chief of the armed forces. The leftists were gaining ground and were expected to win the election. The army feared that the leftists would push Greece, the cradle of democracy, toward communist rule. Colonel Papadopoulos, dedicated to the service of the young King Constantine, predicted civil war if the left succeeded in assuming the leadership.

Sometime around April of the same year, Continental Bank of Illinois, according to Sindona, transferred $4 million to Sindona's Banca Privata Finanziaria. Upon receipt, Sindona immediately wired $4 million to Colonel Papadopoulos through the bank account of Helleniki Tecniki, a construction company controlled by the Greek army. The loan was guaranteed by the Central Bank of Greece.

In the early morning hours of April 21 Michele Sindona was sitting at home in his study chewing on cubes of sugar as he waited for an important phone call. His eyes darted back and forth from the telephone to the portrait of Nunziata. He was nervous, and the pain above his eye was throbbing.

At 2:00 A.M., in Athens, the last light at Tatoi Palace went out. A few minutes later, soldiers slipped from the shadows, took command of every military station in Greece and shut down all radio stations. Three soldiers and an officer appeared at the house of Premier Panayotis Kanellopoulos. The premier barricaded his door, but the officer — after explaining to the premier that he had come to protect him — ordered his men to break into the house. The soldiers grabbed the premier and dragged him into a waiting car. He screamed, "Why don't you kill me here?"

Simultaneously, in the Athenian suburb of Kastri, former premier George Papandreou, father of Andreas Papandreou, was kidnapped from his house and locked up. At the same time, eight soldiers smashed the glass door to Andreas Papandreou's house. The soldiers overpowered Andreas and his bodyguard. They dragged Andreas, wearing only his underpants, across the broken glass and stuffed him into a car.

The "merchants of the right" repeated scenes like these until five thousand communists were in prison. At approximately 2:45 A.M., fifteen minutes before the king would learn details of the coup, Michele Sindona's phone rang. The message was short and precise: "In the name of the king," the voice said, "we have succeeded." The pain above Michele's eye vanished. He was happy. He had assisted in what he considered to be a major defeat of the communists.

At 3:00 A.M., in the same instant that three tanks positioned themselves in front of the palace gates, the Greek army ended the radio silence and announced to the rest of the world that it had, "in the name of the king," taken control of the country.

Two years later, in December 1969, a letter published in the London *Times* revealed a plot to overthrow the government of Italy and establish an Italian fascist state backed by sympathetic forces within Greece. The document was titled "Ministry of Foreign Affairs, Minister's Office, Ref. No. 600 A-47" and was labeled "Strictly confidential. To be opened only by the ambassador."

The document explained that a report from Greece's agents in Italy "indicated that events are developing in a direction very favorable to the national revolution." It went on to say that Premier George Papadopoulos, the former colonel who had organized the 1967 coup in Greece, wanted to prevent "any possibility of linking the activities of our Italian friends with the official Greek authorities."

The report also quoted a mysterious man from Italy identified only as "Mr. P." (believed to be Licio Gelli) appealing to Premier Papadopoulos "to continue the supply of both moral and material help from Greece as well as advice on the development of action groups." Mr. P. is reported to have concluded, "Conditions are much more favorable than in the past. Many people in Italy want to see the establishment of order and peace in their own country."

The Colonels' Coup validated Michele Sindona's position in the world as a man who held in his hand the secret keys to real power. And as history demonstrates, many powerful men do indeed believe themselves to be above the law. So it was for Michele Sindona, as his business prospered from 1967 through 1974 and he reached the height of his power, influence, and growth.

What is not commonly known, however, is that after 1967, according to medical opinion, Michele Sindona suffered a continually diminishing functional capacity of his central nervous system, which affected his cognitive processes: in short, he suffered from manic depression and a degenerative organic brain disease that affected his judgment, moods, and logical processes. Attempting to camouflage his weakened psychological state, Michele suppressed his fear that he was losing his mind, a fear that appears to have caused him to react to stress with emotional instability. Manifestations of rage, unreasoning hatred, and finally depression increased. Medical records suggest the possibility of epileptic episodes, and

they add the possibility that the "process of aging coupled with dysrhyth-
mia . . . decreased the supply of oxygen to his brain and over a period of
time . . . affected his mental performance."

Michele Sindona rejects all psychological explanations for his downfall, but he admits that he was from time to time treated with antidepressants, gastric enzymes, and a drug to reduce high blood pressure. Nothing
seemed to work, and it was probably the use of drugs that caused him to
hallucinate. When the headaches and gastric problems were most painful,
Michele imagined Nunziata scolding him for using medicinal drugs: "A
man must not be afraid of pain. He must not pollute himself with drugs. A
man must be himself."

During this seven-year period, Michele's craving for excitement dramatically increased. Business deals were not enough. Headaches became
less tolerable and more frequent, and when they occurred, his face would
visibly swell. Fatigued much of the time, he needed rest but, paradoxical-
ly, when he rested he felt guilty for not working. As he worked on financial deals, he began to realize that his ability to handle complex tasks and
deal with multiple variables had diminished. Confused and frightened, he
desperately needed to prove to himself and his associates that he could still
harness the intellectual power necessary to pull off big deals. Because of
this drive, this volcanic desire to prove himself a man of great vision,
coupled with the success of the Colonels' Coup, he joined with Licio Gelli
and the Vatican in the financing of right-wing movements.

The day before Ash Wednesday, in 1972, one of Sindona's personal aides
left the Banca Privata Finanziaria and rode the night train from Milan to
Rome. A tiny man with shiny black hair, a white mustache, and large
brown eyes, the aide carried with him a brown leather briefcase stuffed
with 50,000- and 100,000-lire notes. Twice in the same week he had made
the trip. This delivery would bring the total to the equivalent of $2 mil-
lion.

Michele Sindona, punctual as always, sat at a corner table in the Café
de Paris on Rome's fashionable Via Veneto, sipping a fresh espresso sweet-
ened with five teaspoons of sugar as he watched the *carnevale*. There were
thousands of people, some dressed as clowns and others wearing the masks
of characters created by the Venetian writer Carlo Goldoni. As the aide
made his way through the crowded streets, he was perspiring both from
the heat and from the fear that a bandit on a motor scooter might snatch
the case from his grip. At the café, he ate a French pastry and drank an
espresso with Michele. Then he pushed the briefcase to Sindona under the
table and left. A few minutes passed; then Don Michele casually walked to
the Grand Hotel, where he turned the money over to Raffaello Scarpetti
and Fillippo Micheli, both leading members of the Christian Democratic

party. The money would be used to create propaganda against the left and help the Christian Democrats in the upcoming elections.

Michele also helped finance Raffaello Scarpetti and the Christian Democrats in other ways. At Banca Unione, Scarpetti had three checking accounts through which Sindona filtered money, and a temporary account (number 75011.94). During 1972 and 1973, some 220 million lire (approximately $360,000) passed through the temporary account. Scarpetti received another 15 million lire in the form of three bank checks drawn on Credito Italiano and paid to the order of Luigi Rossi, a fictitious name. But Michele was not the only one financing the right. According to the 1976 Pike Report, written by the U.S. House Select Committee on Intelligence, Chairman Otis Pike discovered that the U.S. government had spent $10 million in 1972 backing the Christian Democrats and the right in Italy.

While Graham Martin was U.S. ambassador to Italy during the Nixon administration, the CIA poured millions of dollars into Italy to support right-wing activities. Of that money, $800,000 went directly to SID chief Vito Miceli, a member of P-2 who has since been charged with political conspiracy in the "Tora Tora" coup attempt led by the late Prince Junio Valerio Borghese. General Miceli was not the only member of P-2 who participated in the coup, however. Carlo Bordoni says that Michele Sindona, in the middle of an argument, boasted that he was one of the masterminds of the aborted coup.

Borghese, also known as the "Black Prince," a friend of Licio Gelli, had been head of Decima Mas, a group of fascists who operated during 1944 and 1945. Borghese, like Gelli, was a strong supporter of Mussolini and Hitler. During World War II Borghese received his country's highest award for gallantry as a naval officer.

As the leader of Decima Mas, the Black Prince ordered the assassination of partisans and of civilians suspected of protecting partisans. After the war Borghese spent four years in prison for his pro-Nazi affiliations. Confinement, however, did not diminish the prince's political ambitions. And the clash between the far left and the distant right during 1970 set the mood for Borghese's planned coup.

In February 1970 Italian Premier Rumor and his Christian Democratic minority cabinet resigned. President Giuseppi Saragat immediately instructed Rumor to form a new four-party left-of-center coalition government. The process, however, was complicated by a dispute between Pope Paul VI and parliament over the issue of whether Italians should have the right to divorce. The pontiff sent a letter to Rumor claiming that the passage of the divorce bill would violate Italy's treaty with the Vatican. This stand caused a clash between moderate and rightist Christian Democrats and leftists who rejected the pope's warning, declaring it "an unwarranted interference in internal affairs." The conflict proved too difficult for Rumor to overcome. On March 1, he announced his failure to resolve the crisis and form a new coalition government.

On March 4, former Premier Aldo Moro accepted a mandate from President Saragat to form a new cabinet. At the same time, Jesuit priests publicly denounced the pope's stand on the divorce bill. Pope Paul, the Jesuits said, was interfering in politics while also "violating the principles of religious liberty expressed by Vatican II." Pope Paul, nevertheless, remained steadfast. So the Christian Democrats blocked the vote on the divorce bill, demanding that negotiations between the Vatican and the senate be concluded first. Frustrated by the Vatican's pressure, on March 12, Moro abandoned efforts to form a new four-party coalition government. President Saragat turned to Senate President Fanfani, but Fanfani also failed to establish a new government. Then, on March 21, Rumor announced the formation of a new four-party, left-of-center government, ending Italy's longest postwar political crisis.

In late June and early July groups of neo-fascists organized citizens of Reggio Calabria in armed protest over Rome's decision to name Cantanzaro instead of Reggio Calabria as the Calabria region's new capital. Police used teargas to disperse stone-throwing and fire-bombing demonstrators. One person was killed and some 150 were injured. On July 5, labor unions called for a nationwide strike. Premier Rumor, fearing that his government would collapse as a result of the strike, pleaded with labor leaders to call it off. But on July 6, Italy's thirty-first government since World War II fell.

Finally, on August 4, Emilio Colombo formed a new four-party coalition government. In September, in an attempt to end the violence, the new central government sent six thousand policemen from other parts of the nation to Reggio Calabria. Nevertheless, rioters continued to build barricades and attack the government. Neo-fascists also moved to organize a general strike. At the same time, ultra-leftist students denounced the Communist party as a member of the establishment. Though both the neo-fascists and the leftist students wanted reform through armed conflict directed against the government, they turned the streets of Rome and Milan red with their own blood as they battled one another.

Reggio Calabria, however, was not the only trouble spot. In Trento, on October 4, bombs exploded in three theaters. In Rome and Milan, student-workers turned over automobiles and marched through the streets wearing helmets and carrying chains.

By December of 1970 the will of reform had swung Italian politics completely toward the left. Pro-Nazi and pro-fascist groups continued in conflict with university students. Warnings persisted that rightists were planning to overthrow the government and establish a presidential dictatorship. Most politicians believed that no one group could or would attempt a coup d'etat. But Communist party leaders thought differently.

Fearing that a rightist coup was in the making, they ordered several stand-by alerts, directing members to safe houses in the event that the right succeeded in establishing a dictatorship.

On December 7, 1970, two hundred military forest rangers stood armed for battle in the mountains near Rieti, about 30 kilometers from Rome. By order of Prince Borghese, twenty rangers entered the Ministry of the Interior. Another group of fascists stood prepared to receive an order to kidnap the president of the republic, Giuseppe Saragat. At the last moment, however, the coup, for reasons unknown, was canceled.

It is unlikely that the coup could have been successful, because Borghese lacked the manpower necessary to pull it off. Nevertheless, had he given the order for his men to march on Rome, there would have been bloodshed. Perhaps he realized this. Whatever the reason, after Borghese fled to Spain, a fourteen-page document was discovered that detailed the plot and subsequent acts of violence planned through 1974. The report also revealed that Vito Miceli had known of the coup but had not informed parliament. The reason may be that Licio Gelli, his superior in P-2, supported Borghese's attempt.

In spite of all this obscurity, one thing is clear: on five different occasions during the seventies factions of the extreme right planned to seize control of the Italian government and establish a fascist state. And in at least one other plot, the Rosa dei Venti, Vito Miceli and Licio Gelli were named as principals.

Numerous journalists have reported that part of the $10 million that the CIA spent on Italy's 1972 elections was filtered through banks controlled by Michele Sindona, and Sindona confirms this. The CIA, however, will not state whether or not it had a fiduciary relationship with Sindona. Nevertheless, a secret court document now makes it possible to show how, in January 1972, Michele Sindona and John McCaffrey, chief of the European resistance movement for Britain during World War II, planned a coup.

In an affidavit taken by one of Sindona's lawyers on February 3, 1981, in Donegal, Ireland, John McCaffrey said:

> Italy's passage from the post-war economic miracle created by the dynamism and inventiveness of private enterprise to her present state of palsy and chaos has been brought about by the pervasive and continuous operations of left-wing, anti-Western forces. These forces have used their customary well-known range of instruments, including the penetration and corruption of individuals and groups which should have been achieved, though they have been greatly helped, by the existence of an overt, numerically strong Communist Party. As always, the Communists have cloaked their allies and fellow-travellers with membership in established political parties and institu-

tions, and have infiltrated individuals into key posts. The battle for control of Italy, which is now more than half won for the Left, was and is still being fought with subtlety and cohesion on all fronts.

Efforts to combat the Left-wing take-over have been fragmented and completely unorganized. Many of those who should have been natural leaders of the opposition were corrupt, docile, and inept. Those who were intelligent, strong and successful posed formidable threats to the Leftist movement and were targets for elimination. Michele Sindona was a member of the latter group.

During my association with Sindona I did, in fact, witness a number of attempts in Italy and abroad to unseat him. Ugo La Malfa, Minister of the Italian Treasury, personally influenced many decisions calculated to harm or disrupt Western policies, free enterprise in Italy, and Michele Sindona. Furthermore, during the absence of Jocelyn Hambro, Chairman of Hambros, the British bank, Italian Left-wing bankers went to the offices of Hambros to sow seeds of distrust for Sindona and to predict disaster for his pro-American, pro-capitalism enterprises.

In the context of these events and his pro-American stance, Sindona approached me, fully aware of my own background in the Resistance movement, early in 1972 with his plan for a coup, the purpose of which was to establish a government in Italy and Sicily which would be closely allied with the United States. Shortly thereafter I met with Sindona and a high-ranking Italian military official in Rome, where we discussed the coup being planned by Sindona and the military. At this meeting I presented a detailed plan for the take-over of the government and for the new administration's first year in office. In view of my background, my collaboration had not only the value of technical competence, but also could be considered as a guarantee of excluding any attempt at neo-fascist dictatorship. Neither the United States nor the United Kingdom could have accepted any such outcome, nor indeed would they have wanted a purely military take-over, even with the best intentions. The idea was to secure the backing of the armed forces for orthodox democratic politicians who wanted a proper Parliamentary government and not a branch office of the Kremlin. The military men involved were fully aware of this and did not aspire to any autonomous action but merely wanted to be the defenders of the Western democratic system. Their part in what was envisaged as a political coup was to provide the authority and control which would have ensured that there was no organized outbreak of anarchy and subversion by the numerous trained squads of rioters and guerrilla fighters which the Communists had at their disposal. Among the Communists' other most formidable weapons were those who supported them from outside the official party. It is my considered opinion that one of their chief allies was Ugo La Malfa.

Following this meeting Sindona spoke with me on several occasions regarding the proposed coup. It was clear to me from these conversations with Sindona that he was the key to the entire operation.

I am sure to a moral certainty that Sindona spoke about the proposed coup with important figures in the American Central Intelligence Agency and with top level officials in the American Embassy in Rome. I would think it highly probable that the existence of the planned coup was known by Graham Martin, then American Ambassador to Italy. There is no doubt but that there exist numerous documents in America which reflect the benevolence on the part of the United States towards the coup organized by Sindona.

The coup failed for a variety of reasons:

— For the lack of security criteria among those who were to take part in the coup;

— For the lack of know-how, courage, and conviction on the part of Italian politicians;

— By the reflection this lack of courage had on the Italian military leaders;

— In the Italian setting, by La Malfa's and others' attacks on Sindona; and

— On the American scene by the emergence of the Watergate upheaval which effectively destroyed any possibility of support. (The American support would not have been military, of course. This would not have been necessary. But I did learn that the Italian military men involved in the coup wanted a United States fleet to find itself in the vicinity of Naples while the coup was being launched.)

— Of the overall picture of this proposed coup and of the overwhelmingly positive and pro-American role played in it by Michele Sindona there can be no possible doubt.

What McCaffrey did not know when he was assisting Sindona in the formalities of organizing a coup was that behind Michele Sindona were members of Propaganda Due. The Sicilian financier has always been credited with having an ability to keep secrets not only from his opponents but from his friends as well. Had he revealed the support of P-2 and its neofascist elements, Sindona might not have received John McCaffrey's assistance.

For Michele Sindona, the prospect of jailing members of the Communist party and leftist parties and establishing a pro-Western presidential form of government was both exciting and therapeutic. In some ways, his concentration during meetings and planning sessions had the same effect on him as a heavy work schedule has on those who throw themselves into their work to avoid dealing with their personal troubles. Like Charles Darwin, Marcel Proust, and Florence Nightingale, Michele Sindona was ill when idle or when there was an interruption in his daily work schedule. During the months of planning and revising plots, however, Michele was mentally and physically sound. Then, when the coup was canceled and the meetings came to a sudden halt, Michele Sindona again began to suffer from headaches, indigestion, and insomnia. Frustrated, he decided that he had to make a dramatic environmental change.

11

THE TURNING POINT

ALMOST AS AN ACT of rebellion, in 1972 Michele Sindona left his children in Milan and, with Rina, established permanent residence in Geneva, Switzerland. Their apartment was on the fifth floor above Finabank, which occupied the first three floors of the building at Rue de la Bourse, in the business district. It was a large suite, handsomely decorated with modern furniture. There was a master bedroom with a sitting room and a large bath and shower. A low wall divided the dining room and living room. The maid's quarters included a bedroom, a small parlor, and a full bath. Throughout the penthouse, the carpeting was deep blue. The curtains in the living room were also deep blue and were held back with gold ties.

Rina, however, did not like the apartment because all of the furniture belonged to the bank. There were a few antiques that she liked, but they also had been purchased by the bank. In such a setting, Rina recalls, she felt like a stranger or a guest in someone else's home. And she did not like the terrace, which wrapped completely around the building, for she always had the feeling that someone dangerous had climbed up to the balcony and was waiting for her.

Having established himself as a foreign resident, Michele needed the apartment more to circumvent Italy's income tax laws than to live in. In reality, Sindona usually rented a suite at the Hôtel des Bergues on the Quai des Bergues at the edge of the Rhone River, one block from Lake Geneva. It was the kind of place Michele Sindona liked. Its bars and restaurants were gathering places for Swiss bankers, families representing old money, and diplomats.

When Michele Sindona moved to Geneva in 1972, he was one of the wealthiest men in the world. He could buy and do anything that he desired. He had a loyal wife and a mistress. He knew heads of states and the world's leading financial figures on a first-name basis. And businessmen would go to elaborate extremes in order to win an audience with Don Michele.

The boy from Patti, Sicily, with the red birthmark on his face and the lopsided ears had risen higher than even Nunziata might have dreamed. He could have retired and enjoyed his success. Had he done so, the secrets of the Vatican, the Freemasons, and the Mafia might have remained hidden inside his mind, and his financial chicanery might never have been discovered. Men like Michele Sindona do not retire, however. They cannot live in peace without risk and excitement and recognition. Such men challenge the world, test their power, and match their intelligence against the combined will of government and society. They stop when they die or when they are beaten and destroyed. Howard Hughes, J. Paul Getty, A. P. Giannini, Aristotle Onassis—they all connived and manipulated until the end. Michele Sindona was one of them, and he could not have lived the life of a recluse, for he was addicted to playing the game.

In fact, whenever pressures became overbearing, the only way Sindona could find relief was to take a long, solitary drive in the mountains— but not to relax. With classical music blaring from the four speakers in his Mercedes sedan, Michele would think of deal after deal until he came up with one that seemed impossible to accomplish. Then, while he maneuvered his car at high speeds through the Alps, his brilliant and cunning mind would construct a means of rendering the otherwise inconceivable plot feasible. Having reconfirmed his greatness, the Machiavellian knight would drive home anticipating the glory of battle.

During his first few months in Swiss exile, Michele formulated a plan to take over Bastogi, Italy's largest financial holding company. This undertaking involved a great risk. Michele would be challenging Enrico Cuccia, Guido Carli, president of the Bank of Italy, and all those who favored nationalization. If his bid to acquire Bastogi succeeded, Michele would pull off the largest of all possible victories against Cuccia, the foremost banker on the left. If Sindona lost, Cuccia would be acknowledged as the more powerful and Michele would be considered a fool.

Michele directed all of his energies toward devising a strategy. He was not hindered by family or business. His son Nino had left home in search of adventure in the Caribbean — though after discovering civilization there instead of wilderness, he had settled for attending a small college in Montreal, Canada. Pier Sandro Magnoni, his son-in-law, was overseeing the Sindona Group's operations in Italy with the help of Massimo Spada, who was by then again in a powerful position on the boards of directors of those corporations in which the Vatican held an interest; he was also a member of the board of directors of Sindona's banks. John McCaffrey, head of Hambros Bank's Italian operations and also a member of the board of Sindona's Banca Privata Finanziaria, helped to keep things in order. And Carlo Bordoni was laundering tax money and illegal profits through the Bank of the Vatican and Finabank of Geneva for Licio Gelli and the Freemasons.

Società Italiana Strada Ferrate Meridionali, more commonly known as Bastogi, was a $200 million holding company that held an equity position in Italy's most important industrial enterprises. Among the stocks in Bastogi's portfolio was a pivotal block of shares in Montedison, the giant chemical company whose control was divided between government and private sectors controlled by Enrico Cuccia. Sindona wanted to take over Bastogi and turn it into a privately owned merchant bank. In essence, he wanted to denationalize it.

Sindona's interest in Bastogi, however, was also directly tied to Licio Gelli and Propaganda Due's plans for Real Action. Though the Sindona-McCaffrey-Freemason coup had not succeeded, neither had it failed; it was simply stalled. Another plan was developing to end nationalization and destroy the parliamentary form of government. Part of that plan, which fit into phase two of Real Action, was to reinforce the base of power through the acquisition of Bastogi. In order to do this, Michele Sindona engaged the support of John McCaffrey, Jocelyn Hambro of Hambros Bank of England, and Roberto Calvi, majority stockholder of Banco Ambrosiano and a member of Propaganda Due.

While John McCaffrey met Michele in his suite at the Hôtel des Bergues, Rina went to lunch at a small restaurant on the Rhone River with Laura Turner (not her real name), a forty-year-old American citizen who had worked in Italy for sixteen years as an executive assistant for Group Sindona. Although Rina had heard rumors of Michele's many affairs, she did not know that Laura Turner was Michele's current mistress.

This extremely bright woman, with her short, boyish haircut and walnut-colored eyes, had become Sindona's lover in 1972, six months after Britta Behn died of cancer. Laura Turner says that Michele Sindona was the only man she never became bored with. "Michele had tremendous courage," she says with admiration. "He was a great champion, a wonderful lover, and a kind person to his friends. But at the same time, he was driven to be godlike. He did what he wanted. He did not live by the laws and morals of others. How could he? He was above all of us. He was a fantasy that lived. He was like the Godfather."

Turner says she realizes that Sindona used her to relax, to get away from pressures. Yet she is grateful to have shared his thoughts, "to have experienced the energy that surrounded him." She believes that Sindona had a purpose that he had to accomplish, that he was a "change agent" who was destined to affect the course of history. Turner says that she realized "there were no boundaries" for Michele, "no laws, no division between right and wrong. There cannot be for men who are born to fight, fight, fight." She says that she saw this quite clearly after Sindona moved to Switzerland and began to collaborate with John McCaffrey and Robert Calvi to take over Bastogi.

Sindona and McCaffrey sipped Campari and soda and nibbled on grapes and fresh fruit while they discussed Michele's plan.

"Bastogi is a sick whale," Sindona said. "Its management is not aggressive, and so its power is not being utilized. Acquiring control of Bastogi would make the Sindona Group the most powerful financial combine in Europe, because we will have established the first privately owned merchant bank in Italy. That will make us more effective in fighting Cuccia and protecting free enterprise."

"It's an ambitious idea, but I don't see any possible way for the Group to get by the interference Cuccia will certainly organize," McCaffrey said. "You're going straight at Cuccia with this. He won't sit still. There will be a fight, and nobody will want to support us, even if they agree with us, because they'll be frightened of Cuccia. He's powerful, Michele. A coup d'etat would be easier than attacking Cuccia where he's strongest."

"A coup," Michele said, "would have a greater possibility of success if the Group also commanded the financial power that control of Bastogi offers. In order to circumvent and neutralize Enrico Cuccia's power, my strategy is to make a public tender offer for Bastogi shares. The uniqueness of the tender offer [an offer, usually made through a newspaper ad, to buy at a fixed price a certain number of shares within a given period] is that it has never before been done in Italy. No one will be expecting it. And once the offer is made, the momentum in favor of the Group will be so strong that Cuccia will not be able to intercede."

It was a brilliant idea. McCaffrey liked it and agreed to win the support of his boss, Jocelyn Hambro. He understood that secrecy, always an ingredient in any Sindona deal, was particularly important now if their tender offer was to be a success. To make leaks impossible, he and Sindona held all subsequent meetings in limousines as they drove past thousands of tourists along the shores of Lake Geneva. The element of surprise was very much in their favor. Even Sindona's secretary of fifteen years, Xenia Vago, did not know of Sindona's intention until she read about it in the newspaper, and the agreement all three parties signed was hidden in a safe deposit box.

The intensity was overwhelming. Michele feared that one of his partners would make an error and thereby allow Cuccia to learn of their plans and block their efforts. Ultimately the pressure seems to have taken its toll on Sindona, because one evening when he and Laura were in Geneva, Michele suddenly woke up and began stalking back and forth at the foot of the bed. Finally, Turner says, he turned to face himself in the mirror and, with his arms stretched out to form a cross with his body, asked, "What do you mean?" Then he glanced from one hand to the other hand while saying something Laura could not hear and "hell." Something and hell. Something and hell. He kept repeating this for about five minutes, his arms stretched out as if he were being crucified and his head turning from left to right, left to right.

"Heaven and hell. Heaven and hell," he repeated. Then he stopped and with a grin that chilled Laura, he said, "I've got to tell Carli. I've got to take him into my confidence and swear him to *omerta* before Cuccia does. That's what *she* was trying to tell me, I'm sure."

Though Laura was a little frightened by this, it was not the first time she had seen Michele behave this way. Many times, such episodes had caused him to break out in a cold sweat. Laura would hold him close to her, and he would be like a helpless child clinging to her. Each episode lasted about thirty minutes. Then they would make love, and he would be strong and confident. This time, however, Laura got out of bed, removed his robe, and massaged his shoulders.

"Do you think I will ever be able to rest?" Sindona mumbled.

Laura remained silent, rubbing his neck, kissing the back of his head.

"Only when I die will I have peace," Michele was saying. "Only then will I be able to ask you, Is what I have done with my life what it was that you wanted of me?"

Then he turned to face Laura. Holding her in his arms, he said, "I think she will be pleased. I have demonstrated that I am a man of courage. I do not fear battle because she has told me in my dreams that I cannot lose. I can never fail. Bastogi will be mine. But I must speak with the governor."

Then they went back to bed and made love as Michele told Laura how he would take over Bastogi and become the savior of democracy.

Michele shared his secret with Guido Carli, the balding, sophisticated governor of the Bank of Italy. Though Sindona had imposed silence on him,

Carli remained uncommitted, something Sindona did not pick up on. Confiding in Carli proved to be a grave error. The governor did not want non-Italians controlling Montedison, so Carli, though he had no legal authority to intervene, related Sindona's plans to Enrico Cuccia and Tullio Torchiani, president of Bastogi.

In the quiet, unforgiving way that may be unique to Sicilians, Enrico Cuccia had carried a vendetta inside himself while patiently awaiting the opportunity Bastogi presented. In 1964, after Sindona had already embarrassed Cuccia with the purchase of Libby, McNeil & Libby, Cuccia had brought Michele Sindona together with the Belgian group, Sofina. Cuccia had interested Sofina in buying CTIP, an engineering company owned by Group Sindona. This was an important deal for Sindona, and, at the time, Sindona had not been powerful enough to pull the deal off without Cuccia's assistance. Cuccia went so far as to have the auditing firm Reconta, a division of Mediobanca, examine the books of CTIP. Among the projects in which CTIP was involved, the most promising, though extremely speculative, was an uncompleted Suez oil refinery. In its report, Reconta recorded the estimated value of the refinery as it was listed in the company's records.

Shortly after the sale, however, Sofina discovered that the refinery was a loser. Sofina's representatives went to Cuccia and, claiming that Sindona had falsified CTIP's balance sheet, demanded reimbursement. Cuccia suggested that Sindona, who had retained 40 percent of the stock in CTIP, resolve the matter by giving Sofina an additional 5 percent of his stock at no cost. At first, Sindona rejected the idea, explaining that he was innocent and that a settlement of any kind would be a sign of weakness and an admission of guilt. In the meantime, however, Sofina had retained André Meyer, Cuccia's friend, to negotiate a settlement. After putting tremendous pressure on Cuccia, Meyer persuaded him to convince Michele that a fee of 600 million lire (at the time approximately $1 million) was fair. Though Michele thought the figure was high by 100 million lire, he agreed. He refused, however, to issue Sofina any of his stock.

From then on, no accord was possible. Two years passed before all parties finally agreed to allow the dispute to be resolved through arbitration. The president of the Swiss Constitutional Court presided over the board of arbitrators, which included one Italian judge.

Sindona argued to the board of arbitrators that Sofina, not he, had altered figures to reduce the value of his shares. The board then reviewed the books and balance sheet of CTIP. In conclusion, they ruled that Sindona would pay Sofina only 500 million lire, a hundred million less than the figure Michele had already offered Cuccia.

During the negotiations, the press had predicted victory for Cuccia and defeat for Sindona. Since it was Cuccia who brought Sofina and Sindona together, and since it was Cuccia who advised Sofina to reject Sindona's offer of 600 million lire, the decision rendered by the board of arbitrators was a serious blow to Enrico Cuccia's reputation in international banking circles. So when Guido Carli told him about Sindona's plan to obtain controlling interest of Bastogi, Cuccia was quick to close the doors on Sindona.

To protect Montedison, Cuccia arranged the merger of three major industrial corporations with Bastogi. These companies all held large blocks of stock in Montedison, securing Montedison's position in Bastogi. This successfully done, Cuccia and Carli believed Bastogi and Montedison were untouchable. But Michele was not yet stopped.

One Friday, since his intentions were then known, in an attempt to win some support, Michele notified the president of Bastogi that he intended to make his tender offer the following Monday. When Cuccia learned of this, he went to Carli. Guido Carli shared Cuccia's hunch that Sindona was bluffing. Nevertheless, Carli wanted protection against the possibility that Sindona, whom they now regarded as a clown, was serious. So Carli went to the Bank of Sicily, the Bank of Naples, and most of Italy's other leading banks and persuaded them not to sell the Bastogi shares they controlled for their customers even though the price per share that Sindona would offer would probably be much higher than the market price.

By Monday Michele was fully aware of the obstacles that had been constructed to block his success, but he publicized his tender offer nevertheless. Cuccia immediately rushed to Rome to try to persuade Emilio Colombo, then president of the council of ministers, to warn Aletti, president of the managing committee for stock exchange agents in Milan, that the bid was not lawful and should not be permitted. Aletti, however, refused to cooperate. He said that not only did Sindona's procedure not violate any laws but it also respected the principles of fundamental ethics by placing all shareholders on an equal footing, even allowing minority holders to obtain the same price per share as the major stockholders.

So Sindona's tender offer, the first in Italian history, was approved with the support of the committee. Carli's and Cuccia's intervention, however, made it impossible for Sindona to buy the shares required to obtain the majority interest. Sindona's failure became a matter of national interest. "The establishment," Sindona says, "spoke of my defeat, of Bastogi being my Waterloo, and of my disappearance from the financial scene."

Although Michele had been beaten, he was unwilling to accept defeat. He filed a lawsuit in Palermo against principals Italpi and Pavese, two of the companies Cuccia had merged with Bastogi. Unlike Rome, where Guido Carli and Enrico Cuccia could easily have persuaded the courts to side with them, Palermo was a Mafia stronghold and its courts were therefore more willing to protect Sindona's interest.

Sindona supplied the court with records of illegal bookkeeping procedures and false documents involving the Bastogi deal. As the public prosecutor was preparing arrest warrants against the principals involved, however, they reached an agreement. In exchange for dropping the lawsuit, the Carli-Cuccia group bought, at a very high price, all of the shares Sindona had purchased, giving the Sindona group a handsome profit. Nevertheless the settlement proved to be a meaningless victory for Michele Sindona.

Sindona's failure to take over Bastogi and the turmoil his attempt stirred up caused irreparable damage to his reputation. Rumors that he was a swindler, a clown, and a troublemaker whipped through the international banking and financial world. To make matters worse, in the interim John McCaffrey and Jocelyn Hambro had retired from Hambros Bank. This was unfortunate because Charles Hambro, who had replaced his cousin Jocelyn as head of Hambros Bank, decided that his bank could no longer afford to associate with a controversial man like Michele Sindona. So Charles Hambro gave Michele Sindona an ultimatum: buy all of the 1,865,625 shares of Banca Privata Finanziaria that Hambros Bank owned or Hambros would sell them to the highest bidder.

In September 1972, two months after Sindona bought controlling interest of Franklin National Bank, the eighteenth largest bank in America, he used a fiduciary contract to funnel the funds from BPF to his holding company, Fasco, A.G. to purchase Hambros' BPF shares. Giorgio Ambrosoli, who was in charge of investigating the bankruptcy of Sindona's empire, proved that Michele Sindona had illegally used bank funds, not his own, to purchase the shares. In his report to the court, Ambrosoli wrote, "Those shares belonging to Hambros Bank were bought in September by Fasco, A.G., not with its own means but with those of Banca Privata Finanziaria."

Sindona also used this formula, which later became known as the Sindona system, to purchase Franklin National Bank. Although the purchase of Franklin seemed to be a major victory for the Sicilian financier, what Michele Sindona did not realize was that the bank was weak and in trouble. More important, Sindona did not realize that Arthur Roth — who had guided Franklin's development from a small community bank on the verge of bankruptcy into the eighteenth largest in the country — would not allow anyone to control Franklin who could not first answer some tough questions. Although Michele Sindona was brilliant in his capacity to evade serious inquiries about himself and his finances, he was to discover that Roth, even at the age of sixty-seven, was a formidable adversary.

12

ARTHUR T. ROTH:
THE MAN AND HIS BANK

LIKE A. P. GIANNINI, Arthur Roth had directed the growth and investment policy of his bank with a firm hand. The two men were so similar that Giannini's heirs acknowledged Roth's abilities and success by referring to Franklin National Bank as the "little Bank of America of the East."

Further evidence of the respect in which the banking community held Roth was demonstrated in 1971 when First California Company, a securities brokerage firm, published a glowing report on the shares of a California bank that had had an excellent record of growth. Attempting to parallel their client's success with that of great bankers, the brokers prefaced their report with brief sketches of four "master builders" in banking who had created "great economic, corporate and investor wealth in America." The four men were J. P. Morgan (1837–1913), founder of Morgan Guarantee Trust Company, the fifth largest bank in the United States; Andrew W. Mellon (1855–1937), who built Mellon National Bank & Trust Company into the fifteenth largest in the country, served for nine years as secretary of the treasury, and whose art collection formed the core of the collection of the National Art Gallery in Washington, D.C.; A. P. Giannini (1870–1945), founder of Bank of America, the world's largest publicly owned bank; and Arthur Roth, "the spark plug behind [Franklin

National Bank's] growth through brilliant mergers, acquisitions and new branches."

Arthur Roth was born in the Bronx on December 22, 1905, of German Catholic parents who had immigrated from Bavaria. He graduated from Townsend Harris Hall High School in three years and, at the age of seventeen, began his career in banking as a messenger for Manufacturers Hanover Trust Company. Roth's creative thinking and natural leadership ability were quickly recognized by his superiors, and he rose rapidly through various teller positions until he was promoted to a job in the comptroller's office, where he was in charge of key operations for all of the bank's thirty-five branches.

At the time, Roth was a newlywed of less than a year, and his wife, Genevieve, was expecting their first child. The Roths were living in the city in order to be close to Arthur's office at Manufacturers Hanover Trust, but Genevieve was a country girl. She had been raised on an estate in Bayshore, Long Island, where her father was employed as the caretaker. Genevieve had fond memories of her childhood and, rather than raise her child in the city, she wanted her family to enjoy the benefits of living where the air was fresh and where people knew their neighbors.

On Sunday, April 15, 1934, Roth drove to Wantagh, Long Island, with his wife. As the Roths drove east, they passed Arthur's cousin, Fred Schilling, a director and major stockholder in Franklin Square National Bank, who was driving in the opposite direction. Schilling slammed on his breaks, jumped out of his car and, running after Roth's car, signaled for Arthur to stop.

"I've been looking for you," Schilling said, as Roth approached him. "We have an opening at Franklin Bank for a cashier. It's a small bank, but I would like you to take a look. We could use you, and you'd be doing me a favor."

Although Manufacturers Hanover was the twelfth largest bank in the country, and although Roth could look forward to a promising career with Manufacturers, he was unhappy with his job. At the time, one of his responsibilities at Manufacturers Hanover was to reduce overhead by cutting the payroll. Roth simply did not have the heart to terminate people during a time when jobs were hard to find. As a result, considering his wife's desire to live on Long Island, the Franklin proposition looked interesting.

In 1934, at the age of twenty-nine, Roth accepted a position as head teller at the tiny Franklin Square National Bank. The bank had been formed by local businessmen and chartered by the Federal Reserve on October 13, 1926. The original capital and reserve of the bank had amounted to only $62,500, and it made its headquarters in a rented store-front of approximately 1,000 square feet.

During interviews with the president of Franklin Square National Bank, no one, not even his cousin, told Roth that the bank was in serious trouble. What he found was a small bank with four employees and deposits of only $478,000, compared with Manufacturers Hanover's $400 million in assets. Roth sensed the bank had the potential to be much bigger, however, and he decided that the opportunity to help build up a small bank would be beneficial to himself and to the community. "After all," he recalls, "Franklin Square had lived through the ten-day banking holiday of 1933 and was the first bank on Long Island to reopen, so I assumed the federal authorities had determined its solvency." Not until after he had rented a house and moved to Franklin Square did Roth discover several critical letters from the comptroller's office warning the bank's directors "to get their house in order or serious results are likely to follow."

Roth also discovered that the directors had outstanding loans with the bank and that the bank held a dangerously high number of delinquent loans. For a short time, frustration and doubt overwhelmed him. "I wondered," he says, "why I had ever gone there. Not only was Franklin smaller than any of Manufacturers' thirty-five branches but its deposits were shrinking in both time and demand accounts and there was a bond depreciation of close to $200,000 against only $125,000 in capital. But I wasn't about to go back to the city; living in the country was just too important to Genevieve and to me. The only solution was to try to put Franklin back into a position of solvency."

First, Roth attacked the loans made to directors. "These," he explains, "had to be reduced, not only for the money involved but also for the bank's reputation." Roth believed that the way to rebuild Franklin was to serve the community. The first step in serving the people was to build confidence, and the first step in building confidence was to prove to the people that the bank was not just a vehicle for its directors. So in his first week at Franklin, while he was supposed to be feeling his way around and judging his authority, Arthur Roth took command and, acting more like the chief executive officer than the head teller, he ordered the directors to reduce their outstanding loans of $60,000 by $10,000. They did.

That done, Roth concentrated on delinquent loans. Some were behind by four or five years. After interviewing the customers, Roth discovered that they "were not willful delinquents but people who wanted to meet their obligation to the bank. Because of the depression, however, they just could not meet the terms of their loans."

At the time, loans were written as thirty-, sixty-, or ninety-day notes. At the end of the designated period, say thirty days, the customer was to pay back the loan. Most people, however, could repay only a small portion of the amount they had borrowed. A customer who borrowed $500 and could only pay $50 was technically a bad credit risk. In order to keep the loans up to date Franklin, like all banks, would rewrite each loan every thirty days. This method was costly both to the bank, because of the clerical work involved, and to the customer, because of the interest that continued to mount up. Roth did not like this method. He wanted to start a new system that would allow his customers to feel proud of their ability to pay small amounts each month rather than be ashamed of their forced delinquency.

Roth called the office of the Comptroller of the Currency and asked if a bank could legally write an installment loan.

Cyrus Upham, of the comptroller's office, told Roth, "It's not proper for a bank to get into that type of business, especially a bank as small as yours."

Frustrated, Roth said, "All I asked you was: is it legal?"

"Yes," Upham admitted, "but I'm saying you ought not to do it."

"Some of these loans may run as long as six or seven years. Is there anything illegal in that?"

"No, but it's improper," Upham repeated.

Roth wasn't interested in Upham's notion of propriety; he was concerned only for his customers and his bank. So Roth called his debtors into the bank and asked them how much they thought they could pay toward their loans each month. One dollar, ten dollars, fifty dollars a month — it didn't matter. Whatever the figure was, Roth rewrote their notes as installment loans extended over as long a period as his customers needed to resolve their debts, and each customer received a book of monthly payment coupons. So Franklin Square National Bank, thanks to Arthur Roth's creativity and determination, gave birth to the now-common installment loan.

Searching for ways in which the bank could serve the community and also bring in additional revenue, Roth covered each loan customer with life insurance so that, if the principal breadwinner died, the bank would be protected and the family would not be burdened with monthly payments. As a result of this practice, Roth learned that most of the citizens of Rockville Centre did not have any life insurance. At the time insurance companies considered the community, with a population of less than five thousand, too small to warrant the services of a full-time agent.

Again Arthur Roth ran into resistance, this time from both the officer of the Comptroller of the Currency and the insurance industry. Roth had read a book on insurance law and had discovered that banks had the right to sell life insurance in communities with a population of less than five thousand. He started a campaign to convince the people of the importance of life insurance. Roth became so successful at selling life insurance that representatives of the insurance industry complained about him to the banking authorities.

Today many of Roth's innovations are common practice in the banking industry; during the postwar boom, his concept of banking was as unique as his courage. Most bankers were corporate people. They were interested in figures. Like Michele Sindona, they based their investment decisions on the last line of corporate financial statements. For them, everything was black or red. The faces behind the figures were unimportant. Unlike them, Roth cared about his customers. He believed in them and wanted to help them fulfill their dreams.

Roth's background in the building and construction business proved extremely important to the growth of both Long Island and Franklin Bank. His father and brother were partners in a small construction company. Like Michele Sindona, when Roth was young, he took care of the firm's bookkeeping records. This experience and the success of his father's company later led Roth to back builders during a period when most New York banks considered them high risks.

The government agreed with Roth's plan to finance building and home modernization. In 1935 FHA home modernization and home construction loans were approved by the government. Most banks would not make these loans, however, because during the depression they had had bad experiences with builders, and the FHA guaranteed only the interest, not the principal. Roth realized that building loans involved a risk, but he believed that the FHA could not go halfway and would eventually have to back the principal as well as the interest. Roth did not wait for the government or other banks to make a move to help builders. Instead, he started making loans, and to compensate for the risk, he charged the builders 2 percent above the prime rate. For Franklin Bank, this formula ultimately meant the difference between a small, insignificant local bank on the verge of bankruptcy and a major bank with more than $3 billion in deposits.

Although he had acquired a reputation as a sensitive, humane banker, Roth agreed that the bank needed to charge a service fee on checking accounts in order to cover its expenses. This service charge was not well received by the bank's customers. Franklin's response to this situation was typically Rothean. To persuade the public that the charge was both necessary and logical, Roth decided to educate his clients in the realities of banking by first educating their children. He started allowing high school students with an average of 85 percent or better to work at the bank for up to six weeks. The advantage to the students was that they would have an employment record that they could use as a reference once they graduated and began to seek employment. The bank benefited because the students told their parents about the bank and its operations.

After Arthur Roth was named president of Franklin Bank in 1946, he continued to attract national attention with his programs. The next year, Roth ran a promotion to persuade parents to bring their children into the bank to open their own accounts. This proved so successful that he decided to advertise for children's accounts. His ad promotion attracted the attention of the *Oklahoma Express*, which published an article on May 20, 1947, nicknaming Franklin "The Lollypop Bank." Roth framed the article and had a sign painted that read, "The Lollypop Bank". He hung both above a teller's window so that the children would have their own teller.

Arthur Roth cared about children, and not only when they were depositing their nickels in his bank. Every December, while preparing the bank for the Christmas holidays, all of Roth's business activities came to a halt. He decorated the window of the bank with holly and dolls in the native dress of twenty-four countries. On a long table inside the bank an elaborate crèche was on display. Seasonal music filtered out to the street, and Santa Claus gave a gift to every child who came to visit him at the bank. But the highlight of the exhibition was the daily performance of the puppet theater. Schools all over Long Island sent busloads of children to the bank to watch marionettes act out Christmas plays and to sing songs with the other children.

Roth also renovated the basement of the bank so that civic organizations could use it as a meeting place. He installed a business library, which he made available to businessmen. He also organized a speaking bureau, making himself and other bank officers available, without fee, to speak to civic groups, colleges, and high school students. Though Roth did wonderful things to help his community grow, it was his new approach to banking that made him famous and ultimately gave banking a much-needed face-lift. In 1941 Franklin became the first bank in the country to offer its customers the services of an outdoor teller. It was the first bank in the country to offer a bank credit card like VISA. It was the first bank in the country to publish an annual report. And, most important, Franklin was the first commercial bank in the country to refer to a time deposit as a "savings account."

It is important to realize that until Roth fought the superintendent of banking for New York for the right to use the word "savings," the term had been sacredly reserved for savings banks. Concentrated in seventeen northeastern states, savings banks are theoretically owned by their depositors, who in theory share in the banks' benefits, for there are no shareholders in any mutual savings institution. The first savings bank in the country was the Provident Institution for Savings, founded in Boston in

1816. It was not called a bank, although in reality that's what it was. It was founded by the wealthy to provide for the poor. That is, it was a means for the rich to help the less affluent, while protecting themselves against social reform, by promoting financial security through savings.

The original paternal purpose of mutual savings banks has long since been dissipated. Such banks are now well-established businesses, run not by philanthropists but by professionals for the purpose of earning money. Because these institutions have been exempt from income tax during most of their existence, they have an enormous reserve of capital, giving them an unfair advantage over the more aggressive commercial banks. The greatest advantage that savings institutions had over commercial banks was that they were the only organizations allowed by state law to promote the use of savings accounts. Commercial banks had to find other less identifiable terms to attract deposits from the general public.

In August 1947 Roth read a book on banking law and concluded that nationally chartered banks had the right to use the word "savings." At the time, commercial banks such as Franklin, had to use terms like "compound interest account," "thrift account," or "special interest account." Roth believed that most people using the services of a commercial bank did not understand that these were really just savings accounts. Roth decided that the Superintendent of Banks for New York and the Comptroller of the Currency, by forbidding commercial banks to make any reference to savings, were giving savings banks an unfair edge. So, secure in his interpretation of the law, Roth ordered deposit slips and signs that boldly bore the words "savings account." He placed the signs inside the bank and in the parking lot so that every customer would see them. Business prospered, and many customers who had accounts with savings banks moved them to Franklin National Bank.

As soon as the savings banks discovered what Roth had done, they filed a complaint against Franklin Bank. When Roth heard that the state attorney general's office was preparing a suit against Franklin Bank for using the word "savings," he dropped everything and went to the attorney general's office. After several hours of being passed from one assistant attorney general to another, Roth finally met with Robert Springer. Springer had been working in the legal department of the superintendent of banking since he graduated from Princeton in 1939. He was a heavy-set man with a wide grin, and he was respected and liked by his staff.

"Now, Mr. Roth," Springer said, "you understand that you cannot use the word 'savings' in any way whatsoever."

"Yes," Roth assured him, "I understand that."

"That means you cannot use it in the bank's annual report or anywhere."

"Well," Roth said, "we have wrought-iron signs in the parking lot, and one of them has a picture of a thief breaking into a house. The word 'savings' is written across the sign."

"You are going to have to take that down."

"Our withdrawal and deposit tickets say 'savings department' on them."

"You'll have to destroy them and have new ones printed without the word 'savings.' You can't use the word in your advertising; you can't use it anywhere. If you do, we will proceed with the lawsuit."

Roth's face turned red. Although he had already reconciled the conflict within himself, he did not like being threatened. After a few minutes of silence, Roth leaned forward and said, "I have a question about this savings thing that is bothering me. I have a sign inside the bank. It's above the teller's window where we handle the savings accounts, and it says 'savings.' Can I leave that there?"

"No, that will have to come down."

"But it's inside the bank. People can't see it unless they come into the bank. It's just to help our customers. We really aren't advertising savings accounts with it."

"It doesn't matter," Springer assured Roth.

"Are you saying that if I don't take that sign down you are going to sue us?"

"Yes."

"All right, now you've pushed me too far. Go ahead with your lawsuit."

In May 1951, when the case came up for trial, the main issue was whether or not Roth could introduce into evidence a survey Hofstra College had produced for him. Thirty students had polled 928 people. The poll revealed that 85 percent of those questioned knew what a "savings account" was and what a "savings bank" was, whereas only 40 percent knew what "compound interest" meant. Only 24 percent knew that a "special interest account" was a savings account, and only 19 percent recognized a "thrift account" as a savings account. Most people, in fact, thought that a "thrift account" was a trust agreement for the rich.

The case went all the way to the U.S. Supreme Court, which ruled eight to one in Roth's favor in 1954. Although the decision was a victory for all nationally chartered commercial banks, Franklin National Bank had received virtually no financial help from any of the big New York banks. All of the $160,000 spent to take the case to the Supreme Court— except an unrecorded $5,000 donation delivered, in cash, to Roth by a Chase Manhattan executive—was paid by Franklin National Bank. Immediately after the decision was rendered by the Supreme Court, however, every nationally chartered bank in the United States began using the words "savings account" in its literature. So, again, as he had done with the installment loans, bank credit cards, drive-up teller's windows, annual report, building loans, and so on, Roth, through Franklin National, had changed banking.

While Arthur Roth was fighting for the right to use the word "savings," the savings banks started a drive to set up branches in Long Island's Nassau County. Their argument was that, because many of their depositors had moved out to Long Island, they should have the right to follow them. They convinced William Lyon, then superintendent of banking, that they should have the freedom to establish branches within a 50-mile radius of their home office.

To protect his territory and defeat the savings banks, Arthur Roth convinced the members of the state association of commercial bankers to unite and form their own lobby. To everyone's surprise, Roth's efforts resulted in the defeat of the superintendent's first attempt to grant large savings banks the right to branch out into the suburbs.

In 1953 Lyon went back to the state legislature with a compromise bill cutting down to 25 miles the radius within which savings banks could establish branches. This bill, though it narrowed the radius, would still have permitted all the big New York savings banks to set up branches in Nassau County. Once again Roth got the New York Bankers Association to pressure its members to talk to their legislators. As a result, the legislature responded, and the bill was never passed.

The savings banks, however, decided to try again, and at the last possible minute, on February 16, 1954, they introduced a branch banking bill. As soon as Roth heard of this, he helped the commercial bankers' association publish a booklet which revealed that a majority of the fifty-four mutual savings banks in New York City held well over $100 million each in deposits and that Bowery Savings alone held over a billion dollars in deposits. Most commercial banks, the booklet explained, were much smaller. While savings banks had grown since 1925 by nearly 400 percent, commercial banks were actually losing deposits. "The big problem presented by the demand of the mutual savings banks for further branch power," the report said, "is that of the survival of the independent community banks."

In September 1956 the legislative joint committee held hearings throughout New York State. Roth arranged for local commercial bankers in each city to testify at the hearings. Because of his duties at Franklin National Bank, however, Roth could not attend every session, and so he left many of the details to other committee members.

After learning that they were not faring well, Roth attended a hearing in Rochester to see what the problem was. Roth left the session appalled at how poorly the bankers presented their position. Most of them were pleading for sympathy rather than attacking the savings banks with facts and figures. Roth decided that he would testify on Friday, September 28, 1956, before State Senator George H. Pierce, chairman of the joint committee.

In preparation for the hearing, Roth decided to focus on one important issue: "flight money." This was money taken from New York depositors by savings banks and then sent out of state — mostly to California — for investment. Roth thought that this practice showed a blatant disregard for the welfare of the people from whom the savings banks were taking deposits. The fact was that savings banks were sending billions of dollars to a place that was 2,500 miles away simply because the money could earn more interest in California while the savings banks denied loans to their depositors and neighbors at home in New York.

At the hearing, Roth asked Senator Pierce to give him more than the usual fifteen or twenty minutes allotted for testimony. His request was granted, and for the next hour and twenty minutes, Roth explained to the committee members why they should not permit savings banks to set up branches in Nassau County and the other suburbs. From then on, Roth was the most sought-after speaker for bank dinners and meetings. This was an unusual opportunity for Roth, because throughout his career many bankers had slighted him, because his bank was relatively small and because they thought he was Jewish.

No one had ever taken the big New York bankers to task for having officers of savings banks on their boards of directors. In the Great Hall of the City of New York, during a meeting of the heads of the New York Clearing House banks, fourteen of the most powerful bankers in the state, Roth did exactly that. His voice echoed through the hall as he scolded the bankers for allowing interlocking directorates and for accepting millions of dollars in savings banks' deposits.

Roth's speech did not win him any points with the most powerful bankers in New York. In fact, a few weeks later Chase Manhattan and First National City Bank abandoned Roth and filed applications with the comptroller of the currency asking for approval to set up branches in the suburbs. Hearings were scheduled in New York City to decide whether or not to grant approval.

The night before the hearing, Roth prepared his presentation. For an hour he searched the attic of his home until he located an old Chinese checker board that his children used to play with. He added some holes and painted it white. Then he put the board and the marbles into his briefcase and went to bed.

At the hearing, Roth said, "The New York City banks are complaining that they haven't grown nearly as much, percentagewise, as the suburban banks. Those percentages bother me. To understand why they bother me, we should take a look at what the New York banks have."

Roth took the white Chinese checker board out of his briefcase and placed it on the table so that the members of the legislative committee could see what he was doing. He had divided the board into three sections to represent New York City, Nassau County and Westchester County.

"Ten years ago," he said in a soft but forceful voice, "the New York banks held $37 billion in deposits. So we'll give them one marble for each billion. Nassau held $700 million, and Westchester held $600 million. Though neither is entitled to one whole marble, we'll give them each one marble."

Then Roth held the board up so everyone could see that the area representing New York held thirty-seven marbles while the Nassau and Westchester sections had only one marble apiece. After allowing a moment to pass so that everyone could absorb the meaning of what he was doing, Roth went on to say, "Now Nassau's deposits have increased by 200 percent, so we'll give Nassau County two more marbles, bringing the total to three. And Westchester, with an increase of 100 percent, will get one more marble. That makes three for Nassau and two for Westchester. The poor New York banks have grown only 20 percent, but that adds seven marbles to their coffers. They now have forty-four marbles, but they aren't satisfied. They want all the marbles."

Roth then lifted the bag and poured all the marbles onto the checker board. The legislators applauded. When it came time to vote, they denied Chase Manhattan and First National City Bank the right to expand into Roth's territory.

On February 18, 1958, at a meeting of the standing committee on banks of the state senate and assembly in Albany, a new branch banking bill called the Omnibus Bill was introduced. The bill was sponsored by the State Banking Department. If passed, it would permit Chase Manhattan and other New York banks to set up branches in the suburbs. Arthur Roth, of course, was present. When his turn came to speak, he took aim at his most powerful opponent to date: David Rockefeller of the Chase Manhattan Bank. Attempting to undermine Rockefeller's power, Roth accused Chase Manhattan of being the major stockholder in the Westchester Bank, the second largest bank in Westchester.

Angered by the accusation, David Rockefeller stormed into the center of the room and, waving a finger at Roth, argued, "No, it isn't right! I would like an opportunity, if I may, to deny categorically the statement that Mr. Roth made. In fact, I am surprised that he made it because I believe that he made it last year, and Mr. McCloy [then chairman of Chase Manhattan] denied it for the record last year, and I think I am in a good position to deny it categorically today. . . . Chase Manhattan does not control, directly or indirectly, any bank in Westchester County."

"Mr. Rockefeller," Roth retorted, "may I ask whether you and your family corporations control about twenty percent of the stock of the Westchester Bank?"

For a long moment, as the legislators and spectators watched Roth and Rockefeller attempt to stare each other down, there was absolute silence. Both men were experienced in handling situations like this, and both knew that the first one to speak would lose the point. But Roth had the advantage. He knew that while he remained silent his accusation would become a reality in the minds of the legislators. The pressure for Rockefeller to respond built rapidly.

Finally David Rockefeller said, "My family-owned corporations own about twenty percent of the [Westchester] bank, but the Chase Manhattan Bank does not control the investments of my family."

Roth turned away from his opponent, made eye contact with each of the committee members, smiled, and said, "Naturally."

From that day on, David Rockefeller never again took part publicly in the push for branch banking. Roth had again beaten the big New York commercial banks and the savings banks. His territory was safe, at least for a time.

Then in January 1959, when Nelson Rockefeller was sworn in as governor of New York State, both the savings banks and the giant New York commercial banks realized that Rockefeller, who personally owned eighteen thousand shares of Chase Manhattan Bank, would support their efforts to beat Roth. In fact, the governor's new superintendent of banking, G. Russell Clark, announced his support of the Omnibus Bill and soon after his appointment began lobbying in Albany for its success.

Arthur Roth was in the visitors' gallery when the bill came up for a vote in March 1959. Walter Mahoney, Republican majority leader of the state senate, had received instructions from Nelson Rockefeller and G. Russell Clark that the governor wanted the Omnibus Bill to pass, but Mahoney knew that he did not have the votes needed to pass the bill that day. Attempting to destroy Roth's bloc, Mahoney stood up and, pointing to Roth, said, "There's a man here today who has bragged that he has the vote of the legislature in his pocket and that this bill will not pass."

Clearly, Mahoney meant to imply that Roth had been buying votes. Roth, however, had earned a reputation as a strong-willed but clean banker. When the votes were tallied, they showed that, although some of Roth's supporters had switched their support to Rockefeller, many Republicans had been so insulted by Mahoney's cheap trick that they had decided to vote against the passage of the bill.

Nelson Rockefeller was not a man who accepted defeat. Although he had personal financial motives for winning on the branch banking issue, the battle was no longer just a matter of pushing the Omnibus Bill through committee. By now, the war was personal: man against man, power versus power. And certainly Rockefeller was the more powerful. Within his grasp were all the weapons of the state and his family's connections and fortune. He appeared too strong for even Arthur Roth. But as everyone had already come to realize, although Arthur Roth did not command the wealth and power of Nelson Rockefeller, he had the mind of a great chess player. And although Roth was ultimately defeated, and the Omnibus Bill became law, he had one exhilarating moment of triumph when Governor Rockefeller, though he was only in his first year of office, began to promote himself as the 1960 Republican candidate for President.

The possibility of Nelson Rockefeller assuming the office of President of the United States bothered Roth. He believed that Rockefeller was too easily swayed by the pressures from big business, to serve the nation fairly. So, in November 1959, when Roth learned that Rockefeller had rented a large private jet and had invited about thirty reporters to accompany him on a visit to the key state of California, Roth constructed a plan aimed at disrupting the governor's trip.

In a final effort to weaken Rockefeller's support of the Omnibus Bill and, more important, to destroy the governor's presidential dreams, Roth returned to the issue of flight money. To help build his case, Roth sent three officers of Franklin National Bank to California to investigate the savings banks' investments in that state. The officers discovered that Californians were getting 100 percent — and sometimes even higher — financing on their homes. A builder would arrange a mortgage for, say, $15,000, although he needed only $13,000 to build the house. The remaining $2,000 was a cash gift from the builder to help the purchaser buy furniture or pay moving expenses. This was illegal because the entire loan was guaranteed by the federal government. The most damaging part of the Franklin Bank's officers' report, however, revealed that the mortgage money came from the big New York savings banks.

After he received this information, Arthur Roth hired an all-female firm of professional interviewers to apply at New York savings banks for FHA- or GI-guaranteed mortgage loans. The results were more damaging to the savings banks than Roth had anticipated. Of the twenty-six savings banks in New York State, only six were granting FHA or GI mortgages to their New York depositors. Furthermore, although the banks were making better than 100 percent loans in California, they would write a New York mortgage only if the customer made a substantial down payment.

Roth prepared a report of his findings. He included the superintendent of banks' own report, which said that savings banks were lending 60
to 100 percent more money out of state than they were in New York. The
total amount of flight money was estimated at just under $7 billion. Roth
also included a graph illustrating that since 1955, while new housing had
risen sharply throughout the rest of the country, housing construction in
New York State had dropped by 36 percent. Finally, Roth placed a large
ink blot in the center of the report's cover probably to demonstrate that his
report was a stain on the banking community.

On November 10, as Nelson Rockefeller and the reporters were
boarding the governor's rented jet in preparation for the flight to California, a young man Arthur Roth had hired handed each of them a copy of
Roth's report. On the first page of the report was a letter written by Arthur
Roth and addressed to Governor Rockefeller. It read:

> On the eve of your departure, I am sure you are too conscientious a first-term
> governor of New York to forget our problems here at home while you are
> surveying the scene in other strategic states. In your penetrating diagnosis of
> the ailments of New York before the Economic Club this week, you said,
> "Industries of certain types are fleeing the state at an accelerating
> rate . . . [and that] the growth rate of the state has dropped way behind the
> national average." In California, you and the excellent staff of analysts on
> your research team will have a unique opportunity to examine at first hand
> a "flight from New York" that veterans in New York State understand from
> painful personal experience.
>
> This difference in treatment of veterans and other home buyers is the pri-
> mary reason why housing in New York State has declined so fast in contrast
> to the favorable showing for the rest of the country. I know [however, that]
> you would find it impossible to believe that New York savings banks are
> largely responsible for the bright showing in California and the poor show-
> ing in New York State. However, I refer you to the report, and ask you to
> read it, keeping in mind what Alexander Paulsen, president of the Long
> Island Home Builders Institute, said: "Savings institutions have a *moral obli-
> gation* to satisfy the mortgage and other financial needs of their own com-
> munities *before any other considerations.*"
>
> In conclusion, to the extent to which savings banks are draining funds out of
> New York State [which my report demonstrates], [it should be clear to you
> that] they are harming the economy of New York.

Governor Rockefeller was trapped. The reporters asked him nothing
about his political plans. Instead, for several hours they forced him to
confront the issue of flight money and the question of branch banking. By
the time he landed in California he was exhausted, angry, and distraught

by what Roth had done to him. But there was no escaping the issues. Roth had notified radio and television stations in Los Angeles, and they were waiting for him when he got off the plane.

Because of Roth's report and the perfect timing and execution of his plan, Rockefeller was unable to cultivate sufficient political support to carry him through the 1960 Republican National Convention. A friend of the Rockefeller family who had accompanied the governor on his trip to California says, "He was hopping mad at Roth. He was so upset during the trip that he couldn't conduct himself properly in California. The visit was a bust."

13

A CHANGE OF POWER

WITH THE FAILURE of his efforts in Albany, Arthur Roth realized that he was fighting a lost battle. Instead of continuing to fight the Rockefellers and the governor's powerful banking associates, Roth decided to counter their encroachment into his territory by moving into theirs. This decision appears to have been one of his few major errors in judgment.

On September 21, 1961, the board of directors of Franklin National Bank adopted a resolution approving Arthur Roth's suggestion that the bank apply for permission to open a branch office in the city. Two months later the deputy comptroller of the currency granted Franklin its request. Not until three years later, however, did Roth finally move Franklin Bank into the city. Rather than open a new branch, Roth wanted to buy an existing bank. Finally, frustrated by unsuccessful negotiations with Federation Bank & Trust, Roth gave up the idea of buying into the city and, on May 18, 1964, opened not one but three branch offices.

He did it in grand fashion. "Roth came to New York building monuments — impressive and very costly structures," a former Franklin executive told *Fortune* magazine. In a city that was proud of its modern steel-and-glass buildings, Franklin's familiar colonial style was very much in evidence in each of its branch offices. There were terrazzo floors, blue carpeting, patterned draperies, and mahogany furniture. A large pewter chandelier adapted from an eighteenth-century fixture in a Newport, Rhode Island, residence hung inside a ceiling dome over the main floor in one branch. The cost of entering the New York market totaled $3.2 million, and the bank spent another $13 million on the buildings at 410 Madison Avenue (at 48th Street) and on Hanover Square (near Wall Street).

The most unusual and successful branch Roth opened was at 758 Fifth Avenue at the corner of 60th Street. The building was constructed of elegant beige stone. The only identifying features were two bronze plaques on which was inscribed the name, "La Banque Continentale." The interior of the bank was decorated with Persian rugs, fine French furniture, and velvet-upholstered chairs. Flanking the cashiers' counter were two eighteenth-century gilt temple dogs and two red marble urns. Instead of the counter at which most bank customers filled out their deposit and withdrawal slips, clients of La Banque Continentale sat at one of four Louis XV acajou desks.

The idea was to serve the rich in an atmosphere in which they would be comfortable. The wealthy, Roth had decided, had been ignored, taken for granted, not given the special attention they deserved, considering their resources. At the time, banks were concerned only with needs of wealthy corporations; they had ignored wealthy individuals. Franklin's La Banque Continentale, Roth's innovation, was the first bank to serve rich people. Clients were escorted through French doors by a doorman wearing tails and white gloves and were given what many considered the best cup of tea in town, with little imported biscuits.

What made the bank successful, however, was not the decor or the gold and black embossed checks or the 14-karat gold check holder each customer received after opening an account. The branch attracted wealthy clients from all over the world mainly because of the services it offered. Every employee of La Banque Continentale spoke at least three different languages. In addition, a customer of La Banque Continentale could dictate letters to a bank secretary and have them translated into any language desired. Among the bank's many services, the most popular among female clients, who constituted 67 percent of the bank's customers, was that they could have their bills sent directly to the bank and automatically paid. The officer handling their account would check each bill for errors, make adjustments, deduct the correct amount from the client's account, and send the vendor a check.

For that kind of service, because a client had to maintain a minimum balance of $25,000 in an interest-free checking account, each customer had to be willing to forfeit the $1,250 in interest that the money would have earned, in 1966, at a savings bank. The loss in earnings, however, did not matter to most customers. In fact, many clients were so impressed with the way they were treated that the average balance per customer exceeded a million dollars. One woman, says Luiz C. P. Gastel, former vice-president and branch manager, kept between three and four million dollars on deposit — interest free.

Explaining why she was willing to wave such high earnings, one female customer told a reporter: "No jewel has ever given me the same lift as walking into this bank."

"There are advantages that money can't buy and a feeling that is more important than any interest," said another client of the bank.

At the beginning of 1964 Franklin held assets of slightly more than $1 billion. At the end of that year, after opening five branches in the city, Franklin's assets totaled more than $1.521 billion. With that kind of success, Roth was convinced that his decision to enter New York City had been a wise one. Faster than the big New York banks could invade Long Island, Franklin National Bank opened new offices in Nassau County and throughout the city. By the close of 1967 the bank's assets had grown to $2.625 billion in resources, with $2.171 billion in deposits; it had seventy-nine branches, twenty-four of which were strategically located in Manhattan.

During the early 1960s Franklin National Bank granted interim financing to companies that were anticipating a public offering of their stock. In theory, the risks appeared to be few, while the advantages of financing a series of growing enterprises were many. At the time, growth companies were the playthings of the investing public. Having a good number of these companies list Franklin as their bank created prestige for the bank. And once an underwriter sent a company public, the initial loan plus interest would be repaid. More important, however, Roth gambled that each company he helped to go public would not only continue to finance itself through Franklin but would also keep large balances on deposit with his bank. He was right. Following his plan, Roth was not only able to increase the size of the bank substantially but was also able to keep in check the larger New York banks, which had already moved into his suburban domain.

After the stock market collapsed in 1962, however, many companies that Roth had financed were forced to withdraw their offerings. Unable to raise funds in the capital markets, a great many companies folded and, as a result, defaulted on their loans. Because there was no chance of collecting the money, the bank was left with a huge deficit in retained earnings. But the worst was yet to come.

Although most banks regarded construction loans as a high risk, Roth had built Franklin National Bank by making an unusually large number of loans to Long Island real estate developers. When the banking laws changed and the apartment boom started in the metropolitan New

York area, Roth did not hesitate to finance the construction of apartment buildings. For a few years, everything went perfectly. Roth was able to get the interest rate he wanted, and loan losses were below his calculations. Then, at about the same time that the stock market collapsed, the bullish apartment- and home-building industry caved in, leaving Franklin with an even greater number of uncollectable loans.

This was a serious and dangerous moment for Franklin Bank, but Arthur Roth was a quick thinker and a strong leader. Responding to the rise in loan losses, Roth switched his investments from construction loans to Long Island municipal bonds. That was a good decision. Roth doubled the bank's security portfolio by purchasing low-risk tax-free bonds, and town treasurers were so pleased with Franklin for buying so many of their bonds that they poured huge deposits into the bank. Quickly, Roth realized that the more bonds the bank purchased, the faster its deposits would grow.

"But Roth overdid it," says *Fortune* magazine. "He bought so many municipals that in later years the bank was stuck with far more of them than were justified by its tax position." The result was that Franklin did not pay "any federal income taxes for [a] decade. Instead, largely because of its municipal bonds and the slow growth of its taxable revenues, the bank started accumulating a tax-loss carry-forward, which it carried on its balance sheet as an asset."

Though Roth's influence at Franklin was total, what *Fortune* failed to point out was that while Roth was in charge of the bank, Franklin's purchase of municipal bonds was well balanced. Using a mathematical equation that Roth had designed, Franklin carefully acquired bonds that would mature in one, two, and five years. And though part of the reason for Roth's decision to purchase bonds was not only to earn tax-free interest on the bank's money but also to acquire large municipal deposits, Roth was sharp enough to realize that the deposits were short-term (ninety days or less) and demand deposits (funds that can be withdrawn without notice), both of which, by law, had to be secured by the bonds. So, having the perception to predict a possible future liquidity crisis for the bank, Roth not only saw to it that the bank balanced its bond portfolio with long- and short-term bonds but also set in motion a plan to acquire long-term deposits from the general public.

At the time, savings banks were paying 5 percent interest — the highest rate available — on savings accounts. So Roth promoted five-, ten-, and thirteen-year savings certificates that guaranteed an interest rate of 5.75 percent. At this rate, as he pointed out in advertisements, the clients' money would double in thirteen years. The promotion was so successful that, in less than two years, Franklin added $415 million in deposits. The new funds provided Franklin with several advantages: the bank had control of the money for a specific length of time; it did not have to depend on municipal deposits to ensure its liquidity; it could earn good profits by making long-term business loans at higher rates than it was paying its depositors; and, finally, in addition to earning tax-free profits on its bond investments, the bank could record as an expense the interest rate paid on savings accounts, a practice that increased its after-tax profits.

Once again, Arthur Roth had demonstrated his ingenuity. The directors praised him. The stockholders of the bank praised him. Even bankers who were still bitter over the way he had fought the branch banking bill acknowledged his genius.

Yet not everyone was happy with Roth. His drive to attract new deposits had caused the savings banks to lose many of their customers. Eventually, the savings banks persuaded the authorities to prohibit Franklin from offering long-term savings certificates. Of course, this disturbed Roth. And it could have been damaging if the bank had continued to invest in municipal bonds. Roth, however, had already switched the bank's focus from bonds to mortgage loans.

While Roth concentrated on opening new branches and negotiating acquisitions, President Paul E. Prosswimmer directed Franklin's loan department. Prosswimmer knew that Franklin's inability to attract grade-A clients or to become either a lead or major bank in syndicated loans was due to the fact that the big New York banks had blacklisted Franklin. Nevertheless, Prosswimmer was determined to prove to his boss that he could improve profits in the loan department. To achieve this, Prosswimmer recruited several aggressive loan officers from Franklin's competition, the bigger and more firmly established New York banks.

The directive was clear: make loans, produce profits, and steal grade-A clients from the competition. None of this happened. Among the lending giants, Franklin was a baby. The bank needed clients more than borrowers needed it. Grade-A borrowers who could get good interest rates at Chase Manhattan or Citibank would not give Franklin their business — and a bank cannot exist without making loans.

In panic, Franklin's loan officers began making substandard loans at interest rates normally reserved for grade-A clients. Although major banks usually receive a compensating balance of 20 or 30 percent of the face value of the loan, even from a grade-A client, Franklin's loan department was so afraid of losing business that it did not demand reasonable compensating balances.

By the time Roth realized what had happened, there was nothing he could do but terminate most of the loan officers and charge off the losses. Because of a loophole that allowed him to charge the reserve account instead of the capital account, however, Roth was able to preserve the bank's earnings ratio. (The authorities disallowed this procedure in 1969. As a result, in later years, when Roth was no longer at the bank and the bank suffered additional losses, its earnings ratio per share dropped dramatically.)

Nevertheless, Franklin continued to sink into trouble. A federally chartered bank is audited three times during every two-year period. Several times, after examiners from the comptroller's office had completed their audit of the bank, the authorities declared Franklin a "problem bank." The auditors were concerned about the substandard loans and the bonds. In 1964, for example, loans classified and criticized as bad loans had totaled $59.7 million, equaling 48.8 percent of total capital and 8.1 percent of all loans. By October 3, 1966, the bank held $129.9 million in questionable loans; that amounted to 100.8 percent of capital and 10.9 percent of all loans.

In short, Franklin National Bank was insolvent. It should probably have been merged with a larger bank that had better internal management. The comptroller's office, however, did nothing. Instead, the authorities accepted Roth's word that he would resolve the situation. And he did. By 1968, when Roth resigned as chief executive officer, classified and criticized loans had been reduced to $94.0 million, while the percentage of bad loans to total capital had dropped to a more manageable 53.7 percent, equal to 7.3 percent of all loans.

On June 30, 1967, Franklin merged with Federation Bank & Trust, adding resources of $291 million and deposits of $261 million and acquiring thirteen branches in New York City. The merger pushed Franklin National Bank up from the twentieth largest bank in the United States to the eighteenth. This was a moment of glory, an achievement of which Roth was proud. At the time, however, he had no way of knowing that Harold Gleason, a soft-spoken and generous man who, since 1956, had been his protégé, would conspire with two Federation directors to push him out of Franklin.

In 1928, when Harold Gleason was eight years old, he would ride his bicycle through Bellerose, Long Island, to Louie's Rocky Hill Road Gas Station to put air in his tires. Louie's was a tiny wooden shack, and its grease pit was a simple hole in the ground with a wooden ladder.

During the Gatsby era, Rocky Hill Road was the main road linking Queens to the South Shore speakeasies that flourished during Prohibition. "Unfortunately for Louie," Gleason says, "his station lay on the northbound side of the road facing Gus's, his fiercest competitor."

And Gus sold something more than gasoline. Along the road next to the station a sign read "Ask for Teddy." "But there was no Teddy," explains Gleason. "To motorists who knew the code, the sign meant, 'Ask Gus where to go to get a drink.' " This knowledge, of course, gave Gus a tremendous advantage over Louie. The only way Louie could fight back was to sell his gas for less than what Gus charged. Every time Louie lowered the price of his gas, however, Gus would lower his.

One summer day while Louie and Gus stood on opposite sides of the street watching each other change prices, Gleason rode his bicycle toward the air pump. Intrigued by the two men, Harold watched Louie write "8 gals per $1." Then Louie turned to face Harold and, as if looking for sympathy from the boy, proclaimed, "Eight for a buck is what the damn gas cost me!" But Louie was willing to break even as long as he could take business away from Gus. To Louie's amazement, however, Gus wrote on his chalkboard: "8½ gals per $1 . . . All You Can Get." Frustrated, Louie threw up his arms and screamed, "I'll be damned if I am going to sell my gas for less than I pay for it just because that dumb son of a bitch has gone crazy."

At that moment Gleason had what he refers to as his first idea in financial advertising. He thought of the beautiful automobiles that stopped at Louie's for fuel—the Marmon touring cars, the V-12 Lincolns, the Packards. He considered how little the gasoline cost in comparison with the price of these machines. Then he told Louie that he ought to put something on the sign to remind people of the value of their cars. "Okay, kid. You write something," Louie said. "At this point, I don't give a good goddamn!"

Harold erased Louie's price. In its place, he wrote: "DON'T RUIN YOUR CAR WITH CHEAP GAS!"

A few minutes later, a Marmon touring car pulled into Louie's station. As Louie began to pump, the distinguished-looking driver said to him, "I'll put anything in my stomach, but there's no way I'll ruin this buggy with cheap gas."

Harold Gleason believes that this incident somehow led him to choose a career in banking and public relations. Fifty-three years after the episode at Louie's, bankers asked to give their opinion of Harold V. Gleason say, "Gleason was not a banker; he was a brilliant advertising and public relations man."

At the age of nineteen, Harold Gleason started his career in banking as an office boy for Hamburg Savings Bank in Brooklyn. Though he never graduated from college, he took advertising and banking courses at Hofstra University, Empire State College, Adelphi University, and the Rutgers University School of Banking.

In 1956 Harold Gleason was in charge of public relations and business development for the State Association of Savings Banks. That same year he met James Smith, Franklin's vice-president in charge of mortgages, at a class reunion of the Rutgers School of Banking. At the time, Roth was bitterly fighting the savings banks over the issue of branch banking. Smith thought that Gleason would be a good man to have on Franklin's side, and so he persuaded Gleason to meet with Arthur Roth.

Roth immediately liked Gleason and hired him to head the bank's business development program and public relations department. The position kept Gleason in close contact with Roth, and when Roth moved against New York Governor Nelson Rockefeller, Gleason was by his side most of the time.

Gleason and Roth had much in common. They were both aggressive, intelligent, and loyal. They were practicing Catholics, dedicated to helping the church. In a very short time, the Roths and the Gleasons became the closest of friends. Harold was like another son, says Genevieve, Roth's wife.

In time, everyone at the bank recognized that Harold was Arthur's protégé. He was a trim man of medium height, with black hair that had gone gray at the temples, and he moved up rapidly, first becoming divisional president of Franklin's Suffolk County division and then, in 1967, corporate president of the bank. There was no question that, when Arthur Roth retired, Harold Gleason would replace him as chief executive officer.

Things did not work out exactly that way, however. For reasons that remain vague in his own mind, Roth decided, after years of coaching, that Gleason was not the man he had thought him to be. When the time came for Roth to name the man who would succeed him upon his retirement in December 1970, he looked Gleason straight in eye and said, "You don't measure up. I've finally realized that you are a faker, an egotistical incompetent. You will never be chief executive of my bank."

For whatever reasons Roth felt that he had to be so candid with Gleason, his frankness proved to be a tactical error. He had underestimated Gleason's will and his ability to fight back. While Roth was busy searching for his replacement, Gleason, feeling insulted and betrayed, conspired with two directors who had come over to Franklin as part of the merger agreement with Federation Bank & Trust; together the three of them planned to outmaneuver Roth. They persuaded the board to change the bylaws of the bank, making the president, instead of the chairman, chief executive officer.

It was a treacherous but brilliant move. Much of what went on is not known: the many hours of secret meetings with members of the board of directors; the promises and details surrounding side deals that may or may not have been agreed upon in order to persuade directors loyal to Roth to betray their leader, extinguish his power, and elect Gleason chief executive of the bank. The only thing that is clear is that, ultimately, Gleason was triumphant.

So, after spending thirty years directing Franklin National's development from a small-town bank into the eighteenth largest in the country, Arthur Roth was left powerless. In one twisted election, the reputation he had earned was transformed into legend. He became a paper chairman, a leader without power or disciples. Bank employees were ordered not to discuss the bank's business with him. The few who remained loyal to him were afraid to be seen talking with him for fear that they would be fired. For a man like Arthur Roth, solitary confinement in a maximum-security prison would have been no worse.

Though he did not approve of what Gleason was doing with the bank, for two years Roth said nothing, believing that time would prove that Gleason was the wrong man and that he, Roth, should pick and train his successor. That never happened. In 1970, seven months before Roth was to retire, Gleason pushed him off the board.

With Roth completely out of the picture, Gleason did things his way. "An easygoing and generous man," says *Fortune*, "Gleason lacked the disposition to control personnel expenses, and they soared. Under Gleason's guiding hand, the number of employees increased sharply, salaries and bonuses rose, and expense accounts became much more lavish. From 1968 to 1970, the bank's salary expense increased by 50 percent."

On March 6, 1972, four months before Michele Sindona purchased controlling interest of Franklin National, bank examiners listed its classified and criticized loans at $211.1 million — 11.6 percent of total loans and 91.2 percent of capital. Again the bank was in serious trouble and probably should have been declared insolvent or merged with a bigger bank. Although the authorities were maintaining a close watch on the bank, and although they could have forced a merger or at least a change in management, they chose instead to take management's word that the situation would be resolved.

Laurence Tisch, chairman of Loews Corporation, was not so easily convinced. During the 1960s Tisch had quietly purchased 21.6 percent of Franklin New York Corporation. By 1972 he had serious doubts about the soundness of his investment. Being the major stockholder and a member of the board of directors of both the holding company and the bank, Tisch had enough power to order a change in management. In May 1972 he persuaded the young and highly respected Paul Luftig to leave Bankers Trust and join Franklin as its new president and chief operating officer. Part of the deal was that, in a few months, Luftig would replace Gleason as chairman. That never happened.

At about the same time, the Federal Reserve was investigating Loews Corporation's influence over the bank. Though Loews owned less than 25 percent of the stock—ownership of more than 25 percent would have automatically declared Loews a one-bank holding company, forcing Loews to divest itself of its significant and profitable nonbanking holdings—Tisch himself was a director for both the holding company and the bank. The authorities decided that there existed a "rebuttable presumption" that Loews did in fact control the bank. Had the Federal Reserve proved this presumption, Tisch would have had to sell all of Loews Corporation's other interests. Not wanting to risk such a declaration, Tisch instead searched for someone who would buy Loews Corporation's one million shares of Franklin New York Corporation. He did not have to wait very long. On July 20 Michele Sindona paid Tisch forty dollars a share, eight dollars above market value.

14

THE SINDONA SYSTEM

ON A SUNNY AFTERNOON in May 1972 Harold Gleason met Laurence Tisch in the lobby of the Regency Hotel. From there they walked to the Drake Hotel, which, like the Regency, was owned by Loews Corporation. As they strolled along Park Avenue, Tisch informed Gleason that the man they were going to meet, an Italian financier named Michele Sindona, was interested in buying his Franklin New York Corporation stock. Gleason, however, was not to worry about his position with the bank. Tisch assured him that Sindona would give Gleason a contract—anything Gleason wanted. Gleason said nothing.

Sindona was wearing a black suit, a white shirt, and a gray tie. Also present were Dan Porco and a representative of Kuhn Loeb, the brokerage house that introduced Sindona to Tisch. After greeting Tisch and Gleason, Sindona pointed to Porco, whose assignment was to negotiate the purchase price down from $45 per share and said, "He speaks for me."

The meeting lasted fifteen minutes. There was no discussion of the deal. While the others talked about miscellaneous things, Sindona constantly paced as he molded a piece of plain paper into the shape of a papal hat. The only purpose of the meeting was for Sindona to meet Gleason, the chief executive officer of the bank. And for Sindona, that consisted mostly of a few stares.

Gleason soon announced that he had to leave, explaining that his daughter-in-law was expecting him and his wife for dinner. Someone in Sindona's organization must have researched Gleason's family, because Sindona immediately came to life in an odd way. Demonstrating the kind of enthusiastic interest he usually exhibited when anticipating a favorable response, Sindona asked Gleason his daughter-in-law's maiden name. Surprised by what seemed like an odd question, Gleason said that it was Bracco. A smile slowly spread across Sindona's face. Third generation, Gleason said, explaining that she did not speak Italian. That did not seem to matter, however, and Sindona continued to smile as he generously shook Gleason's hand.

The following morning Gleason went to the Park Avenue offices of Sol Kittay to ask Kittay about Sindona. Kittay was a director of Franklin and owned 100,000 shares of stock. He had business contacts in Europe and said that Sindona was "a helluva guy, a good man for the bank." Kittay said that he had had some dealings with the Sindona Group and that the deals had been successful. He repeated, "Oh, yes, Harold, Sindona is a helluva guy, a helluva guy!"

About a month passed before Gleason heard anything more about Michele Sindona. After a Franklin Bank directors' meeting one afternoon in June, Laurence Tisch entered Harold Gleason's wood-paneled office to use the phone.

"Have you heard any more from the Italian?" Gleason asked.

"Now he's monkeying around on price," answered Tisch. "You know. . . . No, nothing."

Then, on July 5, Tisch called Gleason. "Harold," Tisch said, "I've sold my stock to Sindona. Sorry you weren't kept informed, but I tried to reach you earlier."

At about the same time, Michele Sindona called Milan and spoke with Pier Sandro Magnoni and Carlo Bordoni. Both men congratulated Sindona on the acquisition. At the end of their conversation, Michele told Carlo, "When I get back, I will discuss with you how we will have to finance the purchase."

Of Sindona's purchase of Franklin, Carlo Bordoni says, "Michele Sindona was a megalomaniac. He purchased Franklin National Bank because he wanted to merge it with all of his banks and with others that he planned to acquire in England and Spain, so that he would become the largest private banker in the world. Once this was accomplished, Sindona planned to set up headquarters in Messina, Sicily. Knowing this, one should not forget the Mafia angles in this story."

Michele Sindona laughs at Bordoni's statement. "Those are the words of a crazy and evil man," Michele says. "Having seen the difficulty of realizing my plans for creating a company that would ease the way for various countries to invest their capital in Italy, embittered by the illegal and violent opposition to every one of my economic and financial activities, and after being subjected to unheard of fiscal persecution, I decided to move abroad to concentrate my activities in a more hospitable country. When I learned that controlling interest of Franklin National Bank was for sale, I instinctively believed that America wanted Michele Sindona. The bank had a good name. It had financed part of the cost to build the Watergate towers. And the size of its assets attracted me because I felt that it would be possible, especially with my European connections and competent and dynamic leadership, to introduce Franklin into the international arena."

Sindona's explanation, though credible, takes no account of the particularly Sicilian aspects of this entrance into American banking. For a Sicilian to lose face the way Sindona had as a result of his failing to acquire Bastogi is a disgrace second only to being labeled a government informant. The only way an informant can salvage honor for himself and respect for his family is to do one of two things: commit suicide or present himself to the person he is accused of betraying, admit his wrong, and accept death without fear. If he chooses not to follow this course, if he chooses to dishonor himself further by hiding, he will be shot five times in the back of the head when he is caught by those who seek him. This reveals to all that he did not have the courage to face death. In the most brutal cases, his testicles will be cut off and stuffed into his mouth.

The other side to this tribal ritual concerns the man who has been betrayed. For as long as the vendetta goes unresolved there will be a black mark against his name. He will not be cast aside by his friends, but they will consider him weak. Though they will speak with him, they will not share confidences. Soon he will have no one with whom he can do business.

This is the situation Sindona faced. He was not an informant, so death was not a concern. If he did not quickly succeed at another, even bigger deal than Bastogi, however, he would be considered a weak and broken man by his fellow Sicilians.

In reality, Michele Sindona could easily have continued to do business on an international scale. True, some financiers would have been uneasy, at least for a time. But that is the nature of international banking. When one falls backward, one must again prove oneself worthy to play the game. There is no doubt, however, that had Sindona stayed in the shadows for a short time he would have been able to reenter the game with the same respect and power he had had before Bastogi. After all, he was still Pope Paul's confidant, and he still maintained a powerful association with Vatican City.

Nevertheless, Michele had one factor working against him: he did not know how to rest. Though his personal net worth was more than half a billion dollars, he was determined to become the wealthiest man in the world. He was egotistical. Therefore he could not look inside himself and find error. As much as he wanted people to consider him an Italian aristocrat, he was in every sense a Sicilian: loyal to his closest associates, cunning and deceptive with opponents. And most of all, the vendetta he carried for Cuccia corrupted his conscious thoughts. In the final analysis, however, what most contaminated his ability to judge the situation correctly was that unconsciously he was still trying to prove to Nunziata that he had made her dreams for him come true.

There was nothing for Michele to do but find another deal and win. He was convinced that, if he did this, Cuccia and the Italian population as a whole would be forced to acknowledge that he was a great man who had been wronged.

In order to raise the $40 million needed to purchase 21.6 percent of Franklin, Sindona needed to sell all of the shares he held in La Centrale, Credito Varesino, Pacchetti, and Zitropo. The companies named, however, were major industrial and financial institutions important to Licio Gelli's plans for Il Momento di Passare all' Azione (The Time for Real Action). And although Grand Master Gelli relished the idea of infiltrating the American banking community through a high-ranking member of P-2, he was not pleased with the possibility of Propaganda Due losing control.

The only way Sindona could remain faithful to phase two of Real Action was to sell his corporations to another member of P-2. It would also be necessary for that person to have liquid resources outside Italy in order to circumvent Italy's currency restrictions. Roberto Calvi, chairman of Banco Ambrosiano, met these criteria. He was a member of Propaganda Due, and he controlled Cimafin Finanz Anstalt, a Liechtensteinian holding company, and Banca del Gottardo in Switzerland.

"Several months before I purchased Franklin," explains Michele Sindona, "Roberto Calvi paid Fasco, A.G., $90 million for Zitropo and my other companies. The payment was made by Banca del Gottardo to Amincor bank, Zurich, in favor of Fasco, A.G. On July 6, after I had successfully negotiated the purchase of one million shares of Franklin stock from Loews, I instructed Carlo Bordoni to transfer the $90 million from Amincor's house account to Banca Unione's foreign account at Amincor. I did this because I wanted my Italian bank to earn a commission when the $40 million was wired to Laurence Tisch. I wanted to show Guido Carli and Enrico Cuccia that Michele Sindona cared about Italy, that I wasn't like other financiers who did nothing to help the Italian economy.

"On July 20 I told Bordoni to enter a fiduciary contract between

Amincor and Banca Unione for $35 million, using the Fasco, A.G., account as collateral. The purpose for using the fiduciary system was to hide the transaction from bank employees. Had anyone discovered that Michele Sindona was purchasing Franklin Bank, they could have manipulated the stock, and I would have been forced to pay more than forty dollars per share. Handling the transfer in this way protected me from such an enormous risk. As far as anyone could tell, the transaction was simply a time deposit made by Banca Unione with Amincor. The secret fiduciary contract that disclosed Fasco, A.G., as the owner of the funds was known only by myself and Carlo Bordoni."

If what Sindona says is true, then he did not lie to the Securities and Exchange Commission when he said that he purchased control of Franklin National Bank with his own funds; when a bank loan is secured by a customer's cash account that is equal to or greater than the amount of the loan, the bank, in essence, is lending the customer his own funds. This is an important issue. If Sindona did not buy Franklin with his own money, if he borrowed or stole the money from his Italian banks, then he committed a fraud and perjured himself.

After examining the records of Banca Unione, Banca Privata Finanziaria, Amincor, Fasco, A.G., and Steelinvest Holding (a company owned by Group Sindona and managed by Sindona's son-in-law, Pier Sandro Magnoni), it appears, however, that Sindona has attempted to create another illusion by weaving a tale of half-truths and lies. Nowhere can it be verified that Michele Sindona or any of his corporations received $90 million from Roberto Calvi or any of Calvi's banks or corporations on or before July 6, 1972, nor is there proof that Fasco, A. G., deposited $90 million with Amincor or that Amincor transferred funds it had received from Fasco, A.G., to Banca Unione's foreign account.

Confronted with this, Michele Sindona points to a deposit of $29.1 million that Amincor placed at Banca Unione on July 6, claiming that the funds originated from Fasco and were part of the $90 million he used as collateral when he borrowed from Banca Unione the $40 million used to purchase Franklin. This, however, is not true. In fact, it is nothing more than a trick.

On July 6 Sindona told Bordoni that Fasco International would need $40 million to purchase the Franklin shares and that $5 million would be needed the next day as a down payment. Bordoni immediately put into effect a scheme that enabled him to filter bank funds to Sindona. On the same day Bordoni wired a total of $30 million to six different banks: Bank of Nova Scotia ($4.5 million), Banque de Paris et des Pays Bas ($4.75 million), Banco Popular Espanol ($6 million), Cooperative Centrale Raiffeisen ($3 million), the Royal Bank of Canada ($7 million), and Gotenbanken ($4.75 million). On Banca Unione's books, Bordoni listed each transaction as a loan beginning on July 6, 1972, and terminating on July 8, 1973. The six banks involved, however, knew nothing of the loan because Bordoni never intended to leave the money with them—not for a year, not for a month, not even for a day. As soon as the banks received the transfer, Bordoni instructed each of them to send the funds to Manufacturers Hanover Trust. Then he sent a telex to Manufacturers instructing it to wire the entire $30 million to Amincor Bank, Zurich. Amincor received the money, still on July 6, and deposited $29.1 million in Banca Unione's foreign account at Amincor.

In summary, funds that originated from Banca Unione were washed through six different banks and carried on the books of BU as loans so that when they reappeared it would look as if they had come from Fasco's Amincor account. In addition, since BU listed the transactions as loans, Sindona did not have to repay the money for at least a year. This was Sindona's convoluted way of controlling vast fortunes. And, for a time, it was a brilliant and inexpensive way of doing so, because it allowed the Sindona Group to use other people's monies without their knowledge.

Michele has also claimed that a July 13 deposit of $7.9 million from Amincor to BU consisted of funds belonging to him. Like the previous example, however, all of the money originated from BU. On July 10 Bordoni sent $7 million to Uplandsbanken, Stockholm. Again, on BU's books, the amount was listed as a loan running from July 10, 1972, to July 10, 1973. The same pattern was followed. The day the money was sent to Stockholm it was transferred to Manufacturers and then wired to Amincor. At Bordoni's instructions, Amincor added that $7 million to the $900,000 balance that was left over from the first transfer and deposited it on July 13 at BU.

Though it must be said that all of the records of all of the banks and companies involved are not available for examination, it seems strange that the only records missing are those that would prove that Sindona did have $90 million on deposit with Amincor at the time he purchased Franklin New York Corporation. The question that remains unanswered is this: what happened to the $90 million Calvi deal?

Eleven newly available documents prove that Sindona and Calvi had negotiated, on June 23, 1972, a purchase and sale agreement between Zitropo Holding, s.a.; Pacchetti, s.p.a.; and Cimafin Finanz Anstalt. According to a letter dated September 1, 1972, and signed by Pier Sandro Magnoni, however, the agreement did not take effect until August 29, and the payment of $44,317,876 did not have to be paid until February 28, 1973. Nevertheless, there is a letter addressed to the board of directors of Zitropo in which Pier Sandro refers to his resignation as chief executive officer on June 23, 1972. On the surface, this would, it seems, at least confirm that Cimafin, Calvi's company, did take control of the Sindona's companies on that date. There is, however, no document that proves that either Sindona or Fasco, A.G., received payment before July 20, 1972, the day he purchased the Franklin shares.

It may be, says Sindona, that Calvi left the funds on deposit with Banca del Gottardo. There is nothing to support this theory, but if it is accepted as a possibility, it would prove that, at the very least Sindona was liquid — although it does not prove that the funds were on deposit with Amincor at the time Sindona purchased Franklin.

Aside from the fact that Sindona keeps changing his story, the problem with accepting Sindona's theory is that, had the funds already been on deposit outside Italy — whether at Amincor, Finabank, Banca del Gottardo, or any other Swiss bank — Sindona would have had no need to enter into a fiduciary contract with his Italian banks. Sindona's explanation that he wanted to hide the fact that he was purchasing Franklin bank and to allow his Italian banks to earn a commission just does not hold up.

First of all, if Michele Sindona had wanted his Italian banks to earn a commission on the transfer of the $40 million to Loews Corporation, there would have been no need to wire the funds back to Amincor and then have Amincor wire the funds to New York. Doing this cost Sindona a fee that was unnecessary. The only logical reason for handling the transactions in this way, it would seem, was to hide the fact that Michele Sindona through Carlo Bordoni was circumventing both the Italian currency laws and the American security laws.

Sindona has also said that he used fiduciary contracts for security reasons. He says that he did not want to risk anyone discovering his purchase of Franklin before the payment to Tisch was completed for fear that the bank's stock would be manipulated and would, therefore, cost him more than he had negotiated to pay. This argument, however, is also flawed. No matter what a stock does once a purchase and sale agreement is signed, the price is set. In addition, in paragraph two of the fiduciary contracts between Amincor and Banca Unione and between Amincor and Banca Privata Finanziaria, both Italian banks clearly instruct Amincor to credit the funds "in favour of Fasco, A.G., Eschen," not Fasco International, the company that actually purchased Franklin. In fact, on July 13, seven days before Sindona purchased Franklin bank, newspapers in America and Italy printed stories that revealed Tisch's sale of one million shares of Franklin New York Corporation to Sindona.

What appears to have happened is that Sindona did sell Zitropo and his other companies to Roberto Calvi; however, even if Sindona did receive a partial payment on or before July 20, the funds were never offered to Banca Unione or Banca Privata as collateral. This was due, most likely, to conspiratorial negligence. Sindona, true to his nature, was able to construct a method by which he could purchase Franklin while leaving his liquid assets free for other deals. Had the regulatory agencies in the United States requested proof that the $40 million belonged to him "free and clear," as he stated, he would have been able to turn to Carlo Bordoni, who might have back-dated the collaterization papers. At first, however, no one asked Michele Sindona to prove that the money he used to buy Franklin was in fact his, and by the time someone requested proof, Bordoni was no longer Sindona's loyal lieutenant.

So, on July 7, Carlo Bordoni instructed Banca Privata Finanziaria to send $5 million to Privat Kredit Bank, Zurich. He then changed hats: representing Fasco International, Bordoni ordered Privat Kredit to wire the funds to Bankers Trust Co., Park Avenue, New York, with instructions to Bankers Trust to make the funds available to Dan Porco. On July 11 Porco had Bankers Trust draft a check made payable to Loews Theatres and Lawton General Corporation, of which Laurence Tisch was chairman, in the amount of $5 million, which represented a down payment against a purchase price of $40 million for one million shares of Franklin New York Corporation.

On July 11, 1972, Sindona's attorney, Andrew Miller of the law firm White & Case, wrote to the Federal Reserve Bank of New York informing the Bank that Fasco International had been formed by his client for the sole purpose of holding shares of Franklin New York Corporation. Miller included a chart allegedly prepared by Sindona that revealed that Sindona also owned Fasco, A.G., which held Sindona's interest in his Italian and Swiss banks and a number of his American and European companies. The purpose of the letter and chart, as Miller explained, was to support his belief that neither Fasco International nor Fasco, A.G., had control of Franklin National Bank and therefore, should not be declared a bank holding company.

At about the same time that the officials of the Federal Reserve Bank of New York and the office of the Comptroller of the Currency were supposed to be scrutinizing Sindona's purchase of Franklin Bank, Jack Begon, a sixty-two-year-old journalist for ABC in Italy, broadcast a radio report called "Hot Dollars." According to Begon, concrete proof existed to show that Michele Sindona represented American and Sicilian Mafia families looking to invest drug profits into legitimate businesses at the 1957 Mafia summit meeting in Palermo, Sicily.

This should have raised enough suspicion about Sindona for the regulatory agencies to reject Sindona's purchase of Franklin Bank. Nevertheless, without raising one question about Sindona's alleged Mafia connections or about where he got his money, U.S. authorities approved his purchase of the bank. Their only criterion, it seems, was that Michele Sindona was not a director of the bank or of the bank's holding company. Why were the authorities so quick to ignore rumors of some substance? How could they approve the sale of the bank to Sindona so quickly? The answer to these questions may be that Sindona was right when he said, "Banking is a matter of connections."

When Michele Sindona prepared to enter the American banking scene, his connection was David Kennedy. An elder of the Mormon church, former ambassador to the North Atlantic Treaty Organization, ambassador at large, and secretary of the treasury from 1969 to 1971, Kennedy was a loyal friend and a powerful contact for Sindona. Whether Kennedy did any back-room dealing on his friend's behalf is not important. His presence was probably enough to sway the thinking of most officials — and shortly after Michele Sindona purchased Franklin National Bank, James Smith, Kennedy's former undersecretary at the Treasury Department, was appointed comptroller of the currency.

But Kennedy did more than just reveal that he had had a long and successful association with Sindona. "Out of friendship," Michele says, "David Kennedy agreed to become a member of the board of directors of Fasco International Holding, S.A., of Luxembourg, a wholly owned subsidiary of Fasco, A.G., of which I owned one hundred percent of the stock."

According to Sindona, Kennedy never received compensation for any of the work he did for the Group. After the failure of Franklin National Bank, however, government investigators did uncover some $200,000 that Sindona had paid Kennedy and that Kennedy used to buy land in Arizona. When the government questioned Kennedy about this, however, his lawyers successfully argued that the money was a loan that their client had repaid. Sindona confirmed this, and the investigation was stopped.

Of the Kennedy–Sindona connection, Arthur Roth stated in testimony before the Oversight Hearings: "Sindona had entrée . . . to Smith through David Kennedy . . . [and] Smith was incompetent and negligent" in his investigation of Sindona.

In fact, Arthur Roth appears to have been the only one who questioned the sale of stock to Michele Sindona. When he read in the newspapers that Laurence Tisch had agreed to sell his shares of Franklin to Michele Sindona, Roth investigated Sindona. Unhappy with what he learned, Roth then wrote an open letter, dated July 18, 1972, which he sent to all of the regulatory agencies and newspapers:

Dear Mr. Tisch: The newspapers of July 13, 1972, reported Loews Corp. (of which you are its Chief Executive Officer), sale of 1 million shares of stock of Franklin New York Corporation for $40,000,000.00 The sale was to a company controlled by Michele Sindona of Milan, Italy.

Your sale of this stock may have been advisable in so far as Loews is concerned, but, it raises some serious questions for the stockholders and depositors of Franklin National Bank.

1. Do you know enough about Michele Sindona to unconditionally recommend him as a person who will be good for the bank?
2. Will there be a full disclosure of his finances, his backers, and detailed biographies?
3. Why would he pay $40.00 a share for stock that is currently selling for $32.00, having run up from $28.00 per share apparently as a result of rumors of this sale?
4. What are his intentions regarding additional purchases and what role will he play in the operation of the bank?
5. When you sold your holdings at $40.00 a share, did you arrange to see that other stockholders could obtain the same price?
6. Don't you think that you could have found many eminent buyers in the United States if you asked a reasonable price for the stock? Would not these prospective buyers also have offered the same deal to other stockholders?
7. Franklin has a serious problem in covering its $32,500,000.00 tax loss carry over. Would not the sale and merger with a United States corporation aid in resolving this problem?
8. A bank is built on confidence. Have you considered whether or not this transaction will cause a loss of confidence in the bank?
I could ask many more pertinent questions, but this letter is now long enough . . . .

May I hear from you in an open letter because the stockholders, depositors and the banking fraternity will be interested in your answer.

I have written this letter because I feel a continuing responsibility to my family and many loyal stockholders, depositors and employees who helped to build the bank from deposits of less than $1,000,000.00 to become the 18th largest in the nation. I want only good things to happen to Franklin National Bank.

Laurence Tisch never responded to Roth's letter. Neither did the regulatory agencies. Almost everyone regarded Roth as a man who had fallen and who could not be taken seriously.

Dan Porco, however, thought differently. He was concerned, but not because he believed that Roth had the power to stop Sindona's purchase. Porco might have appreciated that because he was convinced that Franklin was a weak bank and that Michele was making a great mistake by purchasing control.

What bothered Porco about Arthur Roth was that he realized that Roth had a legitimate interest in the welfare of Franklin. In addition to having been responsible for Franklin's growth, Roth and his family collectively owned 100,000 shares of Franklin stock. It was clear, at least to Porco, that unless Sindona agreed to meet with Roth and unless he could persuade Roth to trust him, Roth would never retreat from his attack on Sindona's questionable reputation.

Sindona, however, was not interested in what Porco thought about Franklin Bank or about Arthur Roth. It's not that Michele didn't ask; he did. But every time Porco told Sindona that he was making another mistake, Sindona would say, "You don't understand what I am doing! I know what I am doing. I know that Franklin is right." Then, after the purchase had been approved by the regulatory agencies, Sindona was preoccupied with making sure that Bordoni wired the remaining $35 million to Tisch.

On July 20, 1972, Carlo Bordoni transferred $18 million from Banca Unione and $17 million from Banca Privata Finanziaria to Amincor Bank, Zurich. Both transactions were listed as fiduciary deposits in favor of Fasco, A.G. On the same day, Bordoni instructed Amincor to wire the $35 million to Banca Privata's account at Continental Bank International, New York. Then he immediately sent a telex to Continental Bank directing it to send all of the funds to Bankers Trust Co., New York. Louis De Bourbon of Bankers Trust then received a telex explaining that the funds were from Fasco International and that a bank check should be drafted for the total amount and made payable to Loews Theatres and Lawton General Corp.

In New York, at Sindona's apartment at the St. Regis Hotel, Michele Sindona, Dan Porco, and Laura Turner were anxiously awaiting confirmation of the payment to Laurence Tisch. They were all silent. Laura stood by the phone, ready to take the call from Bankers Trust. Michele paced in front of Porco, twisting and molding scraps of paper into papal hats. Porco was slumped in a chair. He had not slept for three days because he was sure that his Sicilian friend was making the biggest mistake of his life. There were dark circles under Porco's eyes. His face looked drawn and unhappy. Sindona was confused because he could not understand why Porco was so negative about the deal.

Suddenly Porco broke the silence. "This is another mistake, Michele," he said. "I'm telling you that this is a sick bank. Franklin has problems that will drown you."

Michele's eyes were cold and challenging as he stared at Porco. It was as if he were condemning his friend for not believing in his judgment. Then, in a soft but rigid voice, he said, "I know what I am doing with this bank."

Then he smiled and added, "Besides, if [Franklin] was in as much trouble as you say, the Comptroller of the Currency would not have approved its balance sheets. This is America, Dan. That's why I was willing to pay eight dollars per share above the market price. I know you think I'm foolish to bid that high but, as I've told you every time you complained, I don't want to lose this one the way I lost Bastogi. My taking control of Franklin will prove to Cuccia and Carli that I am a man who cannot be beaten. They will be sorry they did what they did to me. They will see that in America when you are right, when you follow the law, you can do business and the government appreciates you. The people love you. And they will love me. They will see that my personality and my intelligence are unique to the world. I will take Franklin, and through foreign . . ."

The phone rang. Sindona fell silent.

"The transfer has been received," Laura shouted. Cradling the phone in her arms, she smiled and asked Michele, "Do you want to speak to your attorneys or to Carlo?"

"We have to have a party," Michele laughed. "Call everyone and have them come here for a party."

Reluctantly, Dan Porco congratulated Michele. "It's going to be all right," Michele assured his friend. "We passed the Securities and Exchange investigation. We own just enough to control, but not so much that they can declare Fasco a bank holding company. None of my other investments are in jeopardy. Be happy for me, Dan. Everyone will be glad that Michele Sindona has come to . . ."

"Not everyone," Porco interrupted. "Not everyone is ecstatic about your arrival, Michele."

Michele's face fell. He did not want to hear this, not now. "Who?" he asked.

"You're forgetting about Arthur Roth. The letter he wrote Tisch. The one the newspapers printed. Roth doesn't feel comfortable having an outsider buy his bank."

"Order some wine," Michele said to Laura.

"Dan's right."

"It's not Roth's bank. It hasn't been his for two years, and now it's *my* bank."

"Don't underestimate Roth, Michele," both Laura and Dan warned.

"Order the wine, Laura!"

"Michele . . ."

"Then call my attorney, Andrew Miller, and tell him to arrange a meeting with Roth." Michele put his arm around Porco, adding, "You'll see. When Roth meets me he will be impressed."

In August Michele Sindona sent Dan Porco to see Harold Gleason, chairman of Franklin National Bank. Porco detailed Sindona's history, from lemon dealer during World War II to Vatican representative to worldwide financier. The purpose of the meeting, Porco explained, was to determine what role Michele Sindona and Carlo Bordoni could actively play in the growth of Franklin National Bank. Gleason said that Michele Sindona could not be elected to the board of directors of the bank because American law prohibited noncitizens from holding such a position. He suggested, instead, that the board form an international executive committee to advise the bank on foreign currency matters and foreign deposits. Porco accepted. It was agreed that Sindona would use an office at 130 Pearl Street, headquarters of the international department. Since the position offered no salary, the bank would pay for Sindona's apartment and grant him an expense account.

Shortly after their appointment to the international committee, Bordoni and Sindona were also elected to the board of Franklin New York Corporation, the holding company that controlled 100 percent of the bank. This should have been enough proof for the Federal Reserve Board to raise the issue of "rebuttable presumption." Sindona was in a position to influence the bank's policymaking decisions, and therefore it was reasonable to conclude that Fasco, A.G., and Fasco International should be considered a bank holding company.

Had the Federal Reserve done this, it would have been able to investigate all of Sindona's investments to determine if, in fact, there was a conflict of interest. Or, more to the point, it would have discovered early on that the funds Sindona used to purchase Franklin stock were not his. But after the Board of Governors made inquiries, David Kennedy advised Sindona to retain the law firm of Mudge Rose Guthrie & Alexander. The significance of this move is that then-President Richard Nixon had at one time been a partner in this firm, and former attorney general John Mitchell, after leaving the Justice Department, had joined the same law firm. Furthermore, Sindona and Nixon had known each other for several years. Before Nixon was elected to the presidency, he had referred several clients to Sindona.

Obviously the law firm had clout. Even when Attorney Randolph H. Guthrie informed the Federal Reserve that Fasco, A.G., and not Michele Sindona, owned Fasco International, the Board did nothing.

When Andrew Miller, Sindona's attorney, approached Arthur Roth, he was very direct. "I would like to have you meet Mr. Sindona even though he hates you for what you have said about him and the questions you have asked about him," he said. "But I would like him to get to know you."

Roth accepted the invitation, and finally, at midday on October 25, 1972, Michele Sindona and Arthur Roth met at Sindona's apartment at the St. Regis.

"Franklin has many problems," Roth said. "Loan losses are too high. Management is weak. The biggest problem is Gleason: he is incompetent and should be replaced."

"I don't know Gleason well enough to evaluate his abilities yet. I see Paul Luftig more than I see Gleason," answered Michele.

"Well, suppose you tell me how you plan to straighten out the bank."

"I am going to run the international department. Through my contacts in Europe, I will increase foreign deposits by one to two billion dollars. That's how Continental Bank does it. They earn 55 percent from foreign activity. I will do the same. After all, I am very close to Continental. For twelve years they have been partners with me in one of my banks in Italy. While I concentrate on foreign deposits, Paul Luftig will be reviewing the big loans. In addition, personnel is too high. I have already suggested to Luftig that he reduce personnel by two hundred fifty."

"I think you should cut personnel by six hundred," Roth insisted.

"Perhaps, but this is just the beginning. Give me one year, and you will see my accomplishments."

"You know that Franklin has a huge tax loss carry-forward," Roth said. "This could hurt the bank's earnings."

"I have already sold the Hanover Square building on a lease-buy-back for six million. This will cover the losses for 1972."

"You are still going to have to replace Gleason."

"Give me a chance, Mr. Roth. I appreciate what you are telling me, but I don't know the man."

"One question I have to ask you, Mr. Sindona. Why did you pay forty dollars per share when the market price was less than thirty?"

"Mr. Roth, in Europe bank stocks sell at fifty-two to one hundred times the market value. I paid a premium of only one-third for Franklin. For controlling interest, I feel that I made a good deal. I assure you that I know what I am doing. I have owned many banks. Along with the Vatican, I built the Watergate complex. I understand business. The price was a fair price — as I said — for controlling interest. If I could not have acquired control, I would not have purchased the stocks from Tisch, because I would not have been able to do what I think has to be done. For instance, I want to buy a mortgage company for the bank. Something for about $100 million cash. That will improve the bank's position."

"You say that your objectives are to stop loan losses and to increase foreign deposits," Roth replied. "I would like to repeat that you need a new top executive officer. Every business is the length and shadow of one man, and Gleason's length and shadow are bad. I admit that Harold was my mistake, but you have to correct it. You need efficiency in the bank. And you need esprit de corps, which has gone to pieces."

"I know morale is down," Sindona replied, "but I believe in team play, with myself running things in the background. I repeat, give me all of 1973 and you will see the results."

After the meeting, on the train from Manhattan to Long Island, Roth made notes on his meeting with Sindona. Among them is this comment: "Sindona is good for the bank — is straightforward — appears honest, intelligent, knows where he is going."

15

THE INTERNATIONALIZATION
OF FRANKLIN NATIONAL BANK

No SOONER HAD Michele Sindona bought Franklin National Bank than he used Carlo Bordoni and members of the international executive committee to filter millions of dollars from Franklin to his Swiss and Italian banks. Using conduits like Banco di Sicilia and Interbanca of Milan, he needed only two months to make $15 million vanish: on October 10 and 20, funds in the amounts of $5 million and $10 million, respectively, were transferred to Interbanca as time deposits in favor of Franklin National Bank. Without the knowledge or consent of Franklin's or Interbanca's management, the funds were then illegally deposited with Amincor Bank, which, upon receipt, then deposited the funds with Banca Unione. This was accomplished through the corruption of Interbanca's managing director, Gino Uglietti, whom Bordoni successfully bribed with $105,000 deposited at Amincor under the code name ALNO.

Why this was done is unclear. Authorities claim that BU and BPF, Sindona's Italian banks, were cash poor as a result of having been milked for the $40 million used to buy Franklin, but this is too easy an answer. The records of BU clearly show that it was not insolvent at the time. Most likely the only reason for stealing the money was that it was easy to do. This is supported by the fact that Franklin officials would never have discovered the theft if the bank had not ultimately failed.

After the theft had been executed, and after his meeting with Arthur Roth, Michele Sindona asked his friend David Kennedy to take Harold Gleason's place as chairman of Franklin National Bank. Kennedy refused. Although he was a director of Fasco International, he said he preferred to continue to serve as a consultant to the Sindona Group. This troubled Sindona, for he believed that in order to transform Franklin into an international bank capable of serving the needs of his Group, the bank's credibility within the international community needed to be solidified. This, he believed, could be accomplished only by replacing Gleason with someone equaling the stature of the former secretary of the treasury.

For a couple of weeks Sindona remained unclear about what action he should take. During this period of confusion he gathered additional background on Harold Gleason. He learned that Gleason had replaced Arthur Roth as the dominant banker on Long Island. In fact, in a mock election held shortly after Gleason pushed Roth off Franklin's board, the former public relations man was elected "governor of Long Island." What interested Sindona most, however, was a remark one banker made that during the branch banking war Harold Gleason's style was not abrasive like that of Arthur Roth; instead, he had charmed David and Nelson Rockefeller with his soft voice and smooth manner. If this was true, Sindona thought, then perhaps there was no need to replace Gleason.

In order to confirm this, Sindona decided to test Gleason's relationship with David Rockefeller. To that end, early one morning in November 1972, Michele Sindona entered Harold Gleason's office at Park Avenue and 57th Street. Without saying a word, Sindona sat down and, staring directly at Gleason, began folding a piece of paper into a papal hat. Gleason waited for Sindona to say something. He didn't. What Gleason thought of this odd behavior is unknown, but he must have felt very uncomfortable with Sindona's cold and calculating eyes bearing down on him at 9:30 A.M. Gleason asked if he could be of some assistance. Sindona responded by pacing back and forth like a fox in front of Gleason's desk. Suddenly he stopped, looked Gleason straight in the eye, and asked him to arrange a meeting with David Rockefeller. Gleason, who was was far from stupid, realized that if he failed to arrange the meeting, Sindona would assume he was not respected and would eventually replace him as chairman of Franklin Bank. So when Gleason made the appointment, he related his suspicions to Rockefeller's secretary, knowing she would pass the word to her boss.

Gleason and Sindona arrived at David Rockefeller's office that same day at 12:50 P.M. Rockefeller was courteous. He welcomed Sindona to New York and wished him well with his investment. Before Sindona had a chance to speak, Gleason recalls that Rockefeller added, "With respect to Franklin, Mr. Sindona, in the past there were questions about it, but since

Harold is now there, we feel differently. We have wiped the slate clean."

Although Sindona still would have preferred to have as chairman of Franklin either Kennedy or some other member of his Group, he was now willing to allow Gleason to remain in the position. The experience, however, must have frightened Gleason. From that day forward, he went out of his way to win Sindona's approval. He arranged dinner parties to introduce Sindona to New York, studied Italian, and traveled to Milan to discuss business.

Whenever Rina accompanied her husband to one of the parties, Michele insisted she wear a diamond necklace, bracelet, and ring for which he allegedly paid a million dollars. This caused Rina tremendous discomfort. She was always afraid someone would accuse her of showing off, or worse, that a thief would yank the diamonds from her neck as she walked to the limousine. According to Maria Elisa—who, as her father's interpreter, was always by his side—Rina never enjoyed herself in New York.

Maria Elisa did, though, for wherever Michele was, so was his daughter. She left her husband in Milan so that she could be next to her father. Maria Elisa fulfilled his every wish, desire, and demand. At parties, when Michele was trying to impress someone, she would conspire with her father, pretending he did not understand English well. As she interpreted, Michele had time to decide exactly what he wanted to say to win the person's admiration. They played this drama over and over again. Even when someone knew he was being conned and spoke directly to Michele, Maria Elisa and her father continued to play the game. They understood that for any con to be successful, the first and most important principle was not to acknowledge discovery. Deny, laugh, walk away—but never acknowledge the truth.

One person they were unable to convince was Luiz Gastel, vice-president and manager of La Banque Continentale. A Brazilian with society connections, Gastel often gave small dinner parties for his friends and clients. Among his many guests were Walter Cronkite, Van Johnson, and D. K. Ludwig, the world's richest man. Because of his connections, Gleason assigned Gastel the responsibility of introducing Michele Sindona to New York.

"I held three parties for Sindona at the Hotel Pierre," explains Gastel. "Each one was a catastrophe. Sindona acted like a buffoon. He annoyed everyone. He offered to buy their companies for cash, or he suggested that they would be more successful if they became his partner. I told him New York would not accept him if he continued to act foolishly. But he was Michele Sindona. As far as he was concerned, everyone should have been honored that he wanted them to be partners." At these dinners, Sindona would brag about his association with Pope Paul and the Vatican, praise Western philosophy, and spin tales about his friends in the CIA, the Pentagon, and the Treasury Department. Of course, some were impressed, but Gastel was not. He warned Sindona, explaining that he would have to present a more conservative appearance if he wanted New Yorkers to take him seriously. Gastel even pleaded with Gleason to intervene, but the chairman refused to advise Sindona that he was committing even the slightest gaffe. Eventually, Gastel refused to introduce Sindona to any more of his clients. This angered Gleason, who had by now bought everything Sindona had to sell.

For all his social ineptitude, Michele was, as Gleason observed on three occasions, enormously powerful. One time, for example, the two men were in Sindona's Mercedes, and a Swiss guard waved them through the Vatican gates without hesitation. Another time, Sindona wanted to have lunch at a restaurant in Milan. The restaurant was crowded, and there was a long line of people waiting for tables. Sindona walked past everyone and said something to the owner. A few minutes later, the owner informed the diners that an emergency had arisen. He would not charge anyone for their meals, but they would have to leave. Then the owner closed the restaurant. Don Michele and his guest were seated at a table. For an hour and a half they ate and discussed business in private. But the most dramatic proof of Michele Sindona's power became evident to Harold Gleason when he and Sindona met with James Keogh, governor of the Bank of England (the British counterpart of the Federal Reserve Board) to discuss Keogh's apprehensions about granting foreign exchange privileges to Franklin's London branch.

The Federal Reserve Board had approved Franklin's application for the London branch on March 1, 1971. In order for the branch to compete in the interbank market, however, Franklin needed to obtain from the Bank of England full authority to deal in foreign exchange. This is usually granted once the Office of the Comptroller of the Currency assures British authorities that the bank in question is in good standing. By the time James Keogh requested information regarding Franklin's status, however, the Comptroller's office had again classified Franklin as a problem bank.

For more than a year, from March 1971 to November 1972, while the Comptroller's office knew that Franklin was bordering on insolvency, U.S. authorities had consistently evaded James Keogh's questions about the stability of the bank. During this period United States regulatory agencies maintained a close watch on Franklin. Although reports continued to reveal problems at the bank, records clearly demonstrate that the bank's management convinced the Comptroller's office that any further delays in approving the London branch would cause the public to lose confidence in

Franklin's stability. After accepting renewed assurances from Franklin's management that corrective measures had been taken, the Comptroller's office finally wrote Keogh advising him that "Franklin should be recognized in London."

On June 1, 1972, James Keogh notified Harold Gleason that in three months he would authorize Franklin to deal in foreign exchange. After Michele Sindona purchased control of Franklin, however, the Bank of England decided to withhold final approval until the United States regulatory authorities had an opportunity to investigate Sindona. James Keogh had heard rumors that Michele Sindona was associated with, and financed by, Mafia elements, and he hoped a full investigation by the Comptroller's office would reveal the source of the $40 million that Sindona used to buy control of the bank. At the time, he did not know that U.S. regulatory agencies had no intention of looking into this.

Michele Sindona used political pressure to persuade the Federal Reserve Board to intervene in England. In October 1972 Michele sent word to Maurice Stans, then chief fund raiser for President Richard Nixon, that he wanted to make a contribution. A few days later, Sindona met Stans at New York's University Club. Stans had rented several rooms and was busy getting commitments from bankers and businessmen. He had no time to visit with Sindona, so when he approached the Sicilian, he came right to the point.

"How much?" he asked.

"One million," answered Sindona.

"Why?"

"To demonstrate my confidence in the United States."

"How?"

"In cash."

"In your name?" asked Stans.

"Oh, no. If I did that I'd be shot in Italy."

"Then I can't accept it. All contributions must be identified by law," Stans explained.

"Sorry, but you must know my feelings," Sindona insisted.

Though his offer was refused, Sindona was crafty enough to realize that the Nixon administration would hear of it and consider him a friend. This was his insurance policy. Sindona knew that when the time came for him to ask Nixon's men for a favor, they would not refuse.

Shortly after Sindona offered to donate a million dollars to Nixon's reelection campaign, Harold Gleason and Sindona's attorney, Randolph Guthrie of Mudge Rose Guthrie & Alexander went to Washington to discuss the problem with members of the Board of Governors of the Federal Reserve. What was said is unknown. In November 1972, however, the Comptroller told Keogh that the Bank of England should grant foreign exchange privileges to Franklin's London branch. But Keogh still refused authorization. Frustrated, Gleason ordered Thomas Smith, manager of Franklin's London branch, to seek help from National Westminster Bank, one of England's largest and most respected banks. After looking into the matter, an officer of Westminster told Smith, "Keogh is nervous about Sindona—the Mafia and all that."

Michele Sindona decided that the quickest way to resolve the problem would be to meet James Keogh. And the way in which Sindona manipulated Keogh was brilliant. He realized that anything he said to defend himself against Keogh's suspicions would simply aggravate the problem and weaken his position. Instead, the master of illusion created an atmosphere of respectability by inviting John McCaffrey, Jr., to the meeting. The younger McCaffrey had replaced his father at Hambros Bank when the elder McCaffrey retired to live in Ireland. Sindona had heard that Keogh knew and respected both McCaffreys. By having the son of England's famous World War II intelligence officer present, Sindona hoped to create the impression that if the McCaffreys trusted him then so should Keogh.

In the middle of November 1972 Harold Gleason, Thomas Smith, James Keogh, Michele Sindona, and John McCaffrey, Jr., had dinner at Claridge's Hotel in London. They drank, ate, and laughed. They discussed banking in general. Sindona impressed Keogh with his vast knowledge of international economics, and McCaffrey, following Sindona's earlier instructions, told stories about the many successful deals his father had made with Michele Sindona. Two and a half hours later Keogh seemed relaxed and friendly.

At this point, one of the men asked Keogh why he was withholding approval of Franklin's London branch to deal in foreign exchange. Keogh ignored the question, choosing, instead, to discuss U.S. banking trends. Sindona became impatient. As his eyes moved back and forth from Gleason to Smith, he popped a half-dozen cubes of sugar into his mouth. He wanted someone to force the conversation his way, but no one did. Perhaps, since the real issue was Sindona's reputation, everyone felt that if the evening ended well, if Keogh liked Sindona, the governor would change his mind and allow the London branch full foreign exchange privileges.

Characteristically Sindona's impatience turned to boredom. Though he was confident that his plan had, thus far, succeeded, the central flow of the conversation had drifted. He withdrew, folding pieces of paper into boats and papal hats as he evaluated what had happened and what, if anything, he should do next. He was sure that Keogh liked him, but he wasn't sure that was enough to make Keogh forget the rumors of his association with the Mafia. He couldn't decide exactly how to confront Keogh. Perhaps, he thought, he should betray his instinct and defend himself.

Certainly McCaffrey would support his claim of innocence. He could argue that in Italy he was a victim of political injustice. He could say that the Vatican would never have trusted him if they believed that he was associated with criminals. He could have said a slew of things in his own defense. He said none of them. Instead, he made a very crafty decision: he decided to embarrass Keogh.

Slowly Sindona raised his head until his eyes were level with Keogh's. There was a stern, chilling expression on Sindona's face. He stared into the governor's eyes long enough to cause the conversation to die. The other three men watched, not sure what was happening. Keogh reached for his brandy, but the glass never reached his lips. "Mr. Keogh, I suppose you want to know about me," whispered Sindona. Then, without taking his eyes off Keogh, he placed the papal hat he had made in front of the governor. Keogh attempted a smile, but failed. Then, just as Keogh raised the brandy glass to his lips, Sindona added: "Well, I am the chief of the Mafia." The brandy glass slipped from Keogh's hand and dropped onto the table, but if it spilled, no one noticed. Gleason, Smith, and McCaffrey were speechless, obviously stunned. For a long couple of seconds, no one knew exactly what to say or do. Then, suddenly, Michele Sindona began to laugh. A few seconds later Keogh and the others were also laughing.

What was brilliant about Sindona's move was the clarity in which he perceived the situation. If he had denied being a member of the Mafia, no matter what anyone said in his defense, Keogh would probably not have believed him. Most likely, he would have thought, as most do, that a mafioso will always deny his membership in the "honored society." Michele Sindona realized this, just as he also understood that people generally disbelieve anyone admitting to membership in the Mafia. Of course, there was the risk that Keogh could not be fooled. But the gamble paid off. Approximately a week after they had dinner, the Bank of England granted Franklin's London branch full authority to deal in foreign exchange.

Negative publicity resulting from the delayed approval of the London branch, coupled with speculation that the mysterious Sicilian's background was somehow sinister, caused the price of Franklin's stock to fall almost immediately after Sindona had purchased one million shares. But Sindona was less concerned about the value of his investment than he was about his reputation. Instead of acknowledging his genius, the financial community in Italy and America wondered if he had been a fool. Pathologically obsessed with the need to cultivate the myth that he was the world's greatest expert on acquisition, finance, and banking, Sindona responded to criticism by experiencing tremendous physical and emotional pain. That narcissism stimulated his suffering is partially true. But criticism probably also motivated an unconscious awareness of his criminali-

ty, which he chose to camouflage by forging an image of respectability—
not merely to acquire the esteem of others but for his own comfort as
well.

This urge to exonerate and forgive himself appears to have been the
major cause of his defeat. Had Sindona been willing to accept himself for
what he had become, he would have continued to maintain a low profile.
Instead, he made the devastating error of placing too much value on his
own analytical powers—that is, his ability to scheme. Deciding to court
and seek the admiration of the American public, he hired a public relations man and began making speeches at universities. At the same time,
according to Carlo Bordoni, Sindona attempted to support the price of
Franklin's stock by secretly—and illegally—using his Swiss and Italian
banks to purchase additional shares for customer accounts. This plot, however, failed. As a result, his clients lost a great portion of their liquid assets,
and Sindona continued to be humiliated by his critics: Enrico Cuccia,
Guido Carli, and Ugo La Malfa, Italy's finance minister and a close associate of Cuccia.

Although insecurity and hatred contaminated and shaped Sindona's thinking to such a point that many of his plans seem devious and reckless, his
thought processes were also characterized by the complexity of genius. His
ability to invent and initiate complicated plots to destroy enemies reached
a peak in November 1972 when he constructed a plan designed to bring
about the destruction of the Italian lira. If successful, he would, in one
stroke, disgrace his enemies and force Guido Carli, governor of the Bank of
Italy, to resign.

The birth of what was to become the largest foreign exchange operation ever instigated was probably formed when Michele Sindona was preparing a lecture on the International Monetary System for presentation at
the Harvard Business School the same month the operation began. There
he warned students of the dangers of foreign exchange speculation, but he
also remarked, "Much has been said about the movements and about speculation, and there is no doubt that there has been some speculation. I am,
however, in agreement with Mr. Anthony Barber, chancellor of the
exchequer and governor of the Fund for the U.K., in affirming that anyone
who moves these funds at times of difficulty does so because it is his duty
to protect their value, either on his own behalf or on behalf of the people
whose funds he manages."

Although he and Carlo Bordoni had already mobilized the currency
operation, Sindona concluded his speech with a warning: "I should like to
hope that all men of goodwill employ their energies to create a supreme
international organization with powers to restructure the entire monetary
system and which can avoid the misrepresentations and other similar

measures I have condemned. These are certainly not adopted in the interests of the national and international community, but only to defend centers of power by people who cannot see further than the end of their noses and are thinking only of their own egoistic interests."

This last statement, it seems, was clearly an attack on Enrico Cuccia, Ugo La Malfa, Guido Carli, and the whole Italian system of nationalization and currency restrictions, but Sindona appears to have had another, more self-serving purpose for making such a speech at this time. Michele was creating a record to ensure that, if his involvement in the conspiracy against the lira was uncovered, he would be able to cite proof that he was entirely opposed to such operations. But this problem never materialized.

In November 1972 Michele Sindona ordered Carlo Bordoni to organize a "foreign exchange consortium" to purchase three billion U.S. dollars and, at the same time, sell three billion dollars' worth of lire. Bordoni argued that such a scheme was impossible and said that even if the operation could be accomplished, it would cause the collapse of the lira. That, he said, would ruin Guido Carli, governor of the Bank of Italy. Laughing, Sindona said, "Right! The downfall of the governor is wanted not only by myself but also by Giulio Andreotti." Although Bordoni disapproved of Sindona's motive, he ultimately gave in for fear that Sindona, "the megalomaniac," would accuse him of "betraying the wishes of the Group," which Bordoni believed would have placed his life in jeopardy.

Bordoni knew that the plan could not be implemented without the financial support of several major banks throughout the world. As always, Michele Sindona and his son-in-law, Pier Sandro Magnoni, had already thought of a way to overcome this obstacle. They had Bordoni draft a letter on Westminster Bank's letterhead. The letter, in effect, granted Moneyrex the authority to purchase and sell currencies on Westminster's behalf, for the express purpose of causing the collapse of the lira. Unknown at the time to Bordoni, Sindona then had an employee forge the signature of Westminster's foreign exchange officer. This document lent credibility to Sindona's scheme. As a result, he was able to win the support of several banks. Among them were the First Boston Corporation, Union Bank of Switzerland, Bank of Nova Scotia, and Firestone Bank of Zurich. Of course, Fasco, A.G., and Sindona's banks—Banca Unione, Banca Privata Finanziaria, Finabank, and the German Bankhause Herstatt—were members of the consortium. The two most intriguing members, however, were the Vatican and the Soviet bank, Moscow Marodny.

After Bordoni, through Moneyrex, had taken a $3 billion bearish position in lire, Sindona revealed to him a second plan that was bullish on the U.S. dollar. At the time, the dollar was weak, and many European banks had been establishing a bearish position in dollars. Sindona believed, however, that the dollar would rally, so he told Bordoni to purchase an unlimited number of dollars balanced against a bearish position in any other currency. Risking the wrath that Sindona often vented when challenged or questioned, Bordoni disagreed, explaining that he had acquired secret information that the dollar would soon be devalued. Surprisingly, Sindona did not explode. Instead, he wrapped an arm around Bordoni and in a conspiratorial voice revealed that this "was a special operation ordered by certain U.S. authorities who had guaranteed not only eventual losses but who had also undertaken in writing, both to Fasco and Westminster, to pay them an attractive confidential commission." Sindona and Magnoni went on to say that because they were violating Italy's currency laws, "none of these gigantic operations should appear officially on the books of BU, BPF, or Finabank."

Bordoni did not believe Sindona's story. By now he realized that Sindona—who, he knew, had washed money for the CIA, been involved in at least one coup orchestrated and/or supported by the United States, and established a friendly relationship with U.S. Ambassador to Italy Graham Martin—also liked to "manipulate people through the use of blackmail and well-told lies." He concluded that Sindona was not acting on assurances from the United States. Instead, he believed that Michele Sindona, in a maniacal and devious way, intended to support the dollar—at the full risk of the other banks' and his bank's customers—in order to strengthen his image with the American public. Although Bordoni considered this a valid cause, he did not think it was worth risking the loss of billions of dollars.

Rather than follow Sindona's instructions, Bordoni took it upon himself to sell $1.5 billion and buy an equal amount in deutsche marks. In essence, he was gambling that the deutsche mark would increase in value against the dollar. He also purchased another 3.6 billion dollars' worth of deutsche marks, which he offset by selling an equal amount in Swiss francs. On February 12, 1973, when Treasury Secretary John Connally devalued the dollar by 10 percent, the Swiss franc also fell. Thanks to Bordoni's foresight, this created a $179 million profit for Fasco, A.G., Sindona's holding company. Sindona was extremely pleased that Bordoni had disobeyed his orders and had succeeded.

In the meantime, Sindona's plan to destroy the lira had begun to take effect. The lira rapidly lost value against the dollar, deutsche mark, and Swiss franc. Frantically, the Bank of Italy spent much of its reserves buying its own currency in an attempt to prevent a total collapse of the lira. As a result of continued pressure applied by Sindona's consortium, however, the lira continued to weaken, and Italy's bankruptcy seemed inevitable. Unable to learn where the pressure was coming from or who was behind it, Guido Carli finally acknowledged Michele Sindona's power by asking for his help. Although Sindona was the brains behind the conspiracy, he pretended to know nothing and promised Carli that he would look into the matter.

Sindona took a few days to evaluate the situation. By then, he had earned $30 million betting against the lira. Adding this to the previous earnings, Bordoni had produced a total profit of $209 million—all of which, Bordoni says, disappeared into Sindona's coffers. Of course, Sindona was satisfied with the success of the operations, but he was even more thrilled with the acknowledgment that he, Sindona, was more powerful then Guido Carli. He believed that if he played his hand perfectly, he would be proclaimed a national hero.

How Sindona handled this situation reveals not only how ruthless and cunning he could be but also how quickly he could switch allegiance in order to enhance his own status. Without the knowledge of his conspirators, Michele Sindona abandoned his plan to disgrace and force the resignation of the governor. Adopting the false role of an undercover agent, Sindona pretended that he had successfully infiltrated the organization responsible for attacking the lira and had discovered that Carlo Bordoni was its mastermind. Appearing saddened and ashamed, Sindona told Carli that Bordoni had never asked him for authorization because Bordoni knew that he loved Italy and would consider the plot an act of treason.

Now that he was aware of the conspiracy, Sindona explained, he would use all of his power and money to force Bordoni to close out all foreign exchange positions detrimental to the security of the lira. Because Michele Sindona was the true author of the scheme, this was easily accomplished. As a result of his betrayal of Bordoni and the consortium and his successful deception of Guido Carli, former prime minister Giulio Andreotti declared Michele Sindona "the savior of the lira."

An interesting note is that when inspectors from the Bank of Italy were reviewing the records of Sindona's banks after the collapse of his empire in 1974, they discovered $22 million in a fictitious account. To their surprise, the Vatican claimed the funds, explaining that it had given the money to Bordoni for the purpose of speculating on foreign exchange. Sindona and Bordoni had disguised the Vatican's ownership so well, however, that the Holy See failed to prove conclusively that the funds belonged to the church. Despite the Vatican's angry protest, Giorgio Ambrosoli, the liquidator of Sindona's empire, used the money to pay other creditors.

From the beginning, Carlo Bordoni had warned Michele Sindona and Pier Sandro Magnoni that if the plot to destroy Guido Carli and the lira was ever discovered and if they made him the scapegoat, he would "make them pay a high price." Then why did Sindona betray him? Probably because Sindona knew that Bordoni feared him and therefore lacked the courage to make good his threat. Although Sindona had correctly evaluated Carlo Bordoni, he had not taken into consideration the greed and vengeful will of Bordoni's wife. Virginia Bordoni proved to be as treacherous, devious, and cunning as Michele Sindona.

After learning that Sindona had not only compromised her husband's reputation with the Bank of Italy but had also refused to pay him the $4 million he had been promised for his efforts, Virginia relentlessly accused Carlo of being weak and spineless. She demanded he use his abilities to make them wealthy instead of Sindona. She badgered Carlo almost daily, insisting she deserved to live as well as Rina and Maria Elisa. She wanted the diamonds, the expensive clothes, the villa—all the trappings and prestige of wealth.

Carlo Bordoni was shamed by the frankness of his wife's assault. Wanting desperately to regain her respect, he assured her he would become more forceful. Together he and Virginia rehearsed the exact way in which he would handle Sindona. But their preparations proved to be an exercise in futility. Every attempt Bordoni made to confront Sindona failed miserably. He would freeze as soon as he looked into Sindona's eyes, or he would blurt out the whole story, demand more money, insist that promises be kept and that he be treated with respect. Then, after receiving either a scolding for not being grateful or assurances that things would be better, he would retreat and nothing would change. This was unacceptable to Virginia, who became depressed by her husband's willingness to allow himself to be dominated by Michele Sindona.

Virginia Bordoni eventually succeeded in forcing her husband to betray Michele Sindona. Apparently she destroyed his fear of Sindona by fabricating an incident in which she was the victim of an attempted rape—with Michele Sindona as the would-be rapist. Exactly when she conceived this is unknown. For approximately three months, Virginia withheld affection from Carlo. Finally, in Milan in March 1973, Carlo forcefully demanded an explanation. Virginia began to cry. When she recovered her composure, she told Carlo, "I have a terrible thing to tell you. In November [1972], while you were at the [Franklin] bank, Avvocato Sindona came to our apartment at the St. Regis. He said that he needed to speak with me about some important matters. After I let him in, he began to touch me. When I pushed his hand off my body, he became angry. He said that you were a fool, not a real man, that he could make you do anything—beg like a dog even. He said that he could make me feel like a woman, something you could never do, because a man who lacks courage cannot know how to make love to a woman. He said that I should be honored to have him, because he could have any woman he wanted, but that he had wanted me for so very long. Then he grabbed me and forced me to the floor. Fortunately, I hit him and freed myself. I ran to the door and screamed for him to leave. He smiled, saying that if I ever spoke of this to anyone he would not only deny it ever happened, he would also make his little puppet, meaning you, dance."

Upon hearing of the alleged episode, Bordoni broke into a rage. He immediately called Pier Sandro Magnoni and Nino Pedroni, an associate of the Sindona Group. After they arrived at Bordoni's apartment, Virginia related the story to them. "I cannot believe it," said Magnoni. "If it were true, I wouldn't hesitate one second in abandoning Sindona, and I would [suggest that you and I] work together." Pedroni, however, said, "I'm not surprised at all. Mr. Sindona has been involved in things like this on a number of occasions." Bordoni said that he was unsure what action he would take but that both men should inform Sindona of the matter. "Tell Sindona that he had better not meet with me, at least until I calm down," Bordoni told them, "because in this very moment I could do something irresponsible." Both men left with the clear impression that Bordoni was no longer afraid of Sindona but wanted to kill him.

Virginia was pleased with Carlo's response, for she had finally transformed her husband into a rebel. At the moment of rebellion, anger liberated Bordoni from the psychological bondage of fear, and he refused, no matter what the risk, to allow Michele Sindona to exert authority over him. To deny Sindona the right to humiliate him or make demands on him was not enough for Bordoni, however. Like any slave rebelling against a master, Bordoni wanted to avenge himself — to prove that he was now Sindona's equal.

Yet, although Bordoni had freed himself from Sindona's will, his emancipation was restricted by his love for Virginia, who, being both logical and shrewd, became his new master. She convinced Bordoni that revenge would be best served if he feigned loyalty to Sindona and the Group long enough to steal $45 million, through a complicated system of fraudulent trades in foreign exchange, from Sindona's banks and personal accounts. Virginia also persuaded Carlo to filter the money to a secret account that she controlled at the Union Bank of Switzerland.

To advance her scheme, they agreed that Carlo would pretend to believe Sindona's assertion that the attempted rape had never occurred and that Virginia was probably having a nervous breakdown and should be treated professionally. Their only risk was that Michele Sindona would realize that Carlo loved Virginia too much to take Sindona's word over hers. Fortunately for the couple, Sindona's lack of respect for Bordoni, coupled with his massive ego, neutralized his normally keen instincts and prevented him from uncovering or even suspecting the plot. So from the spring of 1973 to June 1974, Sindona, unaware that Bordoni was a traitor, continued to share secrets, legal and illegal, with him — while still disgracing Bordoni in front of others and refusing to fulfill his promises of financial reward.

16

BREAKING THE BANK

ALTHOUGH MICHELE SINDONA had resolved not to replace Harold Gleason, on the advice of David Kennedy he hired Peter Shaddick to head Franklin Bank's international division. Shaddick, a British subject, was highly respected in the international banking community as an expert in foreign exchange. From 1948 to 1959 Shaddick was employed by the Bank of England as its officer in charge of currency and gold trading. In 1957, while still employed by the Bank of England, he spent six months studying American banking procedures at the Federal Reserve Bank. From 1959 to 1968 Shaddick was vice-president in charge of foreign exchange activities for Continental Illinois National Bank — of which, at the time, David Kennedy was chairman. After Continental purchased an interest in Sindona's Banca Privata Finanziaria, Peter Shaddick represented Continental on the board of BPF and was also appointed to the board of directors of Finabank, Geneva.

Shaddick left Continental in 1968 to become executive vice-president of the Bank of Montreal, in Canada. When he took charge of the international trading department, its assets were $900 million, with net operating earnings representing 7 percent of the bank's earnings. By contrast, when Shaddick left the bank in January 1973 to join Franklin National Bank, the international department of the Bank of Montreal had grown to $2.8 billion and was producing 20 percent of the bank's total profits.

In November 1972 Peter Shaddick's wife, an American, said she was tired of living in Montreal and wanted to return to New York. Knowing that his old friend Michele Sindona had recently purchased control of Franklin National Bank, Shaddick met Sindona at the St. Regis and offered him his services. Had Shaddick been a character in a Paul Erdman novel, his arrival could not have been more timely. Sindona, having already earned substantial profits gambling in the currency market, was convinced that he and Bordoni could produce profits for the bank — which had just reported additional losses in the loan department — through extensive foreign exchange speculation. Until Shaddick made his appearance, however, the problem confronting Sindona was that he could not increase Franklin's foreign exchange activity without risking interference from the bank's management because he did not have control of the bank's international division.

Michele Sindona quickly recognized Peter Shaddick as the solution to his problem and persuaded Harold Gleason to hire him. After Gleason and Shaddick agreed on salary, Shaddick came aboard on January 1, 1973, as executive vice-chairman in charge of Franklin's international division. Although Sindona did not consider the newcomer a Group member, he bought Shaddick's loyalty by depositing $100,000 at Finabank, Geneva, under the code name Mr. New. Sindona told Gleason this transaction was a loan to help Shaddick pay relocation costs. Although this should have been disclosed when the board of directors approved Shaddick's employment contract, it was not mentioned.

A tall man with blue eyes and dark hair, Peter Shaddick ran Franklin's international department with complete autonomy. He did not report to Paul Luftig, president and chief operating officer, or to Harold Gleason, chairman and chief executive officer. In effect, under Shaddick's direction and control, the international department operated as a bank within a bank. And, as records clearly reveal, if Shaddick ever felt a moral obligation to Franklin Bank, it quickly decayed. After having been seduced by Sindona, with total disregard for the law and for the dangerous position in which he was placing the bank, by May 14, 1974, Shaddick had increased Franklin's foreign exchange trading from an average of $11 million, before Sindona, to $3.3 billion.

Reckless as Franklin's traders were, if Shaddick had guessed right, the bank would have made a fortune in foreign exchange profits and probably would not have failed. This, however, did not happen. Although Shaddick was receiving almost daily trading advice from Carlo Bordoni — who at the time was successfully producing profits for the Sindona consortium—Shaddick was unable to produce favorable results for Franklin Bank. His failure appears to have been caused, at least in part, by a scam of greater magnitude than any uncovered by the American and Italian authorities. While Carlo Bordoni advised Peter Shaddick and Andrew Garofalo, Franklin's head trader, to sell certain currencies in anticipation that the dollar would rise in value against those currencies, Bordoni was building a large bearish position against the dollar and the lira while purchasing other currencies. As Bordoni earned profits through the sale of dollars, he used Franklin as the vehicle to close out his positions and secure profits.

Ultimately, Franklin's foreign exchange department was responsible for the loss of $45.8 million. Whether this money found its way into the Bordonis' secret account at Union Bank of Switzerland or was part of the $209 million that Bordoni earned for Sindona is unknown. There is also the possibility that the collapse of Franklin National Bank as a result of foreign exchange losses was premeditated—for, in addition to stealing $45 million from Michele Sindona, Virginia and Carlo Bordoni may have conceived a plot to destroy Sindona's empire by engineering the collapse of Franklin Bank. As outrageous as this seems, one must remember that Bordoni was aware that Franklin was weak and that he considerably influenced Franklin's traders as to which currencies they should buy and sell.

Whatever Bordoni's reason for advising Franklin Bank to take a position opposite to his own position in the market, one must keep in mind that he and Shaddick conspired to conceal trading losses from Franklin's management as well as from the regulatory agencies. For example, although the international department reported a $69,000 profit at the end of January 1973, it had actually lost $436,000. Shaddick's records in May claimed a profit of $241,000 when, in fact, there had been a loss of $3.6 million. And in March 1974, instead of a $1 million profit, as claimed, there had actually been a loss of $19.3 million.

Yet Bordoni and Shaddick were not directly responsible for all of the foreign exchange losses that ultimately caused Franklin's failure. Working under tremendous pressure to produce profits in an atmosphere that promoted deception and fraud, some traders, including Andrew Garofalo, did not fill out the appropriate documents required to register foreign exchange contracts with the bank's processing department and, instead, hid in their desk drawers contracts revealing losses. Added to the Shaddick–Bordoni conspiracy, which blinded Franklin's management to the truth, this practice created duplicity and ignorance, for lack of knowledge prevented even Shaddick from correctly evaluating the bank's position in the extremely volatile currency market. Clearly, this deceit by individual traders had been fostered by the desire to preserve their jobs and, more likely, their reputations as competent currency specialists.

Compared with the rather simple methods of concealment employed by the traders, the techniques that Bordoni, Shaddick, and Sindona employed to mask losses were much more disciplined and criminal. Using fictitious nonmarket rates, they created false paper profits by manufacturing counterfeit foreign exchange contracts between Franklin and Amincor, and Franklin and Banca Unione. At the end of each quarter, Shaddick would report these false profits as real earnings to Franklin's board.

In September 1973 and March 1974, for example, Franklin suffered huge losses, both in foreign exchange speculation and in its bond trading department. To hide these losses from stockholders, management, and the authorities, Shaddick and Bordoni again produced artificial foreign exchange profits between Franklin and Amincor. Both times, however, Michele Sindona authorized an actual transfer of $2 million from Amincor to Franklin. Although this was another illegal and deceitful scheme invented by Sindona, the fact that he felt enough responsibility toward the bank to make a gift of $4 million is remarkable.

As already explained, Sindona's standard procedure was to use currency markets and bank secrecy laws to filter money out of his banks for the purpose of financing Group activities. On the two occasions in question, however, Sindona apparently feared that discovery and disclosure of massive foreign exchange losses would bring about a thorough investigation by the regulatory agencies. As a result, he temporarily altered his course.

In 1970 an unfulfilled and restless Arthur Roth accepted the challenge of building a new bank. By March 1973, as chairman of the Bank of Suffolk County in Stony Brook, Roth had cautiously increased deposits from $20 million to nearly $100 million.

Although he was actively involved in the daily operations of the new bank, Roth remained deeply concerned about the future of Franklin National. He kept constant watch on the direction in which Gleason and Sindona were taking the bank. From what his skeptical eye could see, he feared that Franklin was doomed unless management altered its course. One day in March 1973 Arthur Roth decided it was time once again to confront Michele Sindona.

Roth had not spoken with Sindona for six months. Nevertheless, he decided to pop in on him rather than make an appointment. This tactic, he believed, would produce an atmosphere in which the truth would be more difficult to camouflage, since Sindona would not have the opportunity to prepare evasive answers to his questions.

Roth found Sindona sitting at his desk at Franklin National Bank. To his surprise, Michele greeted him warmly and offered him coffee, which Roth refused.

"It's nice to see you, Mr. Roth," said Sindona. "I want you to feel you are always welcome. Whenever you want, come by and see me. Perhaps, we could even have lunch. There is a place I know that makes the best hamburgers."

"Mr. Sindona, I am worried about Franklin," Roth stated. "You said you were going to make changes, but Gleason is still here, and the annual report is frightening. All this short-term money you've brought into the bank is being lent on a long-term basis at interest rates much below Franklin's cost. It's very dangerous. The bank is growing too fast. It should be a $3.5 billion bank, but these thirty-, sixty-, and ninety-day deposits — they're pushing the bank toward $5 billion, way beyond its natural growth. Loans should be reduced by several hundred million. Too many municipal bonds are being purchased by the trading department. That's Gleason. You've got to replace him."

"Mr. Roth, it's not a year yet," Sindona politely insisted. "I asked you to give me a year and I would show you what would happen. I have a lot of problems here. I'm alone in this bank with a lot of directors who are strangers to me. Let me have a little time to work this out."

"There's too much gambling in foreign exchange. The word is some banks are afraid to deal with Franklin because of all the gambling. When I ran the bank, we never entered the currency market. Manufacturers Hanover never enters the market except on behalf of its customers. It's too risky."

"Give me a year, Mr. Roth. I'll look into everything you have mentioned. But in a year, as I said, you will see my results."

"The bank's stock is at twenty-four dollars a share," Roth said. "That's a whole lot below the forty dollars you bought it for."

Sindona remained silent.

Displeased that Sindona appeared evasive and unwilling to acknowledge the seriousness of the immediate problems within the bank, Roth began to suspect that his original impression of Sindona had been wrong. He sensed that Sindona's sincerity was an act too slick to trust. So he decided it was time to let Sindona know exactly what he intended to do.

"You're going to have a stockholders' meeting in a couple of months," Roth said. "That's why I've come here, Mr. Sindona. I'm thinking of attending that meeting, because I don't like the way things are going. In the past, so not to cause panic, I've stayed away from stockholders' meetings. I've stayed away from the bank. Now I feel things are going badly, and I owe it to the stockholders to go there and express my opinion."

Though Sindona considered this a threat, he successfully hid his anger. "Well, Mr. Roth," he said, "I would be glad to introduce you."

Roth left, both impressed and concerned. That Sindona had remained calm proved to Roth that he was a skilled opponent. He knew that Sindona and Gleason would be ready for him. They would attempt to destroy his credibility. They would make elaborate and misleading speeches, say the bank was crossing an important threshold on its way to becoming a worldwide financial institution. And there would be a trick. Perhaps David Kennedy would be present. If so, he would praise Sindona, and talk about Michele's long association with the Vatican.

None of this worried Roth. He prepared his presentation as meticulously as he had planned all the battles he had won. He gathered hard evidence, facts and figures, to destroy whatever illusion Sindona would try to create. He hoped this would be the greatest of all his victories. He wanted to save Franklin National Bank and its stockholders from disaster.

Arthur Roth evaluated his strategy as he rode the elevator to the ground floor. Later, however, as he walked out onto Park Avenue and looked back at the bank he had worked so hard to build, he suddenly realized that a public showdown could cause stockholders and depositors to lose confidence in the stability of the bank. Since Roth's objective was to save Franklin, not to create a run on the bank, he abandoned his plan to speak at the stockholders' meeting. Instead, Arthur Roth decided to take his evidence to James Smith, the comptroller of the currency. He would persuade Smith to use his authority to replace Franklin's management, stop foreign exchange speculation, and reduce loans. This strategy, Roth believed, would save Franklin and prevent panic.

Some time around March 1973 Michele Sindona told Harold Gleason that Franklin New York Corporation, the holding company that owned Franklin Bank, should buy Talcott National, a Chicago-based financing and factoring company that was losing money. At the time, acquisition of finance companies by bank holding companies was fashionable. Such a move expanded the financial and geographical operations of the bank.

Sindona said that he had arranged for Franklin New York Corporation to buy controlling interest of Talcott at $24 a share. Gleason called a meeting of the senior officers of the bank to discuss the acquisition of Talcott. They rejected the suggestion, deciding that Talcott was "an excessively priced dog."

About two weeks later Gleason was at the bank when the Dow Jones ticker revealed that Laurence Tisch, still a director of Franklin Bank, made a tender offer of $16 a share for Talcott stock on behalf of Loews Corporation. That same night Dan Porco called Gleason at home and advised him that Sindona planned to top the Tisch offer. Gleason warned Porco against Sindona's making any representations involving Franklin. Porco assured him that Sindona would be offering $17 a share through Fasco International, the same Luxembourgian holding company through which Sindona had purchased Franklin. Porco also said that if this bid succeeded, Sindona intended to offer his shares to Franklin at his cost plus interest.

On March 30, when Sindona publicized his tender offer in the *Wall Street Journal* and the *New York Times*, Tisch withdrew his offer rather than enter a bidding war with Sindona. By April 6 Fasco's escrow agent, William O'Neil & Company, had received 1.6 million shares, representing 53 percent of Talcott's outstanding shares. On that same day Carlo Bordoni transferred $27,180,000 from Banca Unione to Amincor in favor of Fasco International. Fasco then wired the funds to the escrow agent. Upon receipt of those funds, controlling interest of Talcott was transferred to Sindona.

Like the purchase of Franklin Bank, the transaction between BU and Amincor was a fiduciary contract. By then, however, Sindona had received the $90 million from Roberto Calvi; the money was on deposit at Finabank, Geneva. Sindona had instructed Bordoni to place a lien against the funds to cover the fiduciary contract, but Bordoni failed to follow Sindona's order. Whether this failure was the result of negligence or a willful oversight, or a combination of both, is unclear.

Was Bordoni's failure to place a lien on Sindona's account at Finabank deliberate? He knew Sindona had offered Talcott to Franklin and that Harold Gleason had accepted the new terms and had requested permission from the Federal Reserve Board to close the deal. Bordoni also knew that the Federal Reserve Board, in order to evaluate the Talcott proposal, had decided to investigate Sindona's role at Franklin to determine if Sindona influenced the policymaking decisions of the bank. Anticipating that the Federal Reserve Board would eventually demand proof that Sindona had purchased Franklin and Talcott with his own money, Carlo Bordoni may have neglected to prepare those documents with the intention of creating legal problems for Sindona. Such a step, of course, would have served his objective, which was to destroy Michele Sindona.

As complex and manipulative as this plan appears, several facts support the theory that this was indeed Bordoni's aim. One is that Bordoni had been stealing from Sindona and the Group. Another is that Bordoni planned to leave the Group, take his money, and move to South America—leaving Sindona to drown in a whirlpool of legal problems. Finally, and this establishes premeditation, Bordoni copied thousands of documents, including the fiduciary contracts used to purchase Franklin National Bank and Talcott National, and hid them in a safe deposit box at Union Bank of Switzerland.

The Federal Reserve Board never asked for documents relating to the purchase of Franklin and Talcott, so the collapse of Franklin Bank and Sindona's empire was stalled for another year. As Carlo and Virginia Bordoni patiently awaited the opportunity to avenge themselves, they continued to steal and hide documents they would one day use against Michele Sindona. In the meantime, unaware of the Bordonis' plot, Michele Sindona was constructing his most ambitious scheme to date.

17

THE TWO HUNDRED
MILLION DOLLAR GAMBLE

IN JULY 1973 Michele Sindona proposed the creation of the largest financial institution in Italian history. His plan was to merge Società Generale Immobiliare — the construction and financial corporation that built the Watergate complex and was owned partly by Sindona and the Vatican — with Edilcentro Sviluppo, another financial corporation owned and controlled by the Group. To accomplish this, both companies would be sold to a third company, which would sell its stock to the public. Getting the approval of the Italian authorities to form a new Italian holding company, however, would have been time-consuming, so Sindona purchased Finambro — a tiny, Palermo-based furniture company controlled by the Mafia.

Although Finambro's capital was only $1,200, Sindona intended to increase it by $200 million through a stock issue. This wonderful idea made Sindona quite happy; while he would earn $22 million, he would also retain enough stock to keep control of Finambro. There was only one obstacle: to increase Finambro's capital, Sindona needed authorization from the Interministerial Credit Committee chaired by Treasury Minister Ugo La Malfa.

A short, dark man with thick glasses and a film of gray blotches covering his eyes, La Malfa was also a vice-governor of the International Monetary Fund and chairman of Italy's left-of-center Republican party. A quiet man who believed in sound economics, he was an idealist tormented and shamed by the political corruption that had infected his country. Although he spent his life fighting for change, many businessmen, including Michele Sindona, attempted to destroy his reputation, claiming he was pro-communist, for La Malfa supported and promoted nationalization and was a close friend and colleague of Enrico Cuccia, Sindona's archenemy.

Though Ugo La Malfa and Michele Sindona never met, a single act caused them to become bitter enemies: when the Finambro application came across his desk, La Malfa discussed it with and sought the advice of Enrico Cuccia.

This was the opportunity Cuccia had been awaiting for nine years. Time and patience, two commodities that shape and feed the extraordinary life of a Sicilian vendetta, had strengthened Cuccia's hate for Michele Sindona. Cuccia had never forgiven Sindona for the Sofina–Suez oil refinery deal, and the years had quietly intensified his desire to get even. He told La Malfa that Finambro appeared to be a typical Sindona scheme, and he insisted that the application for an increase in capital be denied.

Michele Sindona, however, had anticipated Cuccia's interference. To counter his enemy's influence over Ugo La Malfa, Sindona turned to old friends—Giulio Andreotti, then prime minister, and Senator Amintore Fanfani, then secretary of the Christian Democratic party. At the time, the lira was under tremendous pressure because of the currency manipulations devised by Michele Sindona. No one knew, however, that Sindona and his Group were responsible. When Sindona spoke with Andreotti and Fanfani, he blamed the inflation and the weakness of the lira on Enrico Cuccia, Ugo La Malfa, Guido Carli—and on everyone who stood to the left of Andreotti's ruling Christian Democrats.

Furthermore, Sindona said, the only way to strengthen the lira and reverse inflation was to bring new investment capital into Italy. To this end, he said, the capitalization of Finambro had to be approved. Because of his own dynamic personality and powerful contacts, Sindona boasted, a group of foreign investors—whose identities had to remain secret—had committed an amount equal to approximately $150 million to the project. Before the funds would be released, however, Sindona needed Fanfani's and Andreotti's assurance that the Interministerial Credit Committee would approve Finambro.

Convinced that Sindona's plan was advantageous to Italy's economy, and because the majority of members of the credit committee were Christian Democrats, Fanfani assured Sindona that Finambro would be approved. "La Malfa," Fanfani said, "has the obligation to call a meeting of the committee and there the authorization will be granted, because La Malfa will be alone against everyone."

Shortly after receiving their support, Sindona's banks increased the amount and frequency of payments secretly made to the Christian Democratic party. The $150 million in foreign capital was filtered into Finambro and was immediately diverted to one of Sindona's Lichtensteinian corporations as payment for the Immobiliare and Sviluppo shares he had transferred to Finambro. Now all Sindona had to do was wait for the credit committee to meet and authorize the sale of Finambro stock.

Fate, however, had been slowly and methodically turning against Michele Sindona. Just before the committee was to meet and vote on Finambro, Michele's supporters were frightened by a strange and horrifying episode that caused the Italian press to question the legalities of Finambro and to suspect Sindona's Mafia connections.

In July 1973, several months after ABC's Rome correspondent, Jack Begon, age sixty-two, had broadcast his radio report, "Hot Dollars," the journalist was contacted by Angelo Sorino, a Palermo police detective. Sorino told Begon he had documents that conclusively proved Michele Sindona did, in fact, attend the Mafia meeting at the Grand Hôtel des Palmes in Palermo and had made an agreement with Lucky Luciano to become the banker for organized crime in the United States and Sicily. Sorino said he wanted $5,000 for the documents. Begon had received numerous Mafia-style threats when his report was first aired, but now that Sindona was back in the news with the Finambro deal, he could not resist the opportunity that Sorino offered him. He agreed to a secret meeting on Sunday, July 22, 1973.

On the day of the meeting, Begon told his wife he was going to his office to interview Richard Burton and Elizabeth Taylor. While the journalist was in his office making last-minute preparations for his meeting with Angelo Sorino, two men described later as American mafiosi entered the office, ransacked it, and kidnapped Begon. During the next month, the Italian press published rumors that, because of his investigation into the Mafia, Begon had been abducted by the CIA, the FBI, or the Mafia.

On August 18, 1973, Jack Begon suddenly reappeared. Exhausted and frightened, he checked into a clinic in Rome. Two days later, while still recuperating, he was served a warrant of arrest. Later, at a hearing, Begon testified that as a result of his investigation of Michele Sindona's role in washing and reinvesting Mafia drug profits, he had been kidnapped by American gangsters and had been forced to fly to the United States.

Begon said, "After being questioned by a number of different people in several cities, including St. Louis, New Orleans, and Las Vegas, I finally convinced everyone that I had no dangerous information and that I would keep my promise not to attempt to get additional information or follow up the story in any way. I intend to keep my promise, regardless of what may happen to me."

As one American journalist wrote, the Begon incident "reads like a chapter from The Godfather." Initially the Italian magistrate argued that

Begon's story was too sensational to believe, so he charged Begon for sim-
ulating a crime and ordered a full-scale investigation. The authorities ultimately gathered significant proof to support Begon's claim. They had even
discovered Begon's source, but before they could interview Angelo Sorino,
the police officer was shot to death, Mafia-style, on a street in Palermo in
January 1974.

Because of the multiplicity of events — the Jack Begon episode, Enrico Cuccia's interference, the refusal of the governor of the Bank of Italy to
write a report favoring the approval of Finambro — Ugo La Malfa decided
the only way to ensure that he would not be overruled by the Interministerial Credit Committee was to sit on the Finambro application.
Although his party was offered enormous cash payments as an incentive
to persuade him to do otherwise, La Malfa stood firmly behind his decision
for eighteen months and refused to call a meeting of the committee.

In December 1973 Banca di Roma was underwriting an eight-year billion-
dollar bond issue for Crediop, an acronym for Consorzio de Credito per le
Opere Publiche, an Italian governmental agency that financed public projects. The normal practice of an agent bank is to ensure the success of a
bond issue by acquiring purchase commitments from other banks in case
all the bonds are not sold to the public.

Sensing an opportunity to win support for Finambro by helping an
institution owned by the Italian government, Michele Sindona secretly
convinced Peter Shaddick to commit Franklin National Bank as a backup
purchaser of last resort for $200 million. In effect, Sindona and Shaddick
had obligated Franklin to make Banca di Roma a loan. This was illegal
because an American bank's legal lending limit per loan was 10 percent of
its capital, which in Franklin's case was only $15 million. Furthermore,
the offer was invalid because neither Sindona nor Shaddick was authorized
to contract the bank for such an operation without receiving ratification
by the board of directors.

As a reward for his assistance, Michele Sindona allowed Peter Shaddick to open a trading account at Finabank. The conditions agreed upon
were quite unusual and irregular. Shaddick, for example, was permitted to
trade in foreign currency without placing money up for margin. Sindona
also promised that if Shaddick guessed wrong, he would not be forced to
cover losses. As a result, Shaddick earned $476,000 in less than a month.
On January 16, 1974, Bordoni deposited the funds in Shaddick's "Mr.
New" account at Finabank. Shaddick was extremely happy and continued
to conceal the illegal Crediop transaction from Franklin's management.

Only by chance did Harold Gleason learn of Crediop, in February 1974,
while visiting with Walter Page, president of Morgan Guaranty Trust

Company. A large, balding, serious-looking man in his fifties, Page was a typical Morgan president, carefully groomed to represent the bank's high standards and conservative approach to finances. Page's wood-paneled office at 23 Wall Street and his Long Island home in exclusive Cold Spring Harbor, with separate telephone listings for servants, reflected his position as chief executive officer of one of the most respected banks in the world.

With Gleason were Peter Shaddick and Norman Schreiber, former chairman of Walter E. Heller Corporation, an extremely profitable Chicago-based finance company. Recruited by David Kennedy and Michele Sindona to improve Franklin's profits, Schreiber had joined the bank in January 1974 as chairman of the executive committee. A seventy-year-old man of medium height and frame, with rimless glasses, narrow eyes, and sunken cheeks, Schreiber had broad investigative powers in all departments and divisions of the bank, received the same salary as Harold Gleason, and reported to no one except the board. In command of his authority and responsibility, Schreiber raced through the bank, auditing departments, analyzing every single detail, and issuing strong directives outlining changes. Because of his quick, abrupt manner and silver hair, Franklin's staff nicknamed him "the White Tornado."

While Shaddick was chatting with Louis Preston, an associate of Walter Page, Gleason and Schreiber listened to Page as he expressed his concern about Franklin's rapid expansion in foreign operations. An old friend of Gleason and a longtime supporter of Franklin, Page had been instrumental in getting Franklin into the New York Clearinghouse Association, making it the first new member in twenty-eight years. It was therefore natural for Page to worry about Franklin's heavy gambling in foreign exchange and its acceptance of short-term foreign deposits. In a fatherly way, Page counseled Gleason to slow down and consolidate Franklin's position, to strengthen its base and reduce the international division's activities before things got out of hand and other banks became too frightened to deal with Franklin.

As he was calmly advising Gleason and Schreiber that they needed to curtail the international division's momentum, Page overheard Shaddick tell Preston, "Franklin has reduced its foreign operations drastically, to a coins-and-stamps operation."

Immediately, Page turned his attention to Shaddick and asked, "You are? Then what are you doing in that big Italian credit deal?"

"It's been sold," Shaddick quickly but nervously said.

"It has?" Page's soft and steady voice was layered with doubt. "Then what are you doing offering the bonds around town?"

"It's been sold!" insisted Shaddick.

Though Walter Page appeared calm, he must have known that Shaddick was lying. As a result, the conversation became strained, and in a few minutes Gleason, Schreiber, and Shaddick left Page's office.

All three men remained silent until they had settled into Gleason's limousine and were headed back to Franklin National Bank. Finally, Schreiber confronted Shaddick. "What was that Italian-loan business all about?" he asked.

"You heard me," Shaddick said. "They've been sold."

"While Page was cordial and all," Gleason said, "he meant it when he gave us his opinion on our international activity. We've got to go slower. If Morgan refused to deal with Franklin in spot or future contracts, it would spread like wildfire and affect us adversely with other banks worldwide."

Nothing more was said.

On March 3, 1974, with several banks so frightened by Franklin's volume in foreign exchange speculation that they were threatening to stop clearing futures contracts for the bank, Gleason and Shaddick flew to Europe. In fact, the situation was so bad that the Deutsche Bank of Frankfurt had already refused to clear both spot and future contracts for Franklin Bank.

Gleason and Shaddick spent six days on a goodwill tour of banks in Frankfort and London. Upon their return on March 10, Gleason found Schreiber angry, upset, and worried. He told Gleason he had checked into the Italian credit situation mentioned by Page and had discovered that the bonds had not been sold. Instead, Shaddick had executed a scam to make it appear as if they had been sold.

Apparently, in a bearish market, Banca di Roma had been unable to sell $96.5 million of the $200 million in bonds Sindona had guaranteed Franklin would purchase as a buyer of last resort. Because of Shaddick's lie to Page, Gleason, and Schreiber and because Franklin could not legally purchase the bonds, Sindona had to find a way to cover the purchase in order to save face with Banca di Roma.

Sindona decided that a division of SGI, Edilcentro International Limited, a small merchant bank in Nassau, Bahamas, with capital of only $1 million, would assume Franklin's $96.5 million commitment. Following Sindona's directions, Shaddick then ordered Franklin's London branch to credit the account of Edilcentro for $96.5 million. By handling the matter in this way, Sindona had again circumvented the law, for although Edilcentro bought the remaining bonds, it did so with Franklin's money. If Franklin had asked to withdraw the deposit, Edilcentro would not have been able to return the funds.

Immediately after Schreiber related this scheme, Harold Gleason held an emergency meeting in his office. In attendance were Paul Luftig, president; Ray Anderson, new chief loan officer; Peter Shaddick; Norman Schreiber; and Jerry Feller, the bank's attorney. Deciding what action management should take was complicated by the question of whether or not to report the illegal transaction to the authorities. The bankers feared that the resultant publicity might cause a serious panic, which could lead to a great number of withdrawals.

During the meeting, tempers flared. Anderson and Shaddick nearly slugged it out. At one point, Shaddick asked if Gleason wanted him to resign. Recognizing the gravity of the situation, Gleason ignored the question. At the time, he had to make a more important decision, and if he was wrong, his decision could destroy the bank. Furthermore, the longer the meeting went on, the fewer options he had.

Finally, Gleason called Sindona and explained how Schreiber had uncovered the transaction and that it was illegal. He said that he would either have to get Franklin out of the deal or inform the authorities of its existence. Sindona was furious. He could not understand why Gleason and the others were making such a big issue of this situation. Gleason insisted that something had to be done quickly and said that he was immediately sending the bank's lawyer, Jerry Feller, to Rome, to make sure that Sindona resolved the problem.

"They're ganging up on me," screamed Sindona. "Fire Schreiber, fire Anderson, fire the lawyers. I'll personally pay their replacements."

Gleason responded by repeating what had to be done, then put the receiver down.

Later that same day, at Sindona's request, David Kennedy promptly left Chicago for New York. Peter Shaddick picked Kennedy up at the airport and drove him to Sindona's office at Franklin National Bank, where Gleason and Schreiber met him. Though he had already been briefed by Shaddick, it was not until he had reviewed the documents with Schreiber that Kennedy fully realized the imminent danger in which Sindona had placed Franklin.

"He must get the bank out!" Kennedy shouted, as he tossed the papers aside. "Get him on the phone. He must get it out, now!"

Harold Gleason spent the next seven days and nights under intense pressure. The stress was so intense that he was unable to eat or sleep well. His mind must have been fragmented by fear and doubt as he wondered if his decision to try to save the bank was the right one. Was he protecting the bank or Michele Sindona? As each day passed, the stress increased. The fear that an examiner from the comptroller's office would pull a surprise audit left him weak, dizzy, and dry-mouthed. Intimidated by the dark side of reality, he examined the possibility that power and position had corrupted his judgment. Had he betrayed himself? Should he have protected himself by informing the board of directors and the regulatory agencies of the illegality? After all, Sindona had wanted to replace him. How could he have been so stupid? The life of the bank depended on Michele Sindona's ability to untangle the financial mess he had created, and so did Gleason's personal liberty. Then he was left with a question: could Michele Sindona cover the $96.5 million? By the morning of March 17, having heard nothing concrete or encouraging, Harold Gleason must have been tormented by the growing suspicion that the answer to the question was no.

But when Jerry Feller called Harold Gleason from Rome that same morning, he had good news. Franklin National Bank was out of danger. Sindona, Shaddick, and Bordoni had finally resolved the Crediop–Edilcentro contract through a series of complex transactions between Fasco and Banca di Roma. Gleason relaxed. He had gambled with Sindona and had won — at least for now.

Without delay, Gleason placed a call to Michele Sindona to thank him for solving the problem. To his surprise, however, Sindona was still angry.

"This has caused me great embarrassment!" yelled Sindona. "It personally cost me $10 million and has damaged my relationship with Banca di Roma. I have lost prestige just because Schreiber wanted to make a big thing out of nothing."

"While this caused you some embarrassment, Michele, it put the Franklin in a dreadful position," Gleason stated firmly. "Had I been forced to bring the matter to the attention of the directors, I have no idea what the consequences would have been."

Nothing Gleason said seemed to soothe Sindona's temper. "I want everyone fired!" he screamed. "Everyone — Schreiber, Anderson, the lawyer — everyone!"

"Look, Michele," Gleason said, "I have to go to Mexico City for the opening of Franklin's representative office. When I get back, I'll see you. We can talk more."

"All right!"

Ironically, had Franklin's management not disrupted Sindona's Crediop–Edilcentro scheme, had he succeeded without any problems, he still would not have been able to get Finambro approved. In fact, even though the Christian Democrats had forced Ugo La Malfa to resign his post as treasury minister in February 1974, Michele Sindona still could not get approval for Finambro's increase in capital. The gambler's luck had suddenly turned against him.

In March 1974 a new referendum granting Italians the right to divorce had been drafted by the left. In Italy this was a serious political crusade. If the Italians voted in favor of the referendum, they would in effect be striking a blow against the Vatican's thirty-year dominance over

Italian politics through its political arm, the Christian Democrats. Pope Paul VI and the leading members of the Christian Democratic party — Giulio Andreotti, Amintore Fanfani, Raffaello Scarpetti, and Fillippo Micheli, all of whom were among Michele Sindona's strongest allies — had to devote their energy to the campaign against the divorce statute.

This was very unpleasant for Don Michele. It meant that Finambro's approval would be postponed. Furthermore, if the Vatican lost this fight, the Christian Democrats would be politically crippled and Finambro would be permanently lost.

This was the single most nerve-racking period in Sindona's career. He lacked control over a political issue and although he thought the issue was stupid, he knew that it threatened to destroy his entire empire. The $150 million used to purchase Sindona's interest in Immobiliare and Sviluppo — which he claimed had come from foreign investors — had actually been siphoned from the deposits of his Italian banks. Sindona had done this because he anticipated the quick approval of the Finambro stock issue. That approval would have allowed Sindona to replace the funds he had drawn from his depositors' accounts. Now, however, if the Vatican and Christian Democrats failed to defeat the divorce bill, Sindona's banks would face a possible liquidity crisis.

Not comfortable with the odds, Sindona decided to buy insurance. He delivered $2 million in cash to Raffaello Scarpetti and Fillippo Micheli to help cover the cost of the crusade. Then he waited, hoping that on May 12, 1974, the public would support the pope and vote against divorce.

PART
III

THE FALL

PRIVATE ENTERPRISE AND THE ENTREPRENEUR'S RIGHTS SHOULD BE SAFEGUARDED, BUT
NO ONE SHOULD BE IMMUNE FROM BEING PENALIZED FOR HIS OWN INCOMPETENCE.

MICHELE SINDONA,
JUNE 12, 1975, IN A SPEECH AT
THE GRADUATE SCHOOL OF
BUSINESS ADMINISTRATION,
NEW YORK UNIVERSITY

18

THE CRISIS

WHILE MICHELE SINDONA was in Italy struggling to save his empire and preserve the Vatican's power, on the other side of the Atlantic Arthur Roth presented Charles Van Horn, regional director of the Comptroller of the Currency in New York, with a detailed and devastating analysis of Franklin Bank's annual report for 1973. The meeting took place at Van Horn's office on March 19, 1974.

"Hogwash! Cover-up!" Roth declared. "The front page of the annual report tells the story. It shows warm and beautiful sunshine and a nice climate. But it is a setting sun for Franklin National Bank. That is the truth of what it is. If Sindona and Gleason continue to control Franklin's destiny, the bank will soon fail. Read my analysis of the report. It's all there. You can't argue with the figures."

In substance, Roth's report stated that a number of conditions—the size and value of the municipal bond portfolio, the foreign exchange trading account, the loss ratio of loans, the high ratio of loans against volatile deposits, the tax loss carry-forward, and the number of volatile foreign deposits—were unsatisfactory. Management's dependency on high-rate interest funds, certificates of deposit, and federal funds was dangerous because the bank lent the money out for long terms at lower rates than its cost, gambling that the cost of money would drop. The adequacy of capital funds, the retention of earnings after dividends, the liquidity, the profit margin—in other words, all the trends—were dispiriting. Morale was low, and there was no communication between department heads and the board.

"The cause of this," Roth said, "is incompetence stemming from top management, [the failure] of the directors to take full remedial action, and the lack of full disciplinary action by the supervisory authorities."

"I agree with you on everything . . . except one point," Van Horn said. "That is what you say about the lack of disciplinary action by the supervisory authorities."

"I am sorry, but that is my analysis of it and the way I feel about it," Roth insisted. "You have to realize the bank is in a dangerous position. What is the solution? An immediate takeover—promptly!"

Van Horn did not agree that a merger was necessary. "I have some good news for you," he said. "You may have read in the newspapers that the bank has now employed Norman Schreiber, who is the retired chairman of the board of Walter E. Heller, one of the finest finance companies in the country. Schreiber believes he can completely turn the bank around by the end of the year. In fact, he has already made substantial progress in that direction. Do you know him, Mr. Roth?"

"No."

"Why don't you call him?"

"No," Roth said. "You should call him. You tell him exactly what happened here today—that I gave you an analysis of everything I found unsatisfactory and that you said to me that I should meet him because he would have some good news for me."

Van Horn agreed to call Norman Schreiber. He also suggested that Roth go to Washington and meet with the comptroller of the currency, James Smith. Roth said he would see Smith, but first he wanted to talk with Schreiber.

Roth and Schreiber met for dinner on the evening of March 21 at the Westbury Manor, a small, elegant restaurant in Nassau County. Roth told Schreiber that in the past forty-eight hours he had learned many things about him and was impressed.

"You're a doer," Roth said. "That's what the bank needs. Someone who will take charge. I told Mr. Sindona the bank had no right to be a $5 billion bank. It must be shrunk to $3.5 billion. I told him Gleason had to be replaced. I warned Mr. Sindona of all the things I mention in my analysis. He asked me to give him a year. 'In a year, Mr. Roth,' he said, 'you will see my results.' Well, it's been a year, and it's now obvious to me that he conned me into believing he would be good for the bank. My initial concerns about Sindona, where his money came from, the Mafia, that he was a gambler—all of it was true. Why the regulatory agencies did not investigate him, I don't know. Perhaps David Kennedy had influence there. The point is, Sindona has done nothing right. Now it's up to you, Norman. You must stop the speculation in foreign exchange. You know, I have heard that [Franklin is] speculating that the dollar will improve in value when it is constantly going down. Over a billion dollars in currency operations—that's insane. You've got to get Gleason and Sindona out of the bank, Norman. Morgan Guaranty has told [Gleason and Sindona] they would have to stop speculating or [Morgan Guaranty] would stop doing business with Franklin. But nothing has changed. You've got to reduce this speculation to $50 million, and you have to reduce loans by $700 million, municipal bonds by $100 million, and the securities trading account by $100 million because [Franklin] should not own more than $10 million in securities."

Schreiber said he agreed with most of Roth's points, but he believed that loans should be reduced by $500 million instead of $700 million. He explained that he was making up charts outlining a program designed to consolidate the bank's position and reduce speculation. Though Gleason and Sindona controlled the board, he said he was sure the directors would approve his plan.

Roth liked Schreiber. He believed Schreiber knew what he was doing. They would be allies. Sweeping changes would be made.

Later, as Arthur Roth was driving home, he was startled to hear himself cry out suddenly. In that moment he felt the joy of a great burden having been lifted from him. He had won his crusade: Harold Gleason would be removed from the bank and Roth would help pick a new chief executive officer. The plague that had infected Franklin since July 1972 would end: Michele Sindona would no longer influence bank policy. Roth looked forward to the exhausting struggle to reverse the damage Sindona had caused. He was eager to help put Franklin National Bank in order. He would enjoy working with Norman Schreiber.

Emotions, however, could not betray Arthur Roth's mind. He had trained it to record details he otherwise failed to see or hear. As his memory track replayed his conversation with Schreiber, his happiness quickly evaporated, and sadness overwhelmed him. He suddenly remembered that Schreiber had been nervous as they discussed the removal of Michele Sindona. Had Roth been tricked into believing that he had extracted a commitment from Schreiber? Had Schreiber shrewdly evaded the issue by feigning enthusiastic support of Roth's devastating analysis of the bank's position? The questions haunted Roth. He was confused. Instinct told him Schreiber was honest, but it also warned him that something was wrong. He decided to take a closer look at Schreiber.

The next morning, after calling several bankers in Chicago and New

York, Arthur Roth understood why Schreiber had been uneasy and eva-sive while discussing Michele Sindona. He now knew that Michele Sin-dona and David Kennedy had personally recruited Norman Schreiber. This troubled Roth. Although everything bankers said about Schreiber was positive and although he felt that Schreiber honestly intended to try to cure the wounds Gleason and Sindona had inflicted on Franklin, Roth feared that Schreiber's relationship with Michele Sindona would compro-mise his independence, his effectiveness, and his loyalty to the bank.

This would have concerned Roth less if he had known of Schreiber's role in the Crediop episode, for he would have realized that Schreiber had already demonstrated his independence and his moral obligation to the depositors and stockholders of Franklin Bank. Yet, because Schreiber had neglected to admit that Sindona had had a negative influence on the bank, Roth probably would have arrived at the same opinion of Schreiber even if he'd been aware of the Crediop episode.

No matter how honorable Schreiber seemed to be, Roth would not allow the fate of Franklin National Bank to be determined by the strength of one man's character. It was not fair to the stockholders, to the deposi-tors, or even to Norman Schreiber, for Roth had to admit that even he had been temporarily duped by Sindona.

Roth felt that the responsibility was his. He had taken it on in 1934 when he assumed the burden of nurturing a sick bank. Now it was his duty to save his bank and its stockholders. He would go to Washington the first week in April and force James Smith, the comptroller of the currency, to admit that his office had been negligent regarding the approval of Michele Sindona's purchase of Franklin National Bank. Roth would demonstrate that Franklin was headed for disaster and he would motivate Smith to take immediate action by making the comptroller realize that a catastrophe at Franklin would strike a devastating blow to Smith's reputa-tion.

During the first quarter of 1974, as a result of a combination of events, the dollar depreciated against other major currencies. Having bet that the dol-lar would rise, by March 26 Franklin had accumulated a loss of more than $7 million in foreign exchange. This crisis, if exposed, would generate panic worldwide.

At the time, Michele Sindona and David Kennedy were in London, attempting to negotiate the purchase of the Hyatt hotel chain, and Peter Shaddick and Harold Gleason were in Mexico City. From there, Peter Shaddick placed a person-to-person call to Michele Sindona and informed him of the bank's position. Sindona's response was typical: fearing that disclosure might cause the Federal Reserve Board to reject Franklin's pro-posed acquisition of Talcott, Sindona instructed Shaddick to conceal the facts from the regulatory agencies and from Franklin's board of directors. It would be necessary to falsify Franklin's quarterly report, he said, by fabricating profitable currency transactions between Franklin and Amincor. Creating fictitious profits would camouflage the truth, protect the bank from a potentially explosive situation, and, he hoped, ease the Federal Reserve Board's concerns about Franklin and its approval of Talcott. Shaddick agreed.

Sindona said he would discuss the matter with Carlo Bordoni. If there were further instructions, he or Bordoni would be in touch.

Although Harold Gleason had returned to New York two days earlier, he was kept ignorant of the foreign exchange losses. In fact, while Shaddick was talking with Sindona, Gleason was on board a TWA plane bound for London. The purpose of Gleason's trip was to meet with Michele Sindona and David Kennedy at Claridge's Hotel to discuss the Crediop affair.

Gleason was acting in good faith. Sindona was Franklin's major stockholder, he had lost $10 million, and he was still angry and paranoid. As Franklin's chief executive officer—unaware that Sindona and Shaddick had constructed another scheme—Gleason felt an obligation to explain why it had been necessary to release Franklin from the Crediop contract.

Gleason quickly discovered that Michele Sindona did not appreciate his effort. While David Kennedy stood silent, resting his weight on the back of a chair staring directly into Gleason's eyes, Michele Sindona unleashed his wrath. He said that there had been no valid reason for everyone to gang up on him, and he repeated that he wanted Norman Schreiber, Jerry Feller, and Ray Anderson fired.

Gleason was nervous and a bit frightened, for Sindona acted like a psychopath. He would "pace back and forth like a caged animal," screaming profanities and making demands. Then, when one of many phone calls interrupted his rage, he would switch personalities. Instantly, Sindona would gain control of his emotions and thoughts. Rationally, he would speak in Italian to someone—probably Bordoni or Shaddick. (Although Gleason had studied Italian, Sindona spoke too fast for Gleason to understand what was said.) Just as rapidly, at the conclusion of each call, Sindona would again change: his eyes would appear wide and cold, an expression of anger and hate would spread across his brow, and his voice would explode as he continued his assault.

Finally, Gleason was given an opportunity to speak. He said that Crediop was a "serious matter, a grave matter." He repeated what he had told Sindona before leaving for Mexico City. He also suggested that Sindona be grateful he and Schreiber had not reported the illegal transaction to the board, for with all the questions and rumors circulating in the banking community about Sindona, the authorities would have had no choice but to kick him out of the bank.

Sindona said that no one would ever toss him out of the Franklin. He was too powerful. His friends in Washington had always protected his interests and would continue to do so. Again he ordered Gleason to fire everyone. Gleason refused. Inflamed by Gleason's stand, Sindona lowered his voice to a vengeful whisper: "Know what you are doing. It is your decision. One day you will have to answer for it."

The meeting ended. Sindona and Kennedy had another appointment. As Gleason prepared to leave, Sindona added, "At least Crediop has proven to everyone that I have the financial clout to cover a transaction of this magnitude. Who else could afford to lose $10 million? Who else could offer Talcott to Franklin? And tell me, who else could have taken that sick bank into the international market and earned profits in foreign exchange? No one! Because no one can do what I can do."

On March 27, 1974, Paul Luftig discovered that $100 million in government securities had not been transferred from the trading account to the bank's investment account on March 8, as he had ordered. The market value of the bonds was declining, and as long as they remained in the trading account they had to be listed at market value, which drained the bank's earnings. By transferring the bonds to the bank's investment account — according to generally accepted accounting procedures approved by the regulatory agencies — the bank could list them at cost until the date of maturity. This would prevent the bonds from reducing the bank's profits, whether or not the true market value of the securities declined.

Nineteen days had passed since Luftig ordered Howard Crosse — the sixty-nine-year-old vice-chairman who had worked for the Federal Reserve for thirty-three years — to transfer the bonds. During that period the bonds had depreciated by another $2 million. Luftig called John Sadlik, chief financial officer, and asked him what could be done. Sadlik, a distinguished-looking man with gray hair and a thick black mustache, called Franklin's auditors, Ernst & Ernst, and received their approval to transfer the bonds at the higher March 8 market value. But those were not the only bonds switched to the investment account.

On March 27 J. Michael Carter, senior executive vice-president, shifted an additional $62.5 million in U.S. Treasury bonds from the trading account to the investment account. This was done, according to Carter, at Crosse's instructions. On March 31 Peter Shaddick, Carlo Bordoni, and Michele Sindona concluded a series of fraudulent currency trades between Sindona's banks and Franklin, an action that concealed losses and created a false profit of $700,000.

Although these transactions occurred at approximately the same time, they appear to be the product of independent efforts, linked not by a conspiracy but by one common, equally motivating desire: to improve Franklin's quarterly earnings report. How so many illegal activities could have occurred without the knowledge of Gleason or Luftig is not difficult to explain, for the bank had been divided into individual centers of power.

Franklin's directors had appointed several vice-chairmen, and these men, including Gleason and Luftig, were not willing to share information. Their desire to protect individual power bases created a massive void, a managerial gap, from which evolved an unhealthy and competitive atmosphere of secrecy and deceit, making it both easy and desirable to conceal operations from Franklin's directors.

Nevertheless, for all the scheming, Franklin was able to report only a $79,000 profit for the quarter. It was now clear that the Federal Reserve Board would not approve the Talcott acquisition unless Franklin's capital base was improved. So on April 3, 1974, Paul Luftig, acting on what he believed to be a true and accurate balance sheet, convinced Manufacturers Hanover to give Franklin a $30 million three-year unsecured loan. Manufacturers also committed itself to an additional $5 million loan in the event that the Talcott merger was approved.

A tall, handsome man of about forty-five, with light brown hair and an athletic build, James Smith, comptroller of the currency, received Arthur Roth in his Washington office on April 4. Roth handed Smith a copy of the memorandum he had given Charles Van Horn. He told Smith that Franklin was heading for trouble, that Sindona and Gleason had to be replaced. He spoke of the dangers of unregulated foreign exchange speculation. Everything he had said to Van Horn and Schreiber he tirelessly repeated to Smith. Roth talked for more than an hour. Smith, however, did not seem interested and offered no comments.

"He was silent," explains Roth. "He said about fifteen words: 'Thank you' and 'Yes' and 'Is there anything else?' When I got through, he handed my analysis of the annual report of Franklin to me, as if to say, 'Here, I am not interested.' I took the papers, put them on his coffee table, and said, 'These are for you, Mr. Smith.'"

By now Arthur Roth was greatly frustrated. No one wanted to listen to him. Worse, he suspected that Smith was controlled by Sindona through David Kennedy. What Roth did not know was that David Kennedy had called Smith on January 17, 1974, and had arranged an appointment for Michele Sindona. Sindona and Smith had met on January 23 to discuss the Talcott acquisition.

Roth was not about to accept defeat, however. He walked over to the Federal Reserve and spoke with Brenton Leavitt, director of the division of banking supervision and regulation. Roth told Leavitt what had happened during his meeting with Smith. Leavitt said that he did not understand Smith's attitude but that he welcomed Roth's help. Roth gave him a copy of his work papers, and they discussed Talcott.

"Talcott should be approved," Roth insisted, "mainly because Norman Schreiber was chief executive officer of Walter E. Heller & Company and would do a good job. You should not, however, allow Franklin to take [Talcott] over unless [Franklin's] capital is increased by $30 million. And no interest payments or expenses should be made to Sindona. In addition, Sindona has to be taken off the board, and Gleason has to be replaced. Make Schreiber chairman and appoint John Sadlik president. If you do this and if you shrink the bank to $3.5 billion, force Franklin to discontinue cash dividends and pay stock dividends, and prevent them from gambling on foreign exchange — that's Sindona; get rid of him and it will end — I will make a public statement supporting these decisions, and [I will] assure the stockholders, depositors, and other banks that Franklin is solvent."

Leavitt assured Roth that he completely agreed, and he promised to relay his suggestions and concerns to the Board of Governors. But Leavitt's support was a small victory. Although the Federal Reserve Board had the authority to approve or deny the Talcott acquisition, only the Comptroller of the Currency had the power to demand the resignations of Michele Sindona and Harold Gleason.

Realizing this, on April 29 Roth sent a letter to all of the supervisory authorities outlining everything he had said to Smith and Leavitt. He included copies of his analysis and recommendations, his letter to the stockholders, and his July 18, 1972, letter to Laurence Tisch.

"In your present deliberations," wrote Roth, "you may have overlooked the contents of my two letters, copies of which are enclosed." Roth says he hoped this would "again bring to their attention that Sindona was bad."

Once again, James Smith did not respond.

On May 1, 1974, the Board of Governors of the Federal Reserve struck the first blow against the Franklin bank. Although the Federal Reserve Bank of New York had recommended approval of the Talcott acquisition, and although Brenton Leavitt had agreed with Roth's position on the merger, the Board of Governors denied Franklin's application.

The Board's decision did not come as a complete surprise to Franklin's management. In December 1973 and again in April 1974 officials of the Federal Reserve had informed Harold Gleason and Michele Sindona that the Board, based on its examination of the bank, was considering refusing Franklin's proposal. The Board had even warned Franklin officials of the negative publicity such a decision could cause and had suggested that Franklin withdraw its application. Franklin's directors refused to do this, however, for Michele Sindona had convinced them that he was more powerful than the Board of Governors.

Sindona believed that his connections with the Nixon administration would ultimately persuade the Board of Governors to approve the Talcott acquisition. At the time, however, Richard Nixon was facing possible impeachment and, in effect, was a powerless President. As a result, David Kennedy and Nixon's old law firm, Mudge Rose Guthrie & Alexander, had been stripped of their influence. The Sicilian financier failed to realize this.

Like most Europeans, Sindona considered Watergate a silly affair. He could not understand why Americans regarded Nixon's betrayal of their trust as a serious offense. He thought that the uproar would eventually die down and that Nixon's participation in the Watergate cover-up would be swept under the carpet and forgotten. Sindona believed that things would return to normal and that his powerful contacts would successfully lobby for the approval of the Talcott acquisition. That was what experience had taught him. That was the way things were done in Italy.

Officially the members of the Board of Governors stated their reasons for denying Franklin's application to acquire Talcott. Those reasons were the bank's poor earnings record, its unstable management policies, and the weak internal structure. Nevertheless, their investigation into Michele Sindona's background had raised more questions about his character than it had resolved, and this had considerably influenced their decision. In fact, one member of the Board has suggested that if Sindona's control over the bank and the American financial system had not been an issue, Talcott would have been approved. As already explained, however, unless Fasco International was declared a bank holding company, only the Comptroller of the Currency had the authority to remove Michele Sindona from Franklin's board.

The Reserve Board's verdict also disappointed Arthur Roth, for he knew the decision would leave Franklin vulnerable to rumors that the bank was not financially sound. Unfortunately, Roth did not have to wait long for his prophecy to be fulfilled. A lack of confidence quickly began to fester, and the crisis unfolded.

On May 1, 1974, domestic banks and knowledgeable money-market specialists began to withdraw deposits. The following morning Arthur Roth received dozens of calls from large and small depositors—many of them friends and relatives he had persuaded thirty years ago to bank at Franklin—who said they had been advised to pull their money out of the bank. Before acting, however, they wanted to hear what Roth thought of the situation.

Attempting to reinforce confidence, Roth said there was "no question about the solvency of the bank," but if they overreacted, there would be "a problem of liquidity." This was a "critical period," he admitted. But "the Federal Reserve and the other banks will not allow anything to happen to Franklin." Most of the small depositors accepted this explanation and agreed not to withdraw their funds.

Most of those who called Roth, however, were corporate officers concerned about the millions of uninsured dollars their companies had on deposit with Franklin National Bank. They universally claimed no confidence in Franklin's management or in the regulatory agencies. They believed that the authorities had proved their incompetence when they allowed Michele Sindona to purchase controlling interest of the bank. They did, however, trust Arthur Roth. Without exception, all of the executives promised, at least for the time being, not to remove their funds, which amounted to approximately $200 million, until Roth had an opportunity to try to force an immediate change in management.

Later that same day, without having made an appointment, Arthur Roth visited Norman Schreiber at Franklin Bank:

"The situation is getting serious," Roth said, as he walked, unannounced, into Schreiber's office. "You've got to replace Gleason as chairman of the board; Sadlik should become president; Sindona has to get out; and this has to be done before the stockholders' meeting, which means we don't have time to waste. I'm convinced if you become chairman, and if Sindona is gone, we can get the Federal Reserve to reverse their decision on Talcott. This would restore confidence in the bank. But we have to move fast."

"Arthur, I can't do these kinds of things," insisted Schreiber. "Gleason and Merkin control the board. Sindona is too powerful. I can't do anything. I am the chairman of the executive committee, but they control the bank."

At last, frustration overwhelmed Roth; his shoulders sagged, and he collapsed into a chair. He recalls experiencing a spinning sensation, as if he were falling back in time, "back to the beginning." It was Sunday, April 15, 1934, and "my cousin was saying, 'It's a small bank, but I would like you to take a look. We could use you, and you'd be doing me a favor.' "

Presently, he looked at Schreiber and said, "I am shocked that you have been brought into this bank without the control that you should have and that these people who are responsible for the unsafe and unsound banking conditions that exist are still in control. I don't understand it."

"Arthur, I would suggest to you that you don't come in and see me again." His voice stiff and cold, Schreiber added, "I am embarrassed by your walking in like this because Gleason and the others will find out about it."

Roth stared at Schreiber. He was confused. A few seconds passed before sadness twisted a painful knot inside his chest. Later, when Roth was alone, he would cry, but now he struggled to regain composure.

As he left, anger suddenly exploded within him—anger that was directed at himself—for he could not accept defeat without wondering if he had waited too long before acting, wondering if he had honored his responsibility to the stockholders and depositors who had trusted him.

On Friday, May 3, Harold Gleason visited his friend Walter Page, president of Morgan Guarantee. According to Gleason, Page said that he was pleased by what appeared to be a reduction in foreign exchange speculation by Franklin's international division. Gleason looked forward to reporting Page's confidence later that day at a meeting of the Domestic Executive Committee. This, he believed, would boost morale, because if Morgan was willing to stand behind Franklin, other banks would be, too.

The committee meeting was held at noon. In attendance were Harold Gleason, Paul Luftig, Norman Schreiber, Ray Anderson, and Peter Shaddick. Gleason reported his good news. Everyone appeared happy—that is, until Peter Shaddick made a devastating announcement.

Earlier that same morning, Franklin's London branch had notified Shaddick that the National Westminster Bank refused to clear foreign exchange contracts for Franklin. The reason stated was the extremely high daily volume of sterling contracts, which the London branch had been executing at the direction of Donald H. Emrick, Franklin's New York sterling and French franc trader. Shaddick said that, when confronted, Emrick admitted he had concealed unauthorized trades in sterling and French francs. Shaddick added that thirty-nine unregistered foreign exchange contracts had been discovered in Emrick's desk drawer. The amount of the contracts was 325 million French francs ($64,463,692) and 85,387,376 pounds sterling ($132,086,575). Shaddick estimated the bank's loss at $25 million. Then he added that Andrew Garofalo, Franklin's head trader, had taken the trading register home and had uncovered additional unbooked contracts. The potential loss had not been calculated.

The enormity of Franklin's losses—and Shaddick did not disclose the illegal currency transactions that he, Sindona, and Bordoni had committed—shocked the men at this meeting. It was obvious that Franklin National Bank was doomed. Paul Luftig recommended that the Board negotiate a merger with Manufacturers Hanover. The motion was unanimously approved.

That night, rumors of massive foreign exchange losses at Franklin Bank spread through the financial community. Once again, concerned businessmen and bankers turned to Arthur Roth, seeking his assurance that the bank was solvent. Persuading each caller to remain calm was a difficult and exhausting task. "Please don't abandon the bank," Roth begged over and over again throughout the night and the next day. "There is no reason to panic. Everything will be fine. Franklin is too big. The banking community cannot permit anything to happen to it. Don't worry about it."

While Arthur Roth battled depression and exhaustion as he struggled to convince depositors and stockholders not to defect, Harold Gleason and Peter Shaddick attended a dinner at Adelphi University—a dinner honoring Shaddick as a renowned international banker.

On Monday, May 6, Michele Sindona was in Italy, advising Pope Paul, the Vatican, and the Christian Democrats on the final stages of their campaign to defeat the divorce referendum. That morning Harold Gleason called Sindona and told him about the unregistered foreign exchange contracts, the estimated loss, and the decision of the executive committee to negotiate a merger with Manufacturers Hanover. Sindona objected to the merger, insisting, "Do nothing until I arrive."

On Tuesday, May 7, Paul Luftig informed Charles Van Horn, regional director of the comptroller of the currency, and Alfred Hayes, president of the Federal Reserve Bank of New York, of Franklin's foreign exchange losses. With officials of the Reserve Bank, Luftig also discussed the condition of the bank, the negative effect the ruling against the Talcott acquisition had already had on the bank, and his concern that the revelation of foreign exchange losses would promote a drain on the bank's liquidity. Luftig reminded Alfred Hayes that Franklin had become extremely dependent on federal funds, while in recent weeks the bank had encountered increasing difficulty in purchasing funds from other banks. As a result, Luftig said, Franklin would need to borrow between $100 and $200 million from the Federal Reserve Bank to cover its needs for approximately four weeks. Hayes understood the situation and assured Luftig that the Reserve Bank would lend Franklin the necessary funds.

The Franklin crisis began to worsen. In less than twenty-four hours it was evident to the authorities and to Franklin's management that the bank was facing a potential disaster. Corporate and savings account withdrawals had dramatically increased. To cover the demands, Franklin had to borrow $110 million from the Federal Reserve Bank on May 8, much more than had been anticipated. Further evidence that confidence in the bank's solvency was quickly evaporating was illustrated by the rapid decline in value of the common shares of Franklin New York Corporation. In ten days Franklin's stock had fallen a full seven points.

As each day passed, the crisis became more explosive. Roth's efforts to repress the increasing threat of a run on the bank became less effective by the hour, but he refused to quit fighting. On the morning of May 9 he telephoned the regional office of the Comptroller of the Currency and tried once more to motivate Charles Van Horn to intervene.

"This situation is getting to be very serious," Roth said. *"Barron's* and *Financial Chronicle* contacted me. They're going to write a couple of articles about Franklin: the rejection of Talcott, the two cents per share earnings Franklin just reported, the rumors of huge foreign exchange losses. If you don't do something fast to rebuild confidence, this could turn into a real catastrophe. This kind of thing feeds on itself. I have been through runs on banks, and I am worried about this."

"Well, Mr. Smith is not concerned," Van Horn said. "He is very calm about this whole thing."

"Well, I can't explain Mr. Smith, but I do know you guys are not handling this matter correctly. To rebuild confidence, you must have Schreiber as chief executive officer and Sadlik as president."

"I can't run the bank," insisted Van Horn.

"Unsafe and unsound practice is there. You have the right to ask for the removal of these people," Roth persisted.

"Yes, that is so," agreed Van Horn.

"You have been taken in by this fellow Gleason, I think. He is a super con man."

"No, no," Van Horn said, "I know him. We know Gleason, and Smith also knows him."

"There are questions arising because of the Federal Reserve's decision on Talcott and the foreign exchange situation. If something is not done, things will get worse."

"Well, there are many other banks that have problems around the country," Van Horn argued.

"Franklin is the largest. It has immediate problems and may cause national and international repercussions. You don't seem to realize this," Roth said.

The conversation ended. Roth had again accomplished nothing.

At 12:35 P.M. that same day the Franklin episode reached a boiling point: the bank's stock was bid at 8¾. Again Roth called Van Horn, who said that Al Hayes, president of the Federal Reserve Bank in New York, now considered Franklin an international situation. Van Horn was worried. He asked Roth to keep him advised so that he could let Smith know what was happening. Action, Roth said, immediate corrective action had to be taken. If the comptroller got rid of Gleason, Merkin, and Sindona, Roth said he would make a public statement that he hoped would restore confidence in the bank.

If the Comptroller of the Currency, James Smith, needed to be told how dangerous the Franklin affair had become, Roth thought, then he could not depend on Smith. Roth decided to take another step toward saving Franklin National Bank. At two in the afternoon, he telephoned Morris A. Shapiro, a highly respected bank stock specialist.

"Look, Morris, you are the only one who can save this situation," Roth said. "You must call a meeting of the Clearing House banks tonight and request a $100 million loan for Franklin New York Corporation and a standby loan from the Federal Reserve Bank. You have to tell them that Schreiber should be chief executive officer, that Sadlik should be president, and that Gleason, Merkin, and Sindona have to get out."

"Why me?" asked Shapiro. "Why should I do it?"

"You know Al Hayes; you know all the people down there. They all respect you. You know what the consequences are. You take fast action. Get going, Morris. It is getting too late."

It was too late. On Friday, May 10, the Securities and Exchange Commission forced Franklin's management to issue a statement on the financial condition of the bank. At the close of the business day, Harold Gleason announced that Franklin's management had requested the SEC to suspend trading in Franklin New York Corporation shares until first quarter earnings could be recomputed. He also disclosed that the bank had suffered a huge but uncalculated loss in foreign exchange and that the bank would not pay its normal quarterly dividend.

The Franklin crisis exploded. The revelations intensified rumors that Franklin's problems were even more serious than stated. Panic spread through the financial community like a raging beast, completely destroying confidence in the bank's stability.

Anticipating a run on the bank Monday morning, Paul Luftig spent the weekend negotiating an immediate takeover by Manufacturers Hanover. Luftig, the Federal Reserve, and Arthur Roth believed that if a merger could be accomplished before Monday morning, the disaster would be avoided and confidence in the American banking system would be reinforced. But on Saturday, May 11, Michele Sindona — the magician — entered the scene. He made a powerful and successful move to quash Luftig's effort, organized a high-level meeting at the Federal Reserve Board, and proposed a scheme that would allow him to retain control of Franklin National Bank.

19

THE COLLAPSE OF AN EMPIRE:
POPE PAUL VI AND HIS BANKER
FALL FROM POWER

ON FRIDAY EVENING, May 10, Michele Sindona placed Carlo Bordoni in charge of Franklin's international department. Sindona had assigned Bordoni two tasks: to compute unrecorded foreign exchange losses and to block anyone from discovering the illegal transactions Sindona had negotiated. Bordoni, recognizing this as his opportunity to destroy Michele Sindona, made copies of the unrecorded currency contracts, the illegal trades for which he, Shaddick, and Sindona had been the architects. Then he inflicted further damage by entering into additional unregistered and fictitious foreign exchange contracts between Franklin and Edilcentro Sviluppo, a division of SGI managed by Bordoni.

According to the "Hilton file," a secret, fifteen-hundred-page report produced by the Swiss government, Carlo Bordoni had raped Sindona's empire. Through a series of complicated currency transactions between companies controlled by Group Sindona—including Franklin Bank, Edilcentro, and Finabank—Carlo Bordoni had stolen $25,223,301. He used at least three fiduciary contracts to transfer the $25 million to his account at Union Bank in Switzerland (UBS), Chiasso, Switzerland. At the direction of his wife, Carlo then withdrew the funds from his account and deposited them in Virginia's account at UBS.

Blind to these machinations, Michele Sindona depended on Bordoni to protect his back while he manipulated the regulatory agencies so that he could retain control of Franklin Bank. And although Sindona had ordered Bordoni to keep the unrecorded foreign exchange losses confidential, Bordoni attempted to further undermine Sindona's efforts by feeding the information to Paul Luftig, who was still negotiating a merger with Manufacturers Hanover.

Earlier that night Sindona had warned Paul Luftig that if he proceeded to push for the merger, he would "be in trouble." Luftig read violence in Sindona's threat and was frightened, for he, like others, had heard rumors that Sindona was Mafia-connected. Luftig—a soft-spoken, gentle man who never raised his voice—searched his soul and discovered the courage he needed to face fear and remain faithful to his strong sense of moral obligation to Franklin's stockholders.

On Saturday morning Paul Luftig resumed negotiations with John McGillicuddy, president of Manufacturers Hanover, and the entire senior management of Manufacturers Hanover. For two obvious reasons, Manufacturers was interested in Franklin: one was the desire to protect the $30 million unsecured loan Manufacturers had given Franklin in April 1974; the other was Franklin's Long Island branches, considered the finest suburban branch banking operations in the country.

By midday, however, Bordoni had notified Luftig that unrecorded foreign exchange losses of $30 million had been verified. Luftig panicked. He informed McGillicuddy of the losses and asked if he wanted to terminate merger discussions. According to Luftig, McGillicuddy said, "No, it is just a question of price. Let's continue to talk."

John McGillicuddy, however, did impose certain conditions on the merger. A brilliant banker with an outstanding earnings record, McGillicuddy wanted assurance from Washington that the Justice Department would agree to waive potential antitrust violations. He wanted financial assistance from the Federal Deposit Insurance Corporation (FDIC) and the Reserve Bank. This was not an unusual demand, for in the past the regulatory agencies had given financial assistance to similar mergers. Finally, McGillicuddy insisted there be no obligation to retain any senior officer or director of Franklin.

That night Luftig discussed each point with officials of the Federal Reserve. "I was led to assume that the Fed had discussions with the Justice Department or other people in Washington," he explains. "I was also led to believe all through this period, up until Sunday, May 12, that the Fed was very much in favor of trying to merge the banks. . . . And yet sometime during that weekend, regulatory support for the merger dissolved, and support for Mr. Sindona's solution grew."

Michele Sindona spent Saturday night, May 11, forcefully resisting the merger at the Federal Reserve Bank of New York, a dismal, gray stone

building with barred windows. Seated with Sindona at the giant mahogany
conference table in the boardroom of the Federal Reserve were Randolph
Guthrie, Carlo Bordoni, and Harold Gleason. Federal officials in conference with the Sindona team were Alfred Hayes, president of the Reserve
Bank of New York; William Moran, chief of the New York regional office
of the SEC; and Charles Van Horn, regional director for the Comptroller of
the Currency. Having gained control of the situation, Michele Sindona
had barred Paul Luftig and Franklin's law firm (Kaye Scholer Fierman
Hays & Handler) from participating because they had favored a merger
with Manufacturers Hanover.

Sindona was a master craftsman with a powerful presence, and he
spoke with authority. "I am not opposed to a merger," he said, "but I am
opposed to a merger that does not protect the stockholders. I am not speaking only of myself, although I do own 22 percent of the outstanding shares
of Franklin. I am speaking for the interest of all the shareholders. It is my
belief that there is not enough time to negotiate a favorable acquisition
with Manufacturers, nor do I believe there is sufficient time for the regulatory agencies to meet their terms. We must remember we are in the
midst of a critical and volatile situation. The menace caused by these traders . . . I should mention that I have personally seen to it that all the
names of those responsible have been placed in the hands of the FBI. Criminal charges will undoubtedly be brought against each one of them. They
will have to pay for this terrible act of treachery and dishonor. . . . Excuse me gentlemen, I find myself angry. I must ask you all to forgive me,
for this is not what I desire to say.

"What I propose will save the bank. I propose that Franklin New
York Corporation make a $50 million rights offering. This is an amount in
excess of the foreign exchange losses and, therefore, will stabilize the situation. To help restore confidence in the stability of Franklin Bank, I will
allow you to announce that I, Michele Sindona—though I have no legal
obligation to do so, for I am simply a stockholder—through Fasco International will guarantee the purchase of any and all shares not subscribed for
by the stockholders. Furthermore, if the offering is successful, I will match
it by injecting an additional $50 million into the bank."

By the time the meeting ended, Michele Sindona had mesmerized
the New York officials, who agreed to present his proposition to the Board
of Governors. But it was Sindona's nature not to leave an important decision to the discretion of a select group. As he had done so many times in
Italy, he infiltrated the group to muster support for his plan.

Early Sunday morning, May 12, Michele Sindona called Washington
and pitched his program to James Smith, comptroller of the currency. Later that same morning Smith presented Sindona's solution to the Board of
Governors. The Board members were skeptical, for they believed Sindona's reputation had influenced the market's negative reaction to the

bank. That the scheme could potentially increase Sindona's interest in Franklin to 50 percent, they argued, might infect public opinion and, rather than heal the situation, cause the collapse of the bank.

The Board had to consider not only the possible failure of Franklin National Bank—the eighteenth largest in the country and the first major U.S. bank since the depression to miss a regular dividend payment—but also the devastating effect Franklin's collapse could have on the banking community. Many banks had failed during the 1970s—among them the U.S. National Bank of San Diego ($930 million in deposits), the Bank of the Commonwealth of Detroit ($992 million), and Security National Bank of Long Island ($1.3 billion)—but only Franklin National Bank posed a threat to the stability of the American and international banking network. This new risk was the offspring of Franklin's dependency on Eurodollar deposits, the purchase of federal funds, short-term foreign deposits, certificates of deposit, and the vast number of open foreign exchange contracts.

Franklin's liquidity crisis came at a time when rising inflation, tight money markets, OPEC, and governmental controls were suffocating the industrial and financial world. If Franklin's insolvency prohibited the bank from returning deposits and fulfilling currency contracts as they matured, an epidemic could have swept through the international financial system. Many banks, too small to absorb the losses, would have failed; larger banks would have suffered tremendous losses, which would have drained their assets, and the system of floating currencies and Eurodollars would have been disrupted, propelling the world into the worst recession since World War II.

Faced with the kind of disaster that could evolve from the bankruptcy of Franklin National Bank, the regulatory agencies would ordinarily have seriously assisted Paul Luftig's attempt to bring about the takeover by Manufacturers Hanover—or at least one would expect them to take such a step. That is not what occurred. When smaller banks failed, they were swiftly merged or salvaged with federal assistance, but the authorities performed incompetently during the Franklin crisis. This was caused, in part, by the intervention of Michele Sindona and David Kennedy.

Though James Smith agreed with the Board's opinion of Michele Sindona, he continued to insist that there were no alternatives. The Board of Governors approved the Sindona motion on the stipulation that Sindona place his stock in a voting trust and appoint a trustee acceptable to the Board. Smith informed Michele Sindona of the Board's condition and Sindona immediately agreed to place his rights to vote his Franklin shares in trust for one year, naming David Kennedy as trustee. Smith then called David Kennedy, who agreed to "accept the responsibility." The Comptroller reported this to the Board of Governors, and the Board approved the deal, allowing Michele Sindona to retain control of Franklin National Bank.

Interestingly, James Smith testified in 1976 in front of the Rosenthal Committee, which was investigating the failure of Franklin National Bank, that he had always favored a merger with Manufacturers. His decision to support Sindona's proposal, he said, came only after Manufacturers had notified him that it was not interested in Franklin, and was not prompted by Sindona's relationship with David Kennedy. Smith, however, contradicted himself. He admitted he had not been informed of Manufacturers' refusal to proceed with the merger — a decision provoked by the unwillingness of the regulatory authorities to make a concerted and serious effort to promote a federally assisted merger — until noon on Monday, May 13, 1974, more than twenty-four hours after Smith had introduced Sindona's scheme to the Board of Governors.

Paul Luftig arrived at the bank early Sunday morning, anticipating a meeting with John McGillicuddy to clarify final details of the negotiations between the regulatory agencies and Manufacturers Hanover for the purpose of solidifying the immediate takeover of Franklin National Bank. Neither McGillicuddy nor any other official of Manufacturers showed up for the meeting. At about 10:00 A.M. Harold Gleason entered Luftig's office and said, "You might as well go home. There won't be a merger." Luftig was stunned. Gleason, however, offered no explanation.

Between 11:00 A.M. and 11:00 P.M. that Sunday the final terms of Sindona's plan were negotiated. Paul Luftig, Peter Shaddick, and several junior officers of the Franklin were terminated. Kaye Scholer Fierman Hays & Handler resigned as legal counsel, and Sindona's lawyers took over the bank's legal work. Franklin New York Corporation would make two share offerings — the first for $30 million, the second for $20 million — both guaranteed by Fasco International and subject to the approval of the stockholders at the annual meeting on June 27. Sindona also insisted the authorities promise there would be no lawsuits if Fasco's proposal was approved by the stockholders. And finally, because of Franklin's liquidity problem, the Federal Reserve Bank of New York committed funds to cover withdrawal demands.

To revive public confidence in Franklin Bank, the authorities also collaborated with Sindona's team, drafting a joint press release detailing the terms of the agreement, the proposed stock issue, and the support of the Federal Reserve Bank. The statement, issued that night under Harold Gleason's name, also contained several inaccurate comments. For instance, Gleason stated that the bank had suffered exchange losses of $14 million in the second quarter of 1974 and that the losses were covered by insurance. Both statements were false. In truth, bank officials already knew that the losses were close to $40 million, of which $26.7 million had been lost during the first quarter, and that those losses were not covered by insurance. Nevertheless, the authorities approved the release.

Having made their decision, they could now do nothing but wait. Within the next forty-eight hours the durability of the government's support system would be tested; the market would pass judgment on its endorsement of Michele Sindona.

Sindona's empire was intact, his secrets remained hidden, and his superego was saturated with self-esteem. Michele Sindona had battled the system and won. Although he had not slept for nearly seventy-two hours, he was not exhausted; instead, he had a great reservoir of energy, for victory always stimulated Sindona, provoking new ideas and a craving for something sweet to eat.

Michele Sindona did not spend the night celebrating his conquest, however. Instead, he suffered through the early morning hours with indigestion and a migraine, depression and fear, loneliness and disgrace. The cause of this dramatic shift in feelings was the discovery that the Vatican and the Christian Democrats had been defeated in the election in Italy. While Michele was locked up in negotiations on May 12, 1974, the Italians had voted in favor of divorce.

Enrico Cuccia had won. Finambro was dead. For the Vatican, Pope Paul VI, and the Christian Democrats, it was a political disaster that weakened Sindona and made him vulnerable to the left.

The left was quick to take advantage of this opportunity. On May 14, 1974, left-wing Italian newspapers reported Franklin's foreign exchange losses and promoted the rumor that Edilcentro Sviluppo — a division of SGI managed by Carlo Bordoni, which had been merged into Finambro — had been involved in fraudulent currency transactions with Franklin. This rumor provoked a loss of confidence in the Sindona Group and its banks, generating massive deposit withdrawals from Banca Privata Finanziaria and Banca Unione. Hence, a liquidity crisis developed that would ultimately rip open the seams of Sindona's protective sphere and allow his enemies access to secrets they would use to destroy his political patrons, disrupt the security of the Holy See, and bring about the collapse of the Sindona empire.

The verdict of the international banking community came swiftly; on both sides of the Atlantic the walls of Sindona's financial kingdom began to crumble. Deposits disappeared from Franklin National Bank so quickly that by May 24 the bank had borrowed $1.13 billion from the Federal Reserve. On June 20 additional stress was created when Franklin's management announced that combined losses from foreign exchange speculation and the bank's securities portfolio amounted to $65 million. And on June 26 the tension reached a catastrophic high when Bankhaus I. D. Herstatt — one of Germany's largest private banks, with assets of $800 million — suddenly collapsed because of huge, unregistered foreign exchange losses.

By now U.S. banking authorities realized they should not have protected Michele Sindona. Franklin's shareholders had responded negatively to Sindona's proposal, making it clear that they would not approve the $50 million subscription offering (which, in all probability, would not have stabilized the crisis). A majority of the shareholders preferred, at the least, a change in management.

Arthur Roth had devised a more detailed resolution. Early in the crisis, while the authorities remained confused about the correct steps to take, Roth had drafted a proposal and sent it directly to Arthur Burns, chairman of the Federal Reserve. Instead of issuing new stock, Roth recommended that the directors of Franklin contribute $100 million to the bank. This, he wrote, would be a "genuine display of good faith, would prevent a further decrease in the value of Franklin's shares, and would be a major step toward restoring confidence in the bank." He also suggested that the FDIC change its practice of not providing financial assistance until a bank is declared insolvent and, instead, "practice preventive medicine." He went on to recommend that the FDIC purchase Franklin's municipal bonds for $280 million, for which the bank would pay the FDIC a premium of 20 percent of its earnings for ten years. Roth's plan also included a $250 million seven-year loan to Franklin from the New York Clearing House banks. The interest rate on the loan would start at 4 percent and increase to 20 percent, averaging out at 10 percent a year. He called for the elimination of the foreign exchange and securities trading departments and an injection of "new leadership that is sound, knowledgeable, and inspiring."

Roth's plan was innovative, constructive, and challenging—but again no one responded. Franklin Bank continued to slide toward bankruptcy while the comptroller continued to work ineffectively at resolving the crisis.

Although Franklin's deterioration was directly related to negative rumors about Michele Sindona and reports of his problems in Italy, David Kennedy was able to persuade James Smith to adopt a course of action more favorable to Sindona. A conventional merger at the current market value of $8.75 per share, far below the price Sindona had paid for his Franklin stock, would cause Sindona to realize a $31.250 million loss. Michele, said Kennedy, preferred not to sell his stock and, instead, favored seeking a partnership with a London bank. Smith complied with Sindona's request, authorizing Kennedy to deal with London banks on behalf of the comptroller's office.

On June 5, 1974, National Westminster Bank's chairman stated that his bank, which Michele Sindona had fraudulently involved in his scheme to destroy the lira, had no interest in acquiring a partnership position in Franklin with Fasco International. Westminster Bank, however, considered purchasing some of Franklin's branches, but U.S. authorities rejected this proposal. That same week, officials of Barclays Bank, Ltd., which had recently purchased the nineteen-branch First Westchester National Bank in Westchester County, New York, announced that it was seriously exploring the Kennedy–Sindona proposal with the Federal Reserve and the comptroller's office.

Barclays' reported interest in Franklin, plus the commitment made on June 11 by the eleven Clearing House banks to lend Franklin up to $250 million (secured by a lien on Franklin's assets and guaranteed by the Federal Reserve Bank), failed effectively to establish a support system capable of reversing public opinion and reinforcing confidence. Instead, as panic continued to increase, hope of stabilizing the crisis began to disintegrate, for in the midst of an investigation by the FBI and SEC, rumors of criminal misconduct by Peter Shaddick and Carlo Bordoni began to spread.

Michele Sindona's lawyers were the first ones to frighten Peter Shaddick. They questioned him about false foreign exchange transactions at Franklin National Bank. Discussing the situation with Michele Sindona on June 15, 1974, in the privacy of Sindona's study just off the living room in his suite at the St. Regis Hotel, Peter Shaddick said, "Their questions were uncomfortably close to the truth concerning the false entries. You had better get your lawyers off my back."

"I will take care of it," Don Michele assured him. And he did: Shaddick never again hear from Sindona's lawyers.

"I'm also very concerned about the upcoming meetings with the SEC and the FBI," added Shaddick. "In point of fact, what on earth am I going to say about the Amincor deals?"

Sindona glanced at the portrait of Nunziata and said, "Well, you just tell them that Carlo is an adviser to Amincor. This was a bank in Switzerland that wanted to get a foothold in the New York international market, that wanted to become acquainted with a bank in New York actively engaged in international business. Tell them they were paying this $2 million as a commission."

Reluctantly, Shaddick agreed to use the story. "What about Bordoni? Since it is apparent that Bordoni will also be interrogated, it is important to know what he will say."

"I will make sure that Carlo tells the same story," Sindona said with confidence.

Sindona did speak with Bordoni. Carlo did agree to say that he had been an adviser to Amincor and had introduced the Swiss bank to Franklin. Michele even introduced Carlo to attorney Anthony G. Di Falco, son of the late Judge S. Samuel Di Falco. Having Carlo Bordoni retain Anthony Di Falco as his counsel was, Sindona believed, insurance. Sindona thought that Di Falco would protect him and make sure Bordoni said exactly what he had been ordered to say. But Di Falco, a politically ambitious man who looks remarkably like Nino Sindona, did not protect Sindona, and Bordoni did not keep his promise when questioned by the SEC. Instead, he denied ever having been an adviser to Amincor or Franklin. Bordoni was now in the final stages of his plot to avenge his wife's honor and ruin Michele Sindona.

Throughout the six-hour interrogation on July 10, 1974, as the SEC examiners questioned Bordoni about the false currency trades between Amincor and Franklin and compared his testimony with Shaddick's contradictory statements, Bordoni remained firm in his determination to deny participation in or knowledge of the situation. He was on a tightrope. Undoubtedly he could sense this, for the questioning became more intense, more direct and accusing. At one point, proof was provided that he and Shaddick had conspired to deceive Franklin's management through the creation of fraudulent trades. This occurred when the SEC examiners displayed a trading confirmation form issued by Amincor, signed by Carlo Bordoni, and addressed to Franklin Bank's Peter Shaddick.

Slowly but methodically the SEC officials stripped the veil of secrecy from each transaction. As they ripped away the layers of conspiratorial dressing, the conspiracy and cover-up became more evident. Carlo Bordoni grew nervous, for he did not have a well-stocked repository of strength and courage that he could tap during a trial. His eyebrows began to twitch. Perspiration erupted, spreading over his thin upper lip and soaking his fleshy waistline and back. His power of speech also began to fail him.

Bordoni was tempted to tell the authorities all of the secrets hidden in his brain and in that Swiss deposit box, to put an end to the tremendous stress he had been living with ever since he and his wife decided to destroy Sindona. He could have cut a deal with the government, agreed to testify against Michele Sindona, and walked away a free and wealthy man. But the timing was wrong. Carlo and Virginia Bordoni had other plans.

Somehow Bordoni endured. Perhaps his love for Virginia sustained him. Because her plans were not complete, she had instructed Carlo to admit to nothing, hoping his denial would lubricate the government's suspicion that a conspiracy existed between Shaddick and Sindona. To promote this deception, Bordoni feigned ignorance of the currency transactions and false profits. He refuted Shaddick's statement that he, Bordoni, was an adviser to Amincor and was Shaddick's contact. And he insisted that his signature on the foreign exchange confirmation certificate had been forged.

That night, in Di Falco's office, Bordoni tape-recorded a telephone conversation with Peter Shaddick. Shaddick, however, was not aware that Bordoni was recording their conversation. Bordoni's purpose was to con

Shaddick into saying that he, Bordoni, had not been involved in the fraudulent transactions and that Bordoni had never been an adviser to Amincor, Franklin, or Shaddick.

Disturbed by Bordoni's attitude, Shaddick visited Sindona at the St. Regis the following day and reported that Bordoni had denied having ever been an adviser to Amincor. Shaddick also said that Bordoni had "accused me basically of selling him down the river." According to Shaddick, Sindona's reaction was characteristic: "This is Carlo's problem. He is a fool."

But it was Michele Sindona who was the fool. He continued to believe he was so brilliant that he was without peers. He thought of himself as an agent of God and believed, therefore, that no one was capable of outsmarting him. In betraying him, he believed, one risked eternal damnation.

Virginia Cornelio Bordoni, however, did not bow her head when Don Michele entered a room or when his name was mentioned. Sindona was not her golden calf; she saw him as an evil, greedy, and maniacal man who had to be used and then destroyed. Yet even though the time was ripe to resolve a vendetta against Sindona, Virginia was not ready to reveal the damage she and Carlo had brought upon the Sindona Group. The game had now become extremely exciting. The dangers had been enhanced. She was now plotting against the combined intelligence and power of Michele Sindona and two governments. The idea of beating them all intrigued her.

That Anthony Di Falco's family had known Michele Sindona for fifteen years played an important role in Virginia's decision to carry out her plot. She would turn Di Falco against Sindona. She would use him to humiliate Sindona as Sindona had humiliated her husband. She would also use Di Falco as she had her husband and she would siphon liquid resources from Sindona's personal accounts.

While the SEC and FBI were investigating the false trading entries at Franklin National Bank, Virginia ordered Carlo to engineer another system of fraudulent currency trades in order to funnel $26,900,822.57 from Edilcentro Sviluppo International, Ltd., a Cayman Island investment corporation owned by Group Sindona, to five Swiss banks (Private Credit Bank, Zurich; Amincor Bank, Zurich; Finabank, Geneva; New Bank, Chiasso; and Credit Suisse, Lugano). The funds were then transferred to Amsterdam-Rotterdam Bank in Amsterdam. They were then wired to the London branch of Union Bank of Switzerland (UBS) and credited to Carlo Bordoni's Chiasso account. Having received power of attorney over her husband's account on July 15, 1974, Virginia Cornelio Bordoni then instructed UBS to transfer $14,607,000 to her account.

On July 18 and 24, Virginia wired $500,000 and $2 million, respectively, from Carlo's account to Anthony Di Falco's account at Bankers Trust Company in New York. (A payment of $150,000 had been previously transferred to di Falco on July 10.) Then on August 2 Virginia issued twelve bank checks made out to Anthony Di Falco. The funds, which were drawn against Carlo's UBS account, totaled $7,995,940. On August 12 Di Falco received another six drafts for $3,621,352.57. Another draft for $400,000 was issued to Di Falco on August 20. Virginia ordered a final check for $226,530 to be paid to Di Falco on December 19, 1974. All together Anthony Di Falco received $12,243,822.57.

Anthony Di Falco endorsed these checks and deposited the funds in three Swiss banks: $2 million went to Banque Populaire Suisse, Geneva; $6,063,352.57 was deposited at Société de Banque Suisse, Geneva; $2,230,478 was deposited at Credit Suisse, Geneva. The destination of the remaining $2 million is unknown.

It is also unknown whether or not Anthony Di Falco was aware that the $12.3 million he received in checks or the $2.650 million wired to his account at Bankers Trust Company had been embezzled by Carlo Bordoni. Unfortunately, the records of the three Swiss banks in which the $12.3 million was deposited are unavailable for examination. As a result, it is still a mystery whether the accounts were controlled by Anthony Di Falco, Virginia Bordoni, or Carlo Bordoni, or all three of them, or even Virginia's two Liechtensteinian companies, Financial Virginia Investment, A.G., and Kosmin Anstalt.

While Carlo and Virginia Bordoni were robbing Sindona's banks, Michele's empire faced a serious liquidity crisis. So that Banca Unione and Banca Privata Finanziaria could meet withdrawal demands, Sindona was forced to seek financial assistance from the Bank of Italy. At the approval of Guido Carli, governor of the Bank of Italy, Banca di Roma made two loans of $100 million each to Michele Sindona. The first $100 million, paid in U.S. dollars, was deposited at Società Generale Banking Corporation, a small bank in the Cayman Islands owned and controlled by Michele Sindona. The second loan of $100 million (actually 65 billion lire) was made to Finambro and deposited at Banca Unione to cover withdrawals. The liquidity problems at BU and BPF were so devastating, however, that Banca di Roma reported to Carli, "Information supplied verbally by Mr. Sindona and a conviction on the part of Banca di Roma, leads us to believe that the loans granted will never be repaid." With this in mind, Banca di Roma took as collateral all of Sindona's shares in both Italian banks and in Società Generale Immobiliare, the giant real estate conglomerate owned partly by the Vatican.

As part of the terms of the loan agreement, Guido Carli dismissed Carlo Bordoni as managing director of BU and ordered Banca di Roma to replace all of Sindona's men with members of its own staff. At the same time, Carli appointed a team of investigators to review the books and records of Sindona's banks. This team was headed by Giorgio Ambrosoli, a soft-spoken forty-one-year-old lawyer with a receding hairline and a thick mustache. Ambrosoli was unknown to the banking community, but was friendly with Enrico Cuccia.

An early report by Ambrosoli revealed that a number of unrecorded foreign exchange contracts and irregular fiduciary contracts existed at BPF. Net losses, Ambrosoli said, were in excess of $500 million. This figure, however, did not include losses suffered by BU or by any of Sindona's other banks.

As news of the Sindona Group's financial problems bounced back and forth between Italy and America, each crisis fed off the other. Unlike the Italian authorities, who wasted no time taking over Sindona's banks and removing his people, the American regulatory agencies appear to have been placed under a Sicilian spell. As the Sindona scandal grew and continued to contaminate the Franklin crisis, the comptroller, James Smith, continued to seek advice and help from David Kennedy. Kennedy, at Smith's request, persuaded Joseph W. Barr, who had been secretary of the treasury during the last twenty-nine days of the Johnson administration, to replace Harold Gleason as chairman, president, and chief executive officer of Franklin National Bank.

Barr is a conservative man with short curly hair, bushy eyebrows, and a square chin. He was chairman of the Federal Deposit Insurance Corporation from 1964 to 1965. Barr was also a former member of the advisory committee of the Export-Import Bank of the United States, a director of several major corporations, and chairman of the Washington Redskins football team. He was a respected figure in the banking community.

After leaving government service, Barr had become chairman and chief executive officer of American Security & Trust Co. He remained with American Security until 1974 when a dispute with the bank's directors over the growth of the $1 billion bank forced him to resign. He took over Franklin Bank on June 20, 1974, and attempted to keep it alive as an independent bank. Several factors impeded his efforts, however, just as certain conditions had prevented James Smith from resolving the Franklin crisis. By this time, Sindona's troubles had infected the market with so much negative opinion that banks continued to withdraw deposits from Franklin as they came due, and major banks refused to clear foreign exchange contracts for Franklin. In fact, the situation had become so desperate that the Federal Reserve Bank of New York was forced into the unusual position of clearing foreign exchange contracts on behalf of Franklin Bank.

After a few months of stalling, the end came quickly. In August, the Bank of Italy merged BU and BPF to form Banca Privata Italiana, making the new bank one of the largest in Italy. Even this scheme did not work, however. Too many irregularities had been discovered and were leaked to the press. They included illegal payments to the Christian Democrats and the washing of hot money through Sindona's banks in collaboration with the Bank of the Holy See. On September 27, 1974, the new bank was put into forced liquidation.

The revelations caused Pope Paul VI tremendous embarrassment. Rumors flew that the church stood to lose up to $1 billion because of Paul's trust in Michele Sindona. The pope was attacked by the Jesuits, who denounced him for interfering in Italian politics and for placing "the church's future in the hands of Satan." The conservative faction — led by French Archbishop Marcel Lefebvre, who had resisted the sweeping changes that came out of the Ecumenical Council and had publicly battled Paul — demanded that Paul abdicate. The *Traditionalist* had also denounced the decrees of Vatican II, and now, with the Sindona affair exploding, declared Paul "a traitor to the church."

The irony was that Pope Paul had made the same error Sindona had made. Paul held a belief, uncontaminated by doubt, that no one would misuse or betray his trust. As Sindona's arrogance had prevented him from seeing Bordoni's true character, so had the Holy Father's naiveté blinded him from seeing Sindona's true character.

The pope discussed with his confidants the possibility of resigning. Before Paul would agree to abdicate, however, he wanted to mend the wounds his banker had inflicted on the church. He also wanted to retain the right to choose his successor. In this regard Pope Paul made an odd decision: he abolished the 400-year-old decree that prohibited anyone from purchasing the Fisherman's ring with money, promises, or favors. This unusual ruling now made it possible to buy votes and be elected pope. It also raised the possibility that Pope Paul and Michele Sindona had more in common than anyone had imagined.

On October 2, 1974, Franklin Bank borrowed $1.767 billion from the Federal Reserve. This figure equaled nearly 50 percent of all federal funds lent to all national banks that day. It was a signal to the authorities that Franklin's life had come to an end. Six days later, on October 8, 1974, Franklin National Bank was declared insolvent. On the same day, the Federal Reserve received bids for Franklin Bank from Chemical, First National City, European American (a banking conglomerate owned by several European banks), and Manufacturers Hanover. European American won.

Arthur Roth's bank no longer existed. The next day signs were changed, and the bank's branches opened under a new name: European American Bank.

Less than a week later, on October 14, the Italian government placed Banca Privata Italiana in forced bankruptcy. Shortly after that, Finabank, Amincor, and Bankhaus Wolff of Hamburg, all three of which were owned and controlled by Michele Sindona, failed because of unrecorded foreign exchange losses.

Carlo and Virginia Bordoni fled to Venezuela with their millions and purchased new citizenship. Before leaving from Switzerland, however, Bordoni gave an interview and revealed some of the illegal transactions Sindona had conducted, adding, "When I talk, Watergate will seem like just a minor scandal."

On October 4 and 24 the Italian government issued two warrants of arrest for Michele Sindona. Enrico Cuccia had won. The Sindona empire had exploded. Nunziata's grandson had brought shame to the Sindona name. Michele was proclaimed the greatest swindler in contemporary history. But Michele Sindona—the magician—was not ready to stop fighting.

20

THE FUGITIVE

"I WON'T GIVE THEM the satisfaction of arresting me and putting me in jail," Michele said to Nino.

It was the morning of October 4, 1974. In the middle of the night Licio Gelli had called Michele, who was hiding in Switzerland, and told him that the Italian government was preparing the first of two warrants of arrest: one for a false 1971 balance sheet, the other for filing a fraudulent bankruptcy.

"Leave Switzerland before they notify Interpol," Gelli ordered. "Get out of there so that they can't extradite you. If you don't, our enemies will torture you. They may even kill you. Cuccia has already been able to have Massimo Spada's passport pulled. Vittorio Ghezzi and Matteo Maciocco and a dozen others associated with the Group have also lost their passports. It is very dangerous, Michele. Things have changed. Perhaps, if you escape, in time I will be able to use my power to help. If not, if you are caught, you know what you must do."

Quickly, Sindona packed a suitcase. Inside his underwear he wrapped four bottles of pure digitalis, a drug that shrinks a damaged heart so that its muscles become strong enough to pump blood through a patient's body. A toxic dose, however, will cause the heart's muscles to begin to beat arhythmically. This progresses in lethal situations to what is known as ventricular fibrillation, in which the major vessels of the heart merely vibrate at a high rate and do not effectively move blood through the body. As a result, oxygen does not reach the major organs of the body. The result is brain death. Michele was aware of these facts because his father had used digitalis for many years and, at one time, nearly died from an over-dose. After speaking with Licio Gelli, Michele had purchased four bottles—a lethal dose equal to one hundred times the normally prescribed dosage—from a friendly pharmacist.

The stress he had been exposed to over the past few months as he struggled to hold his empire together, the devastating realization that the reputation he had worked so hard to promote was now lost, and his new status as a common criminal fragmented Sindona's emotional stability. As he prepared his escape, his mood swung from cheerfulness, confidence, and self-assurance to anger, resentment, and depression.

"Nunziata will not be ashamed of me," he mumbled as he wrapped each bottle of digitalis and neatly, almost ritualistically, placed them securely in the four corners of his suitcase. "I am a courageous man. I am right. I will win."

"What are the bottles for?" Nino finally asked.

Michele stared at his son—or through him. The conversation stopped. Michele appeared nervous and agitated, then, suddenly, frightened and exhausted.

"I told you, I have courage." Michele's voice shook as he walked toward the window. He may have been crying, but Nino could not see his face.

Maria Elisa and Rina entered the room.

"What is wrong?" asked Rina. "I know what is wrong. Michele. You should have listened to me. I told you Bordoni was not who you thought he was. He is not honorable. People like him do not appreciate all the good you have done for him. Michele, I love you. We all love you. But you have been a fool! You should have been satisfied. You were a great lawyer. But you wanted too much, too much, always . . ."

"Mama!" Maria Elisa said with a look that pleaded for her mother to be silent.

As if he were in a trance, Michele picked up a newspaper and silently read a story titled "Il Crack Sindona."

"I never stole from anybody," Michele said, crying. "I have done good. You all must believe this. You must always believe this."

Rina began to cry.

Because she loved her father, Maria Elisa was angry.

Nino embraced his father, who continued to weep in his arms. Rina and Maria Elisa joined them to form a triangle of love and compassion around Michele. Rina kissed both her husband's cheeks and his hands, and wiped away her tears with the fingers of his left hand. Maria Elisa combed her fingers through her father's hair, kissed his neck, and said, "It doesn't matter, Papa. It never mattered if any of this was true or not. I am yours; I have always been there when you needed me; I will not abandon you, not ever."

They all embraced Michele and each other at the same time. They were all crying except for Nino, who felt ashamed. "I know I have let you down, Papa," he said. "I've acted like a self-centered child. Always, I believed you were a great man, a magician who could do anything. I felt inferior. But now I see you are human. You need me. I will not fail you, I promise."

Then Nino stood up and looked down at his family. "Come on," he insisted. "Look at us. We are a family. Together we are strong. We'll beat them all. We'll win. We will fight these bastards, and we will win! For now, Papa, you must leave. But not with the bottles. This is crazy."

Michele kissed his son on the lips. Then he locked the suitcase. "I told you, I have courage!" he repeated. Gathering strength, he sighed, clenched his fist, and added, "I am not afraid of torture. And I am less afraid to die. I will not give Cuccia the satisfaction . . . I will not allow this feud, this communist conspiracy, these inferior and jealous people to harass and destroy my family. I cannot allow that to happen. If I am caught, I will steal their victory. I will take the digitalis."

"That is crazy!" screamed Nino. "You won't steal victory from Cuccia. Killing yourself will only rob me of the opportunity to prove to you that I am your son."

"Now you want to be his son!" Maria Elisa said in a cold and jealous voice. "Now, when things are bad. I have given my life for our father, and now you think you can step in and become a hero. Instead of running around chasing women and having fun, you should have sacrificed your life for him. I have! I have nothing! I will help, Papa!"

"Stop this!" ordered Rina. "Poor Nino was a sick child. You know that, Maria Elisa."

"Yes, I know all about poor Nino," Maria Elisa said with bitterness. "I have heard about poor Nino all my life. What about me? What about my husband? That poor man, he's so naive. He and I have always granted Papa's wishes while Nino played. Now Pier Sandro faces legal difficulties, and he doesn't understand why. I will support Papa! I will go wherever he goes!"

"I want to help," insisted Nino.

"You are the only one who is safe," Rina said. "You must stay out of this. The family may need you. If you get in the middle, if you become a target of Michele's enemies, then all is lost."

"Mama is right," agreed Maria Elisa. "Besides you do not have the courage Papa has. You've been protected. Only I know what the dangers are."

"*Basta!*" Michele ordered. "This is no good. You see, my enemies have already divided my family. If you want to help me, then love one another. Your love and respect for one another will give me strength to do what I must do. My empire, my reputation — they are ruined. It brings me great pain. I am depressed, true. I may die, this is also true. But whatever happens, I must know my children love me, and that all of you respect and love each other. If you do not, if you allow this disaster to promote jealousy, if you become bitter and betray the love I have tried to teach you, then in time what will your memories be of me? What will my grandchildren know of me? Only that I am a criminal?"

"We would never say that of you, Papa," both Maria Elisa and Nino said.

"You are fools!" declared Michele. "It does not matter what pain I feel. That the world now says I am a thief hurts. But it pains me much more that you both do not realize the greatest sin I could commit has nothing to do with the laws and rules society has decided to enforce. I am above this. If you read Nietzsche, you will realize this. But I am not above the guilt your jealousy has revealed. If you listen to yourselves, as I have, you will discover that you have convicted me of failing to teach you to love one another, to be bound to each other. And if I have failed to teach you the meaning of family, then I am a criminal."

Silence fell upon them. Michele placed Rina's hands to his lips and gently kissed them. Then he passionately kissed her lips. For a moment he stared at her. He loved her. He hoped she knew this, but he did not say so, for he was sad and feared he would again cry.

Michele cradled Nino and Maria Elisa in his arms. He kissed them both on the lips, placing an extra kiss on his daughter's forehead.

"You will both help me," Michele said. "You will protect Marco, for he is the baby. No matter what happens, you must keep the family together. I have courage, but I am weak with shame. And I do not want you to remember me this way. I lived my life the way I chose. It has been filled with glory and excitement. And if there is to be no more, I want you both to promise me that you will tell my grandchildren that I was a courageous man. A brave man. A good father. Not a thief."

Laura Turner left Switzerland with Michele Sindona. Together they took the first flight bound for anywhere but Italy. They landed in Jamaica. Michele gave Laura a sealed envelope containing financial records, secret bank accounts held by Roberto Calvi, and copies of the warrants of arrests. Laura flew to Argentina to hand the file over to Licio Gelli. At the time, Gelli was helping President Isabel Perón organize military support to defend her presidency and to help prevent a coup from the left or right. When Gelli read Sindona's file, he quickly returned to Italy.

Two days later Michele boarded a flight to Hong Kong, a city that did not have an extradition treaty with Italy. There was a scheduled stop in Bangkok, however, and Thailand did have an extradition treaty with Italy. Michele was not concerned, for he was in transit and therefore would not have to pass through customs.

Because of a typhoon, however, the authorities grounded the plane in Bangkok. The passengers were told they would be placed in hotels, at the airline's expense, until the weather cleared. Michele says that he thought, "This is it." He would have to show his passport, and he was sure that Interpol had already notified the Thai authorities. But the Italian police had not yet telexed either Interpol or Bangkok, and Michele had no problems.

He was forced to stay in Bangkok for three days. Each day was more frightening than the one before. Afraid someone would recognize him from photographs in the newspapers, he remained hidden in the hotel. He did not eat or sleep during his stay. On the morning of the third day, he called the airline. The flight to Hong Kong was still grounded and would not leave before the next morning. Depressed, he sat on the floor in a corner of the room. In darkness, he thought of Nunziata. What would she think of him? he wondered. "You are more courageous than I," he recalls saying to himself. His head began to throb. The pain over his left eye was so severe that it blinded him. He took pills to kill the pain, and he felt guilty.

He tried to sleep, but could not. He felt like a caged animal, trapped in a corner, fearful of the master's whip. Sitting there in the dark, he reached for the wastebasket and spilled its contents onto his lap. To relax and regain control of himself, he sat there for several hours practicing his origami, folding pieces of paper into the shape of boats, papal hats, and lotus flowers.

A frightening thought suddenly hit him: the Bangkok authorities were waiting to capture him at the airport. He looked outside. The weather was not bad. Yes, that was it: the police were setting a trap for him. He would not clear customs a second time. They would arrest him, search his luggage, confiscate the digitalis, and send him back to Italy. "Cuccia will win," he thought. "He will embarrass me, make me look like a thief. And he will torment my family."

Michele broke into a cold sweat. One by one he placed the bottles of digitalis on the floor. He filled the empty wastebasket with water and prepared to commit suicide. How long he sat there before he spotted a sewing needle among the trash is unclear. But when he did notice the needle, an idea came to him.

Risking capture, he left the hotel in search of a grocery store, where he bought a box of plastic sandwich bags. Back at the hotel, he poured the digitalis into two bags and sealed them. Then he carefully took apart the lining of his suit jacket, making sure the thread did not break. He placed two bags filled with digitalis inside each side of his jacket and, with the needle he had found among the trash, sewed up the lining. He smiled. Now, if he was captured by the police, he would be able to end his life.

On the fourth day, Michele nervously but successfully passed through customs and went on to Hong Kong. From there he sent a message to his family saying he was with "Harry King." They understood this to mean he was in Hong Kong and, because he had been negotiating to buy the hotel chain, guessed that he was staying at the Hyatt House.

Nino took his mother to Hong Kong to meet his father. Rina cooked Michele some pasta. Michele told Nino that he had placed money in a Swiss trust for the family. Each of his children and grandchildren received half a million dollars. He had also opened two accounts of a million dollars each for Pier Sandro and Rina.

They talked about many of the things Michele had done in his life. Michele refused to discuss the warrants of arrest, but when Nino showed his father what the charges were and what the Italian newspapers were saying about him, Michele again broke down and cried. Nino comforted him, assuring his father that the family would never abandon him.

A week later Michele and Rina flew to Taiwan. David Kennedy, according to Michele and Nino, had strong contacts with the Chiang Kai-shek family, who granted Michele political asylum. In exchange, Michele agreed to become an economic adviser for the government of Taiwan.

Soon, however, Michele began to worry about the investigation in America. He realized that if he was indicted in America, Taiwan would not be able to protect him against extradition. He decided to return to the United States to defend himself. "America," he told Nino, "will protect me against Italy because I have always protected the American interest in Europe. I have many friends there. I will win in America." Michele asked his lawyers and David Kennedy to make arrangements for him to enter America without risking capture by the Italian police or Interpol. This was arranged and in December 1974, U.S. marshals and customs officials escorted Michele Sindona through immigration.

Over the next five years, as Michele Sindona struggled to retain his freedom, he would rely on his American and Sicilian Mafia friends for help. As a result, many of Don Michele's enemies would be threatened, blackmailed, and murdered.

21

GLI AMICI DEGLI AMICI:
THE FRIEND OF FRIENDS

MICHELE SINDONA PURCHASED a $300,000 apartment at the Hotel Pierre in mid-Manhattan. His daughter, son-in-law, and two granddaughters moved in with him. Every evening they ate dinner in the Café Pierre on the ground floor of the hotel. Michele played with his granddaughters. He went for walks, sometimes with Maria Elisa, other times with Pier Sandro to discuss the extradition proceedings that Italy had started. Most often, however, he walked alone.

Michele Sindona was still a free man, but he was unhappy. He found it difficult to focus his cerebral energies. His thoughts, he says, seemed out of his control much of the time, and he drifted, recalling old victories. He felt incomplete, lost, and confused. He began seeing several psychiatrists, though he refused any form of psychotherapy except for psychopharmacological treatment: antidepressants, antianxiety drugs, and antihistamines for insomnia. A negative reaction to antidepressants, which produced a tremor in his hands, visual blurring, and psychotic episodes, forced him to discontinue taking them. But he had become as dependent on the other drugs as he had on laxatives and pain killers. Though he had several emotional setbacks, he was able to concentrate more effectively on rebuilding his life.

The negative press coverage he was receiving inflamed Sindona's obsessive desire to cultivate a new image. He rented a small office on Park Avenue and prepared speeches on banking and economics, which he planned to deliver at American universities. On the advice of his Italian-American friends, Sindona hired public relations man Fred Rosen to organize the lecture tour. Rosen was a personal friend of A. M. Rosenthal, executive editor of the *New York Times*. Sindona's cunning mind had not overlooked this friendship. He believed that Rosen could induce the *Times* to write favorable articles about him.

Michele Sindona delivered his first lecture, "The Phantom Petrodollar," on April 15, 1975, at the Wharton Graduate School of the University of Pennsylvania. He appeared confident, though he refused to answer questions regarding the failure of Franklin Bank, his Italian banks, or his personal legal problems. Yet he accused many of the world's largest banks—including Lloyds Bank, Union Bank of Switzerland, and Chase Manhattan—of "reckless gambling" in foreign exchange and of "cooking their books."

"Many foreign banks and financial companies," he said, "accumulate and use offshore dollars. But [on their balance sheets they often report only their net positions] so as not to disclose to the central banks, to which their parent companies are responsible, that they have carried out operations which are not in line with banking regulations or are sometimes in open contrast with them."

Ironically, he went on to say: "Deposits shown on financial statements or balance sheets at the end of the operating period by some banks are whipped cream. This window dressing is done in order to show the public and the financial community that their results are higher than they really are." He added that the big banks never thought they could lose in the currency market. He warned U.S. banks to use more caution, for if they do not, "the logical conclusion can only be the insolvency of the U.S. banks and their consequent bankruptcy." In his closing remarks, he said that "it is the special duty of a banker to safeguard the money he receives as savings."

To Sindona's surprise, the press did not praise his lecture. Instead, most reporters, including Leonard Sloane, the financial reporter of the *New York Times*, focused on the fact that Sindona's speech had supported the Italian government's explanation of why his banking empire had suddenly crumbled.

Although this depressed Sindona, he continued to promote himself as a distinguished financial and banking expert, making speeches at sixteen different universities and business schools between 1975 and 1977. He also granted several interviews in which he defended himself against the accusations made by the Italian government, and he wrote an unpublished manuscript with the working title *Decade of Shame.*

This work was another effort by Sindona to change his image. In it, he presents himself as a victim of a political conspiracy that emerged from the battle between the Italian left and right. Although there is some truth to this, Sindona does not admit that his problems with the left had any relation to his having been a member of the notorious right-wing Masonic lodge, Propaganda Due. Nor does he claim any responsibility, not even the most obvious — that is, trusting the wrong people — for the irregularities that caused the failure of Franklin National Bank and the Sindona empire.

Instead, Sindona focuses on his pro-Western ideology. He portrays himself as a brilliant financial leader who devoted his life "to the struggle of preserving economic and political freedom in Italy." He insists he was "persecuted for openly resisting nationalization" and for "actively promoting a closer relationship between Italy and the United States." He argues that he opposed what was known as the "historical compromise," a movement by the left, including the left wing of the Christian Democrats, to form a coalition government with the communists. And he emphasizes that his will to "protect democracy and preserve free enterprise conflicted with the goals of Enrico Cuccia and Ugo La Malfa — the two most prominent Italians responsible for the Communist party's increasing influence in Italy over the past decade."

While he worked on his manuscript, Sindona's spirits improved. He became more optimistic about his future, his reputation, and his legal problems. He believed that his anti-communist, pro-American outlook would encourage a more sympathetic view of him by the U.S. Justice Department. Then the American authorities would protect him from this communist conspiracy and thereby block the Italian government from extraditing him.

Michele Sindona was too smart not to have more than one plan working for him at the same time. While he was telling everyone that he would be assassinated if forced to return to Italy, Licio Gelli was trying to get the charges dropped so that he could return if he was indicted in America for the failure of Franklin National Bank.

Gelli loved to demonstrate how powerful he was, so he assured Sindona that he would be able to stop the investigation. Licio Gelli was not one to make promises he could not keep. On his list of P-2 Masons were two of the highest-ranking members of the Italian judiciary. Giovanni De Matteo, head prosecutor in Rome, had succeeded many times in quashing investigations into neo-fascist terrorism that pointed to P-2. This time, however, De Matteo could not help, because Sindona's case was being handled by the public prosecutor in Milan.

So Gelli went even higher. Judge Carmelo Spagnuolo, president of a division of the Italian supreme court, was a member of P-2. Spagnuolo agreed with Gelli that the accusations against Michele Sindona were false. He also endorsed the theory that Sindona had fallen prey to the left, and he promised to use the power of his office to intervene officially. But Spagnuolo was stopped even before he had started.

In February 1975 Italy's Anti-Mafia Commission linked Carmelo Spagnuolo, that nation's highest-ranking judge, with Sicilian Mafia boss Frank Coppola, a major heroin smuggler who had close ties to New York's Gambino crime family and the Palermo-based Gambino, Inzerillo, and Spatola clans, which jointly controlled the flow of heroin from Sicily to America.

American and Italian authorities considered Coppola an extremely intelligent and powerful international gangster. He was believed to have participated in the 1957 "Mafia Summit" at the Hôtel des Palmes in Palermo, when the crime syndicate selected Michele Sindona to reinvest its heroin profits. The seventy-year-old mafioso was also a known associate of Tommaso Buscetta, Graziano Verzotto, and Giuseppe Di Cristina, leading mafiosi who have been connected to Sindona's banks and to the Cosa Nostra.

Although an investigator for the Anti-Mafia Commission and a police informer had accused Judge Spagnuolo of conspiring with Frank Coppola to arrange the disappearance of tape-recorded phone conversations between the capomafioso and politicians, the commission simply censured Spagnuolo for misconduct. In the same month, however, Senator Graziano Verzotto was indicted for receiving kickbacks from Sindona's banks. This, coupled with the commission's report, forced Spagnuolo to retreat from making an official inquiry into the Sindona case.

Then, in the spring of 1975, Graziano Verzotto, former regional secretary of the Christian Democratic party and president of Ente Minerario Siciliano (EMS), was seriously wounded in an assassination attempt. Sicilian authorities believe this was provoked by a rumor that Verzotto was preparing to testify against Michele Sindona and the Palermo Mafia.

The mafiosi knew that Verzotto, a northern Italian, could hurt the syndicate. He was godfather to the son of Giuseppe Di Cristina, a high-ranking enforcer for the Gambino, Inzerillo, and Spatola crime families — all of whom were friends of Michele Sindona. The possibility that Verzotto could reveal that Di Cristina had profited from the scheme to milk EMS deposits from Sindona's banks would have been enough reason for the Mafia to kill him.

Verzotto also knew a great deal about Mafia drug bosses Frank Coppola and Tommaso Buscetta, a relative of Carlo Gambino, then kingpin of the five New York Mafia families. Sources in Palermo believe that Giuseppe Di Cristina was ordered to eliminate Verzotto because he knew too much about the mob's banking connections and heroin trade. Though Verzotto survived his wounds, he got the message and fled to Beirut.

The violence did not help Michele Sindona. The old rumors that he was financed by the Mafia began to fly. Many people, both Italians and Americans, who had remained loyal to him when his empire first crumbled began turning their backs on Sindona for fear their lives would be scrutinized or their families harassed by the authorities.

Despite their doubts, a few old friends did remain faithful; one was Dan Porco, who admits he wondered if the rumors were true. This concern wasn't new. Porco had been troubled many times by the possibility that there was a dark side to Sindona. He had questioned Michele about the Mafia rumors. Why were there so many mobsters at the dinner parties the Italian-American community held in Sindona's honor? What was Sindona's relationship with Johnny Gambino, nephew of Carlo Gambino? Porco never received an answer. Sindona would just resort to his famous gesture: both hands would flip palms up; eyes shut, his head would fall to one side; aggravation would mark his lips and brow.

The Italian-Americans treated Michele Sindona like an *uomo rispettato*. They called him Don Michele. They held fund-raising banquets to help pay his legal fees; the money was divided among Sindona and the mafiosi introduced to him by Johnny Gambino. The mobsters took a special interest in Sindona's affairs. "They were always coming to my father," says Nino, "and saying, 'Don Michele, you are the greatest of all Sicilians. We are proud of you. Let us help you with your problems. Tell us whom you want killed. Tell us who these bastards are. We will do this for you because we respect you. No money, Don Michele. We murder only for our friends.'"

Don Michele loved the admiration, the respect, and the sincerity with which these men embraced him. Unlike the northern Italians or the Americans he had done business with, these Italian-Americans were more Sicilian in their thinking. They understood one another. He became their business partner, financial adviser, and *consigliere*.

Through banking contacts Sindona arranged financing and a bond for a construction project for Johnny Gambino. He obtained building permits and financial assistance for Gambino's partner and cousin, Palermo Mafia chief Rosario Spatola. Spatola had risen to become overboss of the Gambino, Inzerillo, and Spatola clans—families that specialize in drug trafficking, tobacco smuggling, and extortion—when he orchestrated the arrest of Tommaso Buscetta.

Sindona also became partners with Joseph Macaluso, a friend of Gambino and Sindona. Macaluso's brother, Salvatore, was an associate of Rosario Spatola. A tall, full-faced, big-bellied Sicilian who speaks no English, Joseph Macaluso had fought with the Allied troops against the fascists during World War II and had been the *capocosca* of the building trade in Catania before moving to Staten Island in 1950. Macaluso and Sindona jointly owned Sipam Corporation, a holding company whose principal property was the Conca d'Oro Motel on Staten Island, a two-story red building with a dining room and pool. Many politicians and mafiosi attended several dinners at the Conca d'Oro that were organized to honor the fugitive financier.

Macaluso also owned a real estate and construction company. He and Sindona developed a scheme to sucker wealthy Italians who wanted to get their money out of Italy and invest it in America. Macaluso and Sindona successfully purchased cheap land and houses and resold them at excessively high prices. But what Sindona did with their profits made even more money. The proceeds were transferred to the control of Intercontinental Bridge, a construction company owned by Macaluso and Sindona, which negotiated large building contracts in the United States, Libya, and Turkey.

In America things seemed to be going well for Michele Sindona. In Italy, however, the legal situation was growing worse. Pictures of Sindona living it up with New York politicians — Mayor Abraham Beame and Mario Biaggi included — and mafiosi appeared in Italian newspapers. Those pictures angered Enrico Cuccia, for the news of Don Michele's activities in America coincided with threats that had been made against Cuccia and his friend Giorgio Ambrosoli, the liquidator of Sindona's Italian banks.

Ambrosoli had received a number of anonymous phone calls threatening him if he continued to dig into Michele Sindona's financial transactions. In fact, Sindona's Italian lawyer, Rodolfo Guzzi, was in Ambrosoli's office one day when someone called and threatened to kill Ambrosoli. Guzzi had listened in on the conversation. He was shocked. He called Sindona immediately and demanded an explanation. Sindona said, "Some people are helping. I tell them my problems; they try to help. What they do, I have no control over."

Although Ambrosoli had admitted that he feared for his life, he considered the threats proof that he was on the right track and refused to alter his course. Wondering every time he started his car if someone had placed a bomb under the hood, fearing every knock at his door and every ring of the telephone in the middle of the night, Ambrosoli found himself unable to sleep because of nightmares in which he and his family were gunned down by gangsters. Yet he refused to quit. Some thought of him as courageous; others regarded him as a fool.

At times Ambrosoli himself must have wondered if he was a fool. Michele Sindona seemed to be safely out of the reach of the Italian government, and the U.S. attorney's office appeared to be doing very little. Then, toward the end of 1975, things changed.

In August Peter Shaddick was indicted for fraud by the U.S. attorney's office in New York. A month later, on September 9, Carlo Bordoni was also indicted. Shaddick pleaded guilty in December and agreed to testify against Michele Sindona in exchange for leniency. The U.S. authorities, however, could not locate Carlo Bordoni.

Bordoni was enjoying life in Caracas, Venezuela, where he had purchased a $3 million estate called Villa Virginia. He and his wife had formed an investment company, Inversiones Malfa, C.A., and were making huge land purchases. (Carlo Bordoni later testified that while living in Venezuela he received several death threats by telephone from people with Italian-American accents.)

At about the same time, Ambrosoli seized four thousand shares of Fasco stock from a safe deposit box at Finabank, Geneva. The discovery enabled Ambrosoli to take over control of Fasco, which led him to documents that allowed him to begin to unravel the mystery of Sindona's empire. He was able to trace many millions of dollars stolen from the depositors of BU and BPF to forty-eight companies controlled by Fasco, thirty-six of which Ambrosoli had never heard of before.

The indictments and the discovery of the Fasco accounts opened the door to communication between the Italian and American governments. Guido Viola, the prosecutor in Milan, brought before the U.S. Justice Department evidence proving that Michele Sindona had bought his Franklin shares with money illegally removed from the Italian banks. And Giorgio Ambrosoli and John Kenny, assistant U.S. attorney in charge of investigating the failure of Franklin National Bank, started collaborating to build a case against Michele Sindona.

Evidence of Sindona's criminal acts secretly moved back and forth between Ambrosoli and Kenny. A graduate of Fordham Law School, John Kenny had joined the U.S. attorney's office in 1971. A tall, balding, unpretentious but hard-driving prosecutor, Kenny would spend hundreds of hours over the next three years reviewing Ambrosoli's reports. Kenny learned to admire Ambrosoli for his courage and his diligence. It was Ambrosoli who patiently taught Kenny the intricacies of Italian and Swiss banking.

With both governments now working against him, Michele Sindona realized he would have to do something dramatic to support his claims that the Italian charges were politically motivated and that any evidence the U.S. prosecutor received from Italy was tainted. This time Naja Hannah (Licio Gelli) was able to assist his Masonic brother. Gelli introduced

Michele Sindona to Count Edgardo Sogno and Luigi Cavallo. Both had been accused of planning the aborted 1972 Golpe Bianco, the White Coup, a nonviolent attempt by the extreme right to overthrow the Italian government by removing heads of governmental institutions, like Enrico Cuccia, and replacing them with allies of the right. Although the SID, Italy's CIA, had compiled a dossier on Sogno and Cavallo, the charges against them were eventually dropped.

Count Edgardo Sogno was a tall, distinguished-looking man with gray hair and elegant manners. A wealthy industrialist born into an old aristocratic family, he held degrees in law, literature, and political and social science. While fighting as a partisan leader during World War II, Sogno was captured by the gestapo in February 1945. His life was spared at the request of Allen Dulles, who later became chief of the CIA. Sogno was awarded the Medaglia d'Oro al Valore Militare, Italy's highest military award. He later served in Italy's diplomatic corps as consul general in Philadelphia from 1959 to 1961, as first counselor of the Italian embassy in Washington from 1961 to 1966, and as ambassador to Burma from 1966 to 1969.

The alliance between Edgardo Sogno and Luigi Cavallo appears, at first, to have been an awkward union. An odd-looking creature with a crew cut, a massive jawbone, and long, gorilla-like arms, Cavallo was a former member of OVRA, Mussolini's secret police in Germany. After the war, Cavallo moved to Paris and established himself as an agent provocateur. While in Paris he hired himself out to the Communist party, for which he organized protests and printed pro-communist posters. A few years later, he returned to Turin, Italy. There he met Edgardo Sogno, then chief of the Brigadi Bianco, the anti-communist partisan brigade in Turin, and Sogno employed Cavallo to help promote a rightist government. Italian police have described Cavallo as a "dangerous man," a "double and triple agent with high connections in Libya." Although his physical attributes make him appear retarded, he is considered "extremely intelligent." A "professional political antagonist," he is said to be "capable of mobilizing groups from the left and right," is believed to have rented his services, on occasion, to terrorist groups like the Red Brigades, and is "able to create propaganda against anyone."

In March 1976, at the Hotel Pierre, in a meeting that lasted several days, Michele Sindona explained his predicament to Edgardo Sogno, Luigi Cavallo, and Licio Gelli. As a result, Count Sogno wrote an affidavit to the U.S. Justice Department. "Mr. Sindona," he stated, "has always been identified with the resistance to the movement toward communism. Indeed, as is well known and well understood in Italy, Sindona supported and made contributions to the center-right-wing of the present Christian Democrat party. That party has moved leftwards towards official coalition with the communists" and has "joined in an attempt to destroy Sindona, who is a symbol of those who oppose this leftward movement. . . . I understand that the political situation in Italy does not change or excuse the enforcement of the ordinary laws. In regard to Michele Sindona, however, the political situation . . . is the basis of the charges." Sogno concluded that it is "beyond doubt that he will not be afforded a fair trial, if indeed he is afforded any trial." There is, he said, "the gravest risk that he will be killed."

Licio Gelli also wrote an affidavit stating approximately the same things. Ten other prominent Italians were persuaded to give statements. John McCaffrey and Phil Guarino also made formal declarations. Guarino, a seventy-five-year-old American priest who had studied at the Vatican's Pontifical Urban University, was national chairman of the Italian-American division of the Republican National Committee — and an honorary member of P-2.

Grand Master Gelli formed a committee of five Masons to evaluate the charges against Sindona. He put pressure on Italian Supreme Court Judge Carmelo Spagnuolo to chair the committee and, after only six weeks of investigation, to write an affidavit clearing Sindona.

"The conclusions arrived at," Spagnuolo writes, "were not only that the aforesaid accusations were false but also that having been made in haste, they confirmed . . . that Michele Sindona had been continuously persecuted chiefly because of his political convictions." Spagnuolo also condemned Ugo La Malfa for not calling "a meeting of the Interministerial Finance Committee" to approve Finambro, a project to which many "Italian and foreign investors had already made subscriptions exceeding the amount of capital increase." He blamed Sindona's problems on "judges professing left-wing ideologies," adding "that it is not an exaggeration to think that left-wing parties will do whatever is in their power to paralyze Sindona." And Spagnuolo boldly advised the U.S. government not to extradite Michele Sindona to Italy. "I am inclined to think," he said, "that Michele Sindona's return to Italy might mean his life would be in danger."

The most remarkable part of this conspiracy was handled by Luigi Cavallo. To support the statements made by Sogno, Gelli, Spagnuolo, and the others, Sindona paid Cavallo $100,000 to engineer a campaign to demonstrate that the left wanted the financier dead.

Cavallo printed hundreds of thousands of leaflets demanding Sindona's death. He sent these to an extreme leftist group, and its members distributed them throughout Milan and Rome. Cavallo hired leftist students to paint *"Morte a* Sindona" on public buildings and to march in the streets of Rome and Milan chanting and carrying signs with the same message. By June 1976 the campaign took off and other political activists joined in. Then Cavallo set in motion the second stage of his scheme to document the violence of the left. He printed and distributed posters calling for workers to burn down their plants and kill their superiors, whom he described as "right-wing capitalists." Cavallo took pictures of the demonstrations and sent them to Sindona.

Back in America, Michele Sindona was busy writing and sending letters to his friends in Sicily. Elections were to be held later that same month, and Sindona strongly advised his Italian friends to reject the communist movement and vote for the right-wing Christian Democrats. Ironically, a small group of Masons, unknown to Sindona, were at the same time trying to revive the Sicilian separatist movement. Joseph Miceli Crimi—a plastic surgeon, a member of the Sicilian division of Propaganda Due known as Camea, and a member of the Mafia—was a key promoter of the separatist movement. Three years later, Dr. Crimi would play an important and deceptive role in the disappearance of Michele Sindona.

In the meantime, Michele Sindona was financing Americans for a Democratic Italy. Co-chairmen of the organization were Phil Guarino and Paul Rao, Jr., a prominent member of the Italian-American community and attorney for the head of the Gambino family. The purpose of the organization was to influence their Italian cousins to vote against the Communist party and to promote the right of Italians living abroad to vote in Italian elections.

In November 1976 Michele Sindona gave his lawyers copies of the pictures of Cavallo's work, the affidavits, his letters to his Sicilian *cugini*, and proof that he had bankrolled Americans for a Democratic Italy. The lawyers presented the evidence to the court as proof of the existence of a communist conspiracy against Sindona and as a warning of the danger Sindona would face if sent back to Italy.

The tactic backfired. When news of the affidavits reached Italy, Count Edgardo Sogno was arrested, and Judge Spagnuolo was removed from his court and barred from holding any judiciary position. Licio Gelli was accused of being a CIA agent, chief of the Argentine death squad, agent of the Portuguese secret service, coordinator of the Greek, Chilean, and West German secret service organizations, and leader of an international neo-fascist movement. A warrant of arrest was issued for Luigi Cavallo, but when the police finally found his printing shop, he was gone. A few days later, police received letters stating that Cavallo had been kidnapped by a group of leftist terrorists who were going to put him on trial for crimes against the people of Italy. Cavallo had, in fact, faked his own kidnapping. He was living in Paris.

Michele's battle for freedom was complicated by the arrest of Carlo Bordoni, who had been picked up by Venezuelan authorities in August 1976 at the request of the U.S. Justice Department. It was time for Bordoni to play his trumps. From a filthy jail cell in Caracas, Bordoni granted to an Italian journalist several interviews in which he revealed the machinations of the Sindona Group. He sent documents to the Italian courts, and his wife gave the authorities the file they had hidden in a Swiss safe deposit box.

From then on, Sindona's problems continued to grow worse. In January 1977 Mario Barone, Sindona's college friend and poker partner, after spending twenty-six hours in jail for refusing to cooperate with the authorities, betrayed Sindona by revealing to prosecutors the existence of what was to become famous as the "List of 500." The document, said Barone, listed five hundred politicians, industrialists, and mafiosi who had used Sindona's banks to smuggle hot money out of Italy. Barone promised to produce the list in exchange for his freedom. But when he opened the safe deposit box at Banca Privata that was supposed to contain the list, it was empty.

The list was safely hidden in a spot known only to Michele Sindona, but the knowledge of its existence led the authorities to intensify their search for documents that would tie Sindona to Mafia drug smuggling and political crimes. Carlo Bordoni added fuel to these investigations by providing both the U.S. and Italian governments with more evidence of Sindona's crimes. At the same time, Anthony Di Falco, Bordoni's attorney, was negotiating a plea-bargain agreement with John Kenny. Although Bordoni would not be extradited from Venezuela to the United States until June 1979, he had already agreed to testify against Michele Sindona.

22

IL MOMENTO DI SICILIA AZIONE:
THE TIME FOR SICILIAN ACTION

MICHELE SINDONA FINALLY ADMITTED to Rina that she was right about Carlo Bordoni, but now there was nothing he could do about it. The scandal angered many of Sindona's friends, for now that the magician's financial tricks had become public knowledge, his associates were embarrassed. No longer willing to participate in Sindona's con, they rebelled. Some brought evidence forward, but most of his associates in the financial sector defied Sindona, refusing to pay fees owed to him or send him money they were holding for him.

Even Roberto Calvi refused to pay Sindona some $30 million due him, but Licio Gelli intervened and an agreement was made. Whenever Sindona needed money, he would send Maria Elisa to see Naja Hannah. Gelli would order Calvi to release the requested funds to Umberto Castelnuovo, Michele's cousin. Castelnuovo would withdraw the funds from a special account at Calvi's Swiss bank, Banca del Gottardo. With cash in hand, Umberto would then enter a branch of Union Bank of Switzerland with Maria Elisa and transfer the funds to New York.

Although she remained loyal, Maria Elisa became more critical of her father. She accused him of being a fool, of allowing people to take advantage of him. She said he demonstrated poor judgment when evaluating character and that he was not helping his situation by associating with Johnny Gambino and Rosario Spatola. Michele was unwilling to admit to having even relatively minor faults, however, even after he was ordered extradited to Italy on May 18, 1978 (an order he appealed). He still had a strong need to be seen by others, and perhaps himself, as an unusually bright and virtuous person. Defensively, he would ramble on, emphasizing his integrity and stressing moral issues while he berated Maria Elisa whenever she criticized him.

A psychiatric test that Michele took during this period reveals an inner struggle. He wrote, "When I am with people I am bothered by hearing very queer things. I am afraid of losing my mind. I do many things which I regret afterwards, and much of the time I feel as if I have done something wrong or evil. Much of the time my head hurts all over. I suffer with attacks of nausea and vomiting. Life does not seem worthwhile anymore. I wish I were dead."

Michele Sindona rejected his family's advice and continued to align himself with the underworld. His reason seems clear. Once a powerful and respected member of the High Mafia, Sindona had been abandoned by most of his political and financial friends. Then his strongest protector, Pope Paul VI, died on August 6, 1978. Once again Michele Sindona was left without anyone. Only the underworld—the lower Mafia, a group of common gangsters—continued to treat Don Michele with respect and honor.

Never a good judge of character, Michele Sindona was blinded by their affection. He did not see that Johnny Gambino and Rosario Spatola were his pals only because he was rich and because he paid them to threaten Cuccia, Ambrosoli, Bordoni, and others. The Gambinos and the Spatolas regarded Michele Sindona as a broken man—without friends, without power, and with no place to run. In mob language, Sindona was a "prime sucker."

Spatola—a muscular, shrewd, treacherous man—represents the shift from the old to the new Mafia. Gone are the days of the legendary Don Vito Cascio Ferro, the greatest leader the Sicilian Mafia has ever had. At the turn of the century, Don Vito organized all crime, making it respectable by establishing unwritten laws. In the old Mafia of his day, murder was acceptable only as retribution against those who had committed an *infamità*; one did not kill for money—the Mafia's men were not that kind of murderers. During Don Vito's regime, Michele Sindona would have been protected; the Mafia of that era would have done anything, without charge, to help its friend.

With the advent of huge profits in heroin and extortion, however, men like Rosario Spatola abandoned many of the unwritten laws. In Spatola's Mafia, friendships have no value, honor without power has no merit, greed is all-consuming. This Mafia exploits friends and commits murder without regret. Once a friend gets into trouble, loses his power and money, this Mafia deserts him, but if he loses his power base and yet retains his wealth, things are much different.

Spatola and Gambino persuaded Sindona to invest a large sum of money in an Italian-American newspaper they said would fight communism, but after they received the money—more than $150,000—they abandoned the idea. Michele lent the Gambinos money for their construction company. He financed operations that never existed. Millions disappeared. Still, Rosario Spatola and Johnny Gambino continued to hug Michele every time they met. They still called him Don Michele. And they praised his crazy, hallucinatory schemes.

In the opinion of psychiatrists, a confused and emotionally unstable Michele Sindona desperately wanted to prove to himself that he was not losing his mind. He dreamed up complex plots with multiple variables to prove that he had the intellectual power necessary to pull off big deals. He drafted a plan to control the silver market, which he says he had proposed to the Hunt family long before they ever entered that market. He hatched a scheme to restructure Iran's economy and bragged that his proposal would save the shah, who, he claimed, was seriously considering it. He also talked about Naja Hannah, Propaganda Due, and Il Momento di Passare all' Azione (The Time for Real Action). One day soon, he said, he, Licio Gelli, and their Masonic brothers would mobilize Real Action.

Spatola and Gambino praised Don Michele for having a brilliant and fertile mind. Rosario Spatola applauded Real Action. And during a trip to Sicily, Spatola constructed an evil and complicated plot against Michele Sindona.

In the meantime, however, the mobsters continued to employ strong-arm tactics against Sindona's enemies so that Sindona would not suspect their betrayal.

On November 22, 1978, two large men wearing dark suits and no ties entered the Wall Street office of Nicola Biase. Biase had worked at Banca Privata Finanziaria before the bank collapsed and had discovered several illegal transactions Sindona had committed. Biase later presented these documents to the U.S. courts and testified against Sindona at an extradition hearing.

The two men were Luigi Ronsisvalle, a self-proclaimed hired killer, and his partner Bruce McDowall. They made sure there was no one else in the office besides Biase. Satisfied they were alone, Ronsisvalle, an associate of Rosario Spatola, said, "Mr. Biase, we represent the interest of Mr. Sindona."

Biase felt a chill at the back of his head. He recalled the anonymous letters and phone calls threatening to kill him and his family if he did not withdraw statements he had made in court against Sindona. He thought of escaping, but there was only one door and McDowall had shut it and was standing in front of it.

"I just did my duty," Biase pleaded.

"Mr. Biase, Don Michele would appreciate it if you would retract your statement and meet with him to discuss your problems. Think about it, Nicola. Do yourself a big favor and think hard. Do the right thing. You're a smart guy. You got a nice business here. A nice wife. A family. I don't want to have to kill you."

Ronsisvalle placed a small papal hat on Biase's desk. He looked Biase straight in the eye and smiled. "You could be dead," he said. "It's that easy."

Both men left.

Shaking, Biase immediately called his wife and asked if anyone had bothered her. No one had. A few days later, after having thought the situation through, Biase called John Kenny and reported the incident.

On January 23, 1979, three more men became victims of the Justice Department's aggressive efforts to punish anyone associated with Michele Sindona or with Franklin Bank's failure. Harold Gleason, Paul Luftig, and J. Michael Carter, former senior vice-president of the bank, were convicted of conspiracy to falsify Franklin's earnings. There is strong evidence, however, to suggest that Gleason, Carter, and especially Luftig were convicted by an unsophisticated jury made up of people who did not understand banking and finances and who therefore found the three men guilty of causing the failure of the bank—a charge for which they had not been indicted. Furthermore, the testimony of prosecution witnesses Peter Shaddick and Howard Crosse was tainted. Both had lied in front of the grand jury, both had lied to the SEC, and both had changed their testimony in order to avoid long sentences. Finally, David Kennedy, who had been called to testify by Gleason's lawyers, failed to recall the purpose of Gleason's trip to London on March 26, 1974, to meet with Michele Sindona. The government maintained that Gleason had met with Sindona to receive instructions to be delivered to Peter Shaddick, ordering Shaddick to create fraudulent profits in foreign exchange. This was not true. If Kennedy had been able to recall Gleason's discussion with Sindona about Crediop, Gleason and the others might not have been convicted. They were sentenced on March 27, 1979, nearly five years after the bankruptcy of Franklin Bank, to three years in prison.

One day toward the end of January 1979 Michele Sindona was in his Park Avenue office reading an article in the Italian magazine, *Panorama*. The story reported a meeting of two men on a yacht off the coast of Palermo.

The two men were identified as Licio Gelli and Dr. Joseph Miceli Crimi, both members of Propaganda Due. The article claimed that Crimi was delivering messages to Gelli for Michele Sindona. Michele laughed. At the time, he "never even knew a Dr. Joseph Miceli Crimi even existed."

Ironically, later that same day, Sindona's secretary announced, "Don Michele, there is a Dr. Joseph Miceli Crimi here to see you."

"My messenger," Sindona laughed. "I must meet this Miceli Crimi. Send him in."

The first thing Dr. Crimi noticed was the different-colored origami figures spread across the top of Sindona's desk. Crimi appeared nervous, rambling on about the article and their mutual benefactor, Naja Hannah. Sindona quickly became bored.

"What is it you came to see me about?" he asked.

Crimi moved his chair next to Sindona. He leaned forward and whispered: "We, a group of Sicilian patriots, mostly Masons, need your assistance to overthrow the Italian government in Sicily. We are aware of your hatred for the communists, the persecution you face both here and in Italy. We need you. Your financial expertise, your personality, the charisma you have would help to make the coup happen. The people of Sicily do not think of you as a criminal, Don Michele. Sicilians are proud of you. You are a great man, a leader. People will follow you. Will you help us free the island of the economic and political prejudice of the North?"

Michele smiled. He liked hearing such praise. He did not know Crimi, however, so he remained cautious:

"Dr. Crimi, what you ask of me is a serious crime. I must think about this. Promise me you will not tell anyone we have talked, and I will give you my answer in a few days."

"We are ready to move. Please do not let our people down, Don Michele," Crimi begged.

As soon as the doctor left his office, Sindona placed a call to Italy and spoke with Licio Gelli. Grand Master Gelli told Sindona that Crimi was an "honest and reliable man, though not very bright, no genius." But as far as Gelli knew, "Crimi was a man of good faith."

Two days later Gelli met with Sindona in New York. Sindona told Gelli of Crimi's plan. He asked Gelli if he thought it was possible to pull a coup off in Sicily and if Gelli would agree to mobilize Real Action. Gelli said the idea was insane. A coup, he said, could be successful only if the military and political members of P-2 approved. They would never go along with it unless the time was right to topple the Italian government and install a presidential dictatorship in Rome. The time was not right. He advised Michele to forget the idea.

But Michele did not forget about the Sicilian coup. He told Joseph Miceli Crimi he would finance the separatist uprising, but that he needed

time to gather additional support. Crimi was pleased. He promised to organize the effort in Sicily while Sindona worked on the American angle.

Sindona studied the political situation and concluded that, because of
the communist conspiracy, America faced a threat of losing its military
bases in Greece, Turkey, and Sicily. "A catastrophe," he told Max Corvo,
former U.S. intelligence officer and member of the Allied forces, "which
would transform the Mediterranean into a Soviet sea." He asked Corvo to
turn over to him the list of partisans and to help organize the coup.

By now Corvo was retired and operating a small newspaper in Mid-
dletown, Connecticut. He said that Sindona was hallucinating. First, he
insisted, they were both too old to participate in clandestine operations.
Second, the Italian and American governments would send troops into
Sicily to quash the rebellion. Third, the Mafia would never go along with
the plan; it would betray Sindona to protect its power. And finally, who
would lead this Masonic rebellion and win the support of the Sicilian
peasants? Certainly not Danilo Dolci, who believed in reform but not violence.

"I am the charismatic leader," Sindona boasted.

"You're ill, Michele," Corvo said. "Your mind is not working. Do
yourself a favor and see a doctor. The stress has caused you to have delusions."

Michele did not take Corvo's advice. This wasn't the first time someone had thought his ideas were crazy. By his own admission, he says, "I
have always tried to think of schemes that appeared impossible. Then I
would figure a way to do them. And I have usually succeeded."

On March 9, 1979, the Justice Department indicted Michele Sindona and
charged him with ninety-nine counts of fraud, perjury, and misappropriation of bank funds. He posted a $3 million bond and was released with the
stipulation that he check in with the U.S. marshal's office every day.

The indictment was Sindona's scarlet letter: it officially branded him
a thief, a liar, and a fraud. This was the turning point. It precipitated a
series of subsequent episodes that would lead to Sindona's kidnapping. By
now Michele Sindona had convinced himself that he could salvage his
name by causing Sicily to secede from Italy. Such an accomplishment
would make him a national hero. America would honor him as a courageous defender of democracy. In trade for dropping all criminal charges,
Sindona would offer to make Sicily the fifty-first state in the Union.

It is important to realize that the planned coup had truly become
part of Sindona's reality. Psychiatric reports state that Sindona suffered
from a serious emotional disorder and an organic brain disease that made it
increasingly difficult for him to think rationally.

He believed so totally in his version of reality that he searched his files and located a letter he had received from retired Rear Admiral Max K. Morris, dated October 13, 1978. Sindona proudly presented the letter to his family and friends as proof that the U.S. military and the CIA were backing his Sicilian coup.

The letter, however, actually refers to information Sindona had given Admiral Morris regarding Russia's monetary manipulation. It also gives details of financial transactions the Sicilian financier had undertaken on behalf of the CIA, details that Sindona threatened to make public if the intelligence department did not intervene in the Franklin Bank investigation.

In his letter to Sindona, Admiral Morris said that he had "passed along the information" Michele had given to him, to "both a high military figure and a similar person in the intelligence field." He said that there was "no way to determine if either of these people would carry the matter further." But that if they did follow up, it was possible, but not probable, that they would "take some action in the matter without informing either" Sindona or himself.

"In any event," writes Morris, "I hope my efforts prove useful and I wish you the very best of luck. All of us, I know, appreciate your efforts in behalf of this country and of the West."

Maria Elisa told her father, "I don't believe this. You are being taken for a ride. A coup in Sicily just does not make any sense."

Pier Sandro Magnoni said to Nino, "Your father is crazy. I met with Dr. Crimi. He's a megalomaniac, a nobody who has delusions of grandeur. Michele is a lunatic to think he and Crimi can do this. He'll just get himself killed. And he'll get us all in trouble."

Nino, however, liked the idea: "It is brilliant. I like it, because nobody believes it can be done. I want my father to do it because it will prove to the world that he is not a common criminal but a great man."

Michele Sindona decided to advance his plan, which he referred to as Il Momento di Sicilia Azione (The Time for Sicilian Action).

In the meantime, the tide of violence continued to rise. Giuseppe Di Cristina was killed in a Mafia shoot-out on a street in Palermo. On Di Cristina's body the police discovered checks that had been drawn against Swiss banks once controlled by Sindona. This provoked the Italian authorities to concentrate more deeply on Sindona's connection with Mafia-controlled heroin.

The FBI captured Ronsisvalle and McDowall, both of whom confessed that they had been hired by the Mafia to threaten Nicola Biase. Ronsisvalle also revealed a plot to assassinate the assistant U.S. attorney, John Kenny.

According to Ronsisvalle's statement, an unidentified man from Italy, who said he was representing Michele Sindona, asked him to kill Kenny. Ronsisvalle refused the contract but recruited someone else — whom he did not identify — to murder Kenny for $100,000. The plot, for reasons unknown, was then dropped.

Carlo Bordoni was returned to the United States in June 1979. While preparing to testify against Michele Sindona, Bordoni was held at the Metropolitan Correctional Center in New York. There he met Ronsisvalle who told him that Michele Sindona had put a contract out on him. Sindona wanted him dead. The FBI immediately moved Bordoni to a safe house.

In June Dr. Joseph Miceli Crimi paid Sindona another visit. He informed Michele that the Camea Masons and a small group of partisans were ready to move. They were worried, however. They needed more men, and they needed the backing of the Mafia. Could Sindona do anything about that?

"Of course," Michele said. "They [the mafiosi] are my friends. I will offer them amnesty for all crimes committed before the new republic of Sicily is formed. I will do this only if they agree to stop dealing drugs. America will appreciate that. They [the Americans] will see that we have done a good thing. Not only have we saved the Mediterranean, but we will stop crime."

Crimi had another concern. The violence that continued to surround Sindona's cases in Italy and America promoted such an explosive atmosphere that Michele, if convicted, would undoubtedly be given a long sentence. Sindona agreed. The coup would have to happen before his trial in September.

"Everyone goes on a holiday in August," Sindona said. "It will be August."

The Mafia is important, Crimi insisted.

"I am a friend of Johnny Gambino and Rosario Spatola. I will talk with them."

Crimi smiled.

Some time in June Michele Sindona, Johnny Gambino, and Rosario Spatola met in a room at the Conca d'Oro Motel in Staten Island. Sindona disclosed his plan to free Sicily from the mainland.

"I need your help," Sindona explained. "The Masons are behind us. Do you know Dr. Miceli Crimi? He is chief medical officer for the Palermo police department."

Gambino and Spatola said they had never heard of him.

"He is a very important man in the Masonry. He has generals in the Italian army drawing up maps of the military bases that must be taken over. The U.S. military has authorized me to do this. They will not participate in the coup, but there will be a fleet off the coast of Sicily. After we have taken over, they will enter the island to help restore order and protect us from Italy."

Sindona handed them a copy of the letter from Admiral Max Morris.

"See? It is true," he said. "We can do this. But I need two hundred more men. More guns. If you help, I will grant all mafiosi amnesty for crimes committed before the coup. But all drug trafficking must stop. All Mafia crimes must end. I want Sicily to be clean. If any Mafia family does not accept this, I will have soldiers drag the bosses into the streets of Palermo. The peasants will spit on them. They will see that these gangsters are nothing, that they are stupid people, animals. Then I will have the soldiers kill them in front of everybody. No one will fear the Mafia any more.

"If you help me, you will be doing something good for Sicily. In return, I will give the Gambino family control of the orange export business. You will be legitimate, you will not have to fear prison, you can be proud."

Rosario Spatola kissed Sindona's hand, a Sicilian gesture of respect. He said he would do whatever Don Michele thought was right, but first he would have to speak with the head of the Gambino family in New York and with his people in Sicily.

On July 9, 1979, Boris Giuliano, deputy superintendent of the Palermo police department, met with Giorgio Ambrosoli. Giuliano was investigating Mafia heroin trafficking. According to Italian authorities, Giuliano presented Ambrosoli with proof that Michele Sindona was laundering drug profits through Swiss banks for the Gambino-Inzerillo-Spatola crime syndicate.

Three days later, at the request of Sindona's American lawyers, Giorgio Ambrosoli gave a deposition in Milan. His testimony, says John Kenny, was very important to the case the prosecution was building against Michele Sindona. Ambrosoli had documented the way in which Sindona had illegally removed funds from BU and BPF, his Italian banks, to purchase Franklin National Bank. Ambrosoli had evidence of Sindona's fraudulent foreign exchange trades, and he was prepared to come to the United States to testify against Sindona.

Later that same day, an exhausted Giorgio Ambrosoli drove home to spend a quiet evening with his wife and two children. He parked his car in the usual spot just outside the door to his Milan apartment. His wife was looking out the window for him. This was a special occasion, for her husband had been so busy preparing the deposition that he had not been able to have dinner with the family for more than three weeks.

Ambrosoli locked his car. He looked up at the window of his apartment and waved to his wife. She smiled.

"Are you Giorgio Ambrosoli?" a voice asked from behind him as he walked toward the door of his apartment.

"Yes," he turned and answered.

A moment later Giorgio Ambrosoli was dead. Three men had shot him five times in the chest.

Nine days later, on July 21, two men walked up to Boris Giuliano and shot him twice in the head. The murder took place in the middle of the afternoon in the center of Palermo. When police questioned witnesses, every one of them denied having seen or heard anything.

The day before Giuliano's murder, Johnny Gambino and Rosario Spatola met with Michele Sindona. According to Sindona, Gambino said that his family had agreed to support The Time for Sicilian Action. In exchange for giving up the heroin factories in Sicily, however, the Gambino family wanted Sindona to assure them that any member of their family facing a long prison sentence in America would be able to flee to Sicily and live in freedom. In addition to control of the orange trade, Rosario Spatola wanted the right to build a casino in Palermo. If Sindona agreed to the terms, Johnny Gambino would supply Sindona with a passport and a disguise. Rosario Spatola would help get Don Michele to Palermo. Sindona agreed. He accepted the passport and disguise, but explained that Joseph Macaluso and Dr. Miceli Crimi had already made arrangements for his flight to Palermo.

On July 29 Michele Sindona sent Rina and Marco, his younger son, to visit Nino, who was then living in Chicago. At Pier Sandro Magnoni's insistence, he and Maria Elisa and their two children flew to Barcelona so that they would not be implicated in Michele's disappearance.

Joseph Macaluso persuaded Anthony Caruso, manager of the Conca d'Oro Motel, to accompany Michele Sindona to Palermo. Caruso, a former officer of Barclays Bank in New York and a retired lieutenant of the Rome police department, had been skeptical about the coup, but he was intrigued by the possibilities it offered. Mostly out of curiosity, he agreed to help. On the afternoon of July 29 Caruso, following Macaluso's instructions, purchased two airline tickets to Vienna from the Liberty Travel Agency. One was for himself; the other was for Joseph Bonamico—the name that appeared on the passport Johnny Gambino had acquired for Michele Sindona.

Michele Sindona's trial was scheduled to begin on September 10, 1979. Sindona spent the morning of August 2 preparing his defense with his attorney Marvin Frankel. He left Frankel's office around noon with a package of documents his lawyer wanted him to review. He dropped them off at his office and then walked to his apartment in the Hotel Pierre.

Michele cooked two eggs, separating the yolks and frying the whites first. When the whites were well done, he dropped the yolks on top, counted to fifteen, then placed the eggs on a dish. As he ate, he kept checking his watch. He was nervous, he recalls.

At 2:00 P.M. he called Rina. "I don't have much time," he said. "I just wanted to hear your voice and tell you I love you."

At approximately 2:20 P.M. the phone rang.

"I am Mr. Corsini," the caller said.

"I understand," said Sindona.

Michele took a long look at his apartment. He wondered if he would ever see it or his family again. A few minutes later he stepped onto East 61st Street and vanished.

23

"KIDNAPPED"

MICHELE SINDONA WALKED TO the Tudor Hotel at the corner of 42nd Street and Second Avenue, where he met Rosario Spatola. They drove to the Conca d'Oro Motel on Staten Island. In a room at the motel, Sindona disguised himself. He put on a white wig that covered his forehead and ears, and a white mustache and beard. On his cheeks he glued pieces of fake, yellow skin. For a final touch, he put on a pair of glasses. Then he changed clothes. He took off his dark, conservative suit, silk shirt, and tie and put on a bright yellow shirt, which he left open at the neck, a light blue and white checkered jacket, and baggy brown pants. He picked up a black leather shoulder bag that contained the Bonamico passport. Sindona was now unrecognizable even to Macaluso and Spatola. The three men toasted the success of Sicilian Action.

Spatola drove Michele Sindona—now known as Joseph Bonamico—to Kennedy Airport. Anthony Caruso was waiting at the TWA check-in counter when Sindona arrived. Caruso began to laugh uncontrollably, for Sindona's wig and beard kept slipping because of perspiration.

"What kind of a disguise is that?" he asked.

"Control yourself, you idiot!" Sindona ordered. "You'll draw attention to me, and then we'll be in real trouble."

After a three-hour delay due to stormy weather, Michele Sindona and Anthony Caruso boarded TWA flight 740 to Vienna. Gabrielle Irnesberger, a beautiful twenty-four-year-old Austrian who had worked at the Conca d'Oro Motel and was a friend of Macaluso, met Sindona and Caruso at the airport. She identified herself by holding up a sign that read, "Welcome, Joseph Bonamico."

Irnesberger had been hired to smuggle Sindona through the Brenner Pass to Florence. The next day Macaluso would fly to Florence, and he and Sindona would take a train to Catania, then drive to Palermo. Because of the delay, however, Sindona feared that a border guard who had been bribed by Crimi would not be on duty by the time they reached the crossing. So Sindona ordered Guenther Blumauer, a disc jockey whom Irnesberger had hired to drive "two businessmen from America" to Italy, to take them to the Berghof Graml, a hotel in Salzburg. During the trip to Salzburg, Sindona removed the blotches of fake skin and cleaned his face with a handkerchief and saliva, but he kept on the rest of his disguise.

At the hotel Sindona called Dr. Crimi in Palermo and informed him of the problem. Crimi told Sindona to go to Vienna and wait for further instructions.

At dinner Sindona told Caruso he was getting suspicious. "Miceli Crimi did not sound right," he said. "Perhaps I should take a train from Vienna to Catania and make my way to Palermo before anyone recognizes me. Or maybe I should just forget this and go back to the United States. After my trial, we can do the thing. Or maybe I should just shoot myself. That would save my family a lot of headaches and money. Do you know how much the American lawyers have stolen from me? Too much. They always want too much. They think Michele Sindona has hundreds of millions of dollars hidden in Swiss banks. And what if I do? I did not work to make them rich. I better call Crimi and tell him to do something that makes sense. No, I'll wait. Tomorrow we go to Vienna; then we'll know what to do."

Sindona was making Caruso nervous. Caruso could not make sense out of Sindona's rambling. He decided that he had made a terrible mistake in agreeing to escort Sindona. He began to drink. This aggravated Sindona, who ordered Caruso to hide in his room before he caused any problems. There Caruso placed a call to the Conca d'Oro Motel and told Macaluso, "This whole idea is becoming ridiculous. You better come over here and handle the situation."

In the meantime, back in America, Xenia Vago, Sindona's secretary, called the FBI. On August 3, she said, she had received an anonymous phone call. A man had said, "We have kidnapped Michele Sindona. You will hear from us again."

It is not known who placed the call to Xenia Vago. The idea of faking a kidnapping, however, was formulated by Johnny Gambino and Dr. Joseph Miceli Crimi (at the time, Sindona did not know that Crimi was involved). Since Sindona had to check in with the U.S. marshal's office every day, the purpose of the kidnapping ruse, Gambino had told Sindona, was to distract the Italian government from the true purpose of Sindona's disappearance.

Nino Sindona pretended to be shocked when he heard the news. He told the FBI and the press, "I fear my father is already dead." Pier Sandro and Maria Elisa left their daughters with relatives in Spain to protect them from the police and immediately returned to New York. There they also feigned concern for the safety of the family patriarch. Rina, the only one in the family to have no knowledge of the coup or the fake kidnapping of her husband, held her fears inside and carried her grief in a silent, fatalistic, and agonizing way.

On August 4 at 6:45 P.M. Joseph Macaluso arrived in Munich. Gabrielle Irnesberger and Guenther Blumauer drove him to the Berghof Graml in Salzburg, Austria. After eating dinner at the St. Rubert restaurant, Macaluso called a female friend who used to work at his motel. After she joined the group, they drove, in two cars, to Vienna and checked into the Intercontinental Hotel. Sindona was nervous. He filled out the registration card as Joseph Bonamico but signed it Michele Sindona. Caruso and Blumauer stayed in separate rooms, Macaluso and his female friend bedded down together, and Irnesberger stayed with Sindona.

That night, Dr. Crimi told Michele Sindona that plans were being made to bring him into Palermo through Greece. In accordance with this plan, Crimi instructed Sindona to go to Athens and check into the Hilton Hotel. Sindona made reservations at the hotel for Mr. and Mrs. Irnesberger.

The next day Anthony Caruso, disenchanted with Sindona and his plans, flew back to New York. Macaluso, at Sindona's direction, went to Sicily to make sure Crimi organized a safe entrance to the island for the leader of Il Momento di Sicilia Azione. In the meantime, Gabrielle Irnesberger became ill and decided not to go to Athens with Sindona.

On August 5, still wearing his disguise, Sindona took Austrian Airlines flight 381 to Athens and checked into the Hilton Hotel as Joseph Bonamico. Later that same day, for reasons he cannot remember, Sindona checked out of the Hilton and registered at the Park Hotel. From room 608, Sindona called Crimi and told him, "Get yourself organized. I am all over the papers. I am afraid someone will recognize me. We've got to get this thing going."

"We're getting a boat," Crimi said. "Some time between the ninth and the fifteenth I'll be there with some Masons. Don't worry. Rosario Spatola is helping us."

"Good," Sindona said.

That night, Sindona could not sleep. He was troubled by something Dr. Crimi had said. He wondered how Crimi knew Spatola.

On August 9 Sindona's family received a letter postmarked Brooklyn, New York, August 3, 1979. The message, which was written in Italian, was signed: "Proletarian Committee for the Eversion of an Improved Justice." It read: "Michele Sindona is our prisoner. He will have to respond to proletarian justice. Our communication No. 2 will follow."

Two days later, Rina received a letter postmarked Newark, New Jersey: "Dear Rina . . . they are interrogating me at length every day; I am not authorized for the moment to tell what they are asking; they do not give me any newspapers. I absolutely am not afraid. I miss you very much. . . . Michele."

Both messages had actually been written by Joseph Miceli Crimi several days before Sindona disappeared. They were mailed, according to Sindona, by Johnny Gambino and his brother Rosario Gambino.

The abduction of any person from the United States would concern the FBI, but the apparent kidnapping of Michele Sindona triggered one of the most intensive manhunts in recent history. The FBI, the New York Police Department, Interpol, the Italian police, and the carabinieri made a concerted effort to locate the Sicilian financier. Investigators in America and Italy interviewed Sindona's family, friends, and business associates. Agents of the FBI reconstructed Sindona's activities during recent months. Still they failed to produce a single suspect.

This did not surprise the authorities. From the beginning they believed that Michele Sindona had faked his own kidnapping in order to avoid trial. Not once during his disappearance did the FBI formally list Sindona as a kidnap victim.

On August 12 Joseph Miceli Crimi finally arrived in Athens with three men he identified as Masons. In reality, only one of the men, Ignazio Puccio, a butcher, was a member of the Palermo-based Camea Masonry. The other two men were members of Rosario Spatola's crime syndicate. Giacomo Vitale had replaced Senator Verzotto as director of Ente Minerario Siciliano (EMS) after the senator fled to Beirut, and Francesco Fodera had recently been appointed to fill the position once held at EMS by the deceased mafioso Giuseppe Di Cristina. Crimi stayed at the Park Hotel with Sindona, while the others registered at the Hilton.

Crimi explained to Sindona that he had rented a boat from some

Mason friends in Greece. They would travel by sea to Sicily and sneak Sindona onto the island at night. Just a few hours before they were to leave, however, Crimi learned that the Palermo police were boarding boats off the coast of Sicily and searching them for contraband cigarettes (cigarette smuggling was a highly profitable trade controlled by Rosario Spatola).

"It would not be funny," Crimi said, "if the boat was searched and, instead of finding cigarettes, they found Michele Sindona."

Again plans were changed.

"I know the people on the government line in Piraeus," Crimi said. "And I have friends in Brindisi. We'll go that way and then drive to Palermo."

On the ferry from Piraeus to Brindisi, Italy, Crimi told Sindona that he would have to be careful in Palermo. Judge Terranova, former chief of the Anti-Mafia Commission, had been murdered a few days ago because he was investigating the Gambino-Spatola heroin business. As a result, the police and carabinieri were all over the place.

"How do you know Rosario Spatola?" Sindona asked.

"I don't," answered Crimi.

"But when I called you from the Park Hotel, you told me Spatola was helping you," Sindona said.

"Oh. Well, you had mentioned to me one time that you were friendly with Spatola and Gambino. You said that they were going to help us. So, since we had this problem of getting you to Sicily, I thought I would approach them and they would help. But Spatola would not see me."

Their arrival in Brindisi on August 16 marked the first time in five years that Michele Sindona had set foot in Italy. Because they would be safer if they split into two parties, Crimi and Puccio took the train to Palermo, and Vitale rented a car and drove Fodera and Sindona to Palermo. On the way, Sindona made two phone calls. He called New York and asked Johnny Gambino to get a message to Pier Sandro and Maria Elisa that he had been delayed in getting to Palermo but that everything was moving ahead now. Then he called Palermo and asked Macaluso if it was too dangerous for him to enter Palermo. Macaluso told him not to worry. Just enter the city during the night, he said. Spatola, he said, had instructed Vitale and Fodera where to take him.

"Something is wrong," Sindona said to Vitale and Fodera. "Something about this stinks. I am going back to Greece. From there I will go back to America and defend myself."

One of the men pulled a gun out of his pocket. The other said, "You must go with us. The boss wants you in Palermo. If you run, we will kill you and your family."

Michele Sindona arrived in Palermo on August 16. His kidnappers took him to the house of Francesca Paola Longo, an elementary school teacher, a member of the Camea Masonry, and a friend of Crimi and Rosario Spatola. Sindona was tied to the post of a small bed and gagged. Francesca, who was called Kakena, brought Sindona a bowl of soup, but he refused to eat.

Half an hour later Joseph Miceli Crimi, Rosario Spatola, and his brother Vincenzo arrived. Rosario ordered Vitale to remove the gag and wait in another room.

"What do you want of me?" a confused and frightened Michele Sindona asked.

"It will all be explained to you in a few days, Michele," Rosario said, as he removed the beard and wig from Sindona. "You're an old fool, Michele. You were going to drag us into the streets so the peasants could spit on us. Kill us if we did not obey the commands of our charismatic leader. For what? The orange trade? We already control it. In a few days you will see who tells who what to do."

"You betrayed me," Sindona cried. "You all betrayed me. Pretending to be my friends. The coup . . ."

"There is no coup, Michele," Crimi said.

"One warning, Michele," Rosario said. "If you try to escape, if you cause any trouble, you will be disposed of."

"I am not afraid to die. Anything you wanted from me you could have asked of me in America. You did not have to do this. This is stupid. Now my family could be implicated in my kidnapping. Why did you do this? What do you want of me?"

"You may not be afraid to die, Michele," Spatola said, "but if you cause trouble, if you do not do exactly as we say, your family will die. Your daughter, your sons, your wife—one by one we will get them. Believe this. You've seen how we can work."

For the next three days Michele Sindona was not allowed to read newspapers, eat, sleep, or wash himself. In scenes that were almost a parody of the days when Michele Sindona was a young tax lawyer in Messina and Rina would stay up all night reading his notes to him as he tapped away on an old typewriter, Crimi and Kakena dictated extortion letters, which Michele typed on three different machines. The letters were signed "Subversive Proletarian Committee for a Better Justice." During the day a small light remained on so that he could see, for the shades were kept shut even in daylight.

By the fourth day Michele had grown a beard, he had lost weight, and his eyes were red with dark circles under them. It was time to take pictures that would be sent to his family and lawyers. To make him appear even more weary from hours of interrogation, Kakena darkened his sad eyes with mascara and, with makeup, emphasized his sunken cheeks.

They tied him to a chair and hung around his neck a sign that read, "We will give him the right kind of trial." Kakena took approximately fifty pictures of Sindona, which the abductors planned to distribute to the press and to potential victims of extortion.

Johnny Gambino, Rosario Gambino, Crimi, and others carried the letters back to New York and mailed them to Sindona's family, Rodolfo Guzzi, Enrico Cuccia, and others. They did this so that everyone would think Sindona was being held captive in New York. The letters demanded money in exchange for not releasing certain documents—including the famous List of 500—which they claimed to have received from their victim, Michele Sindona. They also demanded additional documents from Rodolfo Guzzi, Sindona's lawyer.

The Spatola clan claimed to have documents proving that many powerful people used Sindona's banks to smuggle billions of lire out of Italy, or received bribes for doing favors for Sindona. Among the names were Amintore Fanfani, Raffaello Scarpetti, Fillippo Micheli, Roberto Calvi, and friends of former president Richard Nixon whose names have not been uncovered, if in fact they existed.

Some paid the price that the extortionists demanded, but others ignored the threats. Rosario Spatola believed that those who refused to pay for protection were doing so because they thought that Enrico Cuccia would protect them. Two of Spatola's soldiers were sent to Milan to threaten Cuccia. Several times a day for two weeks, Cuccia received phone calls advising him to cooperate if he valued his life. Still Cuccia remained strong. Then, tired of playing games, Rosario Spatola sent two of his relatives to Cuccia's house with a letter bomb. The bomb exploded and burned down the front door of Cuccia's house. The police had been guarding Cuccia, however, and they caught both men as they fled from the scene.

On August 23 Kakena told Michele Sindona to put on his wig, because he was being moved to another house. There was no need for the fake beard because Sindona's beard had grown in. While he was waiting to be moved, Kakena fixed him a bowl of pasta. As he ate, the carabinieri entered the house and questioned Kakena about the murder of the judge. She said she had not been in the city the day of the murder. The sergeant stared at Sindona, then asked him if he had any information that would help solve the murder. Sindona said he did not. The sergeant asked to see Sindona's identification papers. Nervous but not shaking, Sindona handed him the Bonamico passport.

"An American," the sergeant said. "Your Italian is very good. Did you study in Italy?"

"No."

"He is a friend of my relatives from the States," Kakena said. "He knows nothing."

The sergeant handed Sindona the passport and turned his attention to Kakena. He tossed a picture of Michele Sindona on the table and said, "I'm sure you know who this man is. Look at the picture. He is a dangerous man, this Michele Sindona. If you've seen him, I want to know."

Kakena picked the picture up and, after examining it for a long minute, she spit on it. The sergeant snatched the photograph out of her hand and stormed out of the house.

"Why didn't you tell them who you were?" Kakena asked Sindona.

"My family," he answered.

Later that day Rosario and Vincenzo Spatola placed a blindfold over Sindona's eyes, handed him a newspaper, and ordered him to pretend he was reading the paper as they drove through the center of Palermo toward the Punta Raisi airport. They arrived at a farmhouse just off the Piano dell Occhio; the house belonged to Antonio Terrana, son-in-law of Rosario Spatola.

Here Sindona learned why the elaborate scheme to kidnap him had been constructed. Still blindfolded, Michele was escorted into a room (probably a den) and introduced to a man identified only as "the padrone."

"Mr. Sindona," the man said, "you have become an embarrassment to us."

"Who are you to say these things to me?" Sindona demanded.

Someone apparently raised his hand to strike Sindona for interrupting, for the padrone said, "No! Mr. Sindona deserves more respect than that. He's been an honorable man, a good friend to us for many years. It is only fair his question is answered."

Then the padrone spoke to Sindona: "I represent the council, an organization that ensures peace and order among the families of the Cosa Nostra and the honored society, not only in Sicily and America but throughout the world. Who the members of the council are does not concern you. That they are mostly Sicilian, that there are no niggers or Cubans or Colombians should give you some peace of mind. We are not animals, like the others. If we were, you would be dead. But instead, we show you respect, even though your actions and your affairs have caused us harm."

"What harm have I caused anyone?" Sindona asked. "I have never revealed names. I have always observed *omerta*. Michele Sindona is not a danger to you, whoever you are."

Again the padrone spoke: "Because of your legal problems, Mr. Sindona, the police are investigating the heroin trade between Sicily, France, America, and other countries. When a thing like this happens, men are arrested because judges are afraid to protect us. This leads to killings. Murder enhances our power, but, Mr. Sindona, murder does not make us any money. Blood only causes the people to become angry and gives the politicians a reason to attack us. Things become messy. It upsets the natural order of life. Take this idea of yours to make Sicily a new state of the Union. Nobody wants that. What good could it possibly accomplish? Things are the way they are because the people want them to be so. But you want to change all of this. You offer the Gambino family ultimatums. You say the bosses will be dragged into the streets, the peasants will spit on them, you will kill them. No one will fear the Mafia once the great Michele Sindona rules Sicily. Why do you want to hurt these people who are just trying to earn a living? To make yourself appear virtuous? This is an insult to your friends. And now they are concerned about your mental state. You are a dead man, Mr. Sindona. You will be convicted, if you return to America, and you will be given a long prison sentence. I understand you like to play cards. Well, this time the deck is stacked, and you cannot win."

"I am a friend of Licio Gelli," Sindona said in a pleading voice. "He has promised to help me. He is powerful, you must know that. Talk to him. I have never revealed a secret. He can tell you this is true."

"Gelli is nobody, Michele," the padrone said. "He is a pawn. Gelli exists only as long as he does not become a problem for us, as you have. This Bordoni, look at the things he has said about you. He calls you the banker of the Mafia. Friends told you to get rid of him, but you were stubborn. You rebelled. Now look what has happened. No, Michele, you must answer for this. We want all of our money transferred to different accounts. We want the names of the politicians who helped you. With this information we can trade. Those who pay for protection will not be touched. The others will be sacrificed. The leftist government is stupid. If they have a few Christian Democrats they can nail to the cross, they will forget about us. As for you, you will stay here until we decide what to do. You will write more letters, including one or two that will let your family know that you have really been kidnapped—without saying where you are—so that they will help our cause."

During the next few weeks Michele Sindona was constantly interrogated by different men, many of whom wore masks. Sindona was drugged several times. He was asked about bank accounts and documents. When Rosario Spatola demanded money to cover the cost of the Mafia's operation, Sindona was beaten twice for claiming to be broke. Finally, as a sign of good faith, Michele Sindona transferred $100,000 into Rosario Spatola's account at the Central Savings Bank of Sicily. Because Sindona's Italian lawyer, Rodolfo Guzzi, refused to respond to demands made by Vincenzo Spatola and a crew of mafiosi who traveled back and forth between Rome, Milan, and Palermo, Sindona was forced to write to his son-in-law requesting assistance.

On September 7 Pier Sandro Magnoni received a note signed by the Proletarian Committee for the Eversion of an Improved Justice. The message read:

> Dear Magnoni: We have telephoned and written to Avvocato Rodolfo Guzzi of Rome to obtain names and documents.
>
> If the life of Sindona is dear to you, collaborate with Rodolfo Guzzi and give out the information in your possession.

The efforts organized and directed by Rosario Spatola were unsuccessful. Sindona's lawyer, Rodolfo Guzzi, refused to give Sindona's kidnappers the List of 500 or other documents and names.

The only success Spatola and his accomplices appear to have had occurred when Joseph Miceli Crimi was sent to Arezzo on September 21, to meet with Licio Gelli at the Hotel Europa. All that is known about their discussion is that Crimi delivered a letter in which Michele Sindona begged Naja Hannah to help. It is believed that Gelli supplied the council with documents and a list of P-2 members that was later used to cause the collapse of the Italian government.

Gelli also persuaded Roberto Calvi to withdraw 30 billion lire ($50 million) from Sindona's account at Banca del Gottardo. The money was then handed over to a messenger representing the padrone. Where the funds were deposited is unknown.

When Crimi returned to Palermo on September 22, he reported to Rosario Spatola that Licio Gelli offered to guarantee assistance if Michele Sindona was freed.

While Michele Sindona was held hostage, the tremendous pain above his left eyebrow at times caused him to become temporarily blind. Because of the headaches and the agony and shame he felt, he entertained himself by inventing ways to commit suicide. He was sure his abductors would kill him, but he wanted to end the torture, and the pain he caused his family to suffer, as soon as possible. For Michele Sindona, suicide represented the final act of a courageous man. Preparing to take his own life, Sindona wrote a letter to his beloved Maria Elisa. He was able to smuggle the letter to her by handing it to Joseph Macaluso, who was flying back and forth between New York and Palermo and who somehow never came to realize his friend had been betrayed.

What Michele wrote his daughter reveals a side of him he had rarely, if ever before, allowed anyone to see. The following are excerpts from that letter:

Maria Elisa, my treasure: I imagine that you are going through a most difficult period. . . . Before now, I have not had a chance to write. . . . [As a prisoner I] "live" and "struggle." But this is my life. What pains me are the problems I have caused you, and the anxieties I have given you. The pains I have brought upon you have been too great and you did not merit them and you do not deserve them. Certainly, I have been egotistical and selfish. Always wanting you near me: I tried at times, in lukewarm fashion to convince you and myself that you would have had a more peaceful life far away from me. But I know that I failed you because I could not live without you near me.

It is difficult, if not impossible, to find a daughter, who is also a mother and wife, who sacrifices herself as you have done for your father. I should not have accepted your sacrifice. I know this now, whatever the price would have been for me.

I know that my behavior is unforgivable. But the affection you have given me since you were a child had been lacking in my life. I did not have the strength or the courage to release you from me. The loneliness I felt each time you were away from me for more than a few days pained me. I will never be able to forget, I think it was in 1952 or 1954, after an absence of more than a month, upon my return from Brazil when you came toward me. The emotion I had while embracing you was so very great that for a moment I feared that I was having a heart attack from joy.

But all this is always on your part. What have I done for you, to repay you for the joy that you have given me by staying near me? For the peacefulness that your smile, your countenance, your help, your counsel gave me? Maybe nothing. Maybe because of your nature, but maybe also because of my faults, you were forced to concern yourself about everybody else to maintain the unity of the family. Now, my dear Maria Elisa, you must absolutely think of yourself. Regain lost time. You are still young. You can and you must do it.

My treasure, you have always known that I would never have been able to live an easy life. I know that you knew this. I know too that in a certain sense even this could be the reason why you stood by me. But I have wanted a very active life. I have wanted to uphold certain ideals. But I have committed serious errors. One must know how to lose, and I have lost. . . . [I] have hit up against a different reality that does not forgive. . . .

I am courageous, Maria Elisa. Soon, I am sure, it will all be over. Then you must live your life. . . . Whenever you think of me, think of all the fun I had, of all the satisfaction I experienced; I lived my own way; it was very tense and a very long life and even if there will not be any more of it, I thank the good Lord that he gave me a chance.

On September 23 Rosario Spatola, Vincenzo Spatola, and Johnny Gambino told Michele Sindona that they were going to release him. This was decided, Rosario explained, for three reasons. First, too many people, including Anthony Caruso, Joseph Macaluso, and Sindona's family, knew that Sindona was in Sicily; therefore, if Gambino and the Spatolas assassinated him, they would have to kill three or four others as well, and that would only bring about a more intensified investigation into their affairs. Second, the extortion scheme had failed miserably; a few victims had paid, but they had not turned over any documents. Third, if Michele Sindona returned to New York, the search for him in Palermo would end, thereby liberating the Mafia from the potential dangers inherent in the investigations conducted by the Italian and U.S. governments.

Before he was released, Michele had to swear an oath of honor that he would work to get the documents his kidnappers wanted. "Don't try any tricks," Rosario Spatola warned. "You've seen our organization. You know we can get to you and your family any time we want. Keep your word, get the documents, and your family will be safe."

Sindona agreed.

When Joseph Miceli Crimi learned of the decision to release Sindona, he said, "He cannot go back like that. We must make sure of what he is going to say, and we must do something to make it look as if he was kidnapped by terrorists. We must shoot him."

Michele Sindona was ordered to bend over a stool. Johnny Gambino held his hands. Kakena pulled his pants down and injected him with a mild anesthetic. Crimi and Rosario Spatola drank half a bottle of whiskey.

"Do it quick!" Sindona demanded. "Do it before you faint."

The doctor took aim. Spatola watched with fascination. Anticipating the shot, Gambino cringed. Finally, Kakena ordered Crimi to shoot. He grabbed a pillow from the bed, pressed it against Michele's thigh, and fired. Michele fell to the floor, bleeding, wanting to cry but determined not to allow his abductors the satisfaction of seeing him show his pain.

Crimi cleaned the wound and bandaged Sindona. While Sindona was recuperating, he was tormented by Crimi, the Spatolas, and Gambino, who took turns brainwashing him by forcing him to repeat the story he would tell to U.S. authorities when he returned to New York.

On October 7 Johnny Gambino, Joseph Miceli Crimi, and Spatola's henchmen, Vitale and Fodera, accompanied Michele Sindona, who was wearing a wig and sunglasses, on a flight from Palermo to Milan. From Milan they drove to Vienna and stayed in a small hotel in Salzburg. Without explaining their reasons to Sindona, they stayed in Vienna for two days.

Then Gambino called his cousin Rosario Spatola. "I have to fly directly to Rome. Vincenzo was arrested delivering a note to Guzzi," Gambino told Sindona. "We were trying to get Guzzi to meet us in Vienna. We thought if he saw you wounded he would cooperate with us."

"That's as stupid as everything else you and your people have done," Sindona said.

"You go to Frankfurt with Dr. Crimi and the others," said Gambino. "My brother has a strong connection with TWA. He'll get you back into America."

Gambino gave Sindona a number in Rome where he could call Gambino for further instructions. Possibly out of guilt, he also handed Sindona $25,000 in $100 bills.

"What's this for?"

"That's what my brother will want to get you through customs," explained Gambino.

"Why?" asked a sad Michele Sindona.

"Because *they* are bigger than I am," Gambino said. "I had no choice."

Sindona, Crimi, and the two enforcers flew to Munich. They were delayed a few days, for reasons Sindona does not remember. Then, on October 12, they took Lufthansa flight 750 to Frankfurt. Sindona called Gambino, who instructed the financier to leave on Saturday, October 13, on TWA flight 741, at 3:45 P.M.

An unidentified woman, believed to work for U.S. Customs, met Michele Sindona at Kennedy Airport and escorted him to a waiting van. Rosario Gambino, Johnny's brother, asked Sindona for the $25,000. Sindona handed it to him. He counted out an unknown amount and handed it to the woman who, without saying a word, walked away. Rosario Gambino then asked Sindona for the Bonamico passport, which Michele gave to him. Then Gambino drove Michele to the Conca d'Oro Motel.

"You wait here until we hear from Johnny," Rosario said.

The next day Joseph Miceli Crimi showed up at the motel. He reviewed Sindona's story, checked his wound, and forced him to stay awake, without food, until Johnny Gambino called to say it was all right to release Sindona.

On October 16 an emotionally exhausted and physically weak Michele Sindona put on his disguise for the last time. At 11:10 A.M. Rosario Gambino drove him to a phone booth on the corner of 42nd Street and Tenth Avenue in Manhattan. Michele took off the disguise and stepped out of the car.

Michele Sindona called his attorney, Marvin Frankel, and said, "I was kidnapped, but I am free now."

The call ended a nightmare that had started seventy-six days earlier as an ideological scheme conceived by Michele Sindona who later, in reference to Il Momento di Sicilia Azione, called himself a "crazy man."

Pier Sandro Magnoni and Dr. George Serban, Sindona's current psychiatrist, picked Michele Sindona up and admitted him to Doctors Hospital. He remained there for eight days, during which time he was visited, at his family's request, by Joseph Miceli Crimi who had been ordered to check on what Sindona was saying.

On October 24 Sindona, though still weak, was released from the hospital and immediately taken before Judge Thomas Griesa. A hearing was held to determine whether or not Michele Sindona would be allowed to remain free on bail. Dr. Serban attended the hearing for the purpose of measuring the stress that testifying would have on Sindona.

Michele Sindona was nervous and afraid that he would say something to endanger his family. As instructed by the Mafia, Sindona testified that at about 2:20 P.M. on August 2 he received a call at his apartment from a man who spoke perfect Italian. The man, Sindona said, identified himself as, "Mr. Corsini, a friend of Mr. Guzzi," Sindona's Italian lawyer. "Mr. Guzzi told me to call you because I need help urgently," the man explained. Sindona said that when Corsini refused to come to his office, he agreed to meet him at the Tudor Hotel. After canceling another appointment, Sindona said he took a taxi to East 42nd Street. There, a man about 6 feet tall with curly blond hair and a hand hidden in the pocket of his suit coat as if he had a pistol, approached him and said, "Stay silent if you don't want to die." Sindona said he was forced into a metallic beige Fleetwood limousine, blindfolded, and handed a newspaper. "Look like you are reading the paper, and cover your face," the kidnapper ordered.

Sindona testified that they drove for many hours. Then he was taken out of the car and placed in the cellar of a house. The kidnappers removed the blindfold and told him to sit down. Two other men, wearing "scarves and dark glasses," told the driver and his partner to leave. The kidnappers, Sindona said, told him they were going to put him on trial for crimes against the people.

Eight or ten days later, explained Sindona, the men moved him to another house. A woman joined the kidnappers. She stood guard over Sindona most of the time, always carrying a gun in her jeans. He said he saw this as a chance to escape, but when he tried to run, the woman shot him in the back of the thigh.

Sindona also testified that he was moved four times to different locations. He said his kidnappers "wanted to convince me that I was completely guilty because I was pro-establishment, pro-American, against the leftists, against the people." They told him if he gave evidence against the rich, "principally the rightest of Democratic Christians," they would not kill him.

Judge Griesa asked Sindona if the terrorists had threatened to harm him if he testified.

"They told me," Sindona said, " 'You saw our organization. You saw that we can kill you and your family if you describe this place.' "

Judge Griesa ruled that Michele Sindona could remain free on bail, but he ordered Sindona to hire a twenty-four-hour guard service to protect himself and his family.

By the end of the hearing, Michele Sindona was hallucinating. Dr. Serban was concerned. He helped Sindona into his limousine and accompanied him back to Maria Elisa's apartment. During the drive, Michele Sindona rambled on about ideologies, about Aristotle and Plato. Suddenly he began to cry.

"They don't understand," he mumbled. "Nietzsche believed there were people who were above the laws of society. Why don't they understand that? Nunziata understood. She always told me I would be a great man."

EPILOGUE

● On March 27, 1980, Michele Sindona was convicted of sixty-eight counts of fraud, misappropriation of bank funds, and perjury. While awaiting sentencing, he was incarcerated at the Metropolitan Correctional Center in Manhattan. On May 13, 1980, two days before he was to be sentenced, Michele Sindona attempted suicide.

Anticipating his arrest, on February 6, 1980, the day he went on trial for the failure of Franklin National Bank, Michele Sindona wore the suit in which he had hidden the digitalis five years earlier. After his conviction, he somehow was able to rip the lining open and sneak the plastic bags of digitalis into his cell without detection by the guards. Around 3:00 A.M. on May 13 he took the digitalis, swallowed an unknown quantity of Darvon and Librium, and slashed his wrist. Although he was in critical condition and refused to cooperate with the attending physicians, Sindona survived this suicide attempt. On June 13, 1980, he was sentenced to twenty-five years in prison and fined $207,000.

On October 7, 1980, Michele Sindona was indicted for perjury and bail-jumping. Also indicted were Anthony Caruso and Joseph Macaluso. Named as unindicted co-conspirators were Johnny Gambino, Rosario Spatola, Vincenzo Spatola, and Joseph Miceli Crimi.

According to court testimony, Michele Sindona financed a bizarre

258

helicopter escape attempt in January 1981 at the Metropolitan Correctional Center. Sindona allegedly recruited Robert Wyler, a convicted drug
dealer, to help him. As of this writing, Wyler's girl friend, Dianne Becker,
and two friends have been charged with hijacking a helicopter and forcing
the pilot to land on the mesh screen that covers the rooftop recreation area
of the correctional center. The attempt failed because Wyler was unable to
cut through the wire.

Michele Sindona was convicted on April 20, 1981, for bail-jumping
and perjury. He was sentenced to two and a half years. He is now serving
his twenty-seven-and-a-half-year prison sentence at the Federal Correction
Institute in Otisville, New York, a medium-security prison.

On July 7, 1981, the Italian government charged Michele Sindona
with ordering the murder of Giorgio Ambrosoli. Named in the warrant of
arrest as one of the three killers was William J. Arico, a convicted bank
robber who escaped from the Rikers Island prison on June 28, 1980. Also
named in the warrant of arrest were Pier Sandro Magnoni and Nino Sindona.

On January 25, 1982, Michele Sindona was indicted in Palermo, Sicily, along with seventy-five members of the Gambino, Inzerillo, and Spatola Mafia clans. They were accused of operating a $600-million-a-year
heroin trade between Sicily and America. Sindona was also charged with
complicity, illegal possession of arms, fraud, using a false passport, and
violating currency regulations.

● In 1980 Licio Gelli offered to help presidential candidate Ronald Reagan. In a letter written to Phil Guarino, dated April 8, 1980, Gelli said: "If
you think it might be useful for something favorable to your presidential
candidate to be published in Italy, send me some material and I'll have it
published in one of the papers here." After Reagan was elected President,
Guarino sent Gelli an invitation to Reagan's inaugural ball, which Gelli
attended. In May 1981 the Italian police raided the home of Licio Gelli and
discovered secret government documents linking Gelli, Sindona, and other
members of P-2 to financial crimes and conspiracies against the state of
Italy. The discovery of the list of P-2 members led to the collapse of Italy's
fortieth government since World War II.

Although Licio Gelli had been indicted for espionage, political conspiracy, criminal association, and fraud, he successfully evaded arrest and
was believed to be living in Argentina. On September 13, 1982, however,
Gelli was arrested in Geneva, Switzerland, while attempting to withdraw
$50 million from a Swiss bank account—funds that had been illegally
transferred from a branch of Banco Ambrosiano. In a related investigation
conducted by the U.S. Justice Department, more than $34 million has
been traced from Italy to Banco Ambrosiano's Nassau subsidiary. Between
April 1981 and April 1982 the funds were withdrawn in cash, smuggled

into the United States, and deposited at two Miami banks, Bankers Trust International (account number 001050018) and South East First National Bank (account number 18221465) — accounts, according to customs agents, controlled by Licio Gelli and Michele Sindona.

● On July 21, 1981, Roberto Calvi was convicted of illegally exporting currency out of Italy. He was fined $13.7 million and sentenced to four years. On July 9, 1981, like Sindona, Calvi attempted suicide but survived. Later the Bank of Italy uncovered $1.4 billion in loans made by Banco Ambrosiano — and authorized by Archbishop Paul Marcinkus, president of the Vatican Bank, Banco Ambrosiano's fourth largest stockholder — to a group of Panamanian companies believed to be controlled by Licio Gelli, Michele Sindona, Roberto Calvi, and the Vatican. Unable to block the inquiry, Calvi disappeared on June 10, 1982. Five days later his secretary jumped to her death from a fourth-floor window of Banco Ambrosiano's Milan headquarters. She left behind a note proclaiming that Calvi should be "twice cursed for the damage he caused to the bank and all its employees." In London three days later, on June 18, Calvi's body was found hanging from the Blackfriars Bridge over the Thames River. In his suit pockets police found $20,000 in foreign currencies, a fraudulent passport, and twelve pounds of bricks and stones.

● Massimo Spada, the Vatican prince, as of this writing, is awaiting trial for fraud and conspiracy in the bankruptcy of Sindona's Italian banks.

● Pier Sandro Magnoni is awaiting trial in Italy on charges of fraud, conspiracy, and violating currency laws. He is also under investigation for complicity in Sindona's disappearance on August 2, 1979, and in Ambrosoli's murder, and for criminal association with the Mafia.

● A warrant of arrest has been issued for Maria Elisa (Sindona) Magnoni in Italy. She is wanted for questioning in the Ambrosoli murder and for association with the Mafia. Rather than join her husband in Italy, Maria Elisa has chosen to remain close to her father. She is living in New York City, where she has filed for divorce from Pier Sandro Magnoni. Her mother, Rina, lives with her.

● Carlo Bordoni was sentenced to seven years in prison for fraud and misappropriation of bank funds, which resulted in the failure of Franklin National Bank. Early in 1981 the U.S. Justice Department turned Bordoni and his wife over to the Italian authorities. Carlo Bordoni was allowed to remain free on bail while preparing to testify against Pier Sandro Magnoni, Michele Sindona, Massimo Spada, and several other associates of Group Sindona. In March 1982, however, Carlo and Virginia Bordoni vanished.

● Joseph Miceli Crimi has been indicted for being a member of the Mafia and for participating in the kidnapping of Michele Sindona. Crimi has testified in Italy against Rosario Spatola, Johnny Gambino, Vincenzo

Spatola, and seventy-two other mafiosi. If he lives, he will be the government's chief witness in the heroin case.

● Johnny Gambino, as of this writing, has not been charged by the American authorities for his participation in the August 2, 1979, disappearance of Michele Sindona. On January 25, 1982, however, Italy indicted Gambino, charging him with complicity and criminal association in a $600-million-a-year heroin-smuggling operation conducted by the Gambino, Inzerillo, and Spatola crime families in New York and Palermo.

● On September 3, 1982, General Carlo Alberto Dalla Chiesa, the highest-ranking police official in Italy and head of the Anti-Mafia Commission, his wife, and bodyguard were ambushed and killed on a street in Palermo by assassins carrying machine guns. General Dalla Chiesa had been investigating the Mafia's heroin trade between Palermo and New York.

● Joseph Macaluso and Anthony Caruso were convicted of conspiracy in the August 2, 1979, disappearance of Michele Sindona. They were both placed on probation.

● Dan Porco owns and operates several companies that once belonged to the Sindona Group.

● David Kennedy was sued by the Italian government, in New York on January 29, 1982. Italy alleges that Kennedy conspired illegally with Michele Sindona to sell Talcott Corporation to a group of Utah businessmen. Italy claims that Talcott belonged to Banca Privata Finanziaria, and is seeking $54 million in damages from Kennedy.

● Harold Gleason and Paul Luftig each served one year of a three-year sentence at Allenwood Federal Prison Camp. They were released in 1981.

● Peter Shaddick testified against Harold Gleason and Michele Sindona. For his cooperation he was sentenced to only three years in prison. He now lives in the Bahamas.

● The Vatican officially reported having lost $30 million as a result of its association with Michele Sindona. Sources inside the Vatican, however, put the figure closer to $200 million. In October 1982 Pope John Paul II appointed a special commission to investigate the Vatican's involvement in the theft of $1.4 billion from Banco Ambrosiano.

● Nino Sindona lives in Chicago with his wife and their two children. Nino Sindona owns a Hong Kong–based exporting company. He does not travel to Italy to do business; he is wanted there for questioning in regard to the murder of Giorgio Ambrosoli.

Nino Sindona has replaced Maria Elisa as his father's confidant and crusader. He works with Michele's new lawyer, fighting extradition proceedings filed by the Italian government and attempting to get his father moved to a minimum-security facility.

Determined to win his father's release, Nino collaborated with Michele to draft a thirty-one-page letter addressed to President Ronald Reagan, requesting that the President reopen Sindona's case in the hope of obtaining a pardon. David Kennedy delivered the letter to President Reagan's personal attorney at the White House.

If all fails, Michele Sindona claims he will commit suicide. He attempted to do so on two occasions while in prison. Once he took sleeping pills; another time he swallowed rat poison. Both times he vomited and survived.

Nino Sindona, however, says that he and his father have another plan. Should Michele Sindona's efforts to win his freedom fail — which seems likely, as the Supreme Court has already refused to review his case — they still hope he will be moved to a minimum-security prison. From there, according to Nino, Michele Sindona will attempt, with the aid of accomplices he has already paid, what he intends to be his final escape.

CAST OF CHARACTERS

MICHELE SINDONA. Pope Paul VI's banker and confidant. Born in 1920 in Patti, Sicily. Sindona became the most successful tax lawyer and the most powerful banker in Italy. Years later, as one of the wealthiest men in the world, Sindona was identified by the Italian and U.S. governments as the Mafia's banker. He was accused of washing heroin profits through his banks and of smuggling currency out of Italy through the Bank of the Vatican. In 1972 Sindona purchased controlling interest of Franklin National Bank. Two years later Franklin Bank collapsed—the largest bank failure in American history. On August 2, 1979, while under indictment, Michele Sindona disappeared and was believed to have been kidnapped by left-wing terrorists. He reappeared on October 16, 1979, was later convicted of bank fraud, and was sentenced to twenty-five years in prison.

CATERINA "RINA" SINDONA. Wife of Michele Sindona. Born Caterina Cilio in Catania, Sicily.

MARIA ELISA (SINDONA) MAGNONI. Eldest child of Michele and Rina Sindona. Born in 1945.

NINI SINDONA. Michele Sindona's father.

NINO SINDONA. Second-born, first son of Michele and Rina Sindona. Born in 1948.

MARCO SINDONA. Youngest child of Michele and Rina Sindona. Born in 1952.

PIER SANDRO MAGNONI. Husband of Maria Elisa. Born in Milan, Italy. Became Michele Sindona's lieutenant.

POPE PAUL VI. Born Giovanni Battista Montini on September 26, 1897, in the northern Italian town of Concesio. Elected pope on June 21, 1963. Died 1978.

DAVID KENNEDY. Former secretary of the treasury. Retired chairman of Continental Bank of Illinois. Director of Fasco International, one of Sindona's holding companies.

ARTHUR ROTH. Born in New York City in 1905. Former chairman of Franklin National Bank. Roth came to Franklin as head teller in 1934 when Franklin was a small community bank. He was responsible for making Franklin the eighteenth largest bank in the United States and for bringing about many changes in banking.

HAROLD GLEASON. Replaced Arthur Roth as chairman of Franklin National Bank in 1968.

PAUL LUFTIG. Former president of Franklin National Bank.

CHARLES BLUDHORN. Chairman of Gulf & Western.

LAWRENCE TISCH. Chairman of Loews Corporation. Sold controlling interest of Franklin National Bank to Michele Sindona in 1972.

CARLO BORDONI. Founded Moneyrex with Michele Sindona. Key operations officer for Group Sindona.

VIRGINIA BORDONI. Born Virginia Cornelio. Wife of Carlo Bordoni.

DAN PORCO. Former executive of Crucible Steel of America. Born in 1922 in Pittsburgh. Became Sindona's adviser and lead man for his American operations.

MASSIMO SPADA. Vatican prince. Former director of the Bank of the Vatican. Member of the boards of directors of Sindona's Italian banks.

BISHOP PAUL MARCINKUS. Born in Cicero, Illinois. Currently the most powerful man in Vatican finances. Pope Paul's bodyguard. Michele Sindona's partner and friend.

GIULIO ANDREOTTI. Leading member of Italy's Christian Democrats. Served as prime minister of Italy more times than any other man in Italian history. Had close ties with the Vatican, Michele Sindona, and Licio Gelli.

LICIO GELLI. Grand master of the renegade, right-wing Masonic lodge Propaganda Due (P-2). Also known as Naja Hannah.

NAJA HANNAH. *See* Licio Gelli.

ENRICO CUCCIA. Chairman of Mediobanca, Italy's government-owned investment bank. Because Cuccia pushed for nationalization, he and Sindona became archenemies.

GUIDO CARLI. Governor of the Bank of Italy.

ROBERTO CALVI. One of Italy's most powerful bankers. A member of Propaganda Due.

JAMES SMITH. Former U.S. comptroller of the currency.

CHARLES VAN HORN. Regional director for the comptroller of the currency in New York.

GIORGIO AMBROSOLI. Appointed by the governor of the Bank of Italy as liquidator of Michele Sindona's empire.

JACK BEGON. American journalist working for ABC in Italy. Investigated Michele Sindona's connections with the Sicilian and American Mafia.

TOMMASO BUSCETTA. Sicilian-born Mafia chief, heroin smuggler, and a relative of Carlo Gambino.

FRANK COPPOLA. Sicilian-born Mafia chief and international heroin smuggler. A close associate of Tommaso Buscetta.

MAX CORVO. Born in Sicily; became an American citizen. Captain of OSS and a member of the American invasion force in Sicily during World War II. A friend of Michele Sindona.

JOSEPH MICELI CRIMI. A member of Propaganda Due. Also identified as a member of the Mafia. An associate of Johnny Gambino and Rosario Spatola.

GIUSEPPE DI CRISTINA. Deceased Mafia assassin. An associate of Tommaso Buscetta, Frank Coppola, and Graziano Verzotto. An officer of Ente Minerario Siciliano.

ANTHONY DI FALCO. Carlo Bordoni's attorney. Son of the late S. Samuel Di Falco.

S. SAMUEL DI FALCO. American judge. A close friend of Michele Sindona. Now deceased.

AMINTORE FANFANI. Senator, prime minister of Italy, and former secretary of the Christian Democratic party.

MARVIN FRANKEL. Former federal judge. Represented Michele Sindona in the Franklin National Bank trial.

JOHNNY GAMBINO. Nephew of deceased crime boss Carlo Gambino and cousin of Rosario Spatola.

VITTORIO GHEZZI. Member of Sindona Group and government auditor for Sindona's banks.

RAFFAELE GIUDICE. Italian general. Member of Propaganda Due. Former chief of Italy's finance guard.

PHIL GUARINO. Leading member of the U.S. Republican party. Honorary member of P-2 and close associate of Michele Sindona and Licio Gelli.

RODOLFO GUZZI. Attorney for Michele Sindona.

JOCELYN HAMBRO. Former chairman Hambros Bank.

KAKENA. *See* Francesca Paola Longo.

JOHN KENNY. Former assistant U.S. prosecutor. In charge of the Franklin National Bank case.

JAMES KEOGH. Governor of the Bank of England.

UGO LA MALFA. Deceased. Former minister of finance in Italy. Once a close ally of Enrico Cuccia.

FRANCESCA "KAKENA" PAOLA LONGO. A member of the Freemasons in Sicily.

JOSEPH MACALUSO. Born in Catania, Sicily. Lives on Staten Island. An associate of Johnny Gambino, Rosario Spatola, and Michele Sindona.

MATTEO MACIOCCO. Member of Group Sindona. President of the board of auditors for Banca Unione.

GRAHAM MARTIN. U.S. ambassador to Italy under Nixon.

JOHN McCAFFREY. Deceased. Chief British organizer of the European resistance movement during World War II. Represented Hambros Bank in Italy and was a close friend of Michele Sindona.

JOHN McGILLICUDDY. President of Manufacturers Hanover Trust Company.

ANDRÉ MEYER. President of Lazard Frères, an investment banking house. A friend of Enrico Cuccia.

VITO MICELI. Italian general. Member of Propaganda Due. Former chief of the SID, Italy's CIA.

NUNZIATA SINDONA. Michele Sindona's grandmother.

WALTER PAGE. President of Morgan Guaranty Trust Company.

LUCIANO ROSSI. Deceased. Member of Propaganda Due.

JOHN SADLIK. Former vice-president of Franklin National Bank.

RAFFAELLO SCARPETTI. Leading member of Italy's Christian Democratic Party.

NORMAN SCHREIBER. Former vice-chairman of Franklin National Bank.

PETER SHADDICK. Former executive vice-chairman in charge of Franklin National Bank's international division. A close associate of Michele Sindona and David Kennedy.

CARMELO SPAGNUOLO. Italian judge and former president of a division of the supreme court of Italy. A member of Propaganda Due.

ROSARIO SPATOLA. Boss of the Palermo-based Gambino, Inzerillo, and Spatola crime families. A relative of Johnny Gambino.

VINCENZO SPATOLA. Brother of Rosario Spatola.

GRAZIANO VERZOTTO. Former Italian senator, Christian Democrat, and president of Ente Minerario Siciliano. Godfather to Giuseppe Di Cristina's son. A member of the Mafia.

GLOSSARY

FASCO, A.G. Michele Sindona's holding company.

FIDUCIARY CONTRACT OR DEPOSIT. A secret Swiss banking document that conceals the identity of an Italian citizen or corporation transferring funds out of Italy by recording only the name of the Italian bank. This gives the appearance that the Italian bank is making a normal currency transaction with a foreign bank, allowing the Italian citizen to circumvent Italy's currency laws and smuggle lire out.

GROUP. In Italy a financial organization is commonly referred to as a group. In most cases, the organization will also carry the surname of its founder, as in "Group Sindona" or "Sindona Group."

HIGH MAFIA. The politicians and financial leaders who were recruited by the Mafia after World War II, when the organization spread from Sicily throughout northern Italy and the rest of Europe.

IRI. Instituto per la Ricostruzione (Institute for Reconstruction), Italy's government-owned holding company. The vehicle by which nationalization was implemented.

MAFIA. A society of secret men more than a secret society itself. Its traditions are deeply rooted in Sicily's two-thousand-year history of foreign occupation. The Mafia is the offspring of violence perpetrated against Sicilians, yet not all Sicilians are invited to become members. The Mafia originated in tribal groups who took from their Arab rulers the notion that life was cheap, vengeful murder honorable, and justice possible only to one who has money and influential friends. In each town, the padrone filled the gap of social injustice. This dark side of lawfulness was accepted by Sicilians who believed that *"A liffi è pri ricca, la furca è pri lu poveru, la giustizia pri li fissa."* ("the law is for the rich, the gallows for the poor, and justice for the fools").

The concept of the family power base within the Mafia is structured after the Spanish Inquisition, which was transplanted to Sicily by the Aragonese, of whom Michele Sindona is a descendant. Mussolini's violence, World War II, and the American invasion of Sicily turned the Mafia into the island's real center of power. The Mafia later rented its power to the Christian Democratic party, whose members agreed to protect Mafia interests. This decision in time led "right-wing of the Christian Democrats" to become synonymous with "Mafia." As mafiosi infiltrated the Christian Democrats and were eventually elected to office, the criminal Mafia became more and more political, giving birth to what is today known as the High Mafia.

MEDIOBANCA. Italy's government-owned merchant bank. Headed by Enrico Cuccia, Mediobanca financed nationalization.

NATIONALIZATION. The infiltration of government into privately owned corporations.

PROPAGANDA DUE (PROPAGANDA 2, P–2). The most powerful, political, and violent secret organization in Italy. As grand master of P-2, Licio Gelli severed this Masonic lodge from the hierarchy of Freemasonry and transformed it into "an underground state within a state" by recruiting important military figures, members of the Italian judiciary, and leading members of the business community — all of whom were sworn to destroy Italy's parliamentary form of government.

IOR. Instituto per le Opere di Religione (Institute of Religious Works), also known as the Bank of the Vatican.

BIBLIOGRAPHY

ARCHIVAL AND GOVERNMENT SOURCES

Board of Governors of the Federal Reserve System. Files on Franklin National Bank and Franklin New York Corporation. Washington, D.C.

Federal Deposit Insurance Corporation. Files on Franklin National Bank and Franklin New York Corporation. New York.

United States District Court, Eastern District of New York, *In re Franklin National Bank Securities Litigation (All Cases)*. M.D.L. 196 (T.C.P.).

Office of the Comptroller of the Currency. Files on Franklin National Bank. Washington, D.C.

Securities and Exchange Commission. Files on Franklin New York Corporation. Washington, D.C.

United States District Court, Southern District of New York. *Securities and Exchange Commission, Plaintiff* v. *Franklin New York Corporation,*

Harold V. Gleason, Paul Luftig, Peter R. Shaddick, Michele Sindona, Carlo Bordoni, Howard D. Crosse, Andrew N. Garofalo, Donald H. Emrich, Robert C. Parepinto, Defendants, 74 Civil Action, File No. 4557.

United States District Court, Southern District of New York, *U.S.* v. *Carlo Bordoni, Peter R. Shaddick, Andrew Garofalo, Arthur Slutzky, Donald Emrich, Martin Keroes, Michael Romersa and Paul Sabatella,* Indictment S. 75 Cr. 948.

United States District Court, Southern District of New York, *U.S.* v. *Harold V. Gleason, Paul Luftig and Michael J. Carter,* Complete Trial Transcript.

United States District Court, Southern District of New York, *Requested Extradition of Michele Sindona by the Republic of Italy,* Supplemental Memorandum of Law and Fact in Support of the Requested Extradition of Michele Sindona, 65 Cr. Misc. 1.

United States District Court, Southern District of New York, *Sindona* v. *Grant, In the Matter of the Requested Extradition of Michele Sindona by the Republic of Italy,* 78 Civ. 2472. Complete File and Trial Transcript.

United States Court of Appeals, for the Second Circuit, *Michele Sindona* v. *George V. Grant, United States Marshall for the Southern District of New York, Acting Under a Warrant Issued at the Request of Italy,* Docket No. 78-2155. Joint Appendix, Volumes I and II.

United States District Court, Southern District of New York, *U.S.* v. *Michele Sindona and Carlo Bordoni,* Indictment S. 79 Cr. 948.

United States District Court, Southern District of New York, *U.S.* v. *Michele Sindona,* Indictment S. 75 Cr. 948.

United States District Court, Southern District of New York, *U.S.* v. *Michele Sindona,* S. 75 Cr. 945. Complete File and Trial Transcript.

United States District Court, Southern District of New York, *U.S.* v. *Michele Sindona,* S. 75 Cr. 948. Complete File and Trial Transcript.

United States Court of Appeals, for the Second Circuit, *U.S. against Michele Sindona,* Brief for Defendant-Appellant, Docket No. 80-1270.

United States Court of Appeals, for the Second Circuit, *U.S. against Michele Sindona,* Brief for the United States of America, Docket No. 80-1270.

United States Court of Appeals, for the Second Circuit, *U.S. against Michele Sindona,* Reply Brief for Defendant-Appellant, Docket No. 80-1270.

United States Court of Appeals, for the Second Circuit, *U.S. against Michele Sindona,* Docket No. 80-1270. Joint Appendix, volumes I through VII.

Supreme Court of the United States, October Term, 1980, *Michele Sindona,* Petitioner, v. *United States Of America,* Respondent, Petition for a Writ of Certiorari to the United States Court of Appeals for the Second Circuit.

United States District Court, Southern District of New York, *U.S.* v. *Michele Sindona, Joseph Macaluso and Antonio Caruso,* 79 Cr. 522. Complete File and Trial Transcript.

U.S. Congress. *Federal Institutions Regulatory and Investment Rate Control Act of 1978.* Public Law 95-630.

International Banking Act of 1978. Public Law 95-369.

Bank Failures, Regulatory Reform, Financial Privacy, Part II, Hearings before the Subcommittee on Financial Institutions Supervision, Regulation and Insurance. 93d Cong., 2d sess., 1974.

Bank Failures, Regulatory Reform, Financial Privacy, Hearings before the Subcommittee on Financial Institutions Supervision, Regulation and Insurance. 94th Cong., 1st sess., 1975.

International Banking: A Supplement to a Compendium of Papers Prepared for the FINE Study. Staff Report, 94th Cong., 2d sess., 1976.

Committee on Government Operations. *Adequacy of the Office of the Comptroller of the Currency's Supervision of Franklin National Bank,* House Report 94-1669. 94th Cong., 2d sess., 1976.

Oversight Hearings into the Effectiveness of Federal Bank Regulation

(Franklin National Bank), Hearings before a Subcommittee on Government Operations. 94th Cong., 2d sess., 1976.

Oversight Hearings into the Effectiveness of Federal Bank Regulation (Regulation of Problem Banks), Hearings before a Subcommittee on Government Operations. 94th Cong., 2d sess., 1976.

Committee on Banking, Housing, and Urban Affairs, *Compendium of Major Issues in Bank Regulation*, 94th Cong., 1st sess., 1975.

The International Banking Act of 1978, Report of the Committee on Banking, Housing, and Urban Affairs to Accompany HR 10899. 95th Cong., 2d sess., 1978.

Problem Banks, Hearings. 94th Cong., 2d sess., 1976.

Federal Bureau of Investigation. FBI 302 reports, *summary of interviews with Michele Sindona* (10/17/79, 10/18/79, 10/19/79, 10/22/79, 10/23/79, 10/24/79, 11/2/79, 11/5/79, 11/13/79, 3/7/80, 6/20/80, 7/7/80).

Federal Bureau of Investigation. FBI 302 reports, *summary of interviews with Joseph Macaluso, Antonio Caruso, Pier Sandro Magnoni, Maria Elisa Magnoni and Nino Sindona*. Various dates between August 1979 and March 1980.

New York Bank Laws of 1893, 1926, 1937, 1938, 1939, 1949, 1952.

Standing Committee on Banks of the Senate and Assembly, Albany, New York. Files on Omnibus Branch Banking Law.

Standing Committee on Banks of the Senate and Assembly, Albany, New York. Transcript of proceedings, February 18, 1958.

SELECTED FOREIGN GOVERNMENT SOURCES

The Republic of Italy, *Relazione Del Commissario Liquidator (Ambrosoli Report)*. Report of investigation into the banks, companies and financial operations of Michele Sindona. Parts I through III, all volumes.

The Republic of Italy, Court of Milan, *Investigation Section*. Testimony of Giorgio Ambrosoli on July 9, 1979. 41 pages.

The Republic of Italy. Bank of Italy, Bank Examiners Department. Complete Record.

Bank of Italy. Files on Banca Privata Finanziaria, Banca Unione, Amincor Bank, Finabank, Fasco, A.G., various corporations owned or controlled by Michele Sindona, and Michele Sindona.

The Republic of Italy, *Parliamentary Commission on Mafia (Antimafia Commission)*. Files on Michele Sindona, Pier Sandro Magnoni, Rosario Spatola. Testimony of government informants.

Antimafia Law of 1982. Public Law 646, 1982.

The Republic of Italy, *Parliamentary Commission on Mafia (Antimafia Commission)*. List of 3,000 high ranking members of the Mafia in Sicily, Southern Italy and U.S. Charts of inter-family relationships, various convictions and arrest records. File on Gambino Crime Family in New York and Palermo.

Antimafia Commission. Files on drug trafficking between Sicily and the United States.

Antimafia Commission. Report of February 1975.

Palermo Police Department, Palermo, Sicily. Files on organized crime.

Palermo Police Department, Palermo, Sicily. Files on Michele Sindona, Pier Sandro Magnoni, Rosario Spatola, Dr. Joseph Miceli Crimi, Tommaso Buscetta, Frank Coppola, Graziano Verzotto and Giuseppe Di Cristina.

The Republic of Italy. Notices of Investigation, Warrants of Arrest and Indictments against Michele Sindona, Pier Sando Magnoni, Rosario Spatola, Johnny Gambino, and Dr. Joseph Miceli Crimi. Public Record.

The Republic of Italy. Notices of Investigation against Nino Sindona and Maria Elisa Magnoni.

Federal Banking Commission, Chamber of Banks, Bern, Switzerland. File No. 232.6. Files on Amincor Bank, Zurich.

AG Fur Banken-und Industriekontrolle (Banking and Industry Auditing Corporation), *Report on the Findings in Connection with the Foreign*

Exchange Transactions between Amincor Bank, Zurich, and the Franklin National Bank, New York, dated August 8, 1974.

Hilton File, *Juge D'Instruction, Canton De Geneve.* An independant investigation into Michele Sindona, his banks, financial operations, Carlo Bordoni and Virginia Cornelio Bordoni.

Transcript of interview of Pietro Olivier, employee of Banca Unione, conducted at Lodi Prison, on July 6, 1977, by Investigating Magistrate Ovillio Urbisci. 32 pages.

August 29, 1974 letter from Banco di Roma to Guido Carli, governor of the Bank of Italy, detailing $200-million loan agreement between Michele Sindona and Banco di Roma. 32 pages, documents attached. Signed by F. Ventriglia.

The Republic of Venezuela, *Citizen Judge Septimo of the first Penal Part of the Judicial District of the Federal District and State of Miranda.* Civil proceedings regarding assets of Carlo Bordoni, Virginia Cornelio Bordoni and Inversionnes Mafal, C.A. Record sealed. Complete file.

INTERVIEWS

There were 452 interviews conducted for this book. The list below does not include the names of confidential sources or those who, out of fear, agreed to talk only after the author guaranteed anonymity.

Father Romano S. Almagno. Scholar, University of Pittsburgh.

Giampiero Azzali. Attorney in Milan representing Michele Sindona.

George Becht. Former corporate secretary of Franklin National Bank.

William Blodgett. Public Relations, Gulf & Western.

Guenther Blumauer. Michele Sindona's chauffeur in Vienna, Austria.

Carlo Bordoni. Associate of Michele Sindona.

Virginia Cornelio Bordoni. Wife of Carlo Bordoni.

James Boshart. Former vice-president of the Suffolk branch division of Franklin National Bank.

Roberto Calvi. Former president of Banco Ambrosiano and former member of P-2.

Antonio Caruso. Friend of Michele Sindona.

Maria Laura Castiglioni. Friend of Sindona family.

Archbishop Giovanni. Permanent Observer of the Holy See to the United Nations.

Frank Coppola. High-ranking member of the Sicilian and American Gambino Mafia Family.

Sol Corbin. Trustee in Bankruptcy for Franklin National Bank.

Max Corvo. Friend of Sindona Family.

Peter Cullen. Public relations, Citibank.

General Carlo Della Chiaso. Former chief of Italy's Antimafia Commission.

Anthony Di Falco. Attorney for Carlo Bordoni.

Luiz C. P. Gastel. Former vice-president of Franklin National Bank and branch manager of La Banque Continentale.

Amadeo Gatti. Attorney for Michele Sindona and the Vatican.

Harold Gleason. Former chairman of the board of Franklin National Bank.

Phil Guarrino. Associate of Michele Sindona and chairman of Italians for the Republican Party.

Rudolfo Guzzi. Former attorney for Michele Sindona.

Gabrielle Irnesberger. Friend of Joseph Macaluso.

William Kelly. Trial attorney for F.D.I.C.

John Kenny. Former assistant U.S. prosecutor.

Irwin Klein. Attorney for Antonio Caruso.

William Lewis. Former director and senior vice-president of Franklin National Bank.

Professor Clara M. Lovett. Scholar of Italian history.

Paul Luftig. Former president of Franklin National Bank.

Joseph Macaluso. Associate of Michele Sindona and Johnny Gambino.

Maria Elisa Magnoni. Michele Sindona's daughter.

Melisenda Marano. Friend of Sindona family.

Graham Martin. Former U.S. ambassador to Italy.

John McCaffrey. Former executive of Hambros Bank and associate of Michele Sindona.

Max K. Morris. Retired rear admiral.

Otis Pike. Former congressman from New York.

Dan Porco. Business associate of Michele Sindona and friend of Sindona family.

Gene Prescott. Business associate of Michele Sindona and friend of Dan Porco and Sindona family.

Luciano Rossi. Former high ranking member of P-2.

Arthur Roth. Former chairman of Franklin National Bank.

Genevieve Roth. Arthur Roth's wife.

John Sadlick. Former comptroller of Franklin National Bank.

Dr. George Serban. Psychiatrist who treated Michele Sindona for many years.

Beverly Sindona. Wife of Nino Sindona.

Caterina (Rina) Sindona. Wife of Michele Sindona.

Enio Sindona. Michele Sindona's brother.

Marco Sindona. Youngest child of Michele and Rina Sindona.

Michele Sindona. International financier.

Nino Sindona. Oldest son of Michele and Rina Sindona.

Charles Van Horn. Former comptroller of the currency for New York.

Myron Washington. Assistant warden, Metropolitan Correctional Center.

Dr. Sheldon Zigelbaum. Psychiatrist who examined, tested, and interviewed Michele Sindona.

AREAS OF INTERVIEWS CONDUCTED
WITH CONFIDENTIAL SOURCES

Federal Bureau of Investigation.

Department of the Treasury, U.S. Customs Service, Office of Investigations.

New York Police Department, Organized Crime Strike Force.

Antimafia Commission, Italy.

Palermo Police Department.

The Finance Guard, Italy.

The Italian Judiciary.

The Italian Parliament.

The Christian Democratic Party in Italy.

CERTAIN OTHER SOURCES

Employees and associates of Michele Sindona, Licio Gelli, Johnny Gambino, Rosario Spatola, Roberto Calvi, Carlo Bordoni, Virginia Bordoni, Nino Sindona, Maria Elisa Magnoni, Pier Sandro Magnoni, Dan Porco, Anthony di Falco, Harold Gleason, Paul Luftig, Arthur Roth, Peter Shaddick and Charles Bludhorn.

Present and former employees of Franklin National Bank, Franklin New York Corporation, Amincor, Finabank, Banca Privata Finanziara, Banca Unione, Gulf & Western, Talcott, Citibank, Union Bank of Switzerland, Banco Ambrosiano (Italy, Switzerland, Bahamas and U.S.).

Attorneys, banking officials and financiers in the following countries: Italy, Switzerland, Luxembourg, Liechtenstein, England, Paris, Germany, Bahamas, Caymán Islands, Panama, Argentina, Venezuela, and the U.S.

Eighteen residents of Patti, Sicily.

Thirty-two residents of Messina, Sicily.

Forty-six residents of Palermo, Sicily.

One hundred and twenty-five residents of Milan, Italy.

Six members of Propaganda Due.

Three members and six associates of the Gambino Crime Family.

Two members and one associate of the Columbo Crime Family.

Four physicians who treated Michele Sindona for medical and psychiatric problems.

SELECTED NOTES AND DOCUMENTS

Michele Sindona: business and personal records, letters, notes, 1968 through 1981. Complete unpublished manuscript.

Universita Degli Studi Di Messina, scholastic record of Michele Sindona, 1940 through 1942.

Medical and Psychiatric records: more than 1,200 pages, including physicians' notes, hospital records, Bureau of Prison records, and a detailed history of the drugs prescribed by Sindona's personal physicians in Italy and U.S.

Arthur Roth: business and personal records, letters, notes, 1934 through 1976. Complete unpublished manuscript.

Arthur Roth: files on Franklin National Bank, 1934 through 1974.

Files, research material and many tape-recorded interviews with government officials, bankers and businessmen, all conducted by journalist Walter Ross while he was helping Mr. Roth write his manuscript.

Maria Elisa Magnoni: files on Fasco, A.G., Banca Unione, Banca Privata Finanziara, and various banks and corporations owned or controlled by Michele Sindona.

Carlos A. Martinez Murga: attorney in Venezuela who represented Carlo and Virginia Bordoni and was an officer and director of Inversiones Mafal, c.a. His complete file.

"Ten Years with Sindona," by Carlo Bordoni. In this 158-page memo, which Bordoni sent to the Italian courts, Bordoni details many of the illegal activities in which he and Michele Sindona collaborated. Written on December 27, 1977, it was later published in two parts (February 15 & 22, 1978) in *Il Mondo*. Later, when Michele Sindona was on trial for the failure of Franklin National Bank, Bordoni's memo was entered into the trial record.

"Observations about the letter–memo sent by Carlo Bordoni to the Investigating Magistrate. . . ," by Michele Sindona. No date. 47 pages.

Seven-page memo written by Antonio Caruso regarding the disappearence of Michele Sindona on August 2, 1979. No date.

Copy of Nino Sindona's personal telephone/address book

Copy of Joseph Macaluso's personal telephone/address book.

Copy of Michele Sindona's personal telephone/address book.

Toll records for ASIPCO, a holding company owned by Michele Sindona and Maria Elisa Magnoni. April 1979 through February 1980.

Travel records (airline tickets, hotel records, various restaurant and bar tabs, telephone toll records for various hotels throughout U.S. and Europe, U.S. Customs declaration forms) for Michele Sindona, Pier Sandro Magnoni, Maria Elisa Magnoni, Rina Sindona, Nino Sindona, Rosario Spatola, Vincenzo Spatola, Johnny Gambino, Rosario Gambino, Antonio Caruso, Joseph Macaluso, William Arico, Licio Gelli, Dr. Joseph Miceli Crimi.

Bank records of Banco Ambrosiano, Milan, regarding thirty-nine wire transfers totaling $10,749,387.00 to Banco Ambrosiano, Nassau, between April 16, 1981 and April 16, 1982.

Records of Banco Ambrosiano, Nassau, regarding cash withdrawals totaling $10,749,387.00 between April 16, 1981 and April 16, 1982, which were hand couriered to Miami, Florida, and deposited at Bankers Trust International, Biscayne Towers, Miami (account number 001050018), and South East First National Bank, Miami (account number 18221465). Cash withdrawals from Banco Ambrosiano, Nassau, and cash deposits made at the two Miami banks were made as follows: 4/16/81 for $24,250.00; 4/30/81 for $24,250.00; 8/11/81 for $85,800.00; 8/21/81 for $87,870.00; 9/18/81 for $300,665.00; 9/29/81 for $353,725.00; 9/30/81 for $504,420.00; 10/5/81 for $126,805.00; 10/8/81 for $95,960.00; 10/9/81 for $991,840.00; 10/13/81 for $288,045.00; 10/21/81 for $193,825.00; 10/23/81 for $72,692.00; 11/2/81 for $192,806.00; 11/16/81 for $169,537.00; 11/19/81 for $453,638.00; 11/24/81 for $317,429.00; 1/14/82 for $193,050.00; 1/15/82 for $268,345.00; 1/18/82 for $90,120.00; 1/18/82 for $250,000.00; 1/19/82 for $131,370.00; 1/20/82 for $192,000.00; 1/21/82 for $192,000.00; 2/1/82 for $145,000.00; 2/2/82 for $94,080.00; 2/3/82 for $95,610.00; 2/8/82 for $92,471.00; 2/9/82 for $208,826.00; 2/16/82 for $119,605.00; 2/17/82 for $216,000.00; 3/8/82 for $220,000.00; 3/10/82 for $192,100.00; 4/2/82 for $285,113.00; 4/5/82 for 1,705,550.00; 4/6/82 for $285,240.00; 4/8/82 for $290,000.00; 4/14/82 for $868,075.00; 4/16/82 for $175,475.00.

FASCO INTERNATIONAL HOLDING S.A., *Minutes of a Board Meeting which was held in Milan on April 20, 1973, at 4:00 P.M.*. Present at Meeting: Mr. Michele Sindona, President and Managing Director; Mr. Pier Sandro Magnoni, Managing Director; Mr. David Kennedy, Director in charge of overseas affairs; Mr. Gian Luigi Clerici di Cavenago, Director; Mr. Carlo

Bordoni, Director, represented by Mr. P. S. Magnoni; Mr. Nico Schaeffer, Director.

FASCO INTERNATIONAL HOLDING S.A. Balance sheet for December 31, 1972.

FASCO INTERNATIONAL HOLDING S.A. Profit and Loss statement for December 31, 1972.

FASCO INTERNATIONAL HOLDING S.A., *Minutes of a circular Board Resolution dated March 26, 1973*. Participants in meeting: Mr. Michele Sindona, President, Delegate Director; Mr. Pier Sandro Magnoni, Delegate Director; Mr. Gian Luigi Clerici di Cavenago, Director; Mr. Carlo Bordoni, Director; Mr. Nico Schaeffer, Director.

FASCO INTERNATIONAL HOLDING S.A., fiduciary deposits, wire transfers, financial documents. Various years.

FASCO, A.G., fiduciary deposits, wire transfers, financial documents. Various years.

EDILCENTRO SVILUPPO INTERNATIONAL, Cayman Islands, fiduciary deposits, wire transfers, financial documents. Various years.

EDILCENTRO SVILUPPO NASSUA, fiduciary deposits, wire transfers, financial documents. Various years. File on legal proceeding filed against Kosmin Anstalt, Vaduz.

INVERSIONNES MAFAL, C.A., Vaduz, corporate records, bank deposits, wire transfers, financial documents, various contracts and agreements. Various years.

KOSMIN ANSTALT, Vaduz, corporate records, bank records, wire transfers, financial documents, letters of correspondence.

Central Savings Bank of Sicily, records of account (159541/20) opened by Rosario Spatola.

Union Bank of Switzerland, Chiasso, deposits, withdrawals, wire transfers and letters of instruction on Carlo Bordoni's account (636503) and Virginia Cornelio Bordoni's account (634612).

Banque De Financement S.A. (Finabank), fiduciary deposits, wire transfers, financial documents, complete records of various accounts. Various years.

Banca Privata Finanziaria (BPF), fiduciary deposits, wire transfers, financial documents, complete and partial records of various accounts. Various years.

Banco Unione (BU), fiduciary deposits, wire transfers, financial documents, complete and partial records of various accounts. Various years.

Bank of Nova Scotia, Westblaak, Rotterdam. Various records and financial documents.

Banque de Paris et des Pay Bas N.V., Herengracht, Amsterdam. Various records and financial documents.

Banco Popular Esparol, Madrid, Spain. Various records and financial documents.

Cooperative Centrale Raiffeisen–Boereleenbank G.A., St. Jacobsstraat, Utrecht. Various records and financial documents.

The Royal Bank of Canada, Montreal, Quebec. Various records and financial documents.

Gotabanken, Stockholm. Various records and financial documents.

Banca Del Gottardo, Chiasso, Switzerland. Various records and financial documents.

MICHELE SINDONA AND HIS BANKS, a memorandum prepared by Mr. Sindona, on May 20, 1979, explaining his relationship with his banks and corporations to his attorneys. 27 pages.

"JORDAN — Financial Center of the Middle East": a thirteen-page proposal written by Michele Sindona, in March of 1976, for King Hussein. Sindona analyzes the financial and banking situation in the Middle East, concluding that Jordan should retain him so that it can become the financial center of the Middle East. Excerpt:

"It has become increasingly clear that the civil disturbances in Lebanon have permanently destroyed the financial reputation of Beirut. This destruction leaves a vacuum in the Middle East that will not persist, owing to the fact that an international money and business center is absolutely vital to the area. Further, such a financial capital is highly desirable to the rest of the world for many specific reasons, but especially as a focus for the emerging importance of worldwide interests throughout the petroleum producing zone.

The Kingdom of Jordan, and specifically Amman, has the best potential to fill that void and assume the central position abdicated by Beirut. . . . To obtain really large deposits for the international banking organizations that already exist in Jordan it will be necessary to safeguard bank secrecy. In no case and for no reason should the Jordanian banks supply, without the consent of the interested parties, information about movements of capital or about holders of accounts to private individuals, governments, political or legal authorities."

"IRAN—Financial Center of the Middle East": a proposal written by Michele Sindona, in March of 1978, for the Shah of Iran. Sindona's theory aimed at "transforming Iran into the Switzerland of the Middle East."

Memorandum dated May, 1978. Michele Sindona explains his opposition to nationalization.

Six memorandums addressed to the Italian Parliamentary Commission by Michele Sindona on October 22, 1981:

"RAPPORTI CON UOMINI O PARTITI POLITICI," 32 pages.

"MASSONERIA–MILITARI–CIA–MAFIA," 6 pages.

"LISTA DEI 500," 4 pages.

"AMBROSOLI," 4 pages.

"VATICANO," 2 pages.

"FALLIMENTO BANCA PRIVATA ITALIANA," 6 pages.

Memorandum of August 3, 1982, written by Nino Sindona. In sixty-three pages, Nino Sindona reconstructs his father's career in an attempt to explain his version of why his father is innocent of all Italian and U.S. charges, both pending and those charges of which Michele Sindona has already been convicted.

Income tax returns for Michele Sindona, 1974 through 1979. Department of the Treasury, Internal Revenue Service, *U.S. Nonresident Alien Income Tax Return, form 1040NR.*

1978 income tax return filed by Associated Metals & Minerals Corporation, Michele Sindona, proprietor. Department of the Treasury, Internal Revenue Service, *Profit (or Loss) From Business or Profession*, form 1040.

1974 state income tax return for Michele Sindona. New York State Department of Taxation and Finance, *NY State Income Tax Nonresident Return 1974*.

1974 return filed by Michele Sindona. The City of New York, Finance Administration Department of Tax Collection, *Nonresident Earnings Tax Return*, form 203.

REPUBLIC OF IRELAND, COUNTY OF DONEGAL, EMBASSY OF THE UNITED STATES OF AMERICA, *Affidavit given by John McCaffrey*, February 3, 1981. 5 pages.

REPUBLIC OF IRELAND, COUNTY OF DONEGAL, EMBASSY OF THE UNITED STATES OF AMERICA, *Affidavit given by John McCaffrey*, February 3, 1981. 1 page.

Letter signed by John McCaffrey, dated February 20, 1979, addressing the United States District Court, Southern District of New York, regarding charges pending against Michele Sindona.

REPUBLIC OF ITALY, MILANO, *Affidavit given by Xenia Vago*, February 10, 1981. 3 pages.

REPUBLIC OF ITALY, MILANO, *Affidavit given by Giampiero Azzali, Professor of Criminal Law and Procedure*, March 3, 1981. 8 pages. Professor Azzali addresses several points of Italian criminal law. Excerpt:

"The defendant . . . is not obliged to tell the truth. . . . [T]he defendant who tells a lie is part of the very function of the interrogation, which in the Italian Criminal Code is conceived essentially as a means of defense for the accused."

Letter signed by Charles M. Carberry, Assistant U.S. Attorney, dated April 27, 1981, requesting an attorney for Michele Sindona to instruct the Sindonas not to call the home of any Assistant U.S. Attorney.

Jail, a list of complaints against the Bureau of Prisons written by Michele Sindona. 7 pages.

Subpoena, issued March 11, 1981, for the testimony of Richard M. Nixon before the United States District Court, Southern District of New York, *United States* v. *Michele Sindona*. No. 80 CR. 634 (PNL).

Subpoena, served on April 14, 1981, for the testimony of Admiral Turner, Office of the General Counsel, Central Intelligence Agency, before the United States District Court, Southern District of New York, *United States* v. *Michele Sindona*. No. 80 CR. 634 (PNL).

Subpoena, served April 13, 1981, to the Department of the Treasury, "Keeper of the Records," for documents regarding *United States* v. *Michele Sindona*. No. 80 CR. 634 (PNL).

Subpoena, issued April 2, 1981, for the testimony of Graham Martin before the United States District Court, Southern District of New York, *United States* v. *Michele Sindona*. No. 80 CR. 634 (PNL).

Subpoena, issued April 2, 1981, to the United States Customs Service, for the testimony of Luigi Cavallo before the United States District Court, Southern District of New York, *United States* v. *Michele Sindona*. No. 80 CR. 634 (PNL).

June 21, 1977 letter on Associated Metals & Minerals Corporation letterhead addressed to Michele Sindona, signed by James C. Slaughter, retaining Mr. Sindona as a consultant for a fee of $1000.00 per month.

Three letters addressed to Michele Sindona and signed by Rear Admiral Max K. Morris. September 20, 1978; October 6, 1978; December 13, 1978.

Letter addressed to Arthur Roth and signed by Senator William Proxmire. October 7, 1974.

Letter addressed to James E. Smith, Comptroller of the Currency. Signed by Arthur Roth. April 29, 1974.

October 17, 1974 letter written by Arthur Roth, addressed to *Fortune* magazine. Never mailed.

Letter addressed to Arthur Roth and signed by U.S. Representative Wilbur D. Mills. March 2, 1973.

SELECTED LETTERS WRITTEN
BY MICHELE SINDONA

March 2, 1980 letter addressed to Maria Elisa Magnoni. In seven pages Michele Sindona recalls his life and love for his daughter as he attempts to explain why he must commit suicide. Signed PAPA.

September 18, 1962 letter addressed to Maria Elisa Magnoni, written on stationary from the St. Regis-Sheraton Hotel, New York, and signed PAPA. Six pages. Michele Sindona wrote his daughter explaining how he desperately missed her.

Addressed to Bishop Paul Marcinkus, President, Instituto per le Opere di Religione, CITTA' DEL VATICANO. One page, dated January 8, 1980. A request for the Vatican to send character witnesses to testify at the Franklin National Bank trial.

To: Giuseppe Cardinal Caprio, President, Admin. of the Beni della Santa Sede, CITTA DEL VATICANO. Three pages, dated January 8, 1980. In summary, a request by Mr. Sindona for Cardinal Caprio to testify on his behalf at the Franklin National Bank trial.

To: Sergio Cardinal Guerri, Governor of the CITTA DEL VATICANO. Three pages, dated January 8, 1980. In summary, a request by Mr. Sindona for Cardinal Guerri to testify on his behalf at the Franklin National Bank trial.

Addressed to Judge Leval. Three pages, dated June 6, 1981. Mr. Sindona describes his gratitude for the way in which he was sentenced, and offers Judge Leval advice. Excerpt:

> "I admired your courage and humility when you expressed your doubts upon delivering my sentence. . . . Please allow me, with the experience of my grey hair, to give my modest advice to a young man. Maintain your humility, personality and courage; and, do not forfeit your mind — as has happened to some of your colleagues — to the coldness of the American bureaucracy or to the vain desire for publicity."

Eight-page handwritten letter addressed to Maria Elisa Magnoni, signed, PAPA. No date. Excerpt:

> "I assure you that I have tried to picture all your movements hour by hour, but, being in the dark as to everything, I have had to make do

with fantasizing. . . . You . . . should get away from New York . . . above all, from all contacts . . . which grate on your nerves. . . . Do not read the newspapers. . . . You know that the so-called journalists have no other means to get read but inventing news of a scandalous nature. They make up for their incompetence by giving vent to their aridness and wickedness. . . . You must come out of the kind of life to which I, albeit somewhat involuntarily, have forced you over the last few years."

Two-page handwritten letter addressed to Xenia Vago, signed MICHELE SINDONA. Dated August 27, 1979.

Five-page handwritten letter addressed to Pier Sandro Magnoni (Maria Elisa, Nino, Marco), dated September 30, 1979, signed MICHELE SINDONA.

One-page handwritten letter addressed to Rina Sindona, postmarked August 11, 1979, signed MICHELE SINDONA.

Four-page handwritten letter addressed to Rina Sindona, signed MICHELE. No date. Excerpt:

"Look around and draw a balance sheet of our lives. We have no right to complain; we have always loved each other, we have been united during the good times as well as during the bad times; you have followed me during very difficult moments, giving me warmth and affection. Many years together: more than 50, with a bottom line which is certainly in the black."

Two-page handwritten letter addressed to Enio Sindona, Michele's brother, signed MICHELE. No date.

Four-page handwritten letter addressed to Marco Sindona, signed PAPA. No date. Excerpt:

"I know that . . . you . . . have an ideology that keeps you busy with principles of honesty and I wish . . . for your sake that you may not have too many big disappointments. . . . In simple words: . . . I have no doubts, materially speaking, . . . your . . . nature will never allow you to take the wrong road."

Two-page handwritten letter addressed to Pier Sandro Magnoni, signed MICHELE. No date.

Three-page handwritten letter addressed to Rina Sindona, signed MICHELE. No date. Excerpt:

> "Ask our friends . . . not to do anything about looking for me. It could be dangerous for me. Let the authorities and the lawyers take care of it. I miss you very much and this is not limited to the "ice cream" and the "foamy stuff!!"

Five-page handwritten letter addressed to Nino Sindona, signed PAPA. No date. Excerpt:

> "I see that . . . you are trying very hard to defend me. I am infinitely grateful to you. . . . However, . . . it is not worthwhile. The blackmailers, the poor in spirit, the so-called journalists who live on scandals (because they do not have the skills necessary to do so with more acceptable ethical methods) are not to be stopped by you or anybody else because they belong to the system that uses them. . . . You're young; you must work; you have a beautiful family and therefore you must think of them serenely. . . . When the children are grown up and you tell them the "story" of their grandfather, recommend that they do not follow his example. . . . [If] they feel like it, they only need to follow one of my qualities: loyalty! (if you believe that I have this quality)."

Letter postmarked September 7, 1979. Addressed: Message for Pier Sandro Magnoni. Signed: COMITATO PROLETARIO DI EVERSIONE *PER UNA GIUSTIZIA MIGLIORE* (Proletarian Committee for the Eversion of an Improved Justice).

August 9, 1979: "Communication No. 1: Michele Sindona is our prisoner. He will have to respond to proletarian justice. Our communication No. 2 will follow."

Letter addressed to Pier Sandro Magnoni, date illegible. Excerpt:

> "We repeat our telephone call to Mr. Gambino. We did not telephone Mr. Guzzi on Friday because we had understood that he wants to make idiots out of us with the agreement of his client and of his son-in-law. We can now state that his client is seriously injured: we have shot him. If you want we will send you proof. This is a last warning." Signed: GRUPPO PROLETARIO DI EVERSIONE PER UNA GIUSTIZIA MIGLIORE.

Letter addressed to Rodolfo Guzzi, October 30, 1979. Excerpt:

"Michele Sindona knows very well that if the promise made is not maintained, we will attack without mercy. Not him but his family as well as the other person in Milan who, it seems, wants to obstruct our mission. We will call in a few days. . . . Otherwise we will send . . . numerous other messengers who are not so stupid." Signed: THE COMMITTEE. (Enclosed with this letter was a list of names, addresses and telephone numbers, the purpose of which is unknown. Some of the individuals named are John J. Kenney, then Assistant U.S. Attorney, Judge J. B. Weinstein, and Deputy U.S. Marshall Pete Spiro.

Twelve-page letter addressed to Dottor Guido Carli, Governor of the Bank of Italy, February 10, 1975, signed Michele Sindona.

Seventeen-page letter addressed to Professor Alberto Martinelli, Universita Commerciale L. Bocconi, Milano, on April 24, 1982. Sindona attacks the Italian financial community accusing it of perpetrating frauds against the public.

Four-page letter addressed to Mr. Pierre Carnitti, head Segretario Generale della CISL, one of the three national labor unions in Italy. April 24, 1982.

Five-page letter addressed to Professor Guido Rossi, president of CONSOB, Italy's Securities & Exchange Commission.

Ten letters Michele Sindona wrote to his attorneys discussing his legal problems. Various dates.

September 7, 1981 letter addressed to the President of the United States. 31 pages. Signed MICHELE SINDONA. In summary, Sindona pleads for President Reagan to review his case.

TRANSCRIPTS OF SPEECHES
GIVEN BY MICHELE SINDONA

"International Monetary System and Balance of Payments," Harvard Business School, November 7, 1972.

"The effect of Foreign Investments on the Balance of Payments," Carnegie-Mellon University, Graduate School of Industrial Administration, February 6, 1973.

"Multinational Companies," Graduate School of Business, Columbia University, February 19, 1973.

"International Monetary and Economic Problems," Adelphi University, June 18, 1973.

"One Hundred National Monies or a Common Worldwide One at the Helm of a New International Monetary System?" University of Chicago, Graduate School of Business, December 1, 1973.

"Aid to Emerging Nations: A Banker's Duty But Also a Pitfall," Bankers, Factors and Finance Division of the Federation of Jewish Philanthropies and United Jewish Appeal of Greater New York, December 13, 1973.

"The Phantom Petrodollar," University of Pennsylvania, Wharton Graduate School, April 15, 1975.

"Inflation Today," New York University, Graduate School of Business Administration, June 12, 1975.

"From Multi-Nationals to Cosmo-Corporation," Graduate School of Business, Columbia University, August 5, 1975.

"Gold and the International Monetary System," Massachusetts Institute of Technology, Sloan School of Management, October 2, 1975.

"Exchange Rates and the International Monetary System," University of San Diego, School of Business Administration, October 22, 1975.

"Aid to Impoverished Nations," University of California at Los Angeles, Graduate School of Management, October 23, 1975.

"Capitalism Today," University of Chicago, Graduate School of Business, November 5, 1975.

"International Liquidity and Special Drawing Rights," Harvard University, Graduate School of Business Administration, November 6, 1975.

"International Economic Détente," Graduate School of Business, University of Minnesota, November 20, 1975.

"International Monetary Upheavals," John Carroll University, School of Business, October 1, 1976.

SELECTED READING LIST

Abbott, Walter M., S.J. (editor). *The Documents of Vatican II*. New York: Association Press, 1966.

Agee, Philip and Louis Wolf. *Dirty Work*. Lyle Stuart, 1978.

Allum, Percy. *Italy: Republic without Government?* London, 1973.

Alongi, Giuseppe. *La Mafia nei suoi fattori e nelle sue manifestazioni, Studio delle classi pericolose della Sicilia*. Turin, 1887.

Barzini, Luigi. *The Italians*. New York: Atheneum, 1977.

Bell, J. Bowyer. *Assassin*. New York: St. Martin's Press, 1979.

Blackmer, Donald L. M. and Sidney Tarrow. *Communism in Italy and France*. Princeton University Press, 1975.

Blanshard, Paul. *Paul Blanschard on Vatican II*. Boston: Beacon Press, 1963.

Blok, Anton. *The Mafia of a Sicilian Village 1860–1960*. Oxford, 1974.

Brancato, Francesco. *Storia della Sicilia post-unificazione—La Sicilia nel primo ventennio del regno d'Italia, Parte I*. Bologna, 1956.

Bruno, Cesare. *La Sicilia e la mafia*. Rome, 1900.

Buttitta, Antonino. *Ideologica e folklore*. Palermo, 1971.

Cavallari, Alberto. *The Changing Vatican*. London: Faber & Faber, 1968.

Ciano, Galeazzo. *Ciano's Diary, 1937–1938*. London, 1952.

Crosse, Howard D. *Management Policies for Commercial Banks*. New Jersey: Prentice-Hall, 1962.

Deakin, F. W. *The Brutal Friendship: Mussolini, Hitler and the Fall of Italian Fascism*. London, New York and Evanston, 1962.

Delzell, Charles F. *Mussolini's Enemies: The Italian Anti-Fascist Resistance*. Princeton and London, 1961.

Dolci, Danilo. *Banditi a Partinico*. Bari, 1955.
Spreco. Turin, 1960.
Inchiesta a Palermo. Turin, 1962.
Conversazioni. Turin, 1962.
Chi gioca sols. Turin, 1967.
Inventare if futuro. Bari, 1968.
Sicilian Lives. New York: Pantheon Books, 1981.

Fallaci, Oriana. *Interview with History*. Boston: Houghton Mifflin, 1976.

Gilbert, Felix. *The Pope, His Banker, and Venice*. Harvard University Press, 1980.

LoBello, Nino. *Vatican, U.S.A.* New York: Trident Press, 1972. *The Vatican Empire*. New York: Trident Press, 1968.

MacKenzie, Norman (editor). *Secret Societies*. New York: Collier Books, 1967.

Martin, Malachi. *The Final Conclave*. Pocket Books, 1978.

Mayer, Martin. *The Bankers*. New York: Weybright and Talley, 1974.

Mussolini, Benito. *Discorso dell' Ascensione—Antologia della mafia*. Palermo, 1964.

Mussolini, Benito. *Fascism: Doctrine and Institutions*. Rome, 1935.

Natoli, Luigi (Galt, William). *I beati Paoli*, Vol. I and II. Palermo, 1971.

Neville, Robert. *The World of the Vatican*. New York: Harper & Row, 1962.

Nolte, Ernst. *Three Faces of Facism*. New American Library, 1969.

Pallenberg, Corrado. *Le Finanze del Vaticano*. Milan, 1969.

Pantaleone, Michele. *Mafia e politica 1943-62*. Turin, 1962.

Powers, Thomas. *The Man Who Kept the Secrets: Richard Helms and The CIA*. Pocket Books, 1981.

Servadio, Gaia. *Mafioso*. Stein and Day, 1976.

Silj, Alessandro. *Never Again Without A Rifle*. New York: Karz Publishers, 1979.

Snepp, Frank. *Decent Interval*. New York: Vintage Books, 1978.

Spero, Joan Edelman. *The Failure of the Franklin National Bank*. New York: Columbia University Press, 1980.

Sterling, Claire. *The Terror Network*. Holt, Rinehart and Winston, 1981.

White, James J. *Case and Statutory Supplement to Teaching Materials on Banking Law*. St. Paul, Minn.: West Publishing, 1980.

GENERAL SOURCES

Allan, John H. "Franklin National Bank Dismisses its President," *New York Times*, May 14, 1974.

Allan, John H. "Reserve is Aiding in Bank Liquidity," *New York Times*, May 16, 1974.

Annual Statistical Digest. Washington, D.C.: Board of Governors, various years.

Annuario Pontificio, Libreria Editrice Vaticana. Various years.

Annuario Statistico della Chiesa, Libreria Editrice Vaticana. Various years.

"Bank Expansion in New York State: The 1971 Statewide Branching Law," Federal Reserve Bank of New York, *Monthly Review* (November 1971), 53(11):266-74.

Bank of International Settlements, *Annual Report*. Basel: BIS, various years.

Barr, Joseph W. "The Last Days of Franklin National Bank," *Administrative Law Review* (Fall 1975), 27(4):301-14.

Becker, Joseph D. "International Insolvency: The Case of Herstatt," *American Bar Association Journal* (October 1976), 62:1290-95.

Bedingfield, Robert E. "Big Stockholder Got Fee of $60,000 in 1973," *New York Times*, May 17, 1974.

Benston, George J. "How We Can Learn From Past Bank Failures," *Bankers Magazine*, (Winter 1975), 158(1):19-24.

Bradshaw, Robert C. "Foreign Exchange Operations of U.S. Banks," in *Conference on Bank Structure and Competition*, pp. 113-23. Chicago: Federal Reserve Bank of Chicago, May 1975.

Brimmer, Andrew F. "International Finance and the Management of Bank Failure: Herstatt v. Franklin National." Paper prepared for presentation before a joint session of the American Economic Association and the American Finance Association. Atlantic City, New Jersey, September 16, 1976.

Burns, Arthur F. "Maintaining the Soundness of Our Banking System," Federal Reserve Bank of New York, *Monthly Review* (November 1974), 56(11):263-67.

Cordtz, Dan. "What's Behind the Sindona Invasion," *Fortune*, August 1973.

De Zulueta, Tana. "How Signor Sindona Swindled the World," *London Times*, January 6, 1980. "Sindona and the Mafia," *London Times*, February 3, 1980.

Earle, John. "The Sicilian Iron Chewer," *London Times*, May 29, 1974.

"Failures of Large Banks: Implications for Banking Supervision and Deposit Insurance," *Journal of Finance and Quantitative Analysis* (November 1975), 10(4):589-601.

Federal Reserve Bulletin, various issues.

Foldessy, Edward P. "Top Officers of Franklin N.Y. Shuffled," *Wall Street Journal*, May 14, 1974.

"Franklin National Bank in Sweeping Reorganization of Four Division Presidents are Appointed," *American Banker*, Feb. 17, 1964.

"Franklin National Bank of New York: A Portfolio and Performance Analysis of our Largest Bank Failure," Federal Deposit Insurance Corporation,

Financial and Economic Research section, Division of Research, Working Papers, No. 75-10, 1975.

Franklin New York Corporation, *Annual Report*. New York: Franklin New York Corporation, various years.

"Hambros at the Helm," *Fortune* (September 1971), 84(3):49.

International Monetary Fund. *Annual Report* (various years), Washington, D.C.: IMF.

"The Italian Connection," *Forbes* (December 1972), 110(11):56-57.

"Italy's Establishment Fights an Outsider," *Business Week* (September 18, 1971), 2194:26.

L'Attivita della Santa Sede, Libreria Editrice Vaticana. Various years.

Mathews, Carol. "192 Banks in Trouble," *New York Post*, June 14, 1973.

Perlow, Austin. "New Management Team Seeks Capital for Franklin National," *Long Island Press*, May 14, 1974.

Pileggi, Nicholas. "The Tycoon Vanishes," *New York Magazine*, September 24, 1979.

Rose, Sanford. "What Really Went Wrong at Franklin National," *Fortune*, October 1974.

Rostron, Bryan. "A Chapter from 'The Godfather'?" *Village Voice*, January, 21, 1980.

Roth, Arthur. "Yesterday's Future Already Tomorrow's Past," *American Banker*, December 9, 1964.

Sheehan, Thomas. "Italy: Terror on the Right," *The New York Review of Books*, January 22, 1981.

"A Sicilian Financier Takes Aim at the U.S.," *Business Week* (April 29, 1972), 2226:34-35.

Sinkey, Joseph F., Jr., "The Collapse of Franklin National Bank of New York," *Journal of Bank Research* (Summer 1976), 7(2):113-22.

"Towards a Theory of International Banking," Federal Reserve Bank of San Francisco, *Monthly Review* (Spring 1976), pp.5-8.

United States Board of Governors of the Federal Reserve System. *Annual Report*. Washington, D.C.: Board of Governors, various issues.

Wille, Frank. *The FDIC and Franklin National Bank: A Report to the Congress and All FDIC Insured Banks*, presented before 81st Annual Convention of the Savings Banks of New York State, Boca Raton, Florida, November 23, 1974. Mimeo.

Wille, Harry F. "Franklin National Bank May Alter Capital Program; 10% Earnings Increase Predicted for 1968," *American Banker*, March 13, 1968.

INDEX